Career Intervention

ARNOLD R. SPOKANE
Lehigh University

Prentice Hall
Englewood Cliffs, New Jersey 07632

Library of Congress Cataloging-in-Publication Data

Spokane, Arnold R.
    Career intervention / Arnold R. Spokane.
        p.   cm.
    Includes bibliographical references and index.
    ISBN 0-13-116450-3
    1. Vocational guidance--Psychological aspects. 2. Counseling.
    I. Title.
    HF5381.S7356 1991
    158.6--dc20   90-47334
                                                                  CIP

Editorial/production supervision: Tara Powers-Hausmann
Interior design: Karen Buck
Cover design: Patricia Kelly
Prepress buyer: Debbie Kesar
Manufacturing buyer: Mary Anne Gloriande

 © 1991 by Prentice-Hall, Inc.
A Division of Simon & Schuster
Englewood Cliffs, New Jersey 07632

Printed in the United States of America
10 9 8 7 6 5 4 3 2 1

ISBN   0-13-116450-3

PRENTICE-HALL INTERNATIONAL (UK) LIMITED, London
PRENTICE-HALL OF AUSTRALIA PTY. LIMITED, Sydney
PRENTICE-HALL CANADA INC., Toronto
PRENTICE-HALL HISPANOAMERICANA, S.A., Mexico
PRENTICE-HALL OF INDIA PRIVATE LIMITED, New Delhi
PRENTICE-HALL OF JAPAN, INC., Tokyo
SIMON & SCHUSTER ASIA PTE. LTD., Singapore
EDITORA PRENTICE-HALL DO BRASIL, LTDA., Rio de Janeiro

To Shelly, Abbe, and Martha, and to my clients, each of whom has taught me something about life and balance.

Contents

Preface

Much of my sensitivity to the career problems of the average person came from watching my father as he made his career choices, and my mother, who had a brief career as a legal secretary, a long period out of the labor market, and then her own business. I concluded, after years of observation, that many of the people around me experienced some confusion about career decisions that they suffered quietly, with no formal and rarely any informal assistance. Career counseling or assistance was almost never available to my parents' generation.

The career difficulties many people face became even more apparent when I interviewed my next-door neighbor for an assignment in my first career course at the Ohio State University with Sam Osipow. My neighbor was a rather ordinary fellow, a high school graduate who in the course of his fifty-three years had held about eighteen different jobs, among which I could find only a few, very loose connections (I did not do well on the assignment). Upon reflection, it occurred to me that most people moved in and out of jobs without much planning. My neighbor, at least, had not given much conscious thought to his career. As a result, his decisions were governed by the external realities of the economy and labor market in central Ohio. This seemingly random movement made theoretical sense in retrospect (my neighbor was a Holland R type), and could have been explained using one or more contemporary career development theories, as I now insist my students do in their life history assignment. But my neighbor, theories notwithstanding, failed to act directly to overcome the barriers and lack of skills that he faced, and the insight that theory might have offered would have been insufficient to move him.

We are at a fortunate juncture in the career development field, for there are now several compelling explanations for career choice and development, and a number have considerable empirical support. These theories and the people who wrote them are more accessible to vocational psychologists than is usually the case in other fields of psychology. In addition, we have a technological armamentarium, unparalleled in modern psychology, with which to assist individuals who are having difficulty making career choices. However, there are fewer bridges between the work of theorists and the interventions of counselors than could easily be the case. As a result, a general therapeutic approach to vocational intervention based upon psychotherapy theory often seems more appealing than a more specific model based upon the formidable but complex advances in theory and research on career behavior achieved across the last two decades. Attempts to fortify the theories with practical implications are more common now than they have been in many years, and more people are now both theorists and practitioners than was once the case. It is my observation that the theorists are listening and that practitioners could be less shy about speaking up; those who would build the bridges between theory and interventions should not be intimidated by the advanced state of large-scale vocational theory and research.

Some of the theoretical principles have become embedded in the language and practice of career intervention. The careful reader will notice the infusion of these principles throughout this volume, even though no separate theory section appears. My goal is to amalgamate my practical and empirical experience from fifteen years as a career counselor with my skills as a researcher and scientist. In this way I hope that I have produced a product that is both practical and empirically sound. As R. A. Myers (1986) so aptly said, advances in career counseling usually proceed from the clinician to the scientist for test, not in the reverse direction. Although there have been several recent theoretical leaps in career development, there have been few counseling advances because clinicians are not making themselves heard. If this volume outlines one counselor's idiosyncrasies but in so doing influences the thinking of a few scientists, I will be satisfied.

This is a generic volume that does not address the particular concerns of special groups unless they are germane to the general process of career intervention. The several excellent books already available on the subject of special populations should always be used to complement this book.

Many individuals contributed directly or indirectly to this effort. Shelly, my wife, spent five years reading drafts, listening to problems, and encouraging me to finish this book. My daughters Abbe and Martha provided a first-hand look at career development and a sense of wonder that I will carry into all of my future writing. The contributions of two colleagues were especially helpful. Tom Magoon guided me through rocky academic waters, encouraged me to take some risks with Chapter 8, and taught me the value of the individual consumer of psychological services. Nancy Schlossberg also suggested that I think about live people, not only data, and then kept after me to write this book, and to be all that I could be as a professional and a person. Both of these remarkable individuals were important role models for me. Sam Osipow and Bruce Walsh have been unusually helpful throughout my career: Bruce Walsh creatively tutored me in person-environment psychology, including the graduate school environment, which I did not always negotiate well; and Sam Osipow, with his commanding critical grasp of the career development field and his willingness to take risks with young talent, encouraged me to think that I might have some contribution to make. John Holland, in addition to supporting and listening to me for years, as he has done with many of my peers, reviewed early drafts of this manuscript and saved me from some embarrassing errors of logic and heart. Laurel Oliver was an exacting and stimulating colleague throughout ten years of trying to understand career intervention and to write about it in convincing ways. Ken and Miriam Clark provided me with steady professional and personal advice. Clark Carney, Bruce Fretz, MaryAnn Hoffman, Charlie Gelso, Zandy Leibowitz, Gary and Linda Gottfredson, Forest Vance, and Franklin Westbrook all contributed ideas in informal ways over the years. My students in the Counseling and Personnel Services Department (CAPS) and my colleagues at the University of Maryland, especially Dave Hershenson, provided a tough crucible in which to fire my ideas as well as a constant source of valuable feedback. My editors, especially Susan Willig, Carol Wada, Tara Powers-Hausmann, and Sherry Babbitt were enormously helpful in style editing and patient beyond reason. Barbara Dantzler, Susan Schwalb, and Robert Davison were my teaching assistants during the writing of this volume. I am also grateful to the three courageous clients who allowed me to audiotape all of their sessions, and to reprint their test results or to excerpt the content of their interventions.

I am indebted to each of these people and for the enormously stimulating environment at University of Maryland from 1978 to 1989, which helped to form and clarify my thinking about career intervention.

Arnold R. Spokane

1

What Is Career Intervention?

THE SOCIAL CONTEXT OF CAREER INTERVENTION

At some point in the history of Western culture, the average person came to perceive the world of work as so complex that navigating a safe and personally enhancing pathway through it required professional assistance. The array and structure of occupations have indeed become more complicated over time. Two world wars, advances in communication and computing technology, and social, economic, and demographic changes have all contributed to the complexity of career patterns in the lives of most American men and women during the twentieth century (Lassalle & Spokane, 1987; for a thorough history of these events, see also Herr & Cramer, 1988). This occupational complexity has often produced avoidance of or ignorance or confusion about the structure of the world of work and possibilities for career mobility. Families, once havens of social support, reassurance, and the transmission of values, have been torn apart by divorce rates in excess of 50 percent, and those that have managed to stay intact often are separated by distance because of job-related relocation. Some of the anxiety associated with the demise of comforting family structures (Kagan, 1988) has been passed from parent to child in the form of career anxiety. In societies in which family structures have remained more stable, careers are still viewed as being inheritable (Tanaka & Ogawa, 1987) or at least as transmittable through familial support and reinforcement. In the United States, however, such predictability of careers has given way to uncertainty, and the role of career counselors in maximizing individual potential has thus become firmly and widely embedded in the social fabric.

Studies repeatedly show that career assistance has been the major concern of adolescents and young adults for decades (Holland, Magoon, &

1

Spokane, 1981). A recent Gallup poll (National Career Development Association [NCDA], 1988) revealed that only 39 percent of Americans had a career plan and that 69 percent would seek additional information if they were choosing a career again. These data suggest that nearly 50 million Americans would say that they did not understand how to interpret and use information to make intelligent career choices. Flamer (1986), in an editorial in the *Journal of Community Psychology*, noted that significant numbers of mature adults "are experiencing some degree of dysfunction with their work experience" (p. 226). Indeed, the 1988 NCDA poll suggested that nearly one in two American workers felt significant job-related stress, and believed that their skills and abilities were not being well used in their current job.

Clinical career intervention with adults is now becoming part of community mental health programs (Flamer, 1986). University career development centers frequently offer assistance to the public on a fee-for-service basis, and there are numerous private career counselors. This emerging adult clientele, combined with the adolescent and college-age populations traditionally served, has produced numbers large enough to warrant increased professional attention. The career problems of adults, however, are often more complex than those of adolescents, and may overlap with mental health concerns.

The Emergence of Career Counseling as a Profession

The issue of careers began to attract serious attention from psychologists, sociologists, and counselors at the turn of the twentieth century, when focus was on the study of vocational interests and development on the one hand and on career intervention or counseling on the other. Parson's (1909) classic *On Choosing a Vocation* and a later, little-known work by Fryer (1925), *Vocational Self-Guidance,* chronicled the ambitious efforts of social reformers who counseled adolescents (usually males) concerning their career choices. From 1900 through the 1960s, most of the effort in the career field was devoted to the measurement of interests, and the analysis of career patterns and development. The research focused on empirical studies of career development theory rather than on counseling process or outcome, although one or two stalwarts still wrote about career counseling (Samler, 1953; Thompson, 1960). From 1960 to 1980, however, the number of counselors and counseling psychologists in the United States increased, and many of them defined career counseling as their principal role. The sheer weight of career clients forced a shift in the literature on careers away from theory and toward more practical interventions.

There is some indication of a leveling off of interest in career counseling among counseling psychologists in the 1980s (Fitzgerald & Oslpow, 1986; Pinkney & Jacobs, 1985), but because other professionals (e.g., social workers, clinical psychologists, and human resource managers) now consider career development to be their specialty, a sizable professional core with an interest in career psychology has been maintained. The relative decline of interest

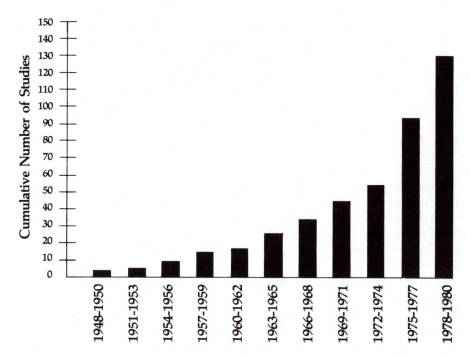

Figure 1-1 Cumulative Frequency of Vocational Intervention Outcome Studies in Published Sources, 1948–80. (Source: A. R. Spokane and L. W. Oliver, "The Outcomes of Vocational Intervention," in W. B. Walsh and S. H. Osipow [Eds.], *Handbook of Vocational Psychology*, Vol. 2 [Hillsdale, NJ: Lawrence Erlbaum, 1983], p. 105. Copyright 1983 by Lawrence Erlbaum, Inc. Reprinted by permission.)

in career issues among counseling psychologists[1] is troublesome and may result in part from their frustration at having to try to apply thirty-year-old models and practices in their daily work with clients, since the clinical literature has long been practically dormant.

New perspectives on career counseling as a mental health intervention (Herr, in press; Spokane, in press, a) have recently revived interest in questions of clinical practice. In the last eight to ten years, theorists and researchers have refocused their attention on the practice and outcomes of career counseling (Spokane & Oliver, 1983). To some degree the steady increase in the number of published outcome research studies of career intervention (see Figure 1-1) reflects greater professional interest and perhaps treatment volume. Although we have no reliable estimates of the actual numbers of clients being served by career professionals, the NCDA (1988) poll does indicate a potentially high demand for services.

This increased attention on the practice and process of career interven-

---

[1] I am not convinced that this proportional decline is not simply a function of the large increase in the number of young counseling psychologists. Other groups, however, such as the American Society for Training and Development, are quickly and vigorously entering the field of career counseling.

tion should result in more attractive and relevant models for use in clinical practice, and several books on the subject have recently appeared (Burck & Reardon, 1984; Crites, 1981; Gysbers & Moore, 1987; Healy, 1982; Raskin, 1987; Yost & Corbishley, 1987; Zunker, 1986). A major review of the field by Myers (1986) and Salamone's (Salamone, 1982; Salamone & McKenna, 1982) articles on difficult cases are excellent examples of the application of recent advances in theory and research to specific client problems. The case study approach has also produced interesting findings about the counseling process (Kirschner, 1988).

The result of this new focus on clinical interventions has been increased concern about diagnosis and treatment (Rounds & Tinsley, 1984), higher quality research (G. D. Gottfredson, 1978; Myers, 1986), a general retooling of extant theories with practice in mind (L. S. Gottfredson, 1986; Spokane, 1985), and a resurgence of interest in the link between vocational theory and counseling practice (Holland, 1985a; Krumboltz, Becker-Haven, & Burnett, 1979).

There is much room for improvement, however. Unfortunately, recent volumes on career counseling vary so widely in content and coverage that readers may wonder if different authors are describing the same general domain of behavior. A review of four recent books (Osipow, 1988) suggests that the approaches offered have little empirical underpinning. Additionally, many of the best and most active researchers, most of whom are also practicing counselors, still conduct basic empirical studies of career development to earn tenure or increase their professional standing, rather than writing about their actual interventions with clients. Figler (1984) has stated that career counselors must define themselves by delineating the overlap between psychotherapy and career counseling, clearly establishing their own knowledge base and standards of practice, sharing intervention methods, and defining successful intervention and outcome.

Ginzberg (1984) observed that although some vocational practitioners may operate under implicit theories, these theories are hard to verify, and it is unlikely that any two practitioners use the same theory. Some career counselors are apologetic or defensive because they feel their methods are untested, and they are reluctant to talk about, much less write about, their practices. In a particularly inflammatory statement about the utility of career counseling, Baumgardner (1977) criticized its scientific basis. Responses to his allegations were unduly defensive, but in 1977 the data did not exist to rebut his charges directly. As this volume will show, the data are now available. There is a problem, however, when counselors do not publicly describe their practices and scientists write but rarely counsel. The result is a separation of science and practice that fuels charges of unsystematic and non-scientific procedures. The scientist cannot draw upon the counselor's wisdom, and the counselor does not find the scientific literature relevant. Neither benefits from the other, and the client benefits least of all. In their search for practical strategies, counselors rather simplistically extract what they consider to be the essence of a theory (Spokane, 1985), but in the process lose the chance to enhance their clinical work with a model sufficiently complex to suit the difficult cases they encounter.

The effective integration of theory, research, and practice is a high priority in the career field. One aim of the present book is to describe a clinical model of intervention that can be related to career development theory and then tested empirically.

CAREER INTERVENTION VERSUS CAREER COUNSELING: A DEFINITIONAL DILEMMA

The literature offers two definitions of career intervention (Spokane, in press-b): The first views career counseling as a variant of psychotherapy that is practiced in dyadic interactions between a counselor and a client, and invokes psychotherapy theory in an attempt to explain and improve client outcomes (Rounds & Tinsley, 1984). The second and more inclusive view of the career intervention process defines career intervention as any activity designed to improve an individual's ability to make improved career decisions. Williamson and Bordin (1941) promoted this restrictive position when they placed the following three constraints on their definition of career counseling: (1) the efforts must be individualized; (2) testing alone was not to be considered counseling; and (3) counseling was not self-analysis, nor was it based upon interview data alone.

In the most restrictive dyadic sense, career counseling is practiced largely in college counseling centers and by a few private practitioners, which serve, respectively, a small number of college students or those adult clients who are able to pay for psychotherapeutic interventions. Counseling centers, normally overburdened with clients, are constantly looking for alternate ways to provide services that do not require one-to-one interventions. The costly nature of traditional career counseling led Lunneborg (1983) to conclude that although it was still productive, this form of intervention had simply become too expensive and therefore was unusable for centers with large constituencies. Time-limited therapy is common in these places, and diversification of the types of treatment is now a necessity, not an innovation. Oliver and Spokane (1988) likewise found that although individual counseling was more than twice as effective per hour as other forms of intervention, it was four times as expensive.

An additional and important problem with traditional one-to-one career counseling was outlined by L. S. Gottfredson (1986), who listed certain groups (e.g., racial minorities, women, and the handicapped) who are at high risk for developing career problems yet either cannot afford to pay premium prices for such assistance or are simply unlikely to seek it out. A final problem with psychotherapeutic models of career counseling is that they assume that there are no substantial differences between personal and career intervention other than the focus of the therapy. While there is certainly some overlap in the process and method of the two kinds of intervention, some differences between the two are also clear.

MISAPPLICATIONS OF PSYCHOTHERAPY THEORY TO CAREER SITUATIONS

A scattering of early articles considered career counseling to be a subset of psychotherapy (Bixler & Bixler, 1945) or social casework (Grumer, 1949), outlined some general principles of counseling (Dolliver & Nelson, 1975; Morrill & Forrest, 1970), or described career counseling as it was then practiced (Samler, 1953, 1966, 1968); an occasional piece delved more deeply into model building (Thompson, 1960). Most of these early efforts lacked the power to explain the change process in career counseling, however, and were difficult to relate to theories of career development. Yet since they failed to spawn full-fledged models or theories of career counseling, to fill the void career development theories were stretched for intervention implications. Because the development theories could not explain the counseling process, psychotherapy theories were thus invoked. Paterson (1964), for example, proposed a client-centered view of career counseling that largely ignored the reality of the labor market. Most recently Keller, Biggs, and Gysbers (1982) have applied cognitive theory, Dorn (in press) has applied social influence theory, and Watkins (1984) has applied Adlerian theory to career counseling. Although these extrapolations make some sense, the theories are borrowed rather than generated from career data, and the fit is rarely optimum, considering the uniqueness of the career situation. Only Bordin (1986) and Krumboltz and Thoresen (1964) have used psychotherapeutic theory (psychoanalytic and behavioral, respectively) with a visible or enduring impact on how career counseling is conducted.

Bordin, who applied psychoanalytic principles to career counseling, argued that clients could best confront career problems when anxiety was minimized. Career problems, according to Bordin, raised conflicts, which then produced substantial anxiety that interfered with the counseling process. This view was also offered by Pepinsky and Pepinsky (1954), and the role of anxiety in career decision making has since been confirmed several times (Mendonca & Siess, 1976).

Krumboltz's work, in which he used behavioral methods to stimulate information seeking, stands as one of the few successful attempts to build a career intervention model from actual situational requirements, even though his cognitive-behavioral prototype has the shortcomings of a purely cognitive model in which environmental constraints during career *implementation* are largely ignored. Krumboltz converted his early work into a theory of career development rather than of career intervention, thus providing more help to theorists than to counselors. Most recently, however, Krumboltz (1983) has suggested that a personal private belief system may govern most career decisions and that these beliefs are not easily tapped by traditional methods. An integration of his latest work on private beliefs with the social learning model he described earlier (Krumboltz, 1976) should account for both environmental constraints and individual career behavior.

Most of the early efforts to find an acceptable therapeutic model of career counseling failed to provide coherent direction for practitioners, partly because of the misapplication of psychotherapy models to career situations and partly because of the restrictive view of career counseling as an intensive, dyadic interaction, a conceptualization that rarely reflected the focused, short-term reality of practice. Crites (1981) has thoroughly catalogued these efforts at model building, but although the structure he provided—trait-factor, client-centered, psychoanalytic, developmental, behavioral, and comprehensive models—is useful, the client-centered and psychoanalytic models share certain shortcomings that account for their failure to offer an acceptable model of career intervention (e.g., inattention to social constraints). The behavioral model shows promise but has not been fully fleshed out, and the developmental model applies well to some preventive and instructional interventions, but is difficult to use in individual and group settings.

Career interventions are rarely designed within the framework of a single theory (for a refreshing exception, see Healy, 1982). Crites's comprehensive prototype comes the closest to the current practical model, but his eclectic synthesis was more theoretical than practical; furthermore, its translation to counseling practice has not been easy for either students or professionals.

DISTINGUISHING CAREER COUNSELING FROM PSYCHOTHERAPY

Among the characteristics that have always distinguished career problems from personal or interpersonal problems, and, therefore, career counseling from psychotherapy, the four most critical are as follows:

1. The social environment forces adjustments in individual career aspirations and impedes sharp changes in choice patterns.
2. The principle of congruence (person-environment fit) is considered in some way in nearly all theories of career development.
3. The public has come to expect a special career intervention technology of interest inventories and computer interventions that is independent of most theory positions and results in a more struc-

tured and predictable course of intervention than is generally the case in psychotherapy.

4. Career development proceeds both continuously and discontinuously, and requires certain critical choices at a predictable number of transition points (e.g., high school graduation), as well as the continuous formation of a vocational identity through a series of small but serial choices (Osipow, 1983).

These four differences between counseling and psychotherapy will be described in more detail below. When practiced as a dyadic intervention, career counseling overlaps with psychotherapy. The extent of overlap between the two is an important question for the field. Other career interventions, however, bear few similarities to psychotherapy. The parent theory bases differ in significant ways. On the other hand, the practice of career intervention without an understanding of the social psychology of career selection and implementation and the influence of lifestyle on careers (Gysbers & Moore, 1987) can result in a sterile and meaningless exercise for the client and for the counselor. We are just beginning to understand the overlap between career intervention and psychotherapy, but we should not overdraw the relationship at the expense of the unique contribution of career development theory and practice to modern psychology.

The Role of the Social Environment in Career Aspirations and Attainment

One major difference between career counseling and psychotherapy is the pervasive constraining influence of the social environment on career choice and attainment. Economists and sociologists have been aware of this for some time (Ginzberg, 1984; L. S. Gottfredson, 1981), but counselors have chosen to minimize this reality and work instead with whatever variance in behavior remains after the social constraints. At the very least, a psychotherapy theory that does not consider the pervasive effects of social constraints will never be successfully applied to career counseling. In an unusually clear paper on this topic, Bucher (1976) described how major social constraints such as position in society and opportunity structures limit the range of career options from which an individual will select. Bucher argued that tightly formed social organizations limit access to their groups by controlling the flow of entry-relevant information to outsiders and by conveying certain core values to potentially desirable recruits. These information barriers are particularly difficult impediments for certain subgroups. Latack, Josephs, Roach, and Levine (1987), for example, studied differences in the transition to permanent employment between female and male carpenter apprentices. They found that although women actually rated their chances of completing the training program as higher than those of their male counterparts, and were performing as well as the men, they had more difficulty in obtaining on-the-job experience, worked less and in more nonconstruction jobs, and earned less. The constraints on women who enter the labor force are undoubtedly more severe than those on men, and as a result female aspiration patterns are more complex (Farmer, 1985; Fassinger, 1985).

L. S. Gottfredson (1986) described the risks faced by many social groups as well as the atttributes of such groups that may impede their career development, including low intelligence, poor education, poverty, cultural isolation, functional limitations, and status as a primary care giver or economic provider (see Table 1-1). Gottfredson defined the clinical tasks as the accurate assessment of such risks, and the use of effective treatments to overcome environmental constraints and barriers.

Gottfredson (1981) also argued that counselors typically underestimate the effects of social constraints in designing their treatments, and suggested that more potent interventions were required to overcome the limiting effects of gender on career development. Regardless of whether one agrees with Gottfredson, she did illustrate that social constraints modify career aspirations by forcing compromises in the level or field of choice and in lowering unrealistically high career goals.

Compromise Versus Persistence in Career Behavior.   Ginzberg (Ginzberg, 1984; Ginzberg, Ginsburg, Axelrad, & Herma, 1951), and to a certain extent Super (Super, 1956; Super & Overstreet, 1960) and Tiedeman (Tiedeman & Ohara, 1963) as well, argued that when social reality produces changes in the career aspirations of adolescents and young adults, compromise is the most frequent response. Compromise was also an explicit factor in L. S. Gottfredson's (1981) theory. It is now clear that most adolescents overshoot in their career aspirations (L. S. Gottfredson & Becker, 1981) and that the social environment forces some degree of alteration in their plans. Gottfredson (1981) argued that occupational interests are more likely to be compromised when faced with an environmental constraint than are gender role or status, which are acquired developmentally earlier. Two recent studies (Holt, 1989; Taylor & Pryor, 1985) also suggested that occupational prestige level is indeed less likely to be compromised than occupational interests. Gender role and interests are so intertwined that the compromise process involving the two may be highly complex.

Super (1956) argued that although *compromise* is an appropriate term to apply to the adaptation process that occurs when reality is encountered late in development (i.e., in adolescence), *synthesis* is more correctly used to describe what takes place when the individual first interacts with the environment and begins to differentiate the "self" from the "other." The influence of the social environment is strongest when an adolescent tries to implement a career aspiration, and especially when an adolescent with a poorly differentiated image of self confronts the reality of the labor force. The shock can force such individuals to reevaluate and reformulate their career plans.

Table 1-1 Special Groups Whose Members Are Hypothesized to Be at Higher-Than-Average Risk (X) Versus Not at Higher-Than-Average Risk (O) of Having Various Attributes That Can Impede Optimal Career Development

EXAMPLES OF SPECIAL GROUPS

Career Choice Risk Factors	"WASP"	White Ethnic	Black	Hispanic	Native American	Asian American	Jewish	Male	Female	Sight	Hearing	Use of Limbs	Dyslexic	Mentally Retarded	III
Different from general population															
Low intelligence	O		X	X	X	O	O	O	O					X	X
Poor academic background	O		X	X	X	O	O	O	O[a]				X	X	
Comes from poor family	O		X	X	X	O	O	O	O				o	x	
Culturally isolated/segregated	o	X	x	x	x	x	x		x / O[b]	X	X	X	X	X	
Functional limitation	O		X		X			O	O		X			X	X
Low self-esteem	O		O					o	o						
Different within own social circle															
Potential nontraditional (i.e., has interests typical of a different sex, racial/ethnic group, or social class)	o								x						
Socially isolated/segregated										X	X	X	X	X	x
Low intelligence compared to family/peers														X	
High intelligence compared to family/peers															
Family responsibilities															
Probable/actual primary care giver	OM		XF	XF				O	X						
Probable/actual primary economic provider		XM	XF / OM	XM				X	O						

Note: X = good evidence that at higher-than-average risk. x = author's estimate that at higher-than-average risk. O = good evidence that not at higher-than-average risk. o = author's estimate that not at higher-than-average risk. Blank = no hypothesis. M = males only. F = females only.

[a] See text for more detailed sex differences in education.

[b] There are sex differences for specific types of functional limitation.

Source: L. S. Gottfredson, "Special Groups and the Beneficial Use of Vocational Interest Inventories," in W. B. Walsh and S. H. Osipow (Eds.), Advances in Vocational Assessment, Vol. 1, The Assessment of Interests (Hillsdale, NJ: Lawrence Erlbaum, 1986), p. 149. Reprinted with permission from Lawrence Erlbaum, Inc.

Astin and Panos (1969) identified a compromise commonly made by college science majors as the "science to non-science shift"; Holland (1985b) called the process of adapting to reality "searching"; and Tiedeman and Ohara (1963) referred to the dual processes of differentiation and integration. Regardless of the term applied to the iterative process of exploring and adapting personal career aspirations to the social reality, most clients, especially younger ones, can anticipate some painful reconsideration of their career dreams in the face of marketplace realities. Tiedeman and Ohara (1963) thought that most of the reconsideration occurred in the critical transition from anticipation to implementation, after the reality of the marketplace had been encountered.

Rather than emphasizing the extent of career compromises, Tiedeman has focused on an individual's force of will, or ego strength, as the critical determinant of eventual career choice. Tiedeman and Miller-Tiedeman (1984) carried this view to its logical conclusion in suggesting that there is a *personal* career reality that is distinct from a *common* career reality. The personal reality is that "thought, behavior or direction that the individual feels is right for him or her, even though someone else may advise that it will never work" (p. 295). Since there is a limited number of jobs in all markets, the common reality is determined by any limits operating when an individual is implementing a career decision. This conflict between the client's aspiration and the labor market's constraints is often the crucial (if hidden) therapeutic issue in career counseling. It would be incorrect, however, to assume that compromise is always proper for a client. There are many examples of individuals who persisted in attempting to implement a desired career aspiration in the face of great odds. This persistent search behavior is a hallmark of the successful career client. Persistence to the point of psychological distress is unwise—but a lack of persistence results in too much compromise.

A clinical example of the problem of persistence versus compromise involves two undergraduate premedical students I once counseled; both had comparable grades, board scores, and socioeconomic backgrounds, and both had just barely missed being admitted to medical school. Both sought counseling for assistance with the issue of compromising their career goals. The first student, obviously distressed by his failure to gain admission, chose to supplement his application by taking advanced courses in biochemistry, and then reapplied to less competitive American schools and to every possible foreign school. This persistent student was eventually accepted to a foreign school, graduated, successfully completed an American internship and residency, and is now a practicing physician. The second student applied to dental school, was readily accepted, and is now a practicing dentist. The differences between these two compromises is clear, and illustrates the variety in individual responses to difficult reality constraints (even though these students were free of the most severe social barriers, and possessed con-

considerable personal and financial resources). Perhaps the second student accepted the *common* reality, whereas the first student pursued a *personal* reality. I did not attempt to intervene to alter these compromises in counseling. Rather, I observed and provided support because I believed that both compromises were reasoned and moderate in nature. No studies have shown convincingly that career interventions that foster persistence cannot overcome some of the more severe social constraints facing a client. In fact some evidence indicates that welfare clients who experience severe constraints will be quite successful in finding work after a behavioral intervention is specifically designed to promote a persistent job search (Azrin, Phillip, Thienes-Hontos, & Besalel, 1980). Common sense, however, tells us that a high proportion of the population cannot overcome such serious barriers no matter how potent the intervention, since the limited availability of many desirable careers must surely dampen unrealistic aspirations. It is still not known the extent to which and under what circumstances career interventions might be able to surmount social constraints.

Tiedeman, Ginzberg, L. S. Gottfredson, and Vondracek, Lerner, and Schulenberg (1986) have all defined the process of career choice as a dynamic interplay between personal aspirations and social reality in which two opposing but more or less continuous forces (differentiation-integration, optimization-compromise, circumscription-compromise, and affordance-selection, respectively) determine the outcome. Osipow (1983) argued that individuals make small serial choices in which every minor decision opens a chain of new options and closes off others, much like the capillary system in the human body. Each persistence or compromise behavior creates or eliminates new choices or options, and the cumulative effect of these serial decisions is a career. In sum, most individuals must make compromises between personal aspirations and the reality of the labor force. The nature of these compromises is not yet clear, but appears to involve occupational status and ability, gender role, and interests. The majority of the compromises seem to be made by age thirty (L. S. Gottfredson & Becker, 1981).

Congruence in Career Intervention

If there is any principle upon which most career development theorists can agree, it is that some degree of fit between an individual and the environment will lead to beneficial career outcomes (Borgen, 1986; Spokane, 1985; Vondracek et al., 1986; Zytowski & Borgen, 1983). This sense of fit, which is usually called *congruence*, is the central tenet in Holland's (1985a) theory of career choice and is implied in most other theories of choice as well, including Super's (1957) in which fit is described as the implementation of the self-concept in a compatible job. According to Super, "holding and adjusting to a job is . . . a process of finding out whether that job permits . . . [the worker] to play the kind of role he wants to play" (p. 191). More recently, L. S. Gottfredson (1981) argued that there is a zone of acceptable career alternatives that an individual will consider, which are determined by the person's level of aspiration and the sextype of the job.

The clearest and most widely studied view of congruence was described by John Holland (1985a), who offered three general propositions:

1. Congruent individuals will be reinforced, satisfied, and less likely to change environments than will incongruent individuals.
2. Incongruent individuals will be influenced by the dominant environment to change in the direction of congruence.
3. When placed in an incongruent environment, persons with consistent and differentiated personality patterns will be more likely to operate to make changes in the environment than will inconsistent and undifferentiated individuals; that is, they will clarify the influence of the environment.

The evidence that individuals select an occupation congruent with their person-environment fit occurs in about 50 percent of the cases. When expressed and measured interests correspond, that predictive power jumps to 70 percent (Borgen & Selling, 1978). Secondly, congruence is correlated with job satisfaction and well-being in the range of about .20 to .55 (Assouline & Meir, 1987; Meir, 1989; Meir & Melamed, 1986; Spokane, 1985).

Two views of congruence exist. The first assumes that fit is a static process in which an individual with a well-defined set of traits selects an environment that most comfortably corresponds to those characteristics; no change process is either implied or necessary (Borgen, 1986). The second view considers congruence to be an interactional process whereby individuals and jobs change and adapt to each other over time (Vondracek et al., 1986).

One troublesome finding in the congruence literature (Schneider, 1987) is that some work organizations may successively narrow the kind of personality inhabiting their environments in a way that jeopardizes the organizations' ability to function creatively; Schneider has dubbed this the attraction-selection-attrition problem. When this process continues for a long period, the work environment may become so homogeneous with respect to skills, competencies, and attitudes that it loses its ability to respond to novel situations. Although some evidence (Prestholdt, Lane, & Matthews, 1987) suggests that this process may be reasoned and helpful, on the whole it is a vexing problem. Congruence may thus not always be beneficial (Muchinsky & Monahan, 1987).

Despite the declining popularity of the strictly static view of person-environment fit, one or two very capable individuals still adhere to this interpretation. The question is whether the next reasonable step is some hybrid model of developmental fit or an interactionist theory that holds that relatively stable individuals influence their environments more than their environments influence them.

L. S. Gottfredson (1981) and Vondracek et al. (1986) provided different views of the nature of person-environment fit. Gottfredson adhered to a more static model in which sex role and prestige level, once acquired, were added to field of interest and then fitted to the ability requirements of jobs, whereas Vondracek et al. offered a continuous interactive or ecological description of the career development process. The two models are still in their formative stages.

Regardless of how one conceptualizes congruence, most counselors and virtually all clients cling tenaciously to the belief one "best-fitting" career option exists for each person, and that the goal of intervention is to make that option sufficiently obvious to permit its implementation.

Expectations of Technical Structure in Career Interventions

An estimated 3.5 million individuals complete interest inventories each year. The SVIB, if one counts both its male and female forms, is one of the most widely used tests in the history of American psychology (Lubin, Larsen, & Matarazzo, 1984). There is an unusually large number of interest inventories, both machine scored and computer interactive, from which to choose, including the "big three" (Borgen, 1986)—the SVIB (Hansen & Campbell, 1985), the Kuder (Kuder & Diamond, 1979), and the SDS (Holland, 1985b)—and a host of new measures such as Johansson's CAI (Johansson, 1982), IDEAs (Johansson, 1980), the ECO (Andberg & Johansson, 1987) (Spokane, in press-b), Jackson's Vocational Survey (Jackson, 1977). Lunneborg's VII (Lunneborg, 1981), and American College Testing Program's (1988) (ACT) UNIACT. More than eighteen major categories of inventories are now used by career counselors, schools, industries, and agencies (see Chapter 4).

Reliance upon Tests.   Nearly 38 percent of Americans have used self-directed career activities, such as library visits, classified ads, or interest inventories (NCDA, 1988). In his review of scaling methods, Dawis (1987) selected one issue of the *Journal of Counseling Psychology* at random and found that all of its twelve articles involved the use of some kind of scale. As an editorial board member, it is my impression that nearly all vocational psychology studies have scaling or testing as a major focus. Does this constitute an overreliance upon tests? The phrase "three interviews and a cloud of dust" has come to symbolize what occurs when the counselor meets with the client for one session, gives the SCII at the second session, and then interprets the results at the third session. This clinical overreliance on tests, not their use in research and theory, has been an important reason for career counselors' dissatisfaction with traditional interventions (Spokane, 1985, in press, b). Clients, however, value tests and more recently computer measures above all other interventions.

The professionals' dissatisfaction with the overuse of tests is probably warranted in view of their effectiveness. Oliver and Spokane (1988) have used meta-analysis to integrate the outcomes of fifty-eight career intervention studies involving 7,311 subjects. They compared the mean effectiveness of individual counseling (Mi), groups (Mg), workshops (Mw), classes (Mcl), and counselor-free (Mcf) interventions; the use of interest inventories alone was reported in the Mcf category. As Figure 1-2 shows, studies reveal small but consistent gains for the individuals who completed inventories alone (Oliver & Spokane, 1988; Spokane & Oliver, 1983). The summarized studies evaluated the effects of these inventories exclusive of any other career intervention, and thus probably underestimated the value of the inventories when part of a comprehensive intervention program. The sobering reality, though, is that no inventory offers particularly superior benefits to clients (L. S. Gottfredson, 1986). Test selection is usually made on the basis of cost, scoring time, or a counselor's proficiency and comfort with an inventory. Although the tests seem equivalent in terms of overall outcome, the studies have not compared the responses of clients with specific presenting problems. In addition, the methodological sophistication of these studies has been very poor (Rounds & Tinsley, 1984). Some differences among tests do suggest varying appropriateness for certain problems and populations (for examples see Chapter 6), at least until the evidential base for their use becomes stronger.

Figure 1-2 Average Effect Sizes of Career Interventions. (Source: L. W. Oliver and A. R. Spokane, "Career Counseling Outcome: What Contributes to Client Gain?" *Journal of Counseling Psychology* 35 (1988):447-462. Reprinted by permission.)

Average Effect Size

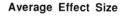
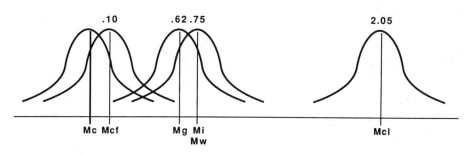

Key:
Mc—mean for control subjects
Mcf—mean for counselor-free subjects
Mg—mean for group counseling subjects
Mi—mean for individual counseling subjects
Mw—mean for workshop subjects
Mcl—mean for class subjects

Although the inventories themselves may not be as effective in promoting change as was once hoped, clients still expect to receive them (Campbell, 1973), and counselors still use them. Clients believe that these technologically sophisticated inventories will provide answers that individuals would not otherwise obtain on their own. In light of such powerful expectations, it is unlikely that the tests' popularity will subside in the foreseeable future. Counselors and researchers must thus now decide which inventories are best for which clients and which problems.

Continuous and Discontinuous Career Development

Career counseling and psychotherapy also differ in their approach to the problem of discontinuity in many career choices. Although individuals may progress through their career stages either continuously or cumulatively, as Tiedeman and Ohara (1963) have described, there are at least a dozen discontinuities, or points, at which a sharply defined decision must be made, such as the following:

1. Selection of part-time employment while in school and afterwards;
2. Selection of subjects to be taken in junior high school;
3. Selection of subjects to be taken in high school;
4. Selection of first full-time position;
5. Selection of another position when dissatisfaction arises over a former position;
6. Retirement.

To Tiedeman and Ohara's position choices, two other discontinuities may be added:

1. Decision to remain in or leave the labor force following childbirth.
2. Selection of a reentry job following childbirth.

Although all of these discontinuities may not be experienced by any one individual, they are often forced on someone by the realities such as firings or layoffs. Many, however, are predictable, and demand decision-making skills and behaviors that are not required in personality developmental progressions. There will always be certain critical choice points at which individuals will feel pressured to take some specific career actions. Because these discontinuities are more regular and marked in career development than in personality development, many clients in career counseling will be feeling a greater sense of urgency than those in personal counseling and psychotherapy. This often results in a more structured and focused intervention than is found in longer-term psychotherapy. Greater structure and support may also characterize career crisis interventions used when a client has been laid off or fired.

Defining career counseling as a subset of psychotherapy ignores this and the three other fundamental differences between career and personal problems: forced adaptation by the social environment, person-environment fit, special career technology, and continuous and discontinuous development. Practice models of career intervention have been few, because applying psychotherapy theories to career situations has serious deficiencies. Restricting our definition of career intervention to the dyadic or group interaction with a counselor limits the populations with which we will work, and decreases the variety and cost efficiency of service delivery. A more moderate definition was outlined by Crites (1981) who distinguished career counseling from guidance and psychotherapy by noting that career counseling was both more and less than personal counseling. All vocational problems are not personal problems, but the two domains do interact. Crites offered five helpful distinctions between career counseling and psychotherapy:

1. The need for career counseling is greater than the need for psychotherapy.
2. Career counseling can be therapeutic.
3. Career counseling should follow psychotherapy.
4. Career counseling is more effective than psychotherapy.
5. Career counseling is more difficult than psychotherapy.

Evidence continues to accumulate to support each of Crites's five propositions, which point toward a broad view of career counseling as therapeutic, but not exclusively so.

CAREER INTERVENTION BROADLY DEFINED

In contrast to the belief that career counseling is merely a subset of psychotherapy, a second and broader definition of career intervention is any activity designed to enhance an individual's ability to make improved career decisions (Fretz, 1981; Spokane & Oliver, 1983). This position recognizes that career counseling is too narrow a term to encompass the wide array of career strategies now in use, including short-term groups, classes, workshops, and self-guided inventories (Myers, 1986). The broader view is not without its problems, however. Since career intervention includes a large and diverse assortment of strategies, it is increasingly difficult to summarize and understand them well enough to predict their effects on the client (Lunneborg, 1983). Perhaps because of this practitioners have simply eclectically chosen those strategies that made sense for the client at hand, rather than developing a more systematic model of career intervention. This eclecticism in turn may have slowed the emergence of a practical model to guide counselor practice. Rounds and Tinsley (1984) argued that until the range of career intervention is narrowed, there will be little progress toward understanding the psychological processes underlying career counseling.

The full range of strategies offered in a hypothetical comprehensive counseling center (Bishop, 1979; Brandt, 1977) that broadly defines career intervention is depicted in Figure 1-3. These interventions are ordered along two dimensions of treatment intensity; the amount of time invested by the counselor and the amount of time invested by the client. The treatment array described in Figure 1-3 was first implied by Magoon (1980), who noted that a complete array of interventions varying in the time investment required from both the client and the counselor would soon be offered in most comprehensive counseling centers. The system also owes a debt to Brandt (1977), who used three major classes of treatments (one to one, small group, and programmed self-instruction) and the developmental nature of the presenting problem (twelve possibilities) to organize the diverse array of career interventions offered in the typical college counseling center. The model shown in Figure 1-3 differs in its attention to treatment intensity, which is viewed as the combination of counselor contact *and* client involvement. Treatments that vary in intensity have also been found to vary in effectiveness (Oliver & Spokane, 1988), which shows the need for some selection according to the severity of the client's problem. The client may participate in brief career interventions by utilizing audiotapes, handouts, self-paced work stations, or the Self-Directed Search (Holland, 1985b) with no assistance from a counselor. The client may also elect to complete an intake process and be assigned to a counselor for a set number of one-to-one or group sessions. Other clients may take either semester-long classes or brief workshops.

To extend the prevailing narrow, dyadic view of career counseling, the NCDA formed a task force to identify a set of counselor competencies that would provide the broadest possible definition of career intervention and demonstrate the wide range of knowledge and expertise, leadership activities, and direct and indirect service that a career counselor might perform. These activities were grouped into the three categories (planning and design, implementation, and evaluation) displayed in Table 1-2.

As the table shows, the traditional psychotherapeutic definition of career intervention is wholly contained in the direct services component/implementation cell. The NCDA competencies are an excellent diagnostic device for counselors who wish to expand their professional role or educate administrators about a more inclusive and appropriate role they themselves may serve.

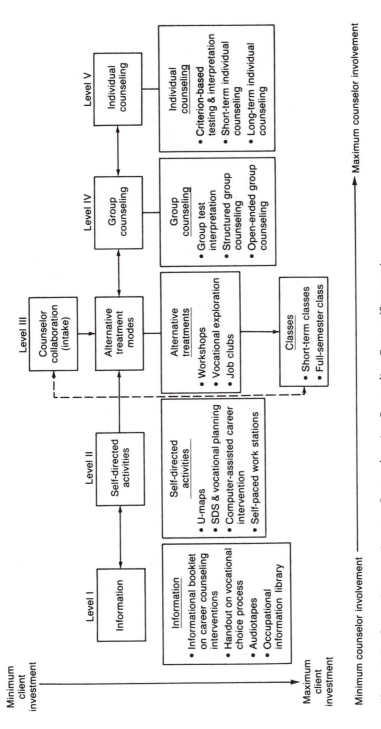

Figure 1-3 Career Intervention at a Comprehensive Counseling Center. (Source: A. R. Spokane, "Self-Guided Interest Inventories: The Self Directed Search," in E. Watkins and V. Campbell [Eds.], *Testing in Counseling Practice* [Hillsdale, NJ: Lawrence Earlbaum, in press].)

Table 1-2 Counselor Competencies

	COUNSELOR KNOWLEDGE/ EXPERTISE COMPONENT	LEADERSHIP COMPONENT	MANAGEMENT COMPONENT	DIRECT SERVICES COMPONENT	INDIRECT SERVICES COMPONENT
Planning/ Design	Understand program management concepts Understand concepts of career education, guidance, and career development Understand staff development and in-service education techniques and procedures Understand community and labor market composition and trends Understand concepts of collaboration in the delivery of educational programs	Involve educational staff and community resource persons in planning and designing activities Institute communication networks among appropriate populations	Assess student career development needs Apply program management concepts Assess the effectiveness of the existing career guidance program Establish program goals and objectives Design specific career guidance services and activities Coordinate career guidance program with career education and total educational thrust at the institution Prepare budgets Develop calendars and time lines depicting sequence of program activities	Plan and design activities and services to facilitate career development needs of students	Participate in the design of school and non-school activities which extend the goals and objectives of the career guidance program
Implementation	Understand career development theories Understand counseling theory and techniques Understand decision-making theory Understand group dynamics Understand needs of specific groups within institutions and the	Coordinate school and community resources Develop program support from administration, board of education, instructional staff, community and students Develop and implement a public relations system	Manage the career guidance program Conduct staff development sessions	Counsel individuals and small groups Conduct student assessment (ability achievement, interest, personality, etc.) Disseminate occupational and educational information Conduct career awareness, explora-	Consult with teachers, parents, and administrators regarding students Conduct information programs for parents and community representatives Provide direct input and technical assistance to persons implementing

	community (women, handicapped, ethnic minorities, etc.) Understand the role and function of information in education and counseling Understand curriculum design and content Understand measurement and appraisal techniques	Provide input to curriculum revision		tions and experience programs Operate student service activities (e.g., career center, job placement program, etc.)	career education activities Conduct staff development training
Evaluation	Understand essential, integral, and continuous nature of evaluation Understand range and variety of data collection and assessment methodologies Understand program standards and guidelines from government agencies and accrediting and professional associations Recognize exemplary career guidance practices, methods, and techniques	Demonstrate exemplary career guidance program aspects	Conduct comprehensive evaluation of the career guidance program Monitor activities conducted by self and others Utilize broad-based input to the evaluation system (students, teachers, parents, etc.) Prepare and disseminate interpretive communication evaluation results Communicate findings to career guidance program decision-makers Improve and modify the career guidance program decision-makers Improve and modify the career guidance program process Identify exemplary practices, methods, and techniques Conduct evaluation of the effectiveness of staff development training	Evaluate the effectiveness and value of specific career guidance activities and services	Disseminate findings from career guidance and career education programs to appropriate populations

Some Definitions

A few definitions may help clarify the specific nature of career intervention. The interpretation to be used in this volume follows that of Spokane and Oliver (1983), which states that a career intervention is "any treatment or effort intended to enhance an individual's career development or to enable the person to make better career-related decisions" (p. 100). We shall refer in this book to three principal career interventions—techniques, strategies, and programs—as defined below.

> *Career intervention:* Any activity (treatment or effort) designed to enhance a person's career development or to enable that person to make more effective career decisions.
>
> *Technique:* A time-limited application of career intervention principles designed to accomplish a focused goal or to alter a specific vocational behavior. A career life line and a vocational card sort are examples.
>
> *Strategy:* A philosophy or plan of action, or a group of techniques intended to change the vocational behavior of an individual, group of individuals, or an organization. Career counseling of an individual by a single counselor is an example.
>
> *Program:* An organized compilation of techniques or strategies with specific and well-defined objectives that is designed to alter systematically the vocational behavior of a group of individuals in a specific behavior setting (e.g., school, work, or community) over time.

Examples of specific techniques, strategies, and programs will be provided throughout this book. Detailed technique descriptions will be labeled sequentially (e.g., Technique 1), and where possible, illustrated with actual case material or transcriptions. Further explanation of the goals of career intervention is provided in Chapter 2.

SUMMARY

Career interventions can be defined broadly as any direct assistance to an individual to promote more effective decision making, or more narrowly focused, intensive counseling to help resolve career difficulties. Several psychotherapy theories have been misapplied to the career counseling situation and ignore the four characteristics of career situations that differentiate career counseling from psychotherapy: forced adaptation by the social environment, person-environment fit, special career technology, and continuous and discontinuous development. There is a full range of career interventions that varies by level of both counselor and client investment of time and energy.

2

The Process of Career Intervention

PHASES IN INDIVIDUAL AND GROUP CAREER INTERVENTION

All career interventions, whether individual, group, workshop, or curricular, benefit from a smooth and skillful execution (Tyler, 1969). Although extensive theory and research have been generated on the process of personal counseling, there is only the beginning of such a literature in career counseling. Osipow (1982) and Rounds and Tinsley (1984) both noted that career intervention research has been focused exclusively on outcome and argued for more process research that would illuminate how career interventions result in client gains, which in turn pave the way for even more potent and efficient interventions. This chapter presents a description of the systematic client changes that occur during a career intervention, and the components of intervention that are associated with those changes.

Describing Career Intervention Process

In an unusually thoughtful and carefully executed study of the career counseling process, Kirschner (1988) conducted seven counseling sessions with a forty-three-year-old woman who was dissatisfied with her career as a speech therapist in the public schools. The client was screened for overt pathology and found to be relatively free of serious disorders. Before the counseling began the client completed the Holland MVS, the Career Exploration Survey (Stumpf, Colarelli, & Hartman, 1983), the Self-Directed Vocational Goal Attainment Scale, and the Strong-Campbell Interest Inventory (SCII). Process analysis done during counseling included measures of the therapist's intentions (see Table 2-1 for a complete description of intentions used in this

Table 2-1   List of Intentions

___

Instructions

    To judge intentions, the therapist should review the tape within 24 hours so that the session is as fresh and vivid in memory as possible. The therapist should stop the tape after each therapist turn (everything the therapist says between two client speech acts, excluding minimal phrases) and indicate as many intentions as applied for that turn. You should strive to remember exactly what was going through your mind right at the time of the intervention *and* be as honest as possible in reporting what you were actually thinking. Remember that there are no right or wrong answers; the purpose is simply to uncover what you planned to do at that moment. Also remember that you should indicate your intentions only for that immediate intervention, rather than report global strategies for the entire session. Note that not every phrase in the definition for each intention needs to fit to judge that the intention applies. In general, the therapist should choose those intentions that best apply, even if all the phrasing is not exactly applicable to the current situation or does not fit the way he or she would say it.

Intentions

1. **Set limits:** To structure, make arrangements, establish goals and objectives of treatment, outline methods to attain goals, correct expectations about treatment, or establish rules or parameters of relationship (e.g., time, fees, cancellation policies, homework).
2. **Get information:** To find out specific facts about history, client functioning, future plans, and so on.
3. **Give information:** To educate, give facts, correct misperceptions or misinformation, give reasons for therapist's behavior or procedures.
4. **Support:** To provide a warm, supportive, empathic environment; increase trust and rapport and build relationship; help client feel accepted, understood, comfortable, reassured, and less anxious; help establish a person-to-person relationship.
5. **Focus:** To help client get back on the track, change subject, channel or structure the discussion if he or she is unable to begin or has been diffuse or rambling.
6. **Clarify:** To provide or solicit more elaboration, emphasis, or specification when client or therapist has been vague, incomplete, confusing, contradictory, or inaudible.
7. **Hope:** To convey the expectation that change is possible and likely to occur, convey that the therapist will be able to help the client, restore morale, build up the client's confidence to make changes.
8. **Cathart:** To promote relief from tension or unhappy feelings, allow the client a chance to let go or talk through feelings and problems.
9. **Cognitions:** To identify maladaptive, illogical, or irrational thoughts or attitudes (e.g., "I must be perfect").
10. **Behaviors:** To identify and give feedback about the client's inappropriate or maladaptive behaviors and/or their consequences, do a behavioral analysis, point out games.
11. **Self-control:** To encourage client to own or gain a sense of mastery or control over his or her own thoughts, feelings, behaviors, or impulses; help client become more appropriately internal rather than inappropriately external in taking responsibility for his or her role.
12. **Feelings:** To identify, intensity, and/or enable acceptance of feelings; encourage or provoke the client to become aware of or deepen underlying or hidden feelings or affect or experience feelings at a deeper level.

13. **Insight:** To encourage understanding of the underlying reasons, dynamics, assumptions, or unconscious motivations for cognitions, behaviors, attitudes, or feelings. May include an understanding of client's reactions to others' behaviors.
14. **Change:** To build and develop new and more adaptive skills, behaviors, or cognitions in dealing with self and others. May be to instill new, more adaptive assumptive models, frameworks, explanations, or conceptualizations. May be to give an assessment or option about client functioning that will help client see self in a new way.
15. **Reinforce change:** To give positive reinforcement or feedback about behavioral, cognitive, or affective attempts at change to enhance the probability that the change will be continued or maintained; encourage risk taking and new ways of behaving.
16. **Resistance:** To overcome obstacles to change or progress. May discuss failure to adhere to therapeutic procedures, either in past or to prevent possibility of such failure in future.
17. **Challenge:** To jolt the client out of a present state; shake up current beliefs or feelings; test validity, adequacy, reality, or appropriateness of beliefs, thoughts, feelings, or behaviors; help client question the necessity of maintaining old patterns.
18. **Relationship:** To resolve problems as they arise in the relationship in order to build or maintain a smooth working alliance; heal ruptures in the alliance; deal with dependency issues appropriate to stage in treatment; uncover and resolve distortions in client's thinking about the relationship that are based on past experiences rather than current reality.
19. **Therapist needs:** To protect, relieve, or defend the therapist; alleviate anxiety. May try unduly to persuade, argue, or feel good or superior at the expense of the client.

Source: C. E. Hill and K. E. O'Grady, "List of Therapist Intentions Illustrated in a Case Study and with Therapists of Varying Theoretical Orientations," *Journal of Counseling Psychology* 32 (1985): 3-22. Copyright © 1985 by the American Psychological Association. Reprinted by permission.

study) and the client's reactions (Hill, Helms, Spiegel, & Tichenor, 1988; Hill & O'Grady, 1985), a session evaluation questionnaire (Stiles & Snow, 1984), and a critical events measure. The client was contacted eighteen months following counseling to study the longer-term process that she was experiencing outside of the sessions.

The beginning phase of counseling concentrated on building the therapeutic rapport, obtaining information, setting limits, and interpreting tests (Kirschner, 1988). This beginning phase seemed more structured, with the counseling dealing with resistance and limit setting, whereas the next phase "began to focus more on the client's self-concept, obstacles to her career development and values and skills assessment" (p. 228). In the last phase, "occupational research, information synthesis, processing of the counseling relationship and . . . termination . . . ," (p. 228) were addressed. At this point the counselor appeared to use more change intentions and increasingly focused on the relationship. Throughout the sessions, insight for this particular counseling intervention was frequently the counselor's intention. Generally, both client and counselor rated as "smooth" those sessions in which more structuring was employed.

Between the fourth and fifth sessions the client showed an increase in hopefulness, self-support, self-understanding, and responsibility taking. This critical break appeared to mark the beginning of real gains for this client. Several components of the intervention were judged by both client and counselor to be particularly effective, with the most important being the counselor's interpretation of the interests, skills and values instruments. Also helpful was the counselor's feedback about the client's organizational and analytic strengths and her tendency to underestimate her abilities. The client's exploratory research appeared to help her decide to stay in her present career and to expand her opportunities within it. Kirschner concluded that the factors that had proved most successful in this situation—social support, information giving, cognitive rehearsal of aspirations, and a framework for understanding self and work—were quite similar to those described by Holland, Magoon, and Spokane (1981) in their review of career interventions. In addition, several of the interventions found also in psychotherapy studies appeared to have been helpful in this career counseling case, especially

1. inspiring and maintaining a client's expectations of help,
2. arousal of client emotions,
3. providing new learning experiences,
4. enhancing a client's sense of mastery,
5. providing opportunities for the client to internalize and maintain the gains experienced in counseling (Highlen & Hill, 1984).

Kirschner's findings for a career intervention parallel those reported for personal counseling in important respects. In a ground-breaking case study, Hill, Carter, and O'Farrell (1983) found that the first four sessions of therapy were somewhat different from the last eight (see Table 2-2). Process measures in their study suggested that in addition to relationship building and minimal encouraging, the counselor used more fact finding, structuring, and clarifying in the first four sessions, but more reframing and analysis in the final eight.

Another study of the psychotherapy process (Hill & O'Grady, 1985) showed similar decreases in counselor intentions to set limits, get information, support, clarify, hope, and cathart, and increases in the insight, change, and reinforce change intentions across the sessions. Hill's (1989) innovative work also suggested that the counselor's interpretation would reliably lead to the client's increased insight. Table 2-3 presents Hill et al.'s (1988) description of possible client reactions to counselor interventions, which indicates that therapist intentions were more strongly related to client reactions in successful therapy cases than in unsuccessful ones. Although this framework draws heavily from the work of Hill and her colleagues on short-term

Table 2-2 Proportions of Counselor Behaviors for First Four Versus Last Eight Sessions of Treatment

Measure	SESSIONS 1–4 M	SD	SESSIONS 5–12 M	SD	TOTAL M	SD
Response modes						
Minimal encourager	.50	.20	.37	.10	.41	.15
Silence	.04	.05	.03	.03	.04	.04
Approval-reassurance	.02	.01	.04	.03	.03	.02
Information	.08	.02	.12	.05	.10	.04
Direct guidance	.02	.02	.01	.02	.01	.02
Closed question	.05	.01	.04	.02	.04	.02
Open question	.03	.01	.03	.02	.03	.01
Restatement	.06	.01	.07	.03	.07	.02
Reflection	.04	.02	.06	.02	.05	.02
Interpretation	.10	.08	.17	.03	.15	.06
Confrontation	.06	.04	.05	.04	.05	.04
Intentions						
Structure	.08	.07	.05	.04	.06	.05
Fact finding	.18	.13	.02	.02	.07	.11
Focus	.07	.07	.03	.03	.04	.05
Support	.08	.05	.10	.08	.09	.07
Ego strengthen	.03	.04	.11	.08	.08	.08
Clarification	.14	.18	.10	.08	.12	.11
Identification	.09	.12	.10	.04	.09	.07
Effects of behavior	.03	.02	.06	.07	.05	.06
Intensification of feelings	.23	.16	.20	.11	.21	.12
Challenge	.10	.08	.11	.08	.11	.08
Insight	.18	.20	.17	.06	.17	.11
Reframing	.06	.08	.18	.07	.14	.09
Direct change attempts	.00	.00	.02	.02	.01	.02
Indirect change attempts	.01	.02	.07	.05	.05	.05
Analysis of relationship	.00	.00	.12	.17	.08	.14
Anxiety	.026	.008	.030	.004	.029	.027

Note: All figures are based on the proportion of each response category to the total responses for the counselor. Higher numbers indicate a greater relative frequency of occurrence.

Source: C. E. Hill, J. A. Carter, and M. K. O'Farrell, "A Case Study of the Process and Outcome of Time-Limited Counseling," *Journal of Counseling Psychology* 30 (1983): 9. Copyright © 1983 by the American Psychological Association. Reprinted by permission.

psychotherapy, it does apply to the more complex career situation and is consistent with a three-stage model of career counseling suggested by Crites (1981).

Table 2-3   Client Reactions System

Instructions

Review the tape immediately after the session. Try to remember what you were experiencing during the session. Stop the tape after each therapist intervention and list the numbers of the reactions that you felt when you first heard what the therapist said. Choose those reactions that best describe your experience, even if every part of the definition does not apply or the phrasing is not exactly accurate.

Positive Reactions

1. *Understood:* I felt that my therapist really understood me and knew what I was saying or what was going on with me.
2. *Supported:* I felt accepted, reassured, liked, cared for, or safe. I felt like my therapist was on my side or I came to trust, like, respect, or admire my therapist more. This may have involved a change in my relationship with my therapist, such that we resolved a problem between us.
3. *Hopeful:* I felt confident, encouraged, optimistic, strong, pleased, or happy, and felt like I could change.
4. *Relief:* I felt less depressed, anxious, guilty, angry, or had fewer uncomfortable or painful feelings.
5. *Negative thoughts or behaviors:* I became aware of specific negative thoughts or behaviors which cause problems for me or others.
6. *Better self-understanding:* I gained new insight about myself, saw new connections, or began to understand *why* I behaved or felt a certain way. This new understanding helped me accept and like myself.
7. *Clear:* I got more focused about what I was really trying to say, what areas I need to change in my life, what my goals are, or what I want to work on in therapy.
8. *Feelings:* I felt a greater awareness or deepening of feelings or could express my emotions better.
9. *Responsibility:* I accepted my role in events and blamed others less.
10. *Unstuck:* I overcame a block and felt freed up and more involved in what I have to do in therapy.
11. *New perspective:* I gained a new understanding of another person, situation, or the world. I understand *why* people or things are as they are.
12. *Educated:* I gained greater knowledge or information. I learned something I had not known.
13. *New ways to behave:* I learned specific ideas about what I can do differently to cope with particular situations or problems. I solved a problem, made a choice or decision, or decided to take a risk.
14. *Challenged:* I felt shook up, forced to question myself, or to look at issues I had been avoiding.

Negative Reactions

15. *Scared:* I felt overwhelmed, afraid, or wanted to avoid or not admit to having some feeling or problem. I may have felt that my therapist was too pushy or would disapprove of me or would not like me.
16. *Worse:* I felt less hopeful, sicker, out of control, dumb, incompetent,

ashamed, or like giving up. Perhaps my therapist ignored me, criticized me, hurt me, pitied me, or treated me as weak and helpless. I may have felt jealous of or competitive with my therapist.

17. *Stuck:* I felt blocked, impatient or bored. I did not know what to do next or how to get out of the situation. I felt dissatisfied with the progress of therapy or having to go over the same things again.

18. *Lack of direction:* I felt angry or upset that my therapist didn't give me enough guidance or direction.

19. *Confused:* I did not know how I was feeling or felt distracted from what I wanted to say. I was puzzled or could not understand what my therapist was trying to say. I was not sure I agreed with my therapist.

20. *Misunderstood:* I felt that my therapist did not really hear what I was trying to say, misjudged me, or made assumptions about me that were incorrect.

21. *No reaction:* I had no particular reaction. My therapist may have been making social conversation, gathering information, or was unclear.

Source: C. E. Hill, S. B. Spiegel, and V. Tichenor, "Development of a System for Assessing Client Reactions to Therapist Intervention," *Journal of Counseling Psychology* 34 (1988): 27–36. Copyright © 1988 by the American Psychological Association. Reprinted by permission.

Martin (in press) maintained that the effects of any therapist intervention were mediated by the client's cognitive reactions to that intervention. Martin argued that the cognitive interplay between counselor and client is so complex as to allow only for probabilistic statements about what client reactions and behaviors could result from a given counselor intervention. There is evidence that career counseling may require more structure than psychotherapy (Holland et al., 1981) and therefore may involve more homogeneous goals and assumptions from both client and counselor than is generally the case with psychotherapy. In career counseling, the focus is clearer, the client's goal is always implicit (even when unstated), and the available technology results in less variable interventions than in psychotherapy. Consider the study by Hampl, Lonborg, Lassiter, Williams, and Schmidt (1987), which found no differences in process or outcome of career counseling for clients of quite differing conceptual level.

A PRELIMINARY MODEL OF THE CAREER INTERVENTION PROCESS

While it may be true that probabilistic statements about which intervention leads to which client reaction are more reliable when microanalysis of actual moment-to-moment experiences is conducted, clinical case material and a few recent articles do suggest a preliminary model of the intervention of short-term career counseling (Table 2-4).

This model has three major phases (beginning, activation, and termination) and eight subphases (opening, aspiring, loosening, assessment, inquiry, commitment, execution, and follow-through). Each subphase involves the

Table 2-4 Phases, Subphases, and Counselor and Client Processes in Individual and Group Career Intervention

PHASE	BEGINNING			ACTIVATION			COMPLETION	
Subphase	Opening	Aspiring	Loosening	Assessment	Inquiry	Commitment	Execution	Follow-Through
Principal therapeutic task	Establishment of therapeutic context	Client rehearsal of aspirations	Perception of incongruence	Acquisition of cognitive structure	Mobilization of constructive behavior	Management of anxiety	Persistent search	Consolidation of gain
Counselor process	Set expectation	Activate hope	Identify conflicts	Generate hypothesis	Test hypothesis	Share hypothesis	Resolve conflicts	Closure
Counselor technique	Structure, acceptance	Fantasy	Reflection, clarification	Test, interpretation	Probing, leading	Reassurance	Reinforcement	Periodic recontact
Client reaction	Relief	Excitement	Anxiety	Progress, insight	Self-efficacy, control, Exploration	Compromise	Withdrawal, adherence	Satisfaction, certainty

principal therapeutic task, the counselor process and technique needed to achieve that task, and the expected client reaction to its successful completion.

Beginning Phase

The beginning phase contains three subphases: opening, aspiring, and loosening.

Opening Subphase.   In the opening subphase, the client brings a certain amount of anxiety and energy to the career counseling process, and the principal therapeutic tasks to establish the therapeutic context, including setting expectations and providing a certain amount of structuring about what will or will not occur during the intervention. We have found that giving clients a brief handout (see Technique 2-1) is an effective way to offer structure and information about the intervention process as well as suggestions from the literature about how to use the time spent during an intervention. But no exaggerated claims or promises are made. This is followed by discussions and contracting, if necessary, to insure that clients understand the time commitment necessary and the kinds of activities usually undertaken during intervention. Typically, clients respond to this first subphase with an immediate sense of relief mixed with the beginnings of some hope about the outcome of the intervention. Larger gains begin to occur around the fourth or fifth session (Kirschner, 1988). In the group setting the initial relief reaction is further enhanced by what Yalom (1985) called universality, or the perception that one is not alone in a difficulty. The opening subphase begins with the first contact at intake or in the first session, and is usually brief (one or two sessions).

Aspiring Subphase.   The aspiring subphase provides the opportunity for clients to rehearse their career aspirations either to themselves or to others, which is an important ingredient in a career intervention (Holland et al., 1981). This rehearsal triggers a broader cognitive exploration and the activation of what has been variously labeled the dream (Levinson, Darrow, Klein, Levinson, & McKee, 1978), the aspiration (L. S. Gottfredson, 1981), or the possible self (Markus & Nurius, 1986). Aspirations may also be rehearsed by using daydream or fantasy techniques. Although, as Morgan and Skovholt (1977) noted, many career counselors may flinch a bit at the term *fantasy* because of the sense of personal pathology or "touchy-feely" tone it may convey, in the career context daydream and fantasy techniques are effective ways to permit clients to explore their dreams and goals using their inner experiences in a relatively nonthreatening manner. The relaxation that is part of these techniques also lessens the anxiety that causes clients to restrict their exploratory process. Even though some of the options generated in such exercises may be unrealistic, we have found that at least one option (usually the second or third option offered) is a fairly plausible future possibility. Technique 2-2 describes a fantasy technique that can be

Technique 2-1

Spokane Career Associates
Arnold Spokane, Ph.D.

To Our Vocational Counseling Clients

For reasons of your own choosing, you have decided to pursue vocational counseling. We feel that there are some basic principles you should know before you begin this important undertaking. These few pointers will help you to make the most effective use of your counseling time, and assist you in making progress toward your career goals. We hope that your reading of this introduction will answer a few of your initial questions, and prepare you for the counseling sessions that will follow.

These are, no doubt, exciting times for you. You have hopes and dreams about what you would like for yourself . . . fears about what lies ahead . . . relief at having finally begun counseling. The suggestions we make here will assist you during this important life transition.

Things You Can Do to Facilitate Vocational Progress

Talk about your situation. Research continues to show that talking about your hopes, dreams, and preferences with family members, loved ones, friends, employers, or business associates, in addition to your counselor, will help to clarify your goals and stimulate your thinking. In particular, you should talk about how you would like your work life to be (what activities you would prefer and what job characteristics seem important to you). The more you talk and think about your choice, the better you will be to implement it.

Share your feelings with supportive people. There will likely be times during counseling when your feelings about your ability to make an effective choice will be particularly acute. You may feel unsure, afraid, depressed, angry—and these moods may alternate with periods of hopefulness, euphoria, or eager anticipation. These shifts are quite normal, given your circumstances. When you have feelings that you are aware of, we encourage you to express them openly to your counselor and, once again, to loved ones or other important people in your life. Ask for their support and take it when it's offered. Expressing and resolving your feelings will provide important additional information to use in making your choices and reviewing your options. Often, when feelings remain unexpressed, progress in career counseling goes more slowly.

Be a reasonable adventurer. Some years ago, Dr. Roy Heath described the ideal learner as a "reasonable adventurer." By this, Dr. Heath meant that one should be open to new experiences and see each new or novel situation as an adventure and an opportunity to acquire new skills and understandings. You may also need to take some calculated risks. These risks will probably be neither trivial nor enormous. Sometimes when people fear failure, they take risks that are either much too small or much too large. We urge you to take well calculated, moderate risks when they are appropriate (e.g., relocating or trying something new).

Explore the occupational world. The best way to clarify your occupational preferences and test them out against reality, is to explore your options as fully as possible. You should engage in *all* of the following exploratory behaviors: (1) Read books, articles, occupational briefs, and any other relevant occupational information about the options you are considering. Get and read a copy of Richard Bolles's *What Color is Your Parachute?* (1988) and investigate the Department of Labor's *Occupational Outlook Handbook* (1988). (2) Visit as many possible occupational sites as you can. Bring along a list of 5 to 10 questions you would like answered. Talk to people in jobs in which you have an interest. Ask them what they do and how they like it. Usually, under pressure to make a decision, most people narrow or restrict their exploratory behavior at the very time they should be expanding it.

Remember that everyone has unique skills and abilities. Even though you might have doubts about your skills, most people have many more abilities than they realize. Recognizing what these skills are and how they translate to job options is a very important part of counseling. Think about what you do well. Write your skills down on 3" × 5" cards, and try to review them in a positive way. Be specific; ask people who know you well for feedback about what skills they believe you have.

Prepare yourself to make a commitment. One of the more difficult tasks you will face is the forging of a new vocational identity that you are willing to commit yourself to, at least tentatively. The choices you make now will probably not be permanent ones. Nonetheless, you should be prepared to make some kind of serious commitment, even though it may be temporary. Making this commitment can be frightening, but it is absolutely necessary to successful career counseling. The first commitment you should make is to set aside adequate time for this career exploration.

Be aware that many people can derive some benefit from counseling. Your success depends upon how hard you work, and your willingness to make a commitment to one or more tentative choices. You could choose simply to "go through the motions" of counseling and not show progress. The more willing you are to invest yourself in making an appropriate choice, however, the more likely you will be to make gains. There is a fair body of research evidence that shows that clients do benefit from career counseling on a fairly consistent basis. The responsibility for your outcome is yours, but your counselor can help in some important ways (e.g., by helping you to integrate knowledge about yourself).

We urge you to follow these few important suggestions and to read them over periodically. During the course of counseling, you may be exposed to new information, including an occupational history, vocational interest inventories, projective techniques to help you understand how you make career decisions, fantasy techniques for projecting into your future, exercises designed to facilitate your exploratory behavior, interview skills training, and other techniques to help you make your decision. If you have questions about any of these procedures during counseling, please ask.

applied in either an individual or group setting. Fantasy techniques can be done silently, with no interaction between client and counselor, or with constant interactive feedback and coaching. Obviously, the silent fantasy is preferable in the group setting. Variations of this technique are consistently rated as the most effective and enjoyable interventions by both clients and counselors (Kirschner, 1988). The following excerpt from an actual counseling session illustrates the use of the fantasy technique:

COUNSELOR   What I'd like to do today is to project you into the future a little bit and to find out something about what you think you'd really like. Now we're not looking for you to put yourself in an exact job necessarily. I'm looking more for some observations about life style, how you like to live. I think that's an important part of who you are; you presented kind of an upbeat, happy life style, and I think that's something you want to continue, even though you may be doing some drudgery that you really hate. So what I want you to do now is to assume that it is a full five years into the future.

CLIENT   O.K.

COUNSELOR   It's 1992; you've made a good career choice, you've made your decision, you're happy about it, you've moved off into your new job, and you like it. You can pick the day, pick the month, pick the year, pick whatever time it is you want. And I'm going to ask you to imagine yourself waking up in the morning and then running through your whole day.

CLIENT   O.K. The type, well, do I have to start with the time of day?

COUNSELOR   Yeah, wherever we locate you.

CLIENT   O.K. Time of year? Geez, ah, well now, is this purely fantasy, or is this something that you expect?

COUNSELOR   Purely fantasy. We don't want what you expect yet.

CLIENT   Well, I could get pretty wild with that.

COUNSELOR   O.K. That's good!

CLIENT   Wake up time, O.K., well, in five years.

COUNSELOR   We want time of year.

CLIENT   Time of year.

CLIENT   I don't know, fall.

COUNSELOR   Fall—September, October, November?

CLIENT   October.

COUNSELOR   O.K., let's make it a Friday.... O.K. You're asleep. How do you get up in the morning? Do you get up on your own? Do you have an alarm clock?

CLIENT   Well, if ideally if I'm not working 9:00 to 5:00, I don't have an alarm clock.

COUNSELOR   O.K. No alarm.

CLIENT   No alarm; I wake up.

COUNSELOR   What time?

CLIENT   Uh, 9:00.

COUNSELOR   O.K. You open your eyes, what do you see around?

CLIENT   Geez, uh, a nice semi-suburban type house.

COUNSELOR   O.K. Are you in the bedroom? You wake up in the bedroom? Look around. What do you see? What colors, what ... ?

CLIENT   In five years probably a wife next to me; I don't think any kids yet, no kids yet.

COUNSELOR   How about the room?

CLIENT   I think the room would have a lot of interesting type statue things. I've been to Jamaica before, and I kind of started collecting these wooden statues and things of that nature. Some of those, some strange paintings that I've maybe ... ah, lot of books.

COUNSELOR   Bookcases, bookshelves?

CLIENT   Yeah.

COUNSELOR   Built-in, freestanding, or ... ?

CLIENT   Geez, this is hard to visualize.

COUNSELOR   Yes, it is, but that's what I want you to do. We want to get as graphic as we possibly can.

CLIENT   O.K., a couple built-in bookcases, a couple freestanding.

COUNSELOR   O.K., good, good. O.K., now what do you do?

CLIENT   I get up. My wife also works, but she works elsewhere. I might work in the house, say in the study or something, typing a manuscript.

COUNSELOR   But you've got to get up first. What do you do when you get up?

CLIENT   Hop in the shower, I go downstairs, eat some breakfast.

COUNSELOR   Do you dress first?

CLIENT   Yeah.

COUNSELOR   What do you wear?

CLIENT   You want the ... O.K., ah, I put on something comfortable. I don't usually wear a suit but something nice though.

COUNSELOR   Like what? It's November, October.

CLIENT   Something comfortable, like maybe nice jeans and a flannel type shirt or something.

COUNSELOR   O.K. Downstairs.

CLIENT   Downstairs I'm eating breakfast, um, maybe listening to the radio.

COUNSELOR   What kind of room is the kitchen? dining room, kitchen?

CLIENT   Probably some kitchen like a modern type kitchen with .... Purely ideal, it's a country kitchen with a thing in the middle—a cooking deal.

COUNSELOR   Right.

CLIENT   Wow, this is pretty fun!

COUNSELOR   O.K. Good, you have something to eat.

CLIENT   Yeah, cereal, fruit, whatever, umm, get finished with that, and then go into my den-study and start typing on my computer, doing a manuscript or some kind of ...

COUNSELOR   O.K. What are we heading into now?

CLIENT   A desk on one side that's not too big and ominous—like a nice walnut or woodsy desk type of deal. And then the computer is under some shelves of books and things. The floor is probably carpeted but it's not thick shag but it's like a kind of a thinner rug.

COUNSELOR   O.K.

CLIENT   Yeah, yeah, probably has two windows. It's not a large room, but it's large enough to move around in. Two windows—one next to the desk and one across from it—and the computer over there. Some pictures, some photography pictures that I've taken, on the desk.

COUNSELOR   Cluttered? neat? Are you cluttered or neat?

CLIENT   Sections of it are neat, and sections are cluttered. The thing that maybe I've been working on late into the morning is still there probably.

COUNSELOR   You're working on a manuscript or something?

CLIENT   A manuscript or some kind of consulting research or something.

COUNSELOR   O.K. How?

CLIENT   There is probably a desk on the telephone, I mean a telephone on the desk. A little awkward, and I have some, a lot of, business contacts while I'm there, and I don't stay in my study all day. I'm out and about doing things, meeting people, and then I go back to the study and I . . . .

COUNSELOR   You mean out in the house?

CLIENT   No, in the business world or . . .

COUNSELOR   O.K. Well, how long do you work on this manuscript? It's what, about 10:00 now?

CLIENT   Probably until 12:30 or 1.

COUNSELOR   O.K. You finish that up and then what do you do?

CLIENT   Then I grab a quick bite to eat, and then I meet with someone that I have an appointment with.

COUNSELOR   O.K. You get in the car and drive?

CLIENT   Uh huh.

COUNSELOR   What kind of car?

CLIENT   It's got to be a Volkswagen; it's got to be a German car.

COUNSELOR   O.K. In you go and drive.

CLIENT   I drive.

COUNSELOR   Where do you drive?

CLIENT   Umm, I drive down a semi-country road, but it's paved and that lasts for about a mile. And then I get on to a suburban road and then a highway, and then I go to an office and meet with a . . .

COUNSELOR   Aauuulright! You drive on the highway, and you get to wherever you are going, and you park the car. You get out. What do you see? We're at about what, 1:30 now?

CLIENT   About 1:30, maybe 2:00. Umm, well, depending on the day, I could see an office complex, or I could see a school type environment or some institution or some ah or government building or ah . . .

COUNSELOR   O.K. O.K., you get out of the car.

CLIENT   Or even a, ah, I don't know about a person's home. Maybe my own office, I don't know, an office somewhere else.

COUNSELOR   What kind of a building?

CLIENT   Ah, probably an office building, but one that's not too huge and concrete and still like a, it's not a city office building its a, ah, outside.

COUNSELOR   Suburban or small city?

CLIENT   Yeah, yeah, something like that, or like maybe even in the little town it's the big office building.

COUNSELOR   You live outside the town, which is a little more country, and you ride into a little town with a substantial building for that town but not like anything you'd see around here.

CLIENT   Right, right!

COUNSELOR   O.K. You get out, you go into the building.

CLIENT   I know the people pretty well there; they are my business contacts, but they're also on a lesser level social companions.

COUNSELOR   O.K. You look around you . . . desks, offices . . .

CLIENT   Yeah, probably some desks, some cubicles, some offices, umm . . .

COUNSELOR   You share office space?

CLIENT   Maybe, yeah, or maybe we all come with our ideas and discuss them. Probably, in some kind of space where everyone is . . . in other words, it's no one's office necessarily, it's but it's a publicly accessible space. Go in there, throw some ideas back and forth, come up with the project that we are doing or discuss what we've just finished. A lot of collaboration, in other words. Get things rolling there, and depending on how they're going, stay an hour or stay four hours. You know, there's no pat schedule.

COUNSELOR   O.K. So let's say that you work for an hour. That would bring you to 3:00, 3:30, or later? What?

CLIENT   3:30.

COUNSELOR   What happens then?

CLIENT   Then I deal, I do something from 4:00 to 5:00 which is physically active; I play racketball or something.

Although the client had difficulty in switching scenarios and was occasionally concerned that his fantasies were too far-fetched, the exercise stimulated him to rehearse his career aspirations in a very direct manner. Skovholt, Morgan, and Negron-Cunningham (1989) wrote that such mental imagery can be used to uncover subconscious material for consideration in career decision making, or to experiment with new roles and decisions under low levels of threat and high levels of relaxation. Their review of the literature on the application of mental imagery in career and life planning led them to the rather cautious conclusion that, when used alone, it is unreasonable to expect mental imagery to do anything more than increase self-awareness and catalyze the cognitive rehearsal of aspirations. Although imagery may not have a substantial effect on traditional outcome measures, this technique is one of the thoroughly examined options in the career counselor's repertoire.

Technique 2-2

"A Day in the Future"–A Typical Guided Fantasy
James I. Morgan, University of Florida
Thomas M. Skovholt, University of Minnesota

Objective: To use a guided fantasy experience to generate possible career options; can be used with individuals making an initial career choice or thinking through a change.

Time Requirement: Approximately 1 hour.

Procedure: The guided fantasy experience consists of three parts: (a) inducing relaxation, (b) the fantasy itself, (c) processing the fantasy experience.

Inducing Relaxation

1. Relaxation training à la Jacobsen can be used (Jacobsen, E., *Progressive Relaxation*, Chicago: University of Chicago Press, 1938).
2. Ask participants to focus on tensing and relaxing each major muscle group sequentially.
3. Emphasize paying special attention to jaws, faces, foreheads, and scalps.
4. Also encourage participants to pay special attention to their breathing and to take deep regular breaths.

The Fantasy Itself

1. As participants remain relaxed, ask them to imagine events during a typical work day 5, 10, or 15 years from now.
2. The following script can then be used:

    Let your imagination take you 10 years into your future. As I talk, just let any images come that will. Don't answer my questions aloud. Just let the images form. (pause) . . . You are just awakening from a good night's sleep. You lie in bed just a minute longer before getting up and doing the things you usually do before going to breakfast. (pause)

    On your way to breakfast now, look around you to see where you are— what this place is like. . . . Perhaps you can begin to sense things now. See if there is anyone with you. Eat your breakfast now and notice how you experience it. (pause) It is nearly time to go to work. . . . perhaps you stay at home, perhaps you leave. If you leave, notice how you get there. Do you walk? . . . drive? . . . take a train or bus? How do things look along the way? Do you see anyone you know? (pause)

    You are approaching where you work if you are not already there. What do you notice? What do you feel as you enter and start about doing your work? Who else is there? What are they doing? Complete your morning's work right up to your lunchtime. (pause)

    It is lunchtime now. Do you stay in or go out? What do you have to eat? Taste it. Smell it. Are you alone or with someone? Is this lunch like your usual one? (pause)

Return to work now and finish the workday. See if anything is different or if it stays the same. Notice what the last thing is that you do before you get ready to quit work for the day. (pause)

Leave your work place and go to where you live. See what you notice along the way. As you arrive where you live, notice how you feel and how your living place looks. Do what you do before your evening meal. (pause) Eat your meal, paying attention to how it tastes, how many help-ings you have, who, if anyone, is with you. (pause)

After your meal do what you do during the evening before going to bed. (pause)

Go to bed now. Just before dropping off to sleep, review your day. Was it a good day? What pleased you in particular? Go to sleep now. I'll help you awaken in a moment. (pause)

You're awakening now . . . but not in your bed . . . in (this place). Open your eyes when you're ready, and just sit quietly for a minute.

Processing the Fantasy

1. Give participants an opportunity to discuss impressions and feelings.
2. Group processing helps participants hear each other and realize the great variety of possible reactions.

Guided Fantasy Variations

"The Award Ceremony" fantasy. In this guided fantasy, participants are asked to imagine themselves the recipient of a special award at a gala banquet. The award is for a special competence the participant possesses. This fantasy at-tempts to help participants crystallize their own goals and think about their motivations. It attempts to tap what White (1959) calls competence motiva-tion, the central motivation of human behavior.

Reprinted with permission of the authors.

Loosening Subphase.   The aspiring subphase gives way to the loosen-ing subphase, as clients begin to uncover or identify conflicts that their aspira-tions engender. For example, the more clearly clients can articulate a positive possible self, the more unsatisfied they may become with their current career situation. The loosening subphase may also cause the client to relive previous painful compromises or old hurts and failures. In addition, during this phase clients may come to appreciate the full complexity and intractability of their particular career problem. As assessment procedures are undertaken, the incongruence between the clients' interest, skills, abilities, and aspirations and the demands of their current job will become even clearer.

The clients' reaction to the loosening subphase is a gradual increase in anxiety as they begin to see that the intervention process may require a difficult and perhaps painful realignment of their past beliefs about what is appropriate or possible to achieve from the career intervention. At this point the counselor's role is to clarify and use reflection of feelings and content.

Activation Phase

As Hill and O'Grady (1985) demonstrated in case studies with short-term psychotherapy clients, as therapeutic interventions proceed, there are decreases in counselor intentions to set limits, get information, support, clarify, activate hope, and cathart. In contrast, later sessions are characterized by increases in counselor intentions to promote insight and change and to reinforce change (see Table 2-1). Hill and O'Grady's work supported a two-phase model of therapeutic intervention in which the first phase is characterized by support and structure, and the second by change, which in psychotherapy is typically called the working phase. In our preliminary model, however (see Table 2-4), it is known as the activation phase, which contains three subphases: assessment, inquiry, and commitment.

In the activation phase, several important therapeutic processes should occur. The counselor who in the beginning phase was primarily engaged in structuring techniques to establish the therapeutic context and encourage the client to start aspiring to new career goals and dreams becomes more active and cognitive intellectually to help the client to see any incongruencies between interests, abilities, and personality and the requirements of specific jobs. Support levels must stay high and even increase in the beginning of the activation stage, since a client's increased anxiety in reaction to a loosening of deeply held beliefs about self and career can result in high levels of dropout or crippling immobility if not addressed directly. Figure 2-1 illustrates this relationship among client anxiety level, counselor structure, and dropout in individual and group career counseling. Typically, just as client anxiety is rising during the activation phase, most prepackaged career interventions are reducing structure, which is seen as less necessary in later phases. The high dropout rates in group interventions, typically in excess of 50 percent (O'Neil, Ohlde, Barke, Gelwick, & Garfield, 1980; Robbins, Mullison, Boggs, Riedesel, & Jacobson, 1985; Zager, 1982), generally result from this increased client anxiety, which is accompanied by diminished hope that a reasonable outcome can be found and implemented.

Assessment Subphase.   During the assessment subphase, the client receives feedback from inventories employed during the counseling process and very rapidly begins to generate hypotheses about what occupations might be reasonably fitting and accessible. The principal therapeutic task during the assessment subphase is to assist the client in acquiring a cognitive structure (i.e., a set of operational rules) for use in evaluating occupations that are explored later in the intervention process. It is during this assessment subphase that the client begins to feel a sense of progress concerning the resolution of the concerns that motivated the client to enter counseling.

Inquiry Subphase.   During the inquiry subphase, a parallel cognitive process, which has been called hypothesis testing by Pepinsky and Pepinsky

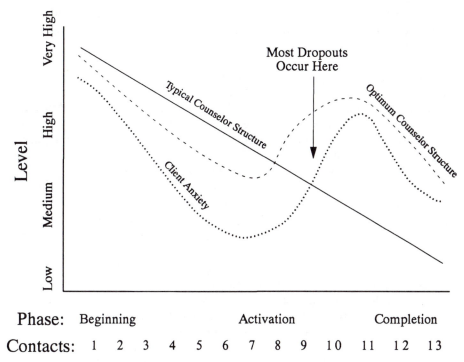

Figure 2-1   Anxiety Level During Phases of Career Intervention.

(1954), begins for both the client and the counselor, as hypotheses are systematically and continuously formed and tested based upon behavioral changes in the client (Blustein & Strohmer, 1987; M. J. Miller, 1985; Strohmer & Newman, 1983). The counselor, according to Pepinsky and Pepinsky, is an applied behavioral scientist who is constantly revising hypotheses in the face of new data. The client is likewise engaging in hypothesis testing, often having come to counseling with a naïve view of the career world that must be unearthed, examined, and revised in the face of input from the counselor and other sources of information. Evidence from instructional psychology, especially the teaching and learning of science and math, suggests that learners often possess such naïve, intuitive theories about the world that may bias their perceptions (Resnick, 1983). Even after exposure to correct, alternative information, these theories will eventually predominate in an individual's thinking unless they are uncovered and examined critically.

ANXIETY AND ACTIVATION.   Anxiety is considered by some theorists to be an irrelevant drive that interferes with the hypothesis-testing process (Pepinsky & Pepinsky, 1954) and that accounts for clients' recurring irrational or nonconstructive actions. Several studies have accordingly demonstrated that treatments to reduce anxiety, although rarely effective in reducing trait anxiety, seem to improve clients' functioning level and ability to make effective career decisions (Mendonca & Siess, 1976; Mitchell & Krumboltz, 1987).

Commitment Subphase. Substantial reductions in state anxiety are necessary for the successful completion of the commitment subphase, in which the client may have to compromise unrealistic aspirations and prepare for the execution of an interim career choice. During the commitment subphase, anxiety that is generated from exploring options and from the inquiry subphase must be managed so that the client can successfully engage in compromise where necessary, and so that the client can make a preliminary commitment to an option (see Table 2–4).

Other research, however, has found that moderate levels of anxiety enhance performance and can lead to productive planning and behavior in career situations (Barlow, 1988). As Barlow noted, "the capacity to experience anxiety and the capacity to plan are two sides of the same coin" (p. 12). If the anxiety about career possibilities reaches crippling levels, Barlow argued that the most effective clinical reduction strategy is systematic exposure to a fear inducing stimulus. Even panic states can be reduced or eliminated through psychological or pharmacological interventions. If undiagnosed, anxiety can abruptly halt the progress in career intervention in a sort of stalemate between the counselor's attempts to mobilize the client to constructive action and the client's heightened anxiety about the career choice process.

THE FEASIBILITY INQUISITION.   As conflicts are unearthed and environmental barriers become apparent, most career counseling clients fear that they will be unable to execute a reasonably fitting option, even if one can be identified. This fear is so powerful that in most cases the client believes that it cannot be overcome by any means. The fear intensifies when the client appreciates the reality of the predicament and constraints acting in a career decision, which usually occurs midway in the counseling process. At this point anxiety increases dramatically, and the client will attempt to persuade or at least to cross-examine the counselor concerning the potency of these barriers. This intense challenge from the fearful client is called the feasibility inquisition. Although the client does not want this inquisition to confirm his or her worst fears, someone in this frame of mind can be very persistent and convincing, as the following excerpt from my seventh session with a thirty-three-year-old client, Donna, illustrates:

CLIENT   I will say that the down side of this, it's been, you know, anxiety ... and not knowing ... and especially when I see my friends and family getting involved with career choices and getting into those rather successfully ... and I, being the oldest, feel like I'm floundering around out here and that gets to be disconcerting.

COUNSELOR   I think to a degree that may be true, because you're in a field that will never look as clear as one of your . . . let's pick a family member . . .

CLIENT   Oh, my sister's staying with us, and I talked to her just this morning. . . She's an attorney, my brother's in medicine.

COUNSELOR   Those are two very clear fields where everything is in a very straight line. That's never going to happen for you. You're in an enterprising field, and it's never going to be that clear.

CLIENT   It's going to be a zigzag!

COUNSELOR   That's right. And that may be something you have to learn to . . .

CLIENT   Adjust to . . .

COUNSELOR   Adapt to, yes . . .

CLIENT   Yeah, that's going to be a tall order, because it's been hard as far as being able to adjust . . .

COUNSELOR   Yes, I think right now it produces a lot of anxiety.

CLIENT   Oh! For sure! I've been just trying to turn this around and just look at this as an opportunity. I've got a chance to get away from this place that I hated.

At this point in the counseling Donna is reexperiencing old sibling rivalries and perhaps some undisclosed private feelings of failure. The reality of how difficult it may be for her to execute a successful enterprising career produces considerable anxiety for Donna. Although I gave her reassurance and did not attend directly to the feasibility inquisition when it was presented, I would have been more astute to have responded with an empathic but direct statement about her obvious fear that she might never find a successful way out of her current, and to her, abominable work situation.

Since to some extent external barriers *are* intractable, a client's argument that it may be impossible to execute any option can be difficult to refute. Usually the effective counter to a feasibility inquisition is to admit that while the client's fears may have some validity, the client can mobilize persistently constructive behavior to overcome many external barriers. Without having seen enough clients who have surmounted such obstacles, an inexperienced counselor often finds it difficult to fend off the feasibility inquisition. I refer such counselors to the evidence on the outcomes of career intervention (see Chapter 9), and advise their competent supervision by an experienced counselor (see Chapter 10). The inquisition described here occurs in all forms of career intervention (e.g., groups, classes, workshops).

Kerr, Olson, Claiborn, Bauers-Gruenler, and Paolo (1983) saw the inquisition as a dual process of *opposition*, or pessimism concerning vocational exploration, and *resistance*, or negative attitudes toward the counseling process. Opposition and resistance could either exist prior to or result from the counseling process. Kerr et al. suggested that a flexible use of counselor social influence power (expertness and attractiveness behaviors) would

		Crisis: No	Crisis: Yes
Commitment	No	Identity diffused	Identity moratorium
	Yes	Identity foreclosed	Identity achieved

Figure 2-2 The Formation of an Ego Identity.

reduce opposition and resistance, or in this analogue, optimism about career exploration and attitudes toward counseling. How a counselor handles the feasibility inquisition may significantly influence the client's ability to implement a career choice. After a brief expertness intervention, many of the subjects improved their attitudes about their career futures and increased their level of career exploration.

Once the feasibility inquisition has been resolved and/or the client has sufficiently managed the anxiety generated by the activation process, the final step in this stage is the development of commitment from the client. This point has been made most effectively by Marcia (1980) in unusually influential research on the development of an ego identity, which, he argued, is a psychosocial task that requires two sequential processes: the experiencing of a crisis and the development of a commitment, which produces reintegration (see Figure 2-2). This model is clinically helpful as the client enters the completion phase of a career intervention. A new measure, called the commitment to career choices scale (Blustein, Ellis, & Devenis, in press) operationalizes the tendency to foreclose described by Marcia, as well as the generalized level of commitment to career choice.

Completion Phase

The completion phase, the final and very critical part of a career intervention, begins when the client has resolved presenting conflicts sufficiently to engage in persistently constructive attitudes, emotions, and behaviors that will lead to a satisfactory career choice. The therapeutic task in this phase, which consists of two subphases (execution and follow-through), is the reinforcement of these changes.

The completion phase, typically called termination in psychotherapy, was described well by Janis (1983), who argued that hope of future contact and extension of the counselor's social support beyond the therapy sessions is crucial for effective client change. Simply stated, it is human nature to resist difficult treatment regimens, whether medical, educational, or psychotherapeutic. This resistance occurs in all phases of career intervention—in groups, in workshops, and especially in long-term classes. Janis held that the counselor is able to move the client toward beneficial outcomes by bolstering the client's self-esteem by maintaining uninterrupted positive regard for the client. The socially supportive aspects of the therapeutic relationship, then, are crucial to the client's sustained improvement beyond the confines of the counseling setting (Janis, 1983; Meichenbaum & Turk, 1987). Janis (1983) listed twelve variables that determine the degree of a counselor's influence, or referent power, over a client (Table 2-5).

Even after the client has successfully mobilized for implementation of a career option, there is no guarantee that the client will be able to maintain a constructive search after counseling ends. In medicine, this problem is called compliance, and usually relates to patients following a prescribed regimen at home (e.g., taking medicine or caring for a wound). In psychology, compliance problems usually arise in programs oriented to changing undesirable behaviors (e.g., overeating or smoking). For example, while it may be possible to lose large amounts of weight, it appears to be much more difficult to keep the weight off than to lose it. Psychology is just beginning to understand how to encourage compliance. Meichenbaum and Turk (1987) offered counselors guidelines for dealing with adherence problems, which are presented here with some rewording to make them appropriate to career situations:

Guideline 1: Anticipate Nonadherence. Life circumstances, particularly a lack of financial resources, can work against constructive behavior during career decisions, as can any educational or learning limitations, feelings of helplessness, or misconceptions about how to mobilize for a career decision. Anticipating nonadherence that might stem from such factors will permit some customizing of interventions to overcome the problems and facilitate gain.

Guideline 2: Consider the Intervention Regimen from the Client's Perspective. Clients begin career interventions with diverse fears, beliefs, and attitudes, which Krumboltz (1983) has called private rules, that may affect their ability to make an effective career decision. For example, in spite of a clear desire for a change, a client may be reluctant to leave a highly prestigious job for fear of losing the esteem of others.

Guideline 3: Foster a Collaborative Relationship Based on Negotiation. Exacting the commitments in time and energy required to make a career change or decision may be difficult, and if not confronted directly, may result in a lack of progress, frustration, or dropout.

Guideline 4: Be Client Oriented. The client's attempts to make strides toward a personally relevant goal should be reinforced, even if they are not perfect from a therapeutic point of view.

Guideline 5: Customize Treatment. Departures from standard interventions are sometimes necessary with a particularly difficult client. The counselor may need to institute anxiety management training if the client

Table 2-5 Critical Phases and Twelve Key Variables That Determine the Degree of Counselors' Referent Power as Change Agents

Phase	Variables
Phase 1: Building up referent power	1. Encouraging clients to make self-disclosures *versus* not doing so
	2. Giving positive feedback (acceptance and understanding) *versus* giving neutral or negative feedback in response to self-disclosure
	3. Using self-disclosures to give insight and cognitive restructuring *versus* giving little insight or cognitive restructuring
Phase 2: Using referent power	4. Making directive statements or endorsing specific recommendations regarding actions the client should carry out *versus* abstaining from any directive statements or endorsements
	5. Eliciting commitment to the recommended course of action *versus* not eliciting commitment
	6. Attributing the norms being endorsed to a respected secondary group *versus* not doing so
	7. Giving selective positive feedback *versus* giving noncontingent acceptance or predominantly neutral or negative feedback[a]
	8. Giving communications and training procedures that build up a sense of personal responsibility *versus* giving no such communications or training
Phase 3: Retaining referent power after contact ends and promoting internalization	9. Giving reassurances that the counselor will continue to maintain an attitude of positive regard *versus* giving no such reassurances
	10. Making arrangements for phone calls, exchange of letters, or other forms of communication that foster hope for future contact, real or symbolic, at the time of terminating face-to-face meetings *versus* making no such arrangements
	11. Giving reminders that continue to foster a sense of personal responsibility *versus* giving no such reminders
	12. Building up the client's self-confidence about succeeding without the aid of the counselor *versus* not doing so

[a]Selective feedback means a combination of (a) negative feedback in response to any of the client's comments about being reluctant, unwilling, or failing to act in accordance with the recommendations and (b) positive feedback in response to all other comments, whether relevant to the decision or not.

Source: I. L. Janis, "Helping Relationships: A Preliminary Theoretical Analysis," in I. L. Janis (Ed.), *Counseling on Personal Decisions: Theory and Research on Short-Term Helping Relationships* (New Haven, CT: Yale University Press, 1982). Copyright © 1982 by Yale University Press. Reprinted by permission.

exhibits excessive anxiety during the course of the intervention. I often arrange special sessions for mock interviews, and these have been very effective tools for teaching job search skills. I videotape the mock interview for study with the client. Other customizations are possible and desirable.

Guideline 6: Enlist Family Support.   Typically, I invite family members to attend one or more sessions with the client. Indeed, if I feel that it will facilitate treatment, I invite these individuals to participate in all the counseling sessions or workshops so that the client's behavior will be reinforced outside the counseling sessions. This familial support is especially important during the beginning phase, when the client is rehearsing aspirations, and in the latter stages of an intervention, when the client is attempting to mobilize constructive behavior to implement a plan of action.

Guideline 7: Provide a System of Continuity and Accessibility.   One reason for the unusual success of Azrin's Job Club approach (Azrin & Besalel, 1980) to career intervention is that it offers the client easy and frequent access to telephone banks and daily counselor contact in support of the job search.

Guideline 8: Use Other Career Personnel and Community Resources.   This tactic increases the number and sources of social support.

Guideline 9: Repeat Everything.   Motivation levels lag over time, on even the most important matters.

Guideline 10: Don't Give Up!   Clients will frequently test you by presenting a hopeless scenario and expect—but not really want—you to agree that the situation they face is intractable. Don't write off such clients. Try to analyze their problems and adjust your intervention to produce the desired gain.

A TYPICAL CAREER INTERVENTION

The following outline of a typical thirteen-hour career intervention can be used to conduct a traditional dyadic (one hour per session), group (two hours per session), or workshop (one or two sessions) encounter.

Prior to First Hour
Client completes a Vocational History Questionnaire (see Appendix A)

First Hour
Client makes a statement about presenting problem and circumstances
Review Vocational History Questionnaire and assess social supports
Set expectations

Second Hour

Use career fantasy to generate cognitive rehearsal (see Technique 1)

Assign assessment inventories (one per session)

Give as a homework assignment to observe others at work and imagine oneself in those jobs

Third Hour

Administer and discuss the Tyler Card Sort

Give the SDS (Holland 1985b) and/or Myers Briggs Type Indicator (MBTI) (Myers & McCaulley, 1985) as homework assignment, following completion of any homogeneous scales

Fourth Hour

Review the SDS and/or MBTI, and discuss preliminary findings of any self-guiding inventories

Give as a homework assignment to develop a list of questions for exploratory interview

Fifth Hour

Interpret any empirically based inventories that have been given, and compare them with self-guiding inventories

Sixth Hour

Decide on three to six options to explore in field interviews (client or counselor should contact persons in the field)

Using a career decision fantasy may help to lower anxiety and anticipate reactions of others in order to mobilize social support

Seventh Hour

Use a decision facilitation technique (decision matrix or force field analysis technique) to narrow choices and understand possible barriers

Determine growing or developing edge of interests

Eighth to Tenth Hours

Client conducts exploratory interviews in field, bringing back answers to questions for discussion and evaluation

Eleventh and Twelfth Hours

Client and counselor together choose an option to pursue in depth

Retool résumé to reflect new direction and begin job search

Conduct mock interviews with videotape feedback

Continue brief weekly contacts until a job offer is received

Final Hour

Review final choice and feelings about it

Discuss salient features of the job search and prescriptions for ensuring success on the job

Discuss the need for continued support through transition and/or work on adjustment on the job

SUMMARY

Individual, group, and workshop career interventions proceed in three overlapping, sequential phases—beginning, activation, and completion—with across-session fluctuations in anxiety, the reduction of which results in more constructive and less destructive client behavior. Resolution of the feasibility inquisition, in which the client challenges the counselor's faith in a positive career outcome, is critical to successful client mobilization. Adherence to constructive behavior patterns will be difficult for the client and nonadherence should be anticipated.

3

Promoting Gains in Career Intervention

Holland (1984) observed that in the past seventy-five years vocational psychologists have developed effective career interventions without the benefit of a "well articulated or substantiated theory of vocational instruction or counseling" (p. 862). As noted in Chapter 1, attempts to detail the intervention theory that Holland advocated have not been well received by either counselors or researchers, and remain untested. The paucity of clinical literature on career counseling over the past twenty years suggests that if counselors possess any personal or implicit theories of intervention, they are not sharing them with other practitioners. Most counselors probably have an eclectic theory amalgamated from various sources, and may be confused, themselves, about how they should conduct their sessions.

In an attempt to move toward the *clinical science* of career counseling (see Osipow, 1988) this chapter provides hypotheses about intervention that are clinically based but empirically verifiable. Six postulates that delineate a testable model of career intervention will be outlined. In an early article, Thompson (1960) touched upon one or two of these ideas, but most of his attention focused on the client's career *choice* process, rather than the career *intervention* process. The problem of promoting client career gain will be discussed throughout this volume, but this chapter is designed to provide a workable clinical model of the gain process that may lead to more powerful treatments. Laboratory analogue studies and research on brief and convenient test interpretations are increasingly less useful to career intervention practitioners or researchers, but we are gradually accumulating a body of case findings that could form the base for a more comprehensive framework. What is needed is more discovery-oriented research (Mahrer, 1988) that directly examines the reactions of actual clients and skilled professionals during interventions.

CLARIFYING PROBLEMS EARLY IN THE CAREER INTERVENTION PROCESS

Clients are rarely clear about why they have come for career assistance. Usually, they report some vague unhappiness at work or a gnawing fear that their career is not progressing as they would like. Thus one important initial step in any career intervention is to clarify the nature of the problem or conflict that brought the client to counseling. This occurs during the beginning phase of intervention and may require simultaneous rapport building with the client, who may be unable to express or even unaware of the extent of the problem being faced.

Tiedeman (1967) argued that an appreciation of the client's problem was an important prerequisite for effective career action. As fundamental a notion as this is, few counselors fully clarify the client's predicament in either the client's mind or their own before proceeding with counseling. Moreover, it is not entirely clear how much of what the client presents as the problem is a reflection of the social constraints placed upon them (L. S. Gottfredson, 1986). Presenting problems may be socially acceptable veneers that cover issues more embarrassing or shame-inducing for the client (Krumboltz, 1983). Whatever the entry route or presenting problem, clarification of the situation is critical in the early phases of career intervention and will pay important dividends later in the process.

In his discussion of problem clarification in career counseling, Thompson (1960) emphasized the need to distinguish personal from vocational problems. He argued that vocational problems could either cause or be caused by personal problems. Personal and vocational problems, he stated, could coexist without much effect on one another, or either type of problem could be a symptom of a deeper underlying concern that the counselor must clarify. Usually, Thompson observed, there was a functional interaction between personal and vocational problems in which adjustment in one area affected adjustment in the other. He also believed that clients had different reasons for requesting counseling and that some clients who asked for vocational counseling were really asking for psychotherapy. Such mistaken presenting problem identifications become clear as counseling progresses, but if not wary, the counselor may be faced with an unexpected change in the nature of the counseling, or discover that the client has suddenly and inexplicably terminated therapy because the misattribution was not discovered. For example, a client who simply lacks information and wants feedback from an interest inventory will not respond well to repeated probing of deeper interpersonal problems and will be impatient to receive the results. Likewise, a client with an underlying conflict with a spouse or family member may respond to attempts to promote exploratory behavior with stubborn immobility.

This brings us to the first postulate about the career counseling process:

Postulate 1. Clients, with the help of the counselor, must clarify the nature and complexities of the decision and the conflict they face before focused career intervention can begin.

This awareness generally comes from a complete exploration of the situation as perceived by the client, accompanied by clarification of the emotions and cognitions that complicate the problem. This can easily be accomplished in the first session or two by taking a complete report of the client's current context and a thorough work and social history (see Appendix A). The client should also indicate how each previous job was secured as preparation for developing search and action strategies. Most of the first session or so is thus spent in clarifying the problem context, understanding the client's emotional and cognitive state and typical behavior patterns, and then ruling out some prohibitive overt pathology. The differentiation of personal problems is a delicate process that requires some familiarity with the range of normal psychological styles that can impede career intervention and some training in psychopathology (see Chapter 11). Inventories, especially those that measure conflict identification (Osipow, Carney, Winer, Yanico, & Koschier, 1976), identity assessment (Holland, Daiger, & Power, 1980a), or career maturity, may help in clarifying the problem.

DESIGNING AND SELECTING CAREER INTERVENTIONS

Once the problem is clarified, decisions must be made about which treatment to select or design for a particular client. Evidence is now accumulating that suggests that the type of treatment may be a factor in the success of the intervention. This is a relatively new field of inquiry that hopes to perfect treatment selection to improve effectiveness. The notion that treatments should vary according to type of client appeared first among developmental theorists (R. A. Myers, 1971). Its application to career counseling treatments was most cogently presented by Fretz (1981), who outlined several domains of client and treatment variables that might interact to affect outcomes (see Table 3-1).

Although the concept of the attribute-treatment interaction is appealing to counselors and researchers hoping to design more effective career interventions, the influence attributable to client variables in outcome studies is generally less than might be expected. The studies that show that certain

Table 3-1   Dimensions of Clients, Treatments, and Outcomes

CLIENT ATTRIBUTES	TREATMENT PARAMETERS	OUTCOMES
Demographic	**Content Domain**	**Career Knowledge and Skills**
Sex	Occupational	Career maturity
Race	information	Accuracy of
Age	Self-knowledge	self-knowledge
Socioeconomic/educational level	Decision skills	Accuracy of occupational information
Urban/rural origin	**Interpersonal Context**	Accuracy of job-seeking skills knowledge
Psychological	One-to-one	Planning and goal selection skills
Intelligence	counseling	Appropriateness of
Cognitive complexity	Group counseling	choices (realism)
Need for achievement	Self- or	Range of choices
Locus of control	computer-administered	Instrumental behaviors
Ego strength		Career information seeking
Self-confidence		Relevant academic
Anxiety	**Degree of Structure**	performance
Dependence		Seeking initial/new job
Defensiveness	Highly structured	Getting initial/new job
Personality type	Semistructured	Being promoted
	Unstructured	Earnings
Career Aspects		Contributions to community
Type of undecidedness		
Career maturity		**Sentiments**
Attitudes toward choices		Attitudes toward choices, certainty, satisfaction, commitment, career salience
Career decision style		Quality of life ratings
Motivation for treatment		Satisfaction with intervention
Expectancies for treatment		Perceived effectiveness of intervention
		Effective Role Functioning
		Self-concept adequacy
		Personal adjustment
		Relapses of career problems

Source: B. R. Fretz, "Evaluating the effectiveness of career interventions," *Journal of Counseling Psychology* 28 (1981): 77–90. Copyright © 1981 by the American Psychological Association. Reprinted by permission.

treatments affect some people more than others generally consider only a portion of a comprehensive treatment. It is not clear, however, that on the whole specifically tailored treatments would be more effective than comprehensive treatments that included all kinds of interventions and all manner of clients.

Theoretically, it is possible that some career interventions could have detrimental effects on a few individuals. There has, however, been no such evidence, and thus there is little basis for withholding a treatment from any client. The practical application of the attribute-treatment interaction studies may lead to the more liberal use of self-help and self-directing interventions with clients who show minimal presenting problems, thus reserving more expensive counselor-intensive interventions for more serious concerns, or for clients with low self-esteem or minimal social skills (Spokane, in press, a). Presently, there is insufficient evidence for firm conclusions about which clients will benefit from specific interventions. The studies on this issue, while not yet conclusive, are beginning to show certain trends and may eventually lead to advances in the differential use of career interventions.

Table 3-2 presents these attribute-treatment studies, the client variable they employed, and the intervention favored for that client type. In Kivlighan, Hageseth, Tipton, and McGovern (1981), a ground-breaking effort to study the differential effects of treatment types, subjects were classified as either people oriented or task oriented using their Holland type and assigned to treatment groups using a stratified random assignment procedure. All subjects received group career interventions, but in half of the groups, member

Table 3-2   Major Blocking Variables Shown to Affect Treatment Selection

STUDY	BLOCKING VARIABLE	PREFERRED TREATMENT
Kivlighan et al., 1981	Holland types high on sociability	Group interaction
	Holland types low on sociability	Individual problem solving
Robbins and Tucker, 1986	High goal instability	Interactional intervention
	Low goal instability	Self-directing intervention
Krumboltz et al., 1986	Rational style	Rational decision-making training
Barak and Friedkes, 1981	Career decision subtypes	
Fretz and Leong, 1982	Low-level career indecision	Self-Directed Search
Zager, 1982	Low self-esteem	Individual intervention
Melhus, Hereshenson, and Vermillion, 1973	Low readiness	Individual counseling

interactions were encouraged, whereas in the other half individual problem solving was emphasized. The outcome measures were career maturity, information seeking, and treatment satisfaction. No treatment effects were found between the group and individual treatments until the Holland type was used to analyze groups separately. Blocking clients according to their sociability (people oriented versus task oriented) unmasked substantial interactions between client type and the use of interaction in the treatment. People-oriented clients fared better in the interactive groups than in individual problem-solving groups. The interaction effects, especially on information seeking, were substantial.

In a similar study, Robbins and Tucker (1986) used level of goal instability as the client attribute, and compared the effectiveness of self-directed or interactional career workshops. The authors employed career maturity and exploration as outcome variables. Subjects with high goal instability faired better in the interactional treatment, whereas those with low goal instability had favorable outcomes regardless of treatment type. Likewise, Krumboltz, Kinnier, Rude, Scherba, and Hamel (1986) used a single, ninety-minute rational decision intervention and classified subjects as rational, intuitive, fatalistic, impulsive, or independent using a decision questionnaire. Results revealed that rational types had higher decision information scores in response to the rational decision training than did intuitive or dependent types. Barak and Friedkes (1981) used the career decision scale to make a differential diagnosis before administering a career intervention. They found that clients who scored higher on lack of structure did better in career counseling than those who scored high on conflicts with others or blocked choices. No interaction was found between the nature of the treatment and the presenting problem, however, which led Barak and Friedkes to conclude that the delivery mode of a career treatment was less likely to result in attribute-treatment interaction than was a dramatic variation in the informational content of the treatment itself.

Fretz and Leong (1982) found that the Self-Directed Search was most effective for subjects with minimal levels of career indecision. Zager (1982) attempted to enhance self-esteem as a career intervention, but inadvertently found that clients with low self-esteem dropped out of group treatment at unusually high rates. Finally, Melhus, Hershenson, and Vermillion (1973) found that low-readiness clients fared better in one-on-one interventions with a trained counselor than with a computer-assisted treatment.

Evidence on the effect of client and treatment variables on outcome is thus slowly accumulating, and reveals that individuals with minimal indecision and stable goals will demonstrate significant gains with a self-directing career intervention, whereas clients with low self-esteem, low readiness, low sociability, or high goal instability should probably receive individual as opposed to group or self-directing career interventions. This is summarized in the second postulate:

Postulate 2. A few major personality and adjustment styles (e.g., sociability, self-esteem, and decisive style and type) should guide the choice of career intervention. In general, the stronger the level of client personality integration, the more educative and less therapeutic the treatment need be.

It should be noted, however, that one might also consider other attributes before choosing a treatment strategy (e.g., obsessive or hysterical personality style; see Shapiro, 1965), and that future research may uncover other salient variables as well.

THE GOALS OF CAREER INTERVENTION

Many clients come to career counseling believing that their major life goals are not realistically attainable. This creates an odd situation, since very few of my clients (except the younger ones) entertain goals that are in fact unrealistic for them. If anything, they *underestimate* their ability. As Markus and Nurius (1986) noted, these clients can imagine both what they would like to become and what they are afraid of becoming, but feel unable to control the actual outcome of their career. This sense of a lack of control often results in inaction, passivity, or what Beck (1967) called paralysis of the will, to such a degree that the clients in fact relinquish control over their careers and thus become subject to the vagaries of chance. This sort of inaction is frequently seen in employees who have been given several months' notice of a layoff, but cannot act to secure alternative positions until the present job has indeed ended. Some of these clients are depressed, and when their depression lifts, they initiate action. More often, however, the immobility results from their lack of faith in their ability to control the outcome of any overt action on their own behalf. The combination of this inaction and lack of faith can lead to a state of career despair.

In addressing the problem of control, Postulate 3 relies heavily on Strong's (1978) compelling work on social influence theory, in which he argued that the goal of psychotherapy is to return control to the client: "Clients are the agents of change in their lives and therapists are like coaches that clients retain to help them do what they must" (p. 103).

Postulate 3. The goal of career intervention is to enhance the mobilization of persistently constructive attitudes, emotions, and behaviors that will improve the client's career attainment.

Strong's view fits well with those of a variety of behavioral theorists who believe that psychologists should study what people actually do when

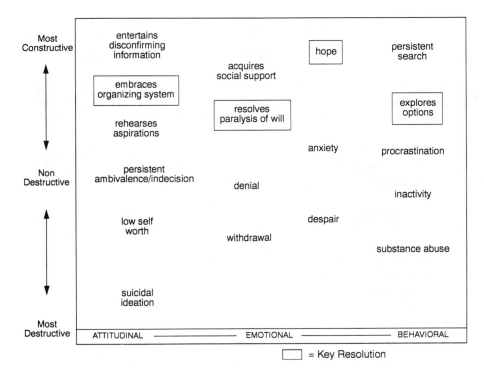

Figure 3-1 Emotional, Attitudinal, and Behavioral Responses to Career Situations.

faced with difficult circumstances in addition to studying "what they say they do, would like to do, or report doing on an inventory" (Pervin, 1983, p. 3). In career situations, the returning of control to the client must be accompanied by a series of constructive behaviors that are associated with the successful negotiation of career situations (see Azrin & Besalel, 1980).

Figure 3-1 presents a range of both constructive and destructive emotional, attitudinal, and behavioral responses to career situations upon which the next two postulates are based. The goal of a career intervention is to promote the constructive responses, especially the four key reactions (embrace of an organizing system, resolution of paralysis of the will, hope, and exploration of options). The most destructive responses are characteristic of moderate to severe depression (Beck, 1967), and are seen during prolonged unemployment (Herr, in press) and difficult career transitions. In Figure 3-1, upward movement is preferable from the professional's point of view, and is generally desired but not articulated by the client.

In spite of the apparent benefits of active strategies on career decisions, some clients will withdraw psychologically from their problems and their work environments, preferring cognitive explanations to overt action as a control strategy (see Rothbaum, Weisz, & Snyder, 1983). In career counseling, this passive or secondary control strategy may be particularly self-defeating, since clients will expend most of their time and energy trying to explain their career difficulties, and will have little energy or desire left to explore new options and collect information needed to make the choice. Janis and Mann (1977) called this strategy defensive avoidance, which, they maintained, led to poor decisions. Denial or withdrawal may occasionally be helpful in adjusting to stressful work environments, and a client's unique predicament may call for some combination of action and denial. Usually, however, mobilization for constructive career action is the appropriate goal for career counseling.

Three recent articles shed some light on the dynamics of persistence in the face of barriers in general (Kernis, Zuckerman, Cohen, & Spadafora, 1982; Koslowsky, Kluger, & Yinon, 1988; Sandelands, Brockner, & Glynn, 1988). Kernis et al. gave subjects several abstract tasks, and manipulated the internality and externality of the subjects' explanations for their success or failure. Persistence and interest in the task at hand were greater when failure was attributed to an external rather than an internal cause, but only when the subjects were highly aware of the actual quality of their own performance. Subjects who were aware of the level of their performance and who attributed failure to an external reason persisted for a longer period and became more invested in the intrinsic benefit of the task itself. Likewise, Sandelands et al. found greater task persistence when subjects were led to believe that continuous behavior and persistence were essential to successful performance. They concluded that management could encourage persistent performance by shaping workers' belief that a specific task required more continuous activity and thereby escalate commitment. Lastly, Koslowsky et al. examined subjects' intention to participate in a specific activity, and found that it predicted eventual behavior as long as no barriers to participation were encountered. When subjects faced impediments, a combination of intention to participate and investment in the activity was a better predictor of eventual behavior than intention alone. Apparently, a high level of investment or commitment in the target behavior resulted in a more realistic appraisal of the person's chances for actually carrying out a specific behavior. Taken together, these three studies suggest that improvements in self-awareness and commitment to a task serve to buffer negative outcomes that might result from environmental barriers. Apparently, however, neither intention (Koslowsky et al., 1988) nor commitment alone (Phillips, 1982) is sufficient to predict positive career outcomes. When exploring career possibilities, the ability to face repeated rebuffs while still maintaining some intentional status and motivation increases the likelihood of a positive outcome and higher quality decision. As Blustein (1988) found, motivational orientations (e.g., autonomy and control) are good predictors of the level of self-determination (Deci & Ryan, 1985).

The reflexive use of denial or avoidance when faced with a difficult career decision can take several forms, including the almost universal wish or expectation that the counselor will somehow provide a perfect solution that will maintain self-esteem and enhance satisfaction and performance. It is striking how many clients come to career counseling looking for a magic pill or answer that will relieve their career conflict. The competent counselor will of course work to overcome rather than react to denial and avoidance. Avoidance or denial is generally preceded by anxiety about the client's ability (or lack of it) to make and implement a satisfactory choice. Once a client begins to mobilize for constructive behavior, that person's approach to counseling changes markedly from one of avoidance and fear to one of challenge and excitement. The resolution of paralysis of will is a critical outcome of a career intervention and an important precondition for the mobilization of constructive behavior. The activation of hope and persistent exploratory behavior are keys to the client's ability to regain control and implement a successful career decision.

It should be noted that most people who come for career counseling are well adjusted and psychologically healthy, with a fairly localized difficulty in making career choices. Their attitudes, emotions, and behaviors will fall within the constructive range, and can be made more so by a successful career intervention. There are, however, those clients who have both career and personal problems, and those who have more extensive emotional problems that must be identified and then either treated or referred. Increasingly, career problems are embedded within a range of personal problems that may make the separation of career and personal domains less desirable and practical. Crites's (1981) comment that career counseling begins where personal counseling leaves off simplifies the work of the career counselor with those clients who have finished or have no need for personal therapy, but excludes those who have career and personal problems, which is an increasing proportion of the clientele seen in most settings.

COGNITIVE FRAMEWORKS FOR ORGANIZING CAREERS

Studies (Osipow et al., 1976) reveal that several factors influence career indecision. In most studies the greatest effect is attributed to a factor that is invariably labeled "lack of structure," which typically means that the client simply has no idea about how to conceptualize the problem and determine an effective solution. This situation is similar to but somewhat different from a lack of control, in that clients seem unable to articulate how they might solve their predicament even if they had the motivation to do so. Subjects for whom a lack of structure is dominant implicitly have relatively few personal problems, and they generally respond most favorably to traditional career interventions (Barak & Friedkes, 1981). Of course clients with this problem will look to the counselor for a solution, which Holland, Magoon, and Spokane (1981) described as a cognitive structure that would provide them with a reference point for understanding themselves, the world of work, and the relation between the two.

Who should supply such a cognitive framework? There is evidence that one that is extracted from the clients' own experiences will most effectively explain their behavior. Clearly, however, counseling outcomes are more effective when a framework is suggested by the counselor than when no framework is provided (Hoffman & Teglasi, 1982).

Not only is it necessary to supply a cognitive framework during the counseling process, but it may also be necessary to refute any inaccurate frameworks the client may have. For example, in her study of the transmission of knowledge in the science classroom, Resnick (1983) found that most students held naïve theories about the scientific world that interfered with their ability to absorb or integrate scientifically based explanations of behavior. She showed that students would revert quickly to these views, which were rudimentary personal beliefs that had never been challenged, unless they were exposed and directly countered during the learning process. Since some of the laws of physics are counterintuitive, it is easy to see how a more intuitive naïve theory would persist, despite its inaccuracy. Similarly naïve and counterintuitive beliefs may be responsible for career intervention failures (Krumboltz, 1983).

In an extension of his social learning theory of career development, Krumboltz (1983) argued that it was not necessarily the accuracy of private career beliefs that made them troublesome, but rather the problems they could produce, including the following: (1) faulty generalizations about the world of work from a single career-related experience; (2) social comparisons with an idealized role model; (3) sustained emotional overreactions to negative career events; (4) erroneous attributions of the causes of specific career outcomes, including the overweighting of low-probability negative outcomes (see also Markus & Nurius, 1986); and (5) self-deception. By countering such erroneous and irrational thinking, and substituting more veridical and constructive beliefs, the client will be prepared for engaging in more constructive behaviors, as Postulate 4 summarizes:

> **Postulate 4. Effective career counseling will provide the client with a clear framework, either self-derived or counselor imposed, that offers an intellectual or cognitive structure for understanding career selection and that will counter any inaccurate theories about the world of work that the client may possess.**

Skillful feedback, whether in group, class, or individual interventions, helps the client to internalize the insights and options that emerge during counseling. This feedback must challenge self-defeating or nonconstructive attitudes and behaviors while encouraging more constructive alternatives. If this feedback process, however, does not result in a clear framework for the client's subsequent use, gains will be shorter in duration and less powerful. Interest inventories or ability measures should be interpreted *after* a cognitive framework is in place, not before or instead of the framework. If the client has no clear framework before the delivery of career information, it is unlikely that such information can be readily absorbed or used (Fogg, 1983). Clients will quickly forget much of what is presented to them (Meichenbaum & Turk, 1987), but the existence of cognitive framework will slow that process if naive theories have first been effectively rebutted.

IDENTIFYING AND IMPLEMENTING REASONABLY FITTING CAREER OPTIONS

Before effective career outcomes can result, the client must come to believe that a reasonably fitting option exists and can be implemented. This process entails two major phases. In the first phase the client identifies, explores, and then successively narrows options until a few remain that fit several of the criteria important to the client (Postulate 5). Clients who are already working will usually conclude that their present job is also a reasonably fitting choice, even though they may have quite negative feelings about it. In the second phase the client recognizes that the reasonably fitting option, once identified, can indeed be implemented (Postulate 6).

> **Postulate 5: The concept of congruence or multidimensional fit (of ability, interests, sex role, and prestige) should guide the exploratory behavior that will increase the number and fit of career options available to the client.**

The idea of congruence or fit is as close to a universal concept as exists in the career development field; it is a theoretical construct that has worked its way into the everyday language of career intervention. What is the nature of this fit, and how is the exploration of reasonably fitting options encouraged? Career development theorists have addressed the searching process that promotes fit and that is so central in career interventions in various ways (see Chapter 1). Super (1984) acknowledged the convergence between developmental and differential vocational theorists on the issue, but noted that developmental theorists examined the emergence of fit over time, whereas differential theorists studied fit at a single moment. Actually, the convergence of the two schools of career theory on the question of congruence is even more complete than Super allowed. Congruence, as originally described by Holland (1985a), is not a static concept. There is a certain reciprocity between the worker and the environment (people change jobs, and jobs change people), but that reciprocity is not presumed to develop in successive or cumulative age-linked stages.

Because many clients come to career counseling seeking a perfectly fitting option that they expect the counselor to unearth, some caution is urged so that the congruence notion will not be misused to reinforce this misconception. The evidence clearly suggests that person-environment congruence will lead to some beneficial outcomes (Assouline & Meir, 1987; Spokane, 1985), although far fewer people will actually be in congruent situations at any specific point than was previously believed (Aranya, Barak, & Amernic, 1981). Indeed, there may be some extreme circumstances under which congruence will neither occur nor affect the outcomes of workers; for example, Heesacker, Elliott, and Howe (1988) found that socioeconomic constraints occasionally predict worker productivity more accurately than does a crude measure of congruence. Several recent studies reinforce the congruence hypothesis, but with a few twists. Grotevant, Cooper, and Kramer (1986) discovered that extensive exploration of career options was more likely to result in a congruent choice, and congruence is generally seen as a comprehensive and dynamic principle rather than a static notion (Greenhaus & Parasuraman, 1986; Savickas, in press; Smart, Elton, & McLaughlin, 1986).

The means of identifying congruence can be as simple as a summary sheet listing a few options that have been gleaned from inventories and discussion. Once a few reasonably fitting choices are available, the second phase in identifying and implementing an option begins, as Postulate 6 describes:

Postulate 6. Effective career counseling will instill in the client a sense of hope about finding and implementing a reasonably fitting career option.

In a theory of the psychology of hope, Stotland (1969) proposed that the perceived probability of attaining a goal is the principal determinant of successful action for achieving that goal. Anxiety, in Stotland's view, interferes with that action. Schemas, or mental sets for action, allow goal-directed behaviors to emerge. Stotland links motivation, cognitive set, and action to the probability that a desired outcome can be achieved. Thus hope is a motivational construct clearly linked to the psychology of goal-directed action. Frank (1976) described this activation of hope as a restoration of morale, which he felt enabled clients to combat destructive states of mind when in the throes of indecision. Most therapeutic approaches provide, according to Frank, some hope for help, which then has the motivating power to produce behavior changes necessary to effective outcomes. Salzman (1976) noted that the capacity for intentionality is weakened in most neurotic states and that many therapists rely on clients to mobilize their own will. Most hope is activated by the quality of the counseling relationship (Marmor, 1976; Strupp, 1976). Regardless of one's view of the career counseling task, the activation of hope for a positive outcome, which N. E. Betz and Hackett (1981) called self-efficacy, will contribute to client gains.

SUMMARY

The six postulates presented in this chapter provide a model of career intervention that draws heavily from the work of John Holland and David Tiedeman. However, although it is based upon existing research, it is not drawn from any existing psychotherapy theory. The model characterizes gain in career interventions as a process of renewing the client's belief that reasonably fitting options exist, and promoting constructive behavior, attitudes, and emotions that will increase the probability of implementing one of those options. The model pertains to all forms of vocational intervention, not solely individual counseling. The high levels of dropout (in excess of 50 percent) in many group settings suggest that in large-scale interventions more attention might be paid to the clients' fears and hopes. The simple conveyance of content in a classroom or curricular intervention, for example, implies that the psychosocial aspects of a career choice are relatively unimportant, and that the goal of preventive or educative interventions should be a broader exploration of the world of work and perhaps some self-assessment. Anyone who has taught one of these classes or conducted a group, however, knows that the issue of gain in a career intervention is emotional as well as cognitive and behavioral, as Figure 3-1 depicts.

4

Assessment and Decision Making in Career Intervention

THE BEGINNINGS OF VOCATIONAL ASSESSMENT

In 1909 Frank Parsons, a social reformer in Boston, published a slim volume entitled *Choosing a Vocation*, in which he described how individuals might learn more about themselves and the requirements of occupations, and then use this information to plan their careers. In 1903, an ocean away, Alfred Binet, the leading French psychologist of the day, had published *L'étude expérimentale de l'intelligence*, and two years later produced the first intelligence scale for use in identifying and educating learning disabled children. Vocational assessment evolved from these two landmark events, developing its goal from early social reformers like Parsons and its measurement techniques from the intelligence testing movement promoted by Binet.

Vocational assessment received a dramatic boost in the early 1920s when E. K. Strong developed a reliable, indirect method for scaling occupational interests. Other measures followed, and these interest inventories, combined with ability assessments, were subsequently used in assigning recruits during World War II and in placing veterans following the war. After the launching of Sputnik in 1957, tests were also used for identifying scientifically talented students. By the 1960s, career assessment had become big business.[1]

After a vigorous period of growth in the use and popularity of interest and ability testing in counseling in the first three decades of the 1900s, E. G. Williamson, a prolific defender of aptitude assessement, found himself in direct conflict with Carl Rogers over the issue. Their argument presaged a prolonged decline in the acceptance of mental testing among both the public and mental health professionals, as Haney (1981) described. Indeed, when Ralph Nader appeared on television in January 1980 to highlight his

---

[1]Borgen (1986), now a leading scholar in differential vocational psychology, provides an excellent chronology of the development of interest inventories.

report criticizing the Educational Testing Service, spontaneous applause broke out when he "gave an impassioned plea for wider consideration of traits like perseverance, wisdom, idealism and creativity—traits that cannot be measured with multiple-choice tests" (Haney, 1981, p. 1021).

Many counselors noted the score differences between blacks and whites on ability tests, and judged such measures to be not only unfair but also of limited predictive utility. It was not unusual to find a career development course or even a textbook that made no mention of ability assessment. Interest testing, which seemed more racially fair but was heavily criticized for sexual bias, evoked fewer negative reactions, and was able to address its deficiencies through heated debate or, simply, survival. Thus as the prestige of ability measurement was in a period of relative decline, vocational assessment prospered. One difference between the two was that the bias question was addressed openly and vigorously in the interest testing literature, which produced some advances and solutions, whereas in the ability assessment field the issue was avoided or suppressed as being injurious to the counseling profession.

In the 1980s, however, ability assessment reemerged as an important concern for applied psychology, although it continues to be plagued by questions of fairness (L. S. Gottfredson, 1988). This resurgence of interest was fueled by two discoveries (Hunter, 1986); (1) that ability screenings devised for specific positions in a company could be successfully applied (generalized) to similar jobs elsewhere; and (2) that the correlation between ability and performance, when corrected for range restriction and the unreliability of the measures employed, was substantially higher than previously thought. The routine administration of ability measures job applicants, however, poses conflicts with legal precedents that deem racially or sexually biased tests that result in disparate impacts on minority groups to be unacceptable for employment screening (see *Griggs v. Duke Power Co*; 1971).

Counselors who are not fully trained to appreciate the complexity of the issues in ability and aptitude assessment continue to use ability assessment far less frequently than is warranted, overrelying instead on interest testing as the basis of predictive and educative assessments. Yet in spite of this limited use of ability measures in vocational assessment, test feedback is repeatedly judged by clients as well as counselors to be the most effective component of vocational interventions (Kirschner, 1988; Wiggins, 1987). How can we use the diverse array of vocational assessments, including ability, without becoming entangled in problems of bias or fairness? Perhaps we can never avoid these issues entirely, but we can specify the appropriate uses of vocational assessment and employ them in conjunction with other sources of information. In this chapter we shall review the purposes and procedures of assessment in vocational interventions, discuss the analysis of presenting problems, and describe thirteen classes of vocational instruments commonly used in career interventions.

THE GOALS OF ASSESSMENT IN CAREER INTERVENTION

In vocational psychology, assessment generally serves two broad purposes. The first is the traditional psychometric goal (Zytowski & Borgen, 1983) of testing and classifying individuals to predict future behaviors of interest, to test formal theories of vocational behavior, or to study the epidemiology of social or psychological problems. This broad purpose was termed "actuarial" by Meehl (1954), who compared the accuracy of statistical predictions of success from tests and clinical judgments.

The second and more familiar general goal of tests and inventories in vocational psychology is to help clients make career decisions. Goldman (1971) described several clinical uses of tests, and others have emerged since the 1960s. These therapeutic uses of vocational assessments, and other purposes outlined in Glaser and Bond (1981), Kapes and Mastie (1988), and Rayman (1982), are the focus of this chapter and are synthesized below.

Unearthing Congruent Career Possibilities

Research suggests that the average client will seriously consider one or two new career options following an intervention, regardless of whether the initial goal was to broaden or to narrow the alternatives under consideration (Fretz & Leong, 1982). These findings appear to hold for women as well as men. Occasionally, the unearthing of these new options translates into the irrational desire for the "perfect" option. A more reasonable use of vocational assessment devices is to identify one or two additional but still reasonably fitting options to add to the two or three possibilities most clients actively consider.

Clients, especially anxious ones, are inclined to distort or restrict the range of career options they are considering. These individuals benefit from increased exploration, which has been found to be an important predictor of the congruence of subsequent choices (see Chapter 3; Grotevant, Cooper, and Kramer, 1986). Since mounting evidence confirms that congruence is related to a variety of work-related outcomes ranging from satisfaction to stress (Spokane, 1987), counselors who motivate constructive exploration in their clients should increase the likelihood of a congruent outcome and positive adjustment. Grotevant et al.'s finding is consistent with Janis and Mann's (1977) view that thorough exploration of disconfirming information improves the quality of resulting decisions.

Discovering the Leading Edge of Interests

In addition to identifying new options, vocational assessment can be used to clarify the client's changing profile of interests and skills (e.g., leading edge). Occupational interests, although stable over long periods (Swanson

& Hansen, 1985), do have a fluid component (Spokane, Malett, & Vance, 1978). Gradual changes in the elevation and shape of interest profiles are detectable. Often these changes are accentuations of existing patterns with age (Walsh, 1973), but they can also result, to a degree, when interests realign in the direction of the dominant environment after a choice has been made (L. S. Gottfredson, 1981; Hershenson & Roth, 1966; Malett, Spokane, & Vance, 1978). For example, Elton and Rose (1967) found that engineering students who transferred to liberal arts became more like the students already in liberal arts after the move. There may be limits, however, to the extent of adaptation that is possible.

These gradual changes in interests can be viewed as having a leading edge that can be identified by retesting a client after several months and analyzing differences in profile shape and elevation. For example, a client with equally high investigative and artistic Holland type scores may show an increase in the latter and a decrease in the former upon retest, revealing a leading edge that is moving toward artistic. This increase in artistic interest could render unsatisfactory an occupation that was previously a reasonable fit. A leading edge can be reflected in secondary interest scores as well.

Figure 4-1 is the SCII profile of a thirty-five-year-old female client with very high enterprising interests, who displayed more moderately similar scores in ES occupations than in EC occupations, and a business management basic interest scale that was somewhat lower than the merchandising and sales scores, which indicates a decided S flavor, even in the absence of particular strength in S criterion scales. Upon retesting two years later (see Figure 4-2), this leading edge was slightly more prominent, even though the client did not respond to four items.

Confirming Congruence of Preferences or Choices

Although the role of assessment in verifying congruence may seem obvious, it is important to rule out interest incongruence as a source of dissatisfaction when a client is struggling with a complex career problem. Clients are reassured when an inventory confirms their present choice (or aspiration) and thus more likely to convert the cognitive and emotional energy tied up in indecision into constructive behaviors aimed at resolving adjustment problems in their current position. As Rayman (1982) suggested, "often clients who are sitting on the fence about choosing a major area of study or a career objective, find the nudge of an interest inventory to be of value in spurring them to action" (p. 9). Commonly, the unhappy client in a congruent work environment, when presented with an inventory that confirms that congruence, will consider acting to insure that other aspects of the environment are more to their liking (e.g., pay, benefits, or colleagial relationships).

This confirmatory role should not be confused with the case in which an expressed choice that the client can verbalize openly, directly conflicts

Figure 4-1 (Source: Reprinted by special permission of Consulting Psychologists Press, Inc., Palo Alto, CA 94306.)

STRONG VOCATIONAL INTEREST BLANK

PAGE 2 **PROFILE REPORT FOR:**

DATE TESTED: 06/07/87

ID: 06157-00087- 262

AGE: 35 SEX: FEMALE

DATE SCORED: 06/15/87

OCCUPATIONAL SCALES	STANDARD SCORES F	M	VERY DISSIMILAR	DISSIMILAR	MODERATELY DISSIMILAR	MID-RANGE	MODERATELY SIMILAR	SIMILAR	VERY SIMILAR

SOCIAL

		F	M							
GENERAL OCCUPATIONAL THEME - S	30 40 50 60 70					15 25 30		40 45 55		
MOD. HIGH (57)		F								
		M								

BASIC INTEREST SCALES	(STANDARD SCORE)		F M	Occupational Scales	F	M	15 25 30		40 45 55	
			SA [AS]	Foreign language teacher	39	(AS)				
			SA SA	Minister	25	41				
			SA SA	Social worker	38	49				
TEACHING		F	S S	Guidance counselor	37	47				
MOD. HIGH (59)		M	S S	Social science teacher	44	40				
			S S	Elementary teacher	34	37				
SOCIAL SERVICE		F	S S	Special education teacher	41	47				
HIGH (66)			SRI SAR	Occupational therapist	32	34				
			SIA SAI	Speech pathologist	45	45				
ATHLETICS		F	SI [ISR]	Nurse, RN	45	(ISR)				
AVERAGE (51)		M	SCI N/A	Dental hygienist	46	N/A				
			SC SC	Nurse, LPN	16	39				
DOMESTIC ARTS		F	[RIS] SR	Athletic trainer	(RIS)	8				
AVERAGE (49)			SR SR	Physical education teacher	15	6				
RELIGIOUS ACTIVITIES		F	SRE SE	Recreation leader	50	34				
LOW (35)		M	SE SE	YWCA/YMCA director	51	43				
			SEC SCE	School administrator	48	48				
			SCE N/A	Home economics teacher	30	N/A				

ENTERPRISING

		F M							
GENERAL OCCUPATIONAL THEME - E	30 40 50 60 70					15 25 30		40 45 55	
VERY HIGH (71)		F							
		M							

BASIC INTEREST SCALES	(STANDARD SCORE)				F	M	15 25 30		40 45 55	
			E ES	Personnel director	61	49				
			ES E	Elected public official	43	39				
			ES ES	Life insurance agent	48	40				
PUBLIC SPEAKING		F	EC E	Chamber of Commerce executive	36	32				
AVERAGE (47)			EC EC	Store manager	57	52				
LAW/POLITICS		F	N/A ECR	Agribusiness manager	N/A	16				
HIGH (61)		M	EC EC	Purchasing agent	63	45				
MERCHANDISING			EC E	Restaurant manager	56	26				
VERY HIGH (68)		F	[AR] EA	Chef	(AR)	35				
			EC E	Travel agent	54	40				
SALES		F	ECS E	Funeral director	46	26				
VERY HIGH (68)		M	[CSE]ESC	Nursing home administrator	(CSE)	52				
BUSINESS MANAGEMENT		F	EC ER	Optician	49	41				
VERY HIGH (68)		M	E E	Realtor	42	51				
			E [AE]	Beautician	27	(AE)				
			E E	Florist	26	32				
			EC E	Buyer	41	51				
			EI EI	Marketing executive	45	32				
			EIC ECI	Investments manager	34	16				

CONVENTIONAL

		F M							
GENERAL OCCUPATIONAL THEME - C	30 40 50 60 70					15 25 30		40 45 55	
AVERAGE (54)		F							
		M							

BASIC INTEREST SCALES	(STANDARD SCORE)				F	M	15 25 30		40 45 55	
			C C	Accountant	34	22				
			C C	Banker	25	31				
OFFICE PRACTICES		F	CR CR	IRS agent	61	44				
MOD. HIGH (55)		M	CES CES	Credit manager	29	35				
			CES CES	Business education teacher	24	38				
			[CS] CES	Food service manager	(CS)	41				
			[ISR] CSE	Dietitian	(ISR)	38				
			CSE [ESC]	Nursing home administrator	34	(ESC)				
			CSE CSE	Executive housekeeper	35	40				
			CS [CES]	Food service manager	25	(CES)				
			CS N/A	Dental assistant	36	N/A				
			C N/A	Secretary	27	N/A				
			C [R]	Air Force enlisted personnel	30	(R)				
			CRS [RC]	Marine Corps enlisted personnel	39	(RC)				
			CRS CR	Army enlisted personnel	41	22				
			CIR CIR	Mathematics teacher	35	16				

CONSULTING PSYCHOLOGISTS PRESS
577 COLLEGE AVENUE
PALO ALTO, CA 94306

ADMINISTRATIVE INDEXES (RESPONSE %)

OCCUPATIONS	50	L %	34	I %	16	D %	
SCHOOL SUBJECTS	50	L %	31	I %	19	D %	
ACTIVITIES	55	L %	31	I %	14	D %	
LEISURE ACTIVITIES	44	L %	26	I %	31	D %	
TYPES OF PEOPLE	67	L %	25	I %	8	D %	
PREFERENCES	30	L %	30	= %	40	R %	
CHARACTERISTICS	36	Y %	21	? %	43	N %	
ALL PARTS	49	%	30	%	21	%	

Figure 4-2 (Source: Reprinted by special permission of Consulting Psychologists Press, Inc., Palo Alto, CA 94306.)

STRONG VOCATIONAL INTEREST BLANK

PROFILE REPORT FOR: **DATE TESTED:** 01/29/89   00001-00001-   78

ID: 78 AGE: 36 SEX: FEMALE   **DATE SCORED:** 02/21/89

	STANDARD SCORES	VERY DISSIMILAR	DISSIMILAR	MODERATELY DISSIMILAR	MID-RANGE	MODERATELY SIMILAR	SIMILAR	VERY SIMILAR

OCCUPATIONAL SCALES

SOCIAL

GENERAL OCCUPATIONAL THEME - S   30 40 50 60 70
AVERAGE (52)

BASIC INTEREST SCALES (STANDARD SCORE)

TEACHING F / M
MOD. HIGH (59)

SOCIAL SERVICE F / M
MOD. HIGH (58)

ATHLETICS F / M
AVERAGE (43)

DOMESTIC ARTS F / M
LOW (42)

RELIGIOUS ACTIVITIES F / M
LOW (35)

		Occupational	F	M
SA	(AS)	Foreign language teacher	30	(AS)
SA	SA	Minister	20	38
SA	SA	Social worker	36	39
S	S	Guidance counselor	32	39
S	S	Social science teacher	35	36
S	S	Elementary teacher	27	45
S	S	Special education teacher	35	32
SRI	SAR	Occupational therapist	22	27
SIA	SAI	Speech pathologist	40	43
SI	(ISR)	Nurse, RN	38	(ISR)
SCI	N/A	Dental hygienist	30	N/A
SC	SC	Nurse, LPN	14	33
(RIS)	SR	Athletic trainer	(RIS)	6
SR	SR	Physical education teacher	6	8
SRE	SE	Recreation leader	37	33
SE	SE	YWCA/YMCA director	43	35
SEC	SCE	School administrator	44	40
SCE	N/A	Home economics teacher	24	N/A

ENTERPRISING

GENERAL OCCUPATIONAL THEME - E   30 40 50 60 70
HIGH (62)

BASIC INTEREST SCALES (STANDARD SCORE)

PUBLIC SPEAKING F / M
AVERAGE (52)

LAW/POLITICS F / M
MOD. HIGH (56)

MERCHANDISING F / M
VERY HIGH (67)

SALES F / M
VERY HIGH (66)

BUSINESS MANAGEMENT F / M
HIGH (60)

			F	M
E	ES	Personnel director	53	42
ES	E	Elected public official	35	36
ES	ES	Life insurance agent	42	33
EC	E	Chamber of Commerce executive	35	26
EC	EC	Store manager	53	47
N/A	ECR	Agribusiness manager	N/A	15
EC	EC	Purchasing agent	52	37
EC	E	Restaurant manager	53	26
(AR)	EA	Chef	(AR)	33
EC	E	Travel agent	45	40
ECS	E	Funeral director	44	22
(CSE)	ESC	Nursing home administrator	(CSE)	50
EC	ER	Optician	42	33
E	E	Realtor	38	46
E	(AE)	Beautician	25	(AE)
E	E	Florist	29	29
EC	E	Buyer	40	50
EI	EI	Marketing executive	39	32
EIC	ECI	Investments manager	34	24

CONVENTIONAL

GENERAL OCCUPATIONAL THEME - C   30 40 50 60 70
AVERAGE (50)

BASIC INTEREST SCALES (STANDARD SCORE)

OFFICE PRACTICES F / M
MOD. HIGH (55)

			F	M
C	C	Accountant	25	16
C	C	Banker	32	34
CE	CE	IRS agent	46	29
CES	CES	Credit manager	31	28
CES	CES	Business education teacher	23	38
(CS)	CES	Food service manager	(CS)	37
(ISR)	CSE	Dietitian	(ISR)	40
CSE	(ESC)	Nursing home administrator	34	(ESC)
CSE	CSE	Executive housekeeper	27	35
CS	(CES)	Food service manager	25	(CES)
CS	N/A	Dental assistant	34	N/A
C	N/A	Secretary	26	N/A
C	(R)	Air Force enlisted personnel	24	(R)
CRS	(RC)	Marine Corps enlisted personnel	31	(RC)
CRS	CR	Army enlisted personnel	31	17
CIR	CIR	Mathematics teacher	21	11

CONSULTING PSYCHOLOGISTS PRESS
577 COLLEGE AVENUE
PALO ALTO, CA 94306

ADMINISTRATIVE INDEXES (RESPONSE %)

OCCUPATIONS	35	L %	48	I %	15	D %		
SCHOOL SUBJECTS	28	L %	53	I %	19	D %		
ACTIVITIES	41	L %	37	I %	22	D %		
LEISURE ACTIVITIES	36	L %	21	I %	44	D %		
TYPES OF PEOPLE	46	L %	42	I %	13	D %		
PREFERENCES	37	L %	33	= %	30	R %		
CHARACTERISTICS	43	Y %	21	? %	29	N %		
ALL PARTS	37	%	41	%	22	%		

71

with measured interests from an inventory. In the confirming case described here, there is doubt about a current choice but no compelling alternative under consideration. Thus the client is assured about his or her current choice and acts to strengthen other aspects of the work environment.

Using Diagnostic Information in Assessing Conflicts or Problems

When a client's clearly expressed aspiration conflicts with measured interests, assessment serves the purpose of providing information for use in clarifying and isolating diagnostic problems. The most common of these conflicts are discrepancies between aspirations and abilities (L. S. Gottfredson, 1986) or between expressed and measured interests. For example, the SDS provides expressed interests in the daydream section, and measured interests in the three letter Holland code. The SCII provides a measure of basic interests and Holland themes, and direct comparisons to workers already in occupations. When these different interest domains agree, the predictive validity of interest inventories generally increases (Borgen & Seling, 1978). But when these sources disagree, what do the discrepancies mean? There is considerable evidence that expressed choices may be the better predictor of eventual choice when the two domains disagree (Slaney, 1980). Measured interests, especially less transparent criterion-based scales, are generally taken to represent the underlying psychological structure of the client's interests, whereas basic interests or verbal expressions of preference may reflect personal desires.

Little is known about the client dynamics that operate when expressed choices disagree with measured interests. Such discrepancies could be the result of a lack of self-knowledge or an unclear self-concept. They could also occur when an underlying choice is blocked, and the client is unable to articulate the barrier, or may be too hurt or embarrassed to recognize the potency of such an external restriction on the preference (Krumboltz, 1983). L. S. Gottfredson (1986) argued that presenting problems rarely reflect the true nature of the client's career difficulty. The conflicts she describes, many of them based upon ability (see Table 1-1), can be explored in depth if they can be accurately diagnosed. An expressed choice that is secondary to the blocked choice may be a more achievable option. Some research suggests that choices based upon these second-letter codes are more realistic (Walsh, Osipow, & Leonard, 1973) than those based upon primary codes.

Motivating Constructive Career Behaviors

A steady stream of evidence suggests that a variety of career interventions—from a directed, twenty-minute, model reinforcement counseling session (Krumboltz & Thoresen, 1964; Thoresen & Krumboltz, 1968) to a sixteen-week intensive career course (Kivlighan, Hageseth, Tipton, & McGovern, 1981; Lent, Larkin, & Hasegawa, 1986; Remer, O'Neill, & Gohs, 1984)—will reliably increase the amount of information seeking the client performs outside of the counseling interview. Clients do seriously consider, explore, and frequently attempt to implement new options suggested by a vocational assessment battery, although there are limits to the motivating potential of such options. For example, two studies found that although a vocational card sort may reduce indecision (Slaney & Lewis, 1986), the card sort alone may be insufficient to stimulate increased information seeking (Slaney, 1983).

Although we know that career interventions will stimulate constructive behaviors, we are just beginning to learn how an option under consideration acquires motivating potential. A suggested option that is seen as having a credible source (e.g., a valid inventory or professional counselor), and as being accessible (i.e., likely to satisfy emotional and vocational needs) will generate more exploratory behavior. Victor Vroom's motivational theory argued this position quite convincingly, stating that the emotional valence attached to an option at the time of the decision determined the direction of that decision (Fletcher, 1966).

Acquiring a Cognitive Structure for Evaluating Career Alternatives

The lack of a cognitive structure for processing and evaluating information about career options appears to be a major component in career indecision (Osipow, 1987b; Shimizu, Vondracek, Schulenberg, & Hostetler, 1988). As indicated in Chapter 3, those inventories that provide a theoretical framework either directly or implicitly help clients assimilate occupational information. For example, the Holland theory (1985a) is the conceptual underpinning for the SCII, the Vocational Preference Inventory (Holland, 1987) (VPI), and the SDS, and is discussed in the Kuder DD interpretive flyer. Super and Crites's notion of career maturity is implicit in some of the decisional status and maturity measures, and Ann Roe's theory is used in the VII and the Ramak inventories. A clever graphic representation of Holland's organizing framework, called UMAPS, was developed at the University of Maryland (Jacoby, Rue, & Allen, 1984). The UMAP contains seven posters announcing the curricular offerings, majors, and activities at the university, organized by Holland type. A brief self-assessment device is also included. The UMAP for the Holland artistic type is reproduced in Figure 4-3. In a study of the treatment utility of the UMAPS, Fogg (1983) showed that subjects who were provided with this cognitive framework showed significantly higher absorption rates ($F = 5.35$, $df = 1,26$, $p < .05$) than those who received no such framework. Those subjects who received the organizer also seemed to need less additional information after the intervention.

Find Yourself??

AT MARYLAND

Realistic · Investigative · Artistic · Social · Enterprising · Conventional

Academic Programs

This is a listing of the academic programs at UMCP that are likely to appeal to students with ARTISTIC interests. Most offer to non-majors interesting courses which fulfill USP requirements and do not have prerequisite courses or knowledge.

Taking some of these courses can help you to choose a major. Admission to starred programs as majors is selective. For further information, consult the Undergraduate Catalog, the Schedule of Classes, and faculty and staff members at the offices listed below.

AFRO-AMERICAN STUDIES
2169 Lefrak x5605
AMERICAN STUDIES
2140 Taliaferro x4661
ARCHITECTURE*
1298 Architecture x3427
ART
1211 Art Sociology x3431
History
CARTOGRAPHY—under
Geography
1113 Lefrak x6659

GEOGRAPHY
1113 Lefrak x2488
HISTORY
2115 F.S. Key x2843
HORTICULTURE
1122 Holzapfel x3607
JEWISH STUDIES
2106 Jimenez x7251
JOURNALISM*
2109 Journalism x2228
Advertising
Broadcast News
News-Editorial
Magazine
Photojournalism
Science Communication
Public Relations
LIBERAL ARTS IN BUSINESS
1101 F.S. Key x6794
MUSIC

Interior Designer
Journalist
Landscape Architect
Librarian
Museum Curator
Organizational Executive
Performer
Performing Arts Manager
Photographer

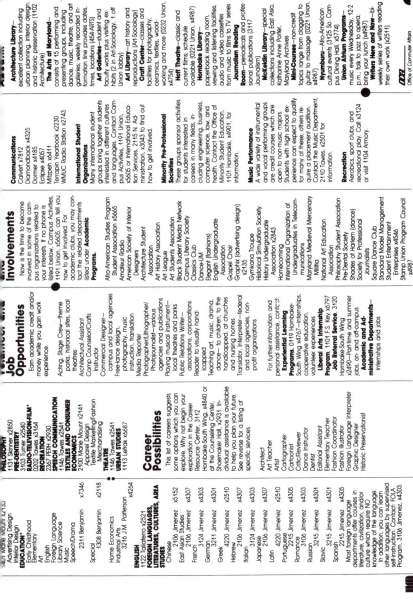

Figure 4-3 The UMAP for the Holland Artistic Type. (Source: Reprinted with permission from the Office of Commuter Affairs, University of Maryland, College Park.)

Using Information in Clarifying Expectations and Planning Treatments

Rayman (1982) found that vocational inventories have a certain consciousness-raising value for clients with an immature career-planning process. He suggested that an important reason for using interest inventories is that they provided structured activity that has some psychometric sophistication. The one or two hours of productive interaction that the inventories generate can help a counselor to structure the counseling process and increase the client's perception of the counselor's expertise. Since clients appreciate and anticipate receiving feedback from inventories (Kirschner, 1988; Wiggins, 1987), their inclusion in an intervention provides the basic structure around which the treatment is built.

Establishing an Ability Range

It may be necessary to ascertain an individual's general ability level as part of a clinical vocational assessment. When there is some question in the client's mind about the range of available options, the ability inventories (see Chapter 5) can be used to document the person's general and/or specific abilities. This assessment will frequently unearth ability-aspiration discrepancies that can be very painful for the client, but if left unaddressed, may sabotage the mobilization process described in Chapter 3. A few inventories employ an ability estimate to narrow the interest findings. The GATB, for example, contains an interest assessment, and the ECO (Andberg & Johansson, 1987) uses an ability estimate to restrict the range of options suggested to the client.

The overarching purpose of a vocational assessment is to provide a logical basis for the resolution of the client's career conflict, which generated enough concern to cause the person to seek counseling in the first place. Generally this involves the consideration—or reconsideration—of one or more alternatives, some debilitating anxiety, or a problem at work such as a conflict with a supervisor. The presenting complaint, however, may be a superficial or socially acceptable way of expressing conflicts between the aspirations and desires of the individual and the expectations and impositions of society (L. S. Gottfredson, 1986; Krumboltz, 1983).

Vocational assessment should thus assist the client in exploring conflicts, generating new career possibilities, and charting the general direction in which the individual's interests are moving. In addition, assessment should confirm congruent options and assist in acquiring and clarifying a framework for implementing realistic choices in the face of the realities of the labor force. Vocational inventories are an effective means of structuring interventions to insure both their attractiveness to the client and their overall effectiveness.

THE CONTENT AND PROCESS OF VOCATIONAL ASSESSMENT

Classifying Vocational Concerns

Early attempts at classifying vocational problems usually involved describing the problems presented by the client or uncovered by the counselor. These early classifications (Apostal-Miller, 1959; Bordin, 1946; Berezin, 1957; Byrne, 1958; Pepinsky, 1948; Robinson, 1963) offered diagnostic constructs that described the problem in psychological terms; for example, a client who was unable to make a career decision independently was considered dependent or immature (see Table 4-1). Such classifications have several weaknesses. First, their accuracy depends upon the counselor's ability to synthesize information from clinical interviews, historical data, and client self-reports (Rounds & Tinsley, 1984). In addition, such diagnoses, while intellectually rich, have not led to research and evaluation, since the link between the categories and existing diagnostic measures and possible interventions is not clear. There is, on the other hand, a certain commonality among the diagnostic categories generated by these psychodynamic classifications that has been confirmed empirically. Indeed, the degree to which factor analyses of the Career Decision Scale (Osipow, 1987b) resemble those outlined in these early systems is striking (Shimizu et al., 1988).

Later vocational diagnostic systems were heavily influenced by either developmental psychology or behavioral psychology. Goodstein (1972) and Crites (1969) distinguished indecision—a superficial and temporary state that is relieved by information or experience—from indecisiveness—a state in which more pervasive and chronic anxiety and conflicts about decisions could be found. Their distinction was important in separating more sustained decisional problems from those that might respond to relatively simple cognitive or behavioral modification.

Five vocational diagnostic models are currently used in career counseling: behavior-analytic, developmental, ability-focused, person-environment interactive, and problem-focused. They all extract data from similar sources, but focus on different aspects of the information to arrive at a diagnosis. All five, used in combination with psychodynamic classifications, offer the most fully developed schemas for understanding career issues in counseling. They are far from complete (Rounds & Tinsley, 1984), but there does seem to be some progress in linking diagnostic schemes to treatment selection, although more research in this area is badly needed.

Behavior-Analytic Career Assessment. A more clinically derived assessment system was outlined by Kanfer and Saslow (1965), who provided a useful general method of functional or behavior-analytic diagnosis. Their model does not depend upon the identification of either a specific cause of disorder

Table 4-1 Psychodynamic Vocational Problem Classifications

BORDIN (1946)	PEPINSKY (1948)	ROBINSON (1950)	BEREZIN (1957)	BYRNE (1958)	APOSTAL-MILLER (1959)	ROBINSON (1963)

Self-conflict
Lack of information
Dependence
Choice anxiety
No problem
	Self-conflict
	  Intrapersonal
	  Interpersonal
	  Cultural-self
	Lack of information
	Dependence
	Choice anxiety
	Lack of assurance
	Lack of skill
		Adjustment problems
		Immaturity
		Problems of skill
			Intrapersonal conflict
			Interpersonal conflict
			Environmental conflict
			Lack of information
			Lack of understanding of self
			Developmental
			Lack of skill
			Self-actualization
				Lack of insight
				Domination by authority person or situation
				Lack of information
				Immaturity in situation
				Lack of assurance
				Lack of problem-solving skill
					Motivational conflict within self
					Conflict with significant others
					Lack of information about or understanding of self environment
					Lack of skill
						Personal maladjustment
						Conflict with significant others
						Lack of information about environment
						Immaturity
						Discussing plans
						Skill deficiency

Source: J. B. Rounds, Jr., and H. E. A. Tinsley, "Diagnosis and Treatment of Vocational Problems," in S. D. Brown and R. W. Lent (Eds.), Handbook of Counseling Psychology (New York: Wiley, 1984), p. 153. Copyright © 1984 by John Wiley & Sons, Inc., Reprinted by permission.

or presenting symptoms that might not focus upon the behaviors producing the problem at hand. Instead, functional diagnosis attempts to determine the explicit environmental factors controlling the observed behavior in order to ascertain some means for altering that behavior. Table 4-2 describes the diagnostic steps in Kanfer and Saslow's system. When applied to career concerns, the behavior-analytic framework presumes certain maladaptive behaviors, but also identifies the client's assets that may help resolve the career concerns. The identification of a target behavior that should be increased or decreased, and the analysis of the conditions that will facilitate promoting the target behavior allow for a very specific analysis of the client's presenting concerns. In this respect the Kanfer and Saslow framework is optimistic and can be closely tied to intervention design. For example, Azrin and Besalel (1980) identified persistent telephone inquiry to be a necessary target behavior for optimum job placement, and so designed their Job Club to promote this behavior directly.

Figure 4-4 presents a behavior-analytic transformation of Bordin's (1946) and Byrne's (1958) earlier psychodynamic systems of vocational classification as a way of comparing the two approaches. As shown, the categories described by Bordin and Byrne can be viewed in behavior-analytic terms as behavioral excesses or deficits that have associated treatment implications. Thus an advantage of the behavior-analytic system is ability to be directly translated to the design of interventions. Although clear and specific, however, this framework has two limitations. The first is a lack of reliability or replicability of a particular functional analysis. For example, two career counselors might not agree in their assessment of a client's assets and deficits, or even in their identification of a target behavior. The second is the fact that behavior-analytic diagnosis is more difficult and time-consuming to perform than a paper-and-pencil or computer-assisted diagnosis.

Developmental Career Assessment.   Were it not for one or two remarkable volumes such as *Appraising Vocational Fitness* (Super & Crites, 1962) and *Occupational Psychology* (Super & Bohn, 1970), it would be tempting to conclude that developmental theorists have considered only developmental stage and career maturity, and have never seriously struggled with the problems of diagnosis. However, assessment, which Super called appraisal, was a fundamental part of nearly all of Super's prolific writings. In addition, the assessment approaches taken by theorists of the various schools have much more in common than is usually thought (Crites, 1981). Developmental career psychologists Super and Crites (1962), for example, as part of the appraisal process utilized data from interviews, questionnaires, anecdotes, personnel records, essays, autobiographies, and formal tests, which are very much the same sources used by differential theorists.

Table 4-2   Diagnostic Steps in Behavior-Analytic Assessment

Initial Analysis of the Problem Situation

Behavioral excess
Behavioral deficit
Behavioral asset

Clarification of the Problem Situation

Problematic response assignment
Who objects to behaviors
Consequences of behaviors
Conditions in which problem behaviors occur
Secondary gains
Problems created by successful treatment
Client's ability to participate in treatment design and implementation

Motivational Analysis

Analysis of client incentives (reinforcers)
Parameters of these reinforcers
Conditions under which reinforcers produce goal behaviors
Verbal/behavioral discrepancies
External behavioral controls (people, etc.)
Understanding of reinforcement contingencies
Analysis of aversive stimuli
Losses associated with treatment
Analysis of potential for arranging positive consequences

Developmental Analysis

Biological changes
Sociological changes
Behavioral changes

Analysis of Self-Control

Extent of client's control over problematic behaviors
Extent to which problem behaviors have been followed by aversive stimuli
Extent of client's ability to avoid situations
Verbal/observational discrepancy of self-control
Situation specificity of self-control
Utility for treatment

Analysis of Social-Cultural-Physical Environment

Analysis of norms in client's environment
Situation specificity of norms
Environmental limitations affecting intervention
Location of most troublesome behaviors
Openness of milieu to intervention

Source: Adapted from F. H. Kanfer and G. Saslow, "Behavioral Analysis: An Alternative to Diagnostic Classification," *Archives of General Psychiatry* 12 (1965): 529–538.

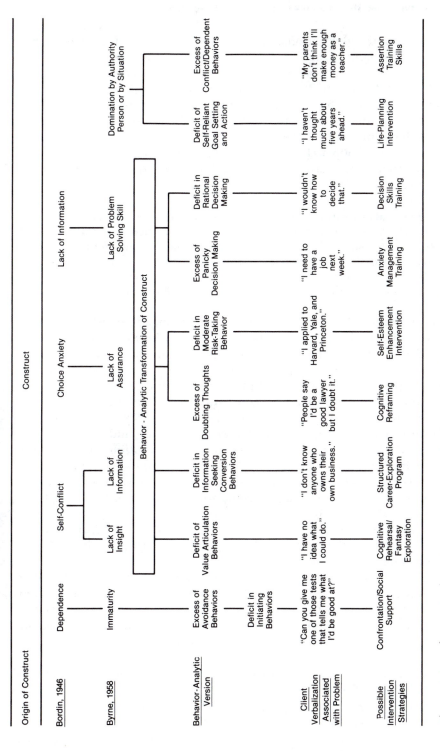

Figure 4-4 Behavior-Analytic Transformation of Psychodynamic Diagnostic Constructs.

81

Developmental vocational appraisal does, however, differ from other forms of assessment in that it is based on the following three notions: First, interests reflect the self-concept, which develops in predictable ways over time (Super & Crites, 1962). Second, career development proceeds in stages that are hierarchical, discrete, and cumulative. Third, career maturity is the successful and timely completion of the vocational tasks required at each stage of development.

According to Super (1957), vocational maturity is an individual's degree of development in reference to sequentially organized tasks required in each career stage:

> Vocational maturity may be thought of as vocational age, conceptually similar to mental age in early adolescence . . . . The place reached on the vocational continuum, may be described . . . in terms of much smaller and more refined units of behavior manifested in coping with the developmental tasks of a given life stage . . . . The vocational maturity quotient may thus be conceived of as the ratio of vocational maturity to chronological age. (p. 186)

Super's definition led to the construction of a number of maturity measures in conjunction with a large longitudinal research investigation called the Career Pattern Study (Super et al., 1957). The most popular of these measures, the Career Development Inventory (Super et al., 1971), postulated six dimensions of career maturity: degree of planning, use of resources, career decision making, career information, information about the world of work, and information about one's preferred occupation (Westbrook, 1983). The most recent version of the original scale (Super, Thompson, Lindeman, Jordaan, & Myers, 1984) is still actively used in career interventions. These newer career maturity inventories consist of an attitude component and a competence component, but it is the attitude scale that is most commonly employed in career counseling outcome studies (Oliver & Spokane, 1988; Spokane & Oliver, 1983).

Crites (1961) described a hierarchical model of career maturity. As the model suggests (see Figure 4-5), career maturity is a complex blend of content, attitudes, and competencies.

A second maturity measure, called Readiness for Vocational Planning (Gribbons & Lohnes, 1982), was used in a twenty year study that employed Markov Chain Analysis to investigate longitudinal models of the development of career maturity. The authors translated their complex data into four patterns of maturity development, or decisional status:

> *Degeneration*—"the progressive deterioration of aspirations and achievement" (p. 93).
>
> *Emerging maturity*—"the passage through the stages and tasks of Super's [1957] developmental model" (p. 99).

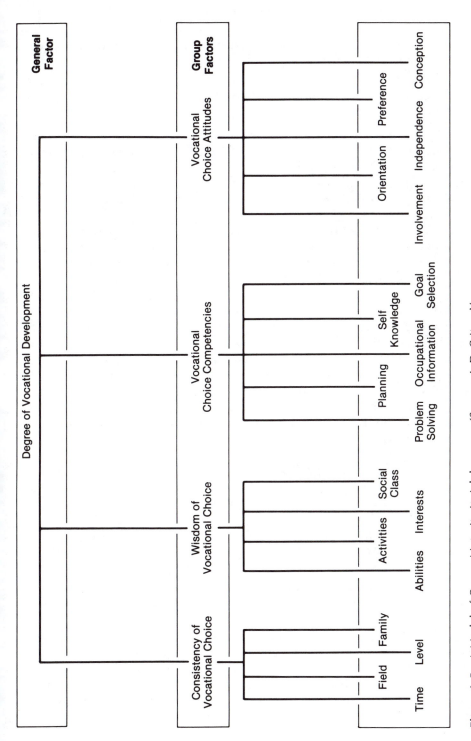

Figure 4-5 A Model of Career Maturity in Adolescence. (Source: J. D. Crites, *Vocational Psychology* [New York: McGraw-Hill, 1969], p. 5. Copyright © 1969 by McGraw-Hill, Inc. Reproduced with permission of McGraw-Hill, Inc.)

Constant maturity—"the consistent, persistent, realistic pursuit of one's first stated goal" (p. 97).

Constant immaturity—"the persistent fixation on fantastic, unrealistic goals with no advances in achieved level" (p. 101).

An alternative model of career maturity, the Cognitive Vocational Maturity Test (Westbrook & Parry-Hill, 1973), identified information about the world of work as the most critical factor in maturity. This instrument was adapted for use in two widely used career assessment programs: the CEEB's Career Skills Assessment Program, or CSAP, and the ACT's assessment of career development (N. E. Betz, 1988).

Career maturity is by far the most commonly employed outcome measure in career counseling research. Although the construct has been well operationalized in inventories, it is not entirely clear what is meant by the term, and the various forms of the measure correlate at an uncomfortably high level with general intelligence, a finding that suggests some cultural limitations. The most appealing aspect of the career maturity research—the competence scale of the Career Maturity Inventory (Crites, 1978) (CMI)—is, unfortunately, the least studied and used of the measures. Competency measures have the advantage of offering an observable link to external behavior and role functioning in which the counselor and the client can determine what the client actually is or is not doing to improve the quality of a career decision, given the environment in which it must be made. So far, developmental diagnosis implies an expected pattern of attitudes that may have limited utility for some subcultures and in some vocational environments.

In contrast to Super, Tiedeman and Ohara (1963) argued that there are at least a dozen predictable points in an individual's career at which a decision must be made, such as "the selection of subjects to be taken in high school" (p. 64). They have emphasized the assessment of decision-making style and stage as the principal diagnostic measure (see the discussion of decisional status below).

Ability-Focused Vocational Assessment.   An alternative framework for assessment, provided by L. S. Gottfredson (1986), argues that interests alone are an insufficient basis for assisting clients with career problems, and must be supplemented with information about ability and the social constraints that accompany membership in certain special groups. Table 4-3 presents Gottfredson's five assessment criteria, which can be posed directly or indirectly to the client, and which focus on the ability fit, or realism, of the client's choices. These criteria presume that presenting problems, such as anxiety or academic failure, are socially desirable, self-reported symptoms of more

Table 4-3   Outline of a System for Assessing Career Choice Problems

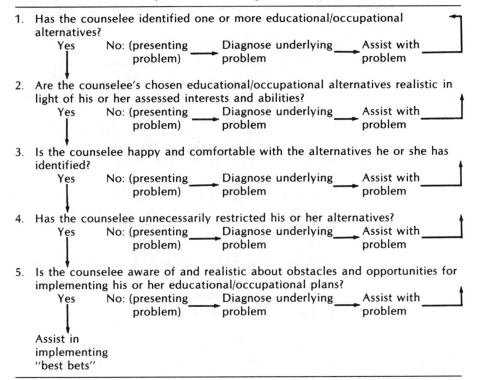

1. Has the counselee identified one or more educational/occupational alternatives?

      Yes   No: (presenting   Diagnose underlying   Assist with
                      problem)   problem   problem

2. Are the counselee's chosen educational/occupational alternatives realistic in light of his or her assessed interests and abilities?

      Yes   No: (presenting   Diagnose underlying   Assist with
                      problem)   problem   problem

3. Is the counselee happy and comfortable with the alternatives he or she has identified?

      Yes   No: (presenting   Diagnose underlying   Assist with
                      problem)   problem   problem

4. Has the counselee unnecessarily restricted his or her alternatives?

      Yes   No: (presenting   Diagnose underlying   Assist with
                      problem)   problem   problem

5. Is the counselee aware of and realistic about obstacles and opportunities for implementing his or her educational/occupational plans?

      Yes   No: (presenting   Diagnose underlying   Assist with
                      problem)   problem   problem

      Assist in
      implementing
      "best bets"

Source: L. S. Gottfredson, "Special Groups and the Beneficial Use of Vocational Interest Inventories," in W. B. Walsh and S. H. Osipow (Eds.), *Advances in Vocational Assessment*, Vol. 1, *The Assessment of Interests* (Hillsdale, N.J.: Lawrence Erlbaum, 1986), p. 167. Reprinted with permission.

serious underlying problems, including lack of self knowledge, internal or external conflicts in life goals and values, and perceived implementation barriers. Gottfredson stated further that certain social groups are at risk for problems that can impede optimal career development, such as cultural isolation, poverty, and primary child care responsibilities. These risk factors and the special groups most at risk for each of them are summarized in Table 1-1.

Gottfredson's system is the only comprehensive diagnostic framework that makes extensive use of ability measures in vocational assessment. It also offers the following nine principles of test usage:

Principle 1: Inventories should be viewed as treatments.

Principle 2: Interest inventories and their interpretive materials constitute packages of interventions, the specific packages differing somewhat from one inventory to another.

Principle 3: Interest inventories are most useful when embedded within a broader career counseling process that recognizes the constraints on career choice.

Principle 4: Treatment should be tied to goals.

Principle 5: Goals for the counseling process, including interest inventories, should relate to the adjustment and welfare of the individual rather than the social groups of which that individual may be a member.

Principle 6: Career counseling strategies, including the use of interest inventories, should be targeted to counselees' career development problems rather than to counselees' special group unless there is some compelling reason to do otherwise.

Principle 7: Interest inventory scores are useful in diagnosing whether career choice is proceeding satisfactorily and why it may not be if it is not.

Principle 8: Interpretive material that accompany interest inventories can be valuable in exposing and treating some underlying problems in career choice.

Principle 9: Interest inventories are useful in developing next-best alternatives when compromises are necessary (Gottfredson, 1986, p. 7.).

Person-Environment Diagnostic Systems.   A final group of diagnostic systems assumes that a complete diagnosis must include information about the client *and* the environment in which the choice is being made. Person-environment interaction systems exist for assessing work adaptation and adjustment (Kulik, Oldham, & Hackman, 1987; Rounds, Dawis, & Lofquist, 1987), work stress (R. D. Caplan, 1987), and general person-environment fit (Moos, 1987). The most popular and complete of these, the Holland system (Holland, 1985a), describes a set of diagnostic indicators (congruence, consistency, differentiation, and identity) derived from the degree of similarity between the person and the environment. Person measures (i.e., Holland codes) are calculated using scores from any of the interest inventories which employ the Holland System. A three-letter code (three of the six Holland code scores in order) or high-point code (the top score of the six) is extracted for each by taking the highest scores for the six Holland types from the inventory. Thus for a three-letter Holland code, a client is classified as a combination of realistic (*R*), investigative (*I*), artistic (*A*), social (*S*), enterprising (*E*), or conventional (*C*) (e.g., *IRC* = investigative, realistic, and conventional). The client's work environment (or major) is then also classified by taking a census of the number of persons from each Holland type inhabiting that environment (see Spokane, 1985, for a detailed description of this procedure). Astin (1964) demonstrated that college environments could be well classified using a combination of student census data and a description of the types of courses and college majors offered at a given institution. Three person-environment diagnostic indicators can then be extracted from the three-letter Holland codes, and the fourth from the Vocational Identity Scale (Holland et al., 1980a) as follows:

THE INDICATORS.   The primary diagnostic indicator, **congruence**, taps the degree of fit between the respondent's three-letter Holland code and the code of that person's environment, such as current occupation, college major, or an option under consideration. An example of a highly congruent individual would be a respondent with a three-letter code of *ASE* (artistic, social, and enterprising) who had selected the occupation of journalist, which is also classified as *ASE*.

Several methods exist for estimating the level of person-environment congruence using the Holland system (Spokane, 1985; in press-b). All use a roughly hexagonal, two-dimensional arrangement, which has been found to exist among the six Holland types (Holland, Whitney, Cole, & Richards, 1969), to estimate each of the four primary diagnostic indices: congruence, differentiation, identity and consistency (see Figure 4-6).

The second indicator, **differentiation**, measures the difference between the high and low scores on the profile to estimate the clarity of the interest pattern in an individual or an environment. To illustrate, a highly differentiated individual might have an investigative (*I*) Holland code score of 41 and a realistic (*R*) code score of 3, for a differentiation level of 97 percent. Another individual, with an *I* code of 18 and an *R* code of 15, would not be well differentiated. Norms for differentiation scores are presented in the SDS manual.

Consistency, the third indicator, is a measure of the harmony of a respondent's scores. Consistency is calculated using the intercorrelations between the first two letters in a three-letter Holland code according to the hexagonal relationship among the six Holland types. The more harmonious the first two letters in a code (either person or environment), the more consistent the individual is.

A final indicator—**identity**—assesses the stability of a person's goals, interests, and abilities (Holland, 1985a), and can be derived by using My Vocational Situation (Holland, Daiger, & Power, 1980a). Holland has applied this same concept to occupational environments by measuring the number of occupations in a work environment (Holland, 1985a), and found that the greater the number of job titles, the lower the identity. Thus a law office employing only lawyers and legal secretaries would have a strong and homogeneous identity.

Problem-Focused Career Assessment.   One comprehensive problem-focused diagnostic system (R. E. Campbell & Cellini, 1981; R. E. Campbell, Cellini, Shaltry, Long, & Pinkos, 1979) has been developed for classifying

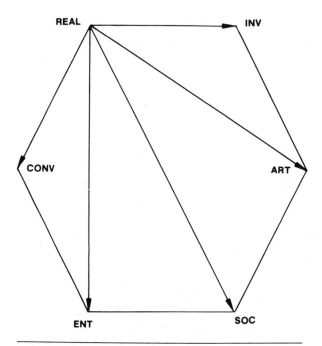

Note: R-person in an R-environment = 4; in a C- or an I-environment = 3; in an E- or A-environment = 2; and in an S-environment = 1.

Figure 4-6   Using the Hexagonal Model to Interpret Person-Environment Relations. (Source: J. L. Holland, *The Self-Directed Search: Professional Manual* (Odessa, FL: Psychological Assessment Resources, 1985). Reproduced by special permission of Psychological Assessment Resources, Inc., Odessa, FL 33556, from the Self Directed Search Professional Manual by John L. Holland, Ph.D. Copyright © 1985 by PAR, Inc.)

adult career concerns. This classification, which is reproduced in its entirety in Appendix B and condensed in Table 4-4, assumes that if specific tasks are not mastered at each stage of career development, problems will result. The system is based upon a review and analysis of developmental theories of psychosocial development that yielded four task themes that are considered necessary to successful career functioning and in which problems might occur: decision making, plan implementation, organizational performance, and organizational/institutional adaptation. As Table 4-4 shows, these categories are more specific and clearer than the psychodynamic classifications, but are also difficult to tie to any existing diagnostic inventories. The system is further constrained by its reliance on hierarchical or cumulative stages of development in which certain tasks are presumed to have been accomplished at each previous stage. It does, however, represent an advance in identifying specific adult career problems, and, when used as a diagnostic check list, can be helpful in clarifying client concerns.

Table 4-4   Diagnostic Taxonomy Outline: Problem Categories and Subcategories

1.0. Problems in career decision making
    1.1.   Getting started
        A. Lack of awareness of the need for a decision
        B. Lack of knowledge of the decision-making process
        C. Awareness of the need to make a decision, but avoidance of assuming personal responsibility for decision making
    1.2.   Information gathering
        A. Inadequate, contradictory, and/or insufficient information
        B. Information overload, i.e., excessive information which confuses the decision maker
        C. Lack of knowledge as to how to gather information, i.e., where to obtain information, how to organize, and to evaluate it
        D. Unwillingness to accept the validity of the information because it does not agree with the person's self-concept
    1.3.   Generating, evaluating, and selecting alternatives
        A. Difficulty deciding due to multiple career options, i.e., too many equally attractive career choices
        B. Failure to generate sufficient career options due to personal limitations such as health, resources, ability, and education
        C. The inability to decide due to the thwarting effects of anxiety such as fear of failure in attempting to fulfill the choice, fear of social disapproval, and/or fear of commitment to a course of action
        D. Unrealistic choice, i.e., aspiring either too low or too high, based upon criteria such as aptitudes, interests, values, resources, and personal circumstances
        E. Interfering personal constraints which impede a choice such as interpersonal influences and conflicts, situational circumstances, resources, and health
        F. The inability to evaluate alternatives due to lack of knowledge of the evaluation criteria—the criteria could include values, interests, aptitudes, skills, resources, health, age, and personal circumstances.
    1.4.   Formulating plans to implementing decisions
        A. Lack of knowledge of the necessary steps to formulate a plan
        B. Inability to utilize a future time perspective in planning
        C. Unwillingness and/or ability to acquire the necessary information to formulate a plan
2.0. Problems in implementing career plans
    2.1.   Characteristics of the individual
        A. Failure of the individual to undertake the steps necessary to implement his/her plan
        B. Failure or inability to successfully complete the steps necessary for goal attainment
        C. Adverse changes in the individual's physical or emotional condition
    2.2.   Characteristics external to the individual
        A. Unfavorable economic, social, and cultural conditions
        B. Unfavorable conditions in the organization or institution central to the implementation of one's plans
        C. Adverse condition of or changes in the individual's family situation

3.0. Problems in organization/institutional performance
    3.1. Deficiencies in skills, abilities, and knowledge
        A. Insufficient skills, abilities, and/or knowledge upon position entry, i.e., underqualified to perform satisfactorily
        B. The deterioration of skills, abilities, and/or knowledge over time in the position due to temporary assignment to another position, leave, and/or lack of continual practice of the skill
        C. The failure to modify or update skills, abilities, and/or knowledge to stay abreast of job changes, i.e., job obsolescence due to new technology, tools, and knowledge
    3.2. Personal factors
        A. Personality characteristics discrepant with the job, e.g., values, interests, and work habits
        B. Debilitating physical and/or emotional disorders
        C. Adverse off-the-job personal circumstances and/or stressors, e.g., family pressures, financial problems, and personal conflicts
        D. The occurrence of interpersonal conflicts on the job which are specific to performance requirements, e.g., getting along with the boss, co-workers, customers, and clients.
    3.3. Conditions of the organization/institutional environment
        A. Ambiguous or inappropriate job requirements, e.g., lack of clarity of assignments, work overload, and conflicting assignments
        B. Deficiencies in the operational structure of the organization/institution
        C. Inadequate support facilities, supplies, and resources, e.g., insufficient lighting, ventilation, tools, support personnel, and materials
        D. Insufficient reward system, e.g., compensation, fringe benefits, status, recognition, and opportunities for advancement
4.0. Problems in organizational/institutional adaptation
    4.1. Initial entry
        A. Lack of knowledge of organizational rules and procedures
        B. Failure to accept or adhere to organizational rules and procedures
        C. Inability to assimilate large quantities of new information, i.e., information overload
        D. Discomfort in a new geographic location
        E. Discrepancies between the individual's expectations and the realities of the institutional/organizational environment
    4.2. Changes over time
        A. Changes over the life span in one's attitudes, values, life style, career plans, or commitment to the organization which lead to incongruence between the individual and the environment
        B. Changes in the organizational/institutional environment which lead to incongruence between the individual and the environment, e.g., physical and administrative structure, policies, and procedures
    4.3. Interpersonal relationships
        A. Interpersonal conflicts arising from differences of opinion, style, values, mannerisms, etc.
        B. The occurrence of verbal or physical abuse or sexual harrassment

---

DEVELOPMENT STAGE SYSTEM   Tiedeman and Ohara (1963) and Tiedeman and Miller-Tiedeman (1984) have shown that clients need career assistance at different positions in their development and in response to different developmentally triggered events. Another problem-focused assessment, presented in Chapter 5 (see especially Figure 5-1), summarizes common presenting problems by client stage. This system borrows from R. A. Myers (1971), who reviewed studies of career counseling based on grade in school and argued that different career interventions were required at different ages and grades. The schema considers special problems associated with occupational level and gender.

Decisional Status and Career Intervention

The extensive and diverse literature on career decision making has historically stumbled through attempts to describe, measure, and dimensionalize career maturity (Phillips & Pazienza, 1988; Westbrook, 1983), to studies comparing decided and undecided students (Slaney, 1988), to systematic attempts to describe, predict, and intervene to facilitate effective career decision making. This history is replete with blind alleys, unfulfilled promises, and disconnected threads of research. Any scholar reviewing the hundreds of studies in the field is immediately struck with the limited number of useful principles that have arisen from this large effort. Organizing this diverse body of work may be the most difficult challenge facing the career development field in the next few years. How, then, is the career practitioner to extract the essence of this research and apply it to clinical intervention?

Beyond Career Maturity to Decisional Status.   In the last one-hundred years, psychology first included, then excluded, and finally rediscovered conscious thought in the study of behavior (Wolman, 1973). Behaviorists such as J. B. Watson, Ian Pavlov, C. L. Hull, and B. F. Skinner were clearly of the opinion that consciousness had no place in the scientific study of human behavior. They argued that the psychologist, rather than explaining the causes of human activity, need only describe the behavior itself and the circumstances under which it could be produced, thereby emulating the natural sciences. Indeed, with his last scholarly breath, Skinner (1987) was still exorcising the cognitive and clinical demons he saw in the modern science of psychology. In spite of or perhaps in reaction to the behavioral movement, however, cognitive and clinical sciences are now stronger than ever. Cognitive psychology is back with a vengeance because it is difficult to explain and predict future behavior by simply observing current behavior (Wolman, 1973). Since private cognitive events cannot be observed directly, a complex set of inferential concepts and methods must be developed for studying cognitive phenomena.

For a time, career psychology was relieved of the problem of fleshing out the inner cognitive experiences associated with career choice, since developmental theory offered logical patterns, stages, and explanatory constructs such as the self-concept and career maturity that described normal development without having even to open the "black box" of the self for inspection. When career maturity proved to be largely unidimensional and uncomfortably correlated with general intelligence, however, we were forced either to define the self in terms of intelligence or to find some other way to account for career decisions. After some fairly superficial attempts to offer prescriptive solutions for how to make career decisions (for a thorough review of these studies, Jepsen & Dilley, 1974), it was discovered that these methods not only were largely ineffective, but also occasionally made matters worse when applied indiscriminately. As a result of the inadequacies of much of this earlier research, theorists and researchers have chosen two somewhat independent routes to attempt to explain career decision making at an appropriate level of complexity.

Indecision and Anxiety. The first approach operationalizes and measures decision status (Harren, 1980; Holland, Daiger, & Power, 1980b; Jones, 1979; Osipow, 1987b) by using brief inventories of individuals' current reactions to their career choice. A series of studies using this strategy have related career indecision to various known constructs of interest in an effort to validate the inventories and explore decisional relationships. These studies now find that indecision and anxiety are heavily intercorrelated (Fugua, Newman, & Seaworth, 1988), much as Goodstein (1972) had predicted. The sheer number and variety of the studies on career indecision attests to the vigor of this issue, but in spite of the volume, some confusion about the problem remains.

Several recent studies, for example, employed the Spielberger State-Trait Anxiety Inventory, STAI (Spielberger, Gorsuch, Lushene, Vagg, & Jacobs, 1983) and a measure of decisional status. A set of factor-analytic studies by Fuqua and his colleagues (Fuqua & Newman, 1989; Fuqua, Newman, & Seaworth, 1988; Fuqua, Seaworth & Newman, 1987; Newman, Fuqua & Seaworth, 1989) confirmed the complex relationship between anxiety and indecision. For example, Fuqua, Newman, and Seaworth performed a factor analysis on the Career Decision Scale or CDS (Osipow et al., 1980) and the STAI. Fuqua, Seaworth, and Newman found that factors such as lack of information, lack of congruence information, and implementation barriers were moderately correlated with anxiety. Likewise, they discovered that measures of career indecision and anxiety had a common variance of 44 percent, and that the relationship between the two domains was simple and linear, which called into question the independence of Goodstein's (1972) two-factor (indecision versus indecisiveness) career indecision model.

In a thoughtful paper, Newman et al. (1989) offered several contrasting models of the career indecision problem (see Figure 4-7). These models are testable views of the relationship between anxiety and career indecision that

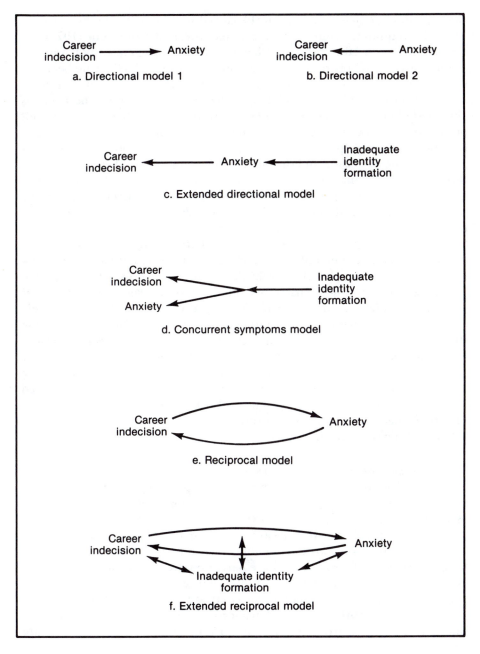

Figure 4-7 Theoretical Models Relating Career Indecision and Anxiety. (Source: J. L. Newman, D. R. Fuqua, and T. B. Seaworth, "The Role of Anxiety in Career Indecision: Implications for Diagnosis and Treatment," *Career Development Quarterly* 37 (1989):225. Copyright © 1989 by the American Association for Counseling and Development. Reprinted with permission.)

should stimulate new research on the causal link between the two factors.

The temporary state of career indecision that Goodstein (1972) described, in which "the individual has never had sufficient opportunity to acquire or learn adaptive or adequate responses, and his inadequate behavior stems from a limitation of experience" (p. 260), may not be very different from the more conflict-engendering indecisiveness in which the client is "undecided not simply because of lack of information either about himself or the world of work but because making a decision or commitment is strongly anxiety arousing" (p. 261). Goodstein observed that in both cases the client avoids making a decision and the anxiety must be reduced. Deciding whether this anxiety is chronic or temporary may be less important than seeing the necessity for reducing the anxiety related to making a decision or taking some constructive action taken. Thus the anxiety, whenever it occurs, is an irrelevant drive (Pepinsky & Pepinsky, 1954).

The tautological nature of this hypothetical indecision construct is frustrating to researcher and practitioner alike. Thus we have attempted first to operationalize decisional status by developing measures of the construct. These measures are now the basis for studies of the construct validity of career indecision, which are designed to determine which variables are closely enough associated with indecision to help us define indecision. But, as these studies proceed, it becomes increasingly evident that most career indecision can be attributed to anxiety. Reduce that anxiety, and the indecision lessens (Mendonca & Siess, 1976). One study, by Berger-Gross, Kahn, and Weare (1983), found that simply being asked to *think* about career choice engendered global anxiety in most individuals. The problem, then, is that nearly all aspects of careers, because they are so central to identity and self-esteem, will correlate with anxiety to some degree.

Indecision as a Cognitive Process.   The second research strategy for studying indecision involves describing the complex cognitive processes used to narrow and eventually select career options (Gati, 1986; Gati & Tikotzki, 1989; Zakay & Barak, 1984); however, it does not explain why some individuals are unable to execute career preferences. Much assisted by computers, these studies use artificial intelligence and decision theory as the base for understanding how selections are narrowed. In these strategies, decision making can be considered to be an intervening cognitive variable that explains how some individuals attain jobs that could not be predicted by social status alone. Since the variety of persons inhabiting similar jobs is considerable, some cognitive operations are presumed to effect how choices are made.

Measures of Career Indecision.   The multidimensional study of career decision-making was advanced significantly by Harren (1980), whose Assessment of Career Decision Making (ACDM) was the first inventory to tap decisional style as well as stage. Harren outlined three basic decision styles—rational, intuitive, and dependent—and although there was considerable inaccuracy in the stages Harren described his concept of styles was a unique contribution to career decision-making research. Prior to the ACDM, decision making was viewed as a rational process that could be simply taught and universally applied. Harren's inventory, and a flood of recent studies that followed, are finally moving the field away from exclusively rational models of decision making and career maturity, and toward more comprehensive psychological models. Although largely ignored by researchers, Fletcher's (1966) view of the career decision-making process as an intuitive-motivational process rather than a rational one helped to pave the way for the comprehensive decision-style models. Two recent such measures, the Career Decision Scale and My Vocational Situation, are used increasingly in vocational assessment.

CAREER DECISION SCALE   (Osipow, Carney, Winer, Yanico, & Koschier, 1976). The CDS was based upon the presumption that career indecision was less a unitary construct than a factorially structured domain composed of the following four factors (Osipow, Carney, & Barak, 1976):

1. *Lack of structure:* absence of a general framework or method for understanding and making career decisions.
2. *External barrier:* the inability to implement a preferred choice option.
3. *Multipotentiality:* or a conflict among several equally attractive alternatives.
4. *Conflict:* conflict with others (e.g., family members), that is generally personal.

Although Osipow (1987b) and Slaney (1985) found a somewhat different factor structure using the CDS, recent work by Shimizu et al. (1988) suggested that when an oblique rather than orthogonal factor-analytic procedure is used, the structure stabilizes and produces a simple solution of four factors (confusion, support, conflict, and barriers) that are very similar to those found in previous studies. The Career Decision Scale seems useful as a diagnostic measure and as an outcome measure for intervention studies. Few studies have used the CDS to diagnose which treatment to employ with a specific client.

MY VOCATIONAL SITUATION   A second career decision-making scale developed for use in selecting and designing interventions is My Vocational Situation, or MVS (Holland, et al., 1980a). Its authors hoped that the scale would permit "the assignment of a client to a category [which] would increase the likilihood of selecting and following an effective treatment" (Holland et al., 1980b, p. 1). The MVS is a brief eighteen-item, true-false scale with three subscales (vocational identity, occupational information, and barriers). The MVS was developed and normed on high school and college students ($N = 824$), and is beginning to be used as an outcome measure in career intervention studies (Slaney, 1988). Holland et al. have defined the three subscales as follows:

> *Vocational identity:* "the possession of a clear and stable picture of one's goals, interests, personality and talents" (p. 1).
>
> *Occupational information:* the "need for vocational information," usually in printed form (p. 1).
>
> *Barriers:* the perception of "external obstacles to a chosen occupational goal" (p. 1).

They assumed that "intrapsychic" concerns were only one area of decisional status, and that environmental constraints and information were equally important in describing career decision making. Unfortunately, the information and barriers scales have minimal internal consistency. The scales are modestly correlated with age, as expected, and low scorers endorsed more career concerns than did high scorers.

Slaney (1988) argued that the evidence of construct validity is still rather weak for the MVS as a measure of decisional status. The evidence may support the scale as a broader measure of personality (Slaney, 1988), and especially as a measure of general level of personal integration, which as suggested in Chapter 3, is a useful variable for selecting and assigning career treatments. Slaney also reviewed the Vocational Decision Scale (Jones & Chenery, 1980).

In a somewhat different approach to the problem of indecision, Lucas and Epperson have used cluster analysis to characterize five types of undecided subjects according to a wide range of psychological variables (Lucas, 1983; Lucas & Epperson, 1986; 1988):

Type 1: Happy and Well-Adjusted.   These students are still undecided, although less so than other types. They have high self-esteem and low anxiety, and probably can make excellent use of less intensive, more self-directing career interventions.

Type 2: Caught in a Dilemma.   These students, who are more likely to be female than male, score low on career salience. They may benefit from informational interventions.

Type 3: Undecided and Limited Interests.   These students have no high scores, and seem to lack motivation, autonomy, and identity. Personal growth interventions seem appropriate for this group.

Type 4: Anxious and Unclear Goals. This type scores high on anxiety and externality, and low on self-esteem. These students may show immaturity and dependence, and may need more psychotherapeutic interventions.

Type 5: Happy and Playful. This type seems well adjusted and close to making a career decision. They seem leisure oriented, and may need some help in making the transition from school to work.

This interesting analysis could be translated into a diagnostic device for treatment assignment in college counseling centers and into a blocking variable for studying attribute treatment interactions (i.e., how treatments affect some individuals more than others) in future research (Fretz, 1981).

Using Decisional Style in Career Intervention

In an interesting analytical departure, Krumboltz (1983) portrayed career decision making as a painful, stressful process in which a set of personal cognitive rules or unfounded beliefs determined most outcomes. Troublesome beliefs are those in which the client forms incorrect or faulty understandings or causal linkages from a limited number of experiences, or creates unrealistic or innappropriate comparison standards that can never be reached. Troublesome private rules may also lead clients to ignore relevant disconfirming information about a choice, focus on low-probability events, and even to engage in self-deceptive or socially acceptable yet counter-productive thinking. This cognitive-behavioral approach to career decision making implies several counseling intervention strategies in addition to the development of a strong, trusting counseling relationship, which Krumboltz detailed:

1. *Carefully examine and challenge the clients' statements about their deeply held beliefs about themselves and their career.* These may include feelings of a lack of control, or mistaken theories about how the world in general and careers in particular operate. This notion is similar to Resnick's (1983) contention that people hold naïve scientific theories that must be exposed, attacked, and replaced if a more valid alternative model is to be fully absorbed. In directly challenging key beliefs on the basis of the evidence supporting them, this strategy also borrows from cognitive behavioral therapy (Beck, 1976).
2. *Attend to the client's actual behavior rather than what they say they would like to do.* This includes looking for discrepancies between expressed preferences and actual choices, and especially to the lack of constructive search, even if the client expresses a high level of positive motivation.

3. *Confront automatic thinking about career problems.* Fairly intrusive techniques, such as paradoxical intention, may be necessary to jolt the client out of simplistic thinking patterns.

4. *Attack hierarchical patterns of irrational thinking at an early stage.* Well articulated but illogical patterns can mushroom from a single irrational belief, and thus must be confronted.

5. *Insist that the client realistically anticipate barriers.* This may result in the discovery of mistaken goals that were more a function of fears about environmental constraints than real aspirations.

In a similar vein, Janis (1982, 1983; Janis & Mann, 1977) outlined a theory of the social psychology of decision making that argues that major decisions engender conflict and stress that in turn adversely affect the quality of the resulting decision. Janis and Mann (1977) described five major coping strategies—unconflicted adherence, unconflicted change, defensive avoidance, hypervigilance, and vigilance—that are differentially used in the face of decisional conflict, depending on the individual's subjective beliefs about the risks associated with the decision and the time frame in which the decision must be made (see Hinkeldey & Spokane, 1986). These five coping styles and the levels of stress and ambivalence associated with each during a decisional conflict are described in Table 4-5.

As Table 4-6 indicates, the five decisional styles are differentially effective in producing high-quality decisional behavior; the table also ranks each style according to the seven criteria for high-quality decision making. The most critical of the criteria appears to be the individual's willingness to consider evidence that contradicts the person's general beliefs about the choice; Janis and Mann (1977) called this the unbiased assimilation of new information.

Table 4-5 Manifestations of Conflict and Related Symptoms of Stress for Each of the Five Basic Patterns of Decision Making

PATTERN OF COPING WITH CHALLENGE	SUBJECTIVE BELIEFS	LEVEL OF STRESS	DEGREE OF VACILLATION OR PREFERENCE FOR ALTERNATIVE COURSES OF ACTION
1. Unconflicted adherence	No serious risk from current course of action	*Low:* persistently calm	No vacillation
2. Unconflicted change	Serious risk from current course of action No serious risk from new course of action	*Low:* persistently calm	No vacillation

Table 4-5 con't

PATTERN OF COPING WITH CHALLENGE	SUBJECTIVE BELIEFS	LEVEL OF STRESS	DEGREE OF VACILLATION OR PREFER- ENCE FOR ALTERNATIVE COURSES OF ACTION
3. Defensive avoidance	Serious risk from current course of action Serious risk from new course of action No better solution can be found	*Variable* from low to high (predomina- ntly pseudo- calm, with break- through of high emo- tional arousal when signs of threat become salient)	Little or no vacillation (except when signs of threat are salient)
4. Hypervigilance	Serious risk from current course of action Serious risk from new course of action A better solution might be found Insufficient time to search for and evaluate a better solution	*High:* persist- ently strong anxiety	Very high rate of vacillation: but occa- sionally practically none as a result of persever- ance
5. Vigilance	Serious risk from current course of action Serious risk from new course of action A better solution might be found Sufficient time to search for and evaluate a better solution	*Moderate:* variations within in- termediate range, with level de- pending upon ex- posure to threat cues or reassuring communica- tions	Moderate to high rate of vacilla- tion (depending on content of new in- formation

Source: I. L. Janis and L. Mann, *Decision Making: A Psychological Analysis of Conflict, Choice, and Commitment* (New York: The Free Press, 1977). p. 78. Reprinted with permission.

Table 4-6 Predecisional Behavior Characteristics of the Five Basic Patterns of Decision Making

			CRITERIA FOR HIGH-QUALITY DECISION MAKING					
	(1)	(2)	(3) Careful Evaluation of Consequences		(4)	(5)	(6)	(7)
Pattern of Coping with Challenge	Thorough Canvassing of Alternatives	Thorough Canvassing of Objectives	a. Of Current Policy	b. Of Alternative New Policies	Thorough Search for Information	Unbiased Assimilation of New Information	Careful Reevaluation of Consequences	Thorough Planning for Implementation and Contingencies
Unconflicted adherence	−	−	−	−	−	+	−	−
Unconflicted change	−	−	+	−	−	+	−	−
Defensive avoidance	−	−	±	±	±	−	−	−
Hypervigilance	−	−	±	±	+	−	−	+
Vigilance	+	+	+	+	+	+	+	+

Key: + = The decision maker meets the criterion to the best of his ability.

− = The decision maker fails to meet the criterion.

± = The decision maker's performance fluctuates, sometimes meeting the criterion to the best of his ability and sometimes not.

All evaluative terms such as *thorough* and *unbiased* are to be understood as intrapersonal comparative assessments, relative to the person's highest possible level of cognitive performance.

Source: I. L. Janis and L. Mann, *Decision Making: A Psychological Analysis of Conflict, Choice, and Commitment* (New York: The Free Press, 1977). p. 77. Reprinted with permission.

Janis and Mann (1977) argued that decision-making counseling is most effective when the seven criteria are used as diagnostic indicators, and the client is asked to express personal views about the decision and what steps have been taken so far. The counselor makes no moral judgments, criticisms, or admonitions, and thus the socially supportive relationship between the client and the counselor can be used to promote adherence to counseling recommendations (Janis, 1982). Most importantly, Janis and Mann (1977) asserted that because most individuals will resist having their pattern of search and decision making altered, simple didactic interventions are not likely to have much of an effect on the quality of the decisional process.

Kahneman and Tversky's (1984) prospect theory highlights the inherent conflict or "mismatch," between the experience value of an option—its "degree of pleasure or pain, satisfaction or anguish" (p. 349)—and the decision value of an option—its rational attractiveness. This position, which asserts that choices can be intuitive as well as rational, was taken quite some time ago by Fletcher (1966), who argued that the emotion attached to an option at the "eleventh hour" of a decision-making process would determine the direction of the choice. Kahneman and Tversky called this process "mental accounting," during which the individual evaluates the balance of the positive and negative consequences of the decision. They also clarified the tendency to make risk-averse choices to avoid losses. The authors predicted, for example, that when two qualities of a job choice are varied, the decision will be to remain in the present job rather than risk a loss in a new one. They further showed that the manner in which the choice is presented (e.g., as a potential loss versus a potential gain) will affect the decision, even when the outcomes are identical.

In an earlier statement of this theory, Tversky (1972) presented decision making as a process of sequential elimination that was rooted in the psychophysical attributes of the alternatives under consideration. Figure 4-8 describes this process in which the decision maker selects acceptable aspects of occupations in a stepwise fashion, eliminating the unacceptable options until only one choice remains. This systematic elimination is an intuitively appealing way to conceptualize career decision making by using general decision theory research and theory.

In an unusually clever and compelling test of the sequential elimination model, Gati and Tikotzki (1989) examined the "dialogue" between career clients and a computer guidance system. They coded the exploratory strategies the subjects employed in shifting among recommended options lists, occupational information about those lists, and information about particular jobs on the lists. The authors found that most subjects did not explore all of the suggested alternatives in depth, and narrowed their search using their interests. These subjects apparently employed a search strategy that combined the sequential elimination of some occupational clusters with a deeper intraoccupational exploration of a subset of alternatives:

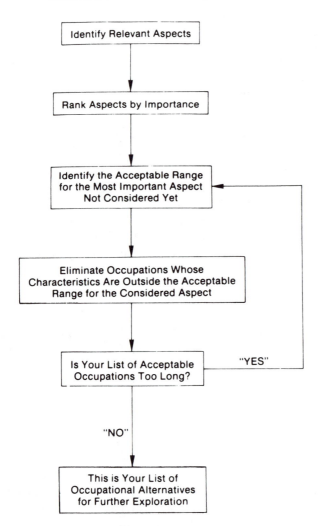

Figure 4-8 A Schematic Diagram of the Sequential Elimination Model. (Source: I. Gati, "Making Career Decisions: A Sequential Elimination Approach," *Journal of Counseling Psychology* 33 [1986]:410. Copyright © 1986 by the American Psychological Association. Reprinted by permission.)

The recorded dialogue of a 22-year-old woman, with 12 years of schooling, reflects this frequent pattern. Her recommended interest fields were Science, General Culture, Service, and Arts and Entertainment, Level 1. She asked for a list of occupations for the first three fields only, but not for the list of occupations of Arts and Entertainment, and she did not ask for information on any occupation of this field. Although for some occupations (including journalist, pharmacist, flight attendant, geographer, medical engineer, and aeronautical engineer), she asked for all available information, on other occupations she explored only part of the available information: for biologist and physician she asked only for the occupational descriptions and training possibilities without exploring the relevant educational institutions, and on earth science expert, behavioral scientist, nurse, and paramedic she asked only for the occupational description, without exploring additional information. (p. 437)

Gati and Tikotzki concluded that this strategy was similar to Simon's (1955) bounded rationality model of decision making, and supported previous findings by Krumboltz, Rude, Mitchell, Hamel, and Kinnier (1982). Their review of compensatory and noncompensatory decision-making models and their implications is clear and helpful. Gati and Tikotzki's breakthrough study reminds us that we must be prepared to consider more complex views of the career decision-making process as well as the larger literature on general decision making to reinvigorate our research efforts. Their work is also an example of one of the rare systematic, long-range research programs that eventually leads to improved understanding of an area of inquiry.

SUMMARY

Assessment has been the foundation of career intervention since its beginnings with the work of Parsons (1909). Although public views on the appropriateness of standardized testing fluctuate, clients continue to request and appreciate feedback from interest inventories, personality inventories, and ability measures, which have several specific benefits in career interventions (e.g., unearthing congruent options, charting changes in interests, confirming preferences, motivating constructive behaviors, diagnosing conflicts, and structuring treatments). In addition to the early psychodynamic classification of presenting career problems, five assessment models are currently in use: behavior-analytic, developmental, ability focused, person-environment, and problem-focused interactive. Research on career decision making has moved from the universal assumption that decision making is and should be rational, to a more comprehensive view of decisions as complex social-psychological events.

5

Considerations in the Selection and Use of Career Inventories

We cannot, of course, expect to fulfill all of the assessment goals described in Chapter 4 with a single inventory. Most researchers agree that multiple measures are required to tap the full range of behaviors, attitudes, and emotions that are involved in career intervention (Oliver, 1979). An unusually broad, high-quality group of inventories is available for use with clients. Indeed, there are so many good inventories with evidence of reliability and validity that even the well-informed counselor has difficulty making an appropriate choice. Several of these instruments are now so comprehensive that they are more of an assessment battery than a single instrument. The extensive array of career-related assessment devices raises several questions for the counselor: What should an intervention battery for career counseling include? Should we employ a standard battery, or tailor the battery for each client's needs? Are the measures needed for research studies different from those used in clinical intervention? Which tests are appropriate for which purposes? What should one look for in a career inventory?

The inventories discussed here are selected for their usefulness as interventions to help clients meet their goals and to improve the overall quality of their career decisions. It is the inventories' contribution to treatment outcome, or their treatment utility (Hayes, Nelson, & Jarrett, 1987), that is the principle concern of this chapter. Hayes et al. define treatment utility as "the degree to which assessment is shown to contribute to beneficial outcome" (p. 963). They argued that clinicians maintain too much separation between their clinical process and the diagnostic classifications conducted in an overall intervention, often seeing very little relationship between the tests administered and the treatment process.

The inventories presented in this chapter must be evaluated with respect to their psychometric adequacy (e.g., validity and reliability) when used either as clinical interventions or as outcome measures in research studies. But it is important to distinguish psychometric properties from clinical or educational utility. A test may meet all of the requirements for psychometric adequacy (e.g., predictive validity, construct validity, and reliability) but still not be documented as a useful educational or clinical intervention (Anastasi, 1985a; Messick, 1980). Conversely, a specific test may lack internal consistency but still show evidence of treatment utility (Hayes et al., 1987). Validity, especially construct validity, or the extent to which an inventory actually taps the construct it is designed to measure, is the bedrock of psychometrics. Treatment utility or the degree to which an inventory interpreted directly to the client will promote an increment in the client's ability to make improved career decisions, is the essence of vocational assessment.

In spite of the extensive use of vocational inventories, there is relatively little empirical evidence on their treatment utility. If this chapter were restricted to inventories whose treatment utility has been well documented, it would be very brief indeed. Instead, it shall present thirteen classes of vocational instruments that clinical experience suggests may be useful in the career intervention process. Any evidence of treatment utility will be summarized for each entry. The psychometric qualities of the inventory class will also be summarized.

At the minimum, a vocational inventory should demonstrate temporal stability. Commonly referred to as test-retest reliability, this property is especially important in a vocational inventory that is used to make long-range career decisions. An unstable inventory that yields different results from one testing to another would be of little assistance in predicting which option might constitute a reasonable fit across time. This second property, called predictive validity, has for years been the acid psychometric test of an interest inventory. An inventory that can predict who will actually wind up in what job and how satisfied they will be is especially useful in career intervention. A related property, concurrent validity, refers to the degree to which the inventory can differentiate individuals inhabiting different occupations (and thereby fitting from nonfitting options) during the brief period immediately surrounding the testing. A final standard, construct validity, is the extent to which a test is a true measure of the phenomenon it seeks to describe. Construct validity is especially crucial in measures of decisional status, where understanding the nature of the problem and its accurate measurement is important in designing effective interventions or in determining the effectiveness of a particular intervention strategy. Prediger and Garfield (1988) have provided a useful summary table and check list of the competencies needed by a counselor to interpret career inventories (see Appendix). Walsh and Betz (1985) have discussed the psychometric properties of career inventories in some depth, and Kapes and Mastie (1988) have made a complete review of inventories.

A MATRIX OF CLIENT PROBLEMS AND INVENTORY CLASSES

Figure 5-1 is a matrix of recommended vocational instrument classes for use with common client presenting concerns. It employs the problem-focused assessment described in Chapter 4, which groups client problems roughly by age, as suggested by Myers (1971). Frequently observed problems are nested within age groups, which are somewhat arbitrary since problems may be age or stage specific. A good bit of evidence suggests that the stages in many developmental theories overlap considerably (Schlossberg, 1983). For example, the three groupings in Figure 5-1—adolescent, young adult, and mature adult—might as easily have been called early, middle, and late career. The system used here is consistent with that presented by Tiedeman and Ohara (1963) and Tiedeman and Miller-Tiedeman (1984), who argued that predictable developmental "triggers" may stimulate movement across developmental stages. The system also borrows from Myers (1971), who summarized studies of career counseling using grade in school (elementary, secondary, and college) and argued that different career interventions were required at different grades. The matrix incorporates, as well, a few of the special client problems that are related to their gender and level of occupational aspiration.

Figure 5-1 lists the client presenting problems commonly seen in clear practice:

Adolescent

Adolescent exploring future career possibilities either upon parental suggestion or self-referral.

College student with situational indecision or identity difficulty during the first two or three years of college.

College student with chronic indecisiveness during the fourth or fifth year of college

Late adolescent, not in college, with situational indecision and/or identity difficulty following the last year of school.

Young Adult

Young working adult, finished with schooling, who is seeking career planning for advancement or because of mild incongruence.

Young person wishing to break into management from the clerical ranks.

Dissatisfied professional/managerial employee with moderate to severe incongruence.

Individual in highly socialized occupation (e.g., Foreign Service or professional sports) with early career failure.

INSTRUMENT CLASS

Instrument Classes:
1. Criterion-Based College Bound
2. Criterion-Based Non College Bound
3. Homogeneous Self-Guiding
4. Homogeneous Hand/Machine
5. Career Maturity
6. Decisional Status
7. Personal Agency
8. Vocational Card Sorts
9. Personal Style, Values, Needs
10. Work Samples
11. Ability
12. Personality
13. Work Environment

Group	Client Presenting Problem	1	2	3	4	5	6	7	8	9	10	11	12	13
Adolescent	Adolescent Exploring Future Career Possibilities			•		•			•	•		•		
Adolescent	College Student with Situational Indecision	•		•	•	•	•		•	•				
Adolescent	College Student with Chronic Indecisiveness					•	•	•		•			•	
Adolescent	Late Adolescent Non-College with Lack of Vocational Identity		•	•	•	•			•	•	•			
Young Adult	Young Adult/Vocational Planning	•							•	•		•		
Young Adult	Woman Wishing to Break Into Management	•						•	•	•				
Young Adult	Professional/Managerial Employee with Job Dissatisfaction						•			•			•	•
Young Adult	Early Career Failure in Highly Socailized Organization	•	•				•	•	•	•			•	•
Young Adult	Young Adult with Excess Occupational Stress									•			•	•
Young Adult	Unemployed Worker Non College		•	•	•					•	•	•		
Mature Adult	Woman Returning to Work Following Child Rearing	•								•		•		
Mature Adult	Displaced Homemaker	•					•	•		•				
Mature Adult	Mid-Career Adult with Perceived Incongruence	•		•					•	•				•
Mature Adult	Mid-Career Plateaued Adult							•		•				•
Mature Adult	Mid-Career Adult with Excess Occupational Stress									•				•
Mature Adult	Worker Planning for Retirement	•		•						•				
Mature Adult	Retiree Seeking Second Career	•		•		•	•		•	•			•	

Figure 5-1 Recommended Instrument Classes for Common Client Presenting Problems.

Young adult with excessive work conflicts, personal strain anxiety, or depression from the work situation.

Worker unemployed or displaced because of economic conditions.

Mature Adult

Worker returning to the labor market following an extended period of child rearing.

Homemaker displaced from the home due to divorce or the death of a spouse.

Adult in mid to late career with perceived incongruence.

Adult in mid to late career who has reached a plateau or been passed over for promotion.

Adult in mid to late career with excessive occupationally induced stress and/or mental health problems affecting work.

Worker planning for retirement.

Retiree seeking a second career.

As Figure 5-1 indicates, somewhat different vocational instruments may be appropriate for several of these problems, and no single inventory is likely to be appropriate for any of the problems. The various classes of inventories are explained below.

CLASSES OF VOCATIONAL ASSESSMENT

The following classification system divides vocational assessment devices into thirteen *distinct* categories that are based upon three considerations: (1) the test construction method; (2) the educational level for which the test is designed; and (3) the clinical purpose of the inventory. This system includes a brief description of the most common inventories and a matrix for determining which assessments are appropriate for which client problems. When available, the stability, validity, and treatment utility of each class is also presented.

Class 1: Criterion-Based Interest Inventories for College-Bound Clients

This class of criterion-based instruments includes two of the "big three" interest inventories (Borgen, 1986)[1]: the Strong-Campbell Interest Inventory, or SCII (Hansen & Campbell, 1965), and the Kuder Occupational Interest

---

[1]Borgen (1986) considered the "big three" to be the Strong Campbell (Hansen & Campbell, 1985), The Kuder OIS (Kuder & Diamond, 1979), and The Self-Directed Search (Holland, 1985b).

Survey, or KOIS (Kuder & Diamond, 1979; Zytowski, 1985). Although these inventories pertain largely to college-bound populations, all three of the examples in this section contain some scales for noncollege-bound individuals as well.

Criterion-based inventories compare a respondent's scores with a preselected normative group who report being happy and stable in a specific occupation. Specific occupational scales (e.g., accountant, engineer, minister, chef, and florist) are the foundation of these inventories. (Several examples of the SCII profile appear in this volume; see Figures 4–1, 4–2.) The 1985 edition (Form T325) of the SCII contains 207 criterion-based occupational scales (male and female combined), 23 noncriterion-based basic interest scales (male and female combined), and the 6 Holland theme scales. The inventory's appendix, which describes the criterion samples, must be read for skilled use of the assessment. The number of workers in criterion groups, their composition, a Dictionary of Occupational Titles code and description (U.S. Department of Labor, 1977), and related occupations are printed for each criterion group. Although it is probably unnecessary to master the complex item selection and scoring systems of the SCII, familiarity with the criterion samples in this kind of inventory is indispensible. For example, knowing that the female farmer sample is composed of 212 women who responded to articles in farm-related publications, or that many of the groups were recruited from professional associations, may help the counselor understand the specific reference group to which a client is most similar. Several new topical reports for the SCII provide information to the respondent on leisure preferences (Hansen, 1989), leadership and management interests (MacAllister, 1989), and organizational specialties (Meyer, 1989).

The KOIS contains sixty male and thirty-nine female criterion-based occupational scales, and twenty-two male and seventeen female criterion-based college major scales that measure the respondent's similarity to a reference group of students enrolled in a particular college major. As with the SCII, the complex item characteristics and scoring may be less important than a thorough understanding of the reference sample on which a score is based. Unlike the SCII, the KOIS does not correct for common responses of a general sample, but instead prints experimental scales that are correlations between the respondent's scores and those of specific reference groups (e.g., men [M], women [W], fathers [F], mothers [Mo], sons [S], and daughters [D]). These experimental scales can be used as measures of gender role identification (e.g., by comparing the men scale with the women scale, or the son scale with the daughter scale). They can also generate information about maturity (e.g., by comparing the father scale with the son scale). The "secrets" of skilled interpretation of the KOIS have been described by Zytowski (1985) in a supplement to its manual, but there is very little research on these experimental scales, in spite of their potential for interesting studies on topics such as parental identification and gender role and career choice.

The criterion-based college major scales on the Kuder are especially useful for adolescents making a career choice and adults considering a return to school, as long as the counselor remembers that the criterion groups are younger than the returning adult students, and that the number of female college major scales is limited and somewhat stereotypic. The KOIS generates scores in rank order, and some research on twin scales—same-named scales for men and women—suggests that the cross-sex twin may be a useful predictor of eventual choices for members of the opposite sex (Zytowski & Laing, 1978).

Figure 5-2 shows the Kuder profile of a late adolescent named Brad, who was entering law school when he sought counseling because he was unhappy with the prospect of practicing law. His broad social and cultural interests were suggestive of a more people-oriented occupation. Brad is now completing a Ph.D. program in psychology and hopes to work with children. He reported being very happy with his decision one year after intervention. His twin scales and occupational scales displayed a similar rank order, and his experimental scales revealed a slighter higher correlation with women (*W*) and daughters (*D*) than with men (*M*) and sons (*S*), which may be common in individuals with nonstereotypic interests.

A third example of a criterion-based inventory, the Jackson Vocational Interest Survey, or JVIS (Jackson, 1977), considered to have state-of-the-art measurement technology (Borgen, 1986), is used as a "bootstrap" technique to construct criterion-based scales from SCII data. The JVIS also contains a mix of other scales, including work styles, basic interest scales, ten theme scales, and college major scales. A female respondent's JVIS profile is presented in Figure 5-3.

Criterion-based inventories almost always require computer-aided scoring, which can be done either by mailing a completed answer sheet to a scoring service or by purchasing software for on-site scoring. Although computer scoring can be cumbersome, many criterion-based inventories offer a comprehensive multipage print-out explaining the scores.

Stability, Validity, and Treatment Utility of Criterion-Based Inventories for College-Bound Clients.   The short- and long-term stability of criterion-based scales and profiles (Kuder & Diamond, 1979) is quite remarkable. Median test-retest reliabilities for the SCII were .92 for two weeks, .89 for thirty days, and .87 for three years (Hansen & Campbell, 1985). Three-week median rank order correlations for the KOIS were .80 (Zytowski, 1985). Median two-week profile stability for the JVIS was .87, and test re-test reliabilities for the individual scales were usually over .90. Thus this group of inventories seems a model of stability.

Studies of the predictive validity of the SCII suggest that the inventory will predict the respondent's occupational choice over a number of years in slightly more than 50 percent of cases. When the information from the basic scales and the criterion scales agrees, the predictive validity jumps to

Kuder Occupational Interest Survey Report Form

Name _____

Sex MALE **Date** _____

Numeric Grid No. _____ **SRA No.** 08132

1 **Dependability:** How much confidence can you place in your results? In scoring your responses several checks were made on your answer patterns to be sure that you understood the directions and that your results were complete and dependable. According to these:

YOUR RESULTS APPEAR TO BE DEPENDABLE.

2 **Vocational Interest Estimates:** Vocational interests can be divided into different types and the level of your attraction to each type can be measured. You may not feel that you know what interests you have already—what you may not know is how strong they are compared with other people's interests. This section shows the relative rank of your preferences on the back of this report form. Your preferences in these activities, as compared with other people's interest, are as follows:

Compared with men

HIGH	
LITERARY	95
SOCIAL SERVICE	86
ARTISTIC	79
AVERAGE	
SCIENTIFIC	60
PERSUASIVE	51
OUTDOOR	46
CLERICAL	33
LOW	
MUSICAL	09
COMPUTATIONAL	03
MECHANICAL	01

Compared with women

HIGH	
LITERARY	94
AVERAGE	
SCIENTIFIC	67
PERSUASIVE	62
SOCIAL SERVICE	61
ARTISTIC	58
OUTDOOR	50
CLERICAL	27
LOW	
MUSICAL	11
COMPUTATIONAL	06
MECHANICAL	02

3 **Occupations:** The KOIS has been given to groups of persons who are experienced and satisfied in many different occupations. Their patterns of interests have been compared with yours and placed in order of their similarity with you. The following occupational groups have interest patterns most similar to yours:

Compared with men

PSYCHOLOGIST	.59
SOCIAL WORKER	.58
JOURNALIST	.56
ELEM SCH TEACHER	.56
AUDIOL/SP PATHOL	.55
LIBRARIAN	.54
FILM/TV PROD/DIR	.53
COUNSELOR, HS	.53
LAWYER	.53
THESE ARE NEXT MOST SIMILAR:	
LAWYER	.53
PHYSICIAN	.51
BOOKSTORE MGR	.50

Compared with women

JOURNALIST	.60
PSYCHOLOGIST	.59
AUDIOL/SP PATHOL	.56
FILM/TV PROD/DIR	.56
SOCIAL WORKER	.55
ELEM SCH TEACHER	.54
LIBRARIAN	.54
FILM/TV PROD/DIR	.53
COUNSELOR, HS	.53
LAWYER	.53

Compared with men — THESE ARE NEXT MOST SIMILAR:

BOOKSTORE MGR, STATISTICIAN, PHYSICIAN, ARCHITECT, COMPUTER PRGRMR, PHOTOGRAPHER, INTERIOR DECOR, RADIO STATION MGR, PHYS THERAPIST, OPTOMETRIST, NURSE

THE REST ARE LISTED IN ORDER OF SIMILARITY:

PERSONNEL MGR, PODIATRIST, MINISTER, ACCT, CERT PUB, CHEMIST, MATHEMATICIAN, TRAVEL AGENT, SCIENCE TCHR, HS, PHARMACEUT SALES, REAL ESTATE AGT, FORESTER, DENTIST, METEOROLOGIST, PLANT NURSERY MGR, AUTO SALESPERSON, CLOTHIER, RETAIL, VETERINARIAN, SCHOOL SUPT, FLORIST, ENGINEER, BUYER, MATH TCHR, HS, PRINTER, TV REPAIRER, EXTENSION AGENT, X-RAY TECHNICIAN, INSURANCE AGENT, BANKER, BOOKKEEPER, POLICE OFFICER, POSTAL CLERK, SUPERVSR, INDUST, BLDG CONTRACTOR, FARMER, PAINTER, HOUSE, BRICKLAYER, WELDER, PLUMBING CONTRAC, ELECTRICIAN

Compared with women — MOST SIMILAR: CONT.

COL STU PERS MKR, DENTIST, ARCHITECT, PHYS THERAPIST, LIBRARIAN

THE REST ARE LISTED IN ORDER OF SIMILARITY:

INTERIOR DECOR, RADIO STATION MGR, PHYS THERAPIST, OPTOMETRIST, NURSE, COMPUTER PRGRMR, COUNSELOR, HS, INTERIOR DECOR, RELIGIOUS ED DIR, INSURANCE AGENT, VETERINARIAN, BANKER, ELEM SCH TEACHER, SECRETARY, ACCT, CERT PUB, NUTRITIONIST, SCIENCE TCHR, HS, NURSE, ENGINEER, FLORIST, OCCUPA THERAPIST, DENTAL ASSISTANT, DIETITIAN, X-RAY TECHNICIAN, BEAUTICIAN, OFFICE CLERK, BOOKKEEPER, BANK CLERK, MATH TEACHER, HS, EXTENSION AGENT, DEPT STORE-SALES

Compared with men — RESTS CONT.

TRUCK DRIVER	.23
AUTO MECHANIC	.22
PLUMBER	.21
MACHINIST	.21
CARPENTER	.20

4 **College Majors:** Just as for occupations, the KOIS has been given to many persons in different college majors. The following college major groups have interest patterns most similar to yours:

Compared with men

ENGLISH	.74
FOREIGN LANGUAGE	.71
SOCIOLOGY	.68
THESE ARE NEXT MOST SIMILAR:	
PSYCHOLOGY	.66
HISTORY	.66
POLITICAL SCI	.63
THE REST ARE LISTED IN ORDER OF SIMILARITY:	
ELEMENTARY EDUC	.60
ART & ART EDUC	.57
BIOLOGICAL SCI	.56
PREMED/PHAR/DENT	.55
MUSIC & MUSIC ED	.54
PHYSICAL EDUC	.53
ARCHITECTURE	.52
HOME ECON EDUC	.52
ECONOMICS	.51
PHYSICAL SCIENCE	.50
MATHEMATICS	.49
SERV ACAD CADET	.47
BUSINESS ADMIN	.47
FORESTRY	.47
ENGINEERING	.41
ANIMAL SCIENCE	.41
AGRICULTURE	.38

Compared with women

ENGLISH	.69
PSYCHOLOGY	.68
FOREIGN LANGUAGE	.65
HISTORY	.63
THESE ARE NEXT MOST SIMILAR:	
POLITICAL SCI	.61
SOCIOLOGY	.60
BIOLOGICAL SCI	.58
DRAMA	.58
THE REST ARE LISTED IN ORDER OF SIMILARITY:	
ART & ART EDUC	.54
BUSINESS EDUC	.53
PHYSICAL EDUC	.53
HEALTH PROFES	.51
HOME ECON EDUC	.51
MUSIC & MUSIC ED	.50
NURSING	.50
MATHEMATICS	.47

Experimental Scales:

V-SCORE 52

M	.47	MBI	.24
D	.55	RO	.63
R	.42	MBI	.25
S	.47	F	.41

7-3881

Figure 5-2 A Sample Kuder Occupational Interest Survey Profile. (Source: Report from Kuder Occupational Interest Survey by G. Frederic Kuder and E. E. Diamond. Published by CTB Macmillan/McGraw-Hill. © 1979 by G. Frederic Kuder and E. E. Diamond. Reprinted by permission of CTB, 2500 Graden Road, Monterey, CA 93940.)

111

```
RESPONDENT-CASE A,                    2124399863    FEMALE

         ******************************************************
         *****   .SIMILARITY TO COLLEGE STUDENT GROUPS   *****
         ******************************************************

                                      FEMALES                MALES

AGRICULTURE                           -0.29 (VERY LOW)       -0.18
ARTS + ARCHITECTURE                   -0.32 (VERY LOW)       -0.05
BUSINESS                              +0.26 (MODERATE)       +0.44
EARTH + MINERAL SCIENCE                                      -0.01
EDUCATION                             -0.11 (VERY LOW)       -0.03
ENGINEERING                           -0.10 (VERY LOW)       -0.00
HEALTH, PHYSICAL EDUC. + RECREATION   -0.24 (VERY LOW)
HUMAN DEVELOPMENT                     +0.00 (LOW)            +0.11
LIBERAL ARTS                          +0.18 (LOW)            +0.36
SCIENCE                               -0.15 (VERY LOW)       +0.05
NURSES                                -0.18 (VERY LOW)
MEDICAL STUDENTS                      +0.16 (LOW)            +0.19
TECHNICAL COLLEGE                                            +0.03


         ****************************************************************
         *****   SIMILARITY TO OCCUPATIONAL CLASSIFICATIONS   *****
         ****************************************************************

BELOW ARE RANKED THE OCCUPATIONAL CLASSIFICATIONS FOUND TO BE SIMILAR
TO YOUR INTEREST PROFILE.  A POSITIVE SCORE INDICATES THAT YOUR PROFILE
SHOWS SOME DEGREE OF SIMILARITY TO THOSE ALREADY WORKING IN THE
OCCUPATIONAL CLUSTER, WHILE A NEGATIVE SCORE INDICATES DISSIMILARITY.

SCORE     SIMILARITY                  OCCUPATIONAL CLASSIFICATION
-----  -------------------  ------------------------------------------------
+0.55 SIMILAR               OCCUPATIONS IN LAW AND POLITICS
+0.50 SIMILAR               OCCUPATIONS IN SOCIAL WELFARE
+0.50 SIMILAR               COUNSELLORS/STUDENT PERSONNEL WORKERS
+0.46 SIMILAR               OCCUPATIONS IN SOCIAL SCIENCE
+0.44 SIMILAR               ADMINISTRATIVE AND RELATED OCCUPATIONS
+0.42 SIMILAR               OCCUPATIONS IN ACCOUNTING, BANKING, AND FINANCE
+0.38 MODERATELY SIMILAR    MILITARY OFFICERS
+0.33 MODERATELY SIMILAR    PERSONNEL/HUMAN MANAGEMENT
+0.33 MODERATELY SIMILAR    OCCUPATIONS IN MERCHANDISING
+0.32 MODERATELY SIMILAR    SALES OCCUPATIONS
+0.29 MODERATELY SIMILAR    OCCUPATIONS IN RELIGION
+0.26 MODERATELY SIMILAR    CLERICAL SERVICES
+0.20 NEUTRAL               TEACHING AND RELATED OCCUPATIONS
+0.18 NEUTRAL               OCCUPATIONS IN WRITING
-0.02 NEUTRAL               MATHEMATICAL AND RELATED OCCUPATIONS
-0.02 NEUTRAL               OCCUPATIONS IN PRESCHOOL AND ELEMENTARY TEACHING
-0.10 NEUTRAL               ENGINEERING AND TECHNICAL SUPPORT WORKERS
-0.13 NEUTRAL               ASSEMBLY OCCUPATIONS-INSTRUMENTS & SMALL PRODUCTS
-0.19 NEUTRAL               OCCUPATIONS IN THE PHYSICAL SCIENCES
-0.26 DISSIMILAR            MACHINING/MECHANICAL AND RELATED OCCUPATIONS
-0.26 DISSIMILAR            PUBLIC SERVICE/PROTECTIVE SERVICE OCCUPATIONS
-0.28 DISSIMILAR            SERVICE OCCUPATIONS
-0.31 DISSIMILAR            OCCUPATIONS IN ENTERTAINMENT
-0.32 DISSIMILAR            MEDICAL DIAGNOSIS AND TREATMENT OCCUPATIONS
-0.33 DISSIMILAR            OCCUPATIONS IN MUSIC
-0.37 DISSIMILAR            HEALTH SERVICE WORKERS
-0.38 DISSIMILAR            OCCUPATIONS IN COMMERCIAL ART
-0.38 DISSIMILAR            LIFE SCIENCES
-0.44 DISSIMILAR            CONSTRUCTION TRADES
-0.46 DISSIMILAR            SPORT AND RECREATION OCCUPATIONS
-0.48 DISSIMILAR            OCCUPATIONS IN FINE ART
-0.50 DISSIMILAR            AGRICULTURALISTS
```

Figure 5-3 A Sample Jackson Vocational Interest Survey Profile. (Source: R. R. Knapp and L. Knapp, *Manual for the Career Occupational Preference System* [San Diego, CA: Educational and Industrial Testing Service, 1980], p. 23. Reprinted by permission.)

70 percent (Borgen & Seling, 1978). Long-term predictive validity for the KOIS is also appreciable (Zytowski, 1976). Although fewer in number, studies of the predictive validity of the JVIS show hit rates as high as the SCII.

However, we know far less than we should about the treatment utility of criterion-based inventories. Since this group of tests is the most complex and difficult to present to the client, it may be that clients absorb less of the sophisticated content than we care to believe. More research, such as that conducted by Zytowski (1977) on the effects of being inventoried, by Hoffman, Spokane, and Magoon (1981) on the role of the counselor in the interpretation process, and by Prediger and Swaney (1986) on the client's reactions to being inventoried, is needed.

The three following criterion-based inventories for the college-bound were discussed in this section:

Strong-Campbell Interest Inventory, or SCII (Hansen & Campbell, 1985)

Kuder Occupational Interest Survey, or KOIS (Kuder & Diamond, 1979; Zytowski, 1985)

Jackson Vocational Interest Survey, or JVIS (Jackson, 1977)

Class 2: Criterion-Based Interest Inventories for Noncollege-Bound Clients

Another class of criterion-based interest inventories also employs a reference group of employed adults to which the client's scores are compared, but here the majority of occupations represented require less than a four-year college education. The Minnesota Vocational Interest Inventory, or MVII (Clark & Campbell, 1965), was the first vocational interest inventory for nonprofessional populations. Developed with a long-term grant from the United States Navy, the MVII emerged from Clark's classic book on the vocational interests of nonprofessional men (Clark, 1961). Because the MVII has no female scales or criterion groups, it cannot be recommended for contemporary use. However, many of its techniques as well as the spirit of this instrument are contained in its successors, principal of which is the Career Assessment Inventory, or CAI (Johansson, 1982). Like the SCII, the CAI contains criterion-based occupational scales, basic interest scales, and Holland theme scales. Its format is very similar to that of the SCII, both in layout and content. The CAI contains the six Holland theme scales, twenty-two basic interest scales, eighty-nine criterion-based scales with test-retest reliabilities ranging from .82 to .95, a fine arts-mechanical scale that appears to be a masculinity-femininity scale and may be useful for studying L. S. Gottfredson's (1981) theory of career aspirations, and educational orientation and extroversion-introversion scales similar to those on the SCII.

Developed to complement the JVIS for "occupationally-oriented individuals," the Career Directions Inventory, or CDI (Jackson, 1986), is similar to the JVIS in its use of vocational roles and styles to formulate items. The CDI contains fifteen basic interest scales, seven occupational themes similar to the Holland types, twenty-two specialty clusters, and over one hundred occupational criterion scales for which the author reports very adequate test-retest reliability, internal consistency, and concurrent discriminative validity, or the ability to differentiate occupational groups. No evidence is reported on the clinical utility of the CDI. Like their counterparts for the college-bound, these inventories also require computer-aided scoring.

A new inventory, Exploring Career Options, ECO, (Andberg & Johansson, 1987), is the first interest inventory developed specifically for direct sale to the public. Although it must be returned to the publisher for scoring, a procedure that takes seven to ten days, the client then receives a computer-generated booklet with personalized interpretive sections on Holland themes, work-place attitudes, personal rewards, career commitment, and verbal and math ability. The material is generally clearly presented, and includes several suggested options that are selected based on field of interest as well as verbal and numerical ability. A case example available from the publisher (Spokane, in press-b) shows the matrix of options for one field of interest by verbal and numerical ability. To measure ability, individuals can either complete a timed ability test or estimate their ability and interests on the basis of personal experience. (Most respondents will probably choose the latter rather than suffer the anxiety of a timed test.)

The use of ability estimates to generate options is both a strength and a weakness of the ECO. There is no evidence in the ECO client report on the accuracy of self-estimates of verbal and math ability. Since the careeer options it suggests seem heavily dependent on these estimates, the use of this procedure could be a serious drawback (Lowman & Williams, 1987). Scale construction, norming, and validity are also impossible to ascertain, since ECO has no technical manual, although a user's guide is planned.

The following criterion-based interest inventories for the noncollege-bound were included in this section:

Career Assessment Inventory, or CAI (Johansson, 1982)

Career Directions Inventory, or CDI (Jackson, 1986)

Exploring Career Options, or ECO (Andberg & Johansson, 1987)

Class 3: Homogeneous Self-Guiding Interest Inventories

The homogeneous self-guiding instruments, or those which contain theoretical scales but no criterion scales, are a popular class of interest inventories, and include the last of the "big three" inventories (Borgen, 1986): the Self-Directed Search, or SDS (Holland, 1985b). The SDS paved the way for a revolution in interest measurement and the delivery of career interventions. It is also the inventory on which the majority of treatment utility research has been conducted.

In a brilliant and controversial departure from measurement tradition, the SDS was designed to be self-administering, self-scoring, and self-interpreting. It was based upon Holland's (1985a) theory of vocational choice. Holland and Rayman (1986) have said that the SDS was developed to help the counselor serve more people and to assist those without access to a counselor. The SDS is appropriate for adolescents over the age of fifteen, and the hand scoring by the client or counselor generally takes about five minutes.

Five booklets can accompany the test: (1) the SDS test booklet (Holland, 1985b); (2) *The Occupations Finder*; (3) the interpretive booklet *You and Your Career* (Holland, 1987b); (4) *The College Majors Finder* (Rosen, Holmberg, & Holland, 1987), and (5) a manual supplement designed to aid interpretation. Also, a revised edition of the *Dictionary of Holland Occupational Codes* (G. D. Gottfredson & Holland, 1989) provides access to the nearly 20,000 jobs listed in the *Dictionary of Occupational Titles* (U.S. Department of Labor, 1977). The SDS is also available in an interpretive format, which is generated when the SDS booklet is sent back to the publisher for additional scoring. At present, the SDS is not marketed to the public, although it is frequently used by laypersons.

The Interest Determination, Exploration, and Assessment System, or IDEAS (Johansson, 1980), is a homogeneous self-directing instrument for noncollege-bound populations. IDEAS generates the six Holland type scores and basic interest scores within each type; combined-sex norms are employed, and the manual offers some evidence of its validity, although the details are not presented. IDEAS is designed for use with the Dictionary of Occupational Titles (U.S. Department of Labor, 1977) and seems to be clear and easily used.

Homogeneous self-directing inventories generally have fewer items and less sophisticated item selection and scoring systems. The scoring systems, since they are transparent, frequently demystify the interest assessment process and educate the client about what an interest is or is not. These inventories are often based upon an earlier machine-scored version of the tests. For example, the SDS followed from Holland's early work on the VPI, and Johansson's IDEAS was extrapolated from early work on CAI. As a result of the success of the SDS, self-guiding interest inventories are beginning to be sold directly to the consumer (Spokane, in press, b). Several can be used with large-capacity personal computers or as a part of a computer-assisted guidance package such as Career Point (Conceptual Systems, 1989). These inventories are called homogeneous because their scales are theoretically rather than empirically derived. Thus on the SDS, for example, a score is produced for the six Holland themes, but no direct comparison is made between the client's scores and those of any occupational group. Because the SDS does list occupations classified in each of the Holland groupings, a result similar to that from a criterion-based inventory is obtained. The obvious advantage of a self-guiding inventory is that no computer is required for scoring and no counselor is needed for adequate interpretation. The disadvantage of such an inventory is the lack of direct comparison to an actual occupational group. It is also important to note that self-guiding inventories, because of their lack of sophisticated scoring, rarely include gender-based norms, which means that women with mixed traditional and nontraditional interests may more often score high in traditionally female occupations than in traditionally male occupations. Thus a female client with gender role questions should not be given self-guided inventories alone.

Stability, Validity, and Treatment Utility of Homogeneous Self-Guiding Interest Inventories.   Because they are briefer, self-guiding inventories may have adequate stability and internal consistency, but will be somewhat less reliable than their longer, machine-scored counterparts. Their construct and predictive validity, on the other hand, is generally comparable to that of the machine-scored versions. For example, IDEAS correlates .91 and higher with the CAI, and in the .80s with the SCII and the MVII. Test-retest reliabilities are described (but not detailed) as being in the high .80s and low .90s (Johansson, 1980). The SDS has a large body of data and studies not only of its psychometric characteristics but also, more recently, of the diagnostic and treatment considerations governing its counseling use. Studies of the treatment utility of the SDS when used as the sole intervention show modest but consistent gains on a wide variety of outcome measures (Oliver & Spokane, 1988), including number of options considered (Fretz & Leong, 1982), information seeking (Krivatsy & Magoon, 1976), and treatment satisfaction, with no evidence of negative outcomes from intervention with the SDS.

Two homogeneous self-guiding interests inventories have been discussed in this section:

Self-Directed Search, or SDS (Holland, 1985b)

Interest Determination, Exploration, and Assessment System, or IDEAS (Johansson, 1980)

Class 4: Homogeneous Hand- or Machine-Scored Interest Inventories

This class of inventories contains homogeneous (theoretical) scales but is normally scored by a complicated hand scoring system or a machine scoring system. One well-documented example of a homogeneous inventory is the unisex edition of the American College Testing (ACT) Interests Inventory (UNIACT). The UNIACT, a ninety-item scale, is the centerpiece of the ACT Career Planning Program (American College Testing Program, 1988) and five additional career exploration devices published by the ACT:

ACT Assessment Program (AAP)

P-ACT + (an adaptation of the AAP for use in tenth grade)

Vocational Interest, Experience, and Skill Assessment (VIESA)

DISCOVER (a computer-assisted device) (American College Testing Program, 1987)

Take Hold of Your Future (a career planning course)

The UNIACT uses those items with minimal response differences between men and women. UNIACT scores are translated to a World-of-Work Map (see Figure 5-4), a clever graphic depiction of a cluster analysis of the more than 20,000 jobs in the *Dictionary of Occupational Titles* (U.S. Department of Labor, 1977).

The California Occupational Preference System, or COPS (Knapp & Knapp, 1980; 1984), is available in both self-scoring and machine-scoring versions. The COPS uses a variant of Roe's classification system consisting of fourteen interest bi-level clusters: science (professional or skilled), technology (professional or skilled), consumer economics, outdoor, business (professional or skilled), clerical, communication, arts (professional or skilled), and service (professional or skilled). An example of the clusters in the self-scoring version appears in Figure 5-5. The clients receive percentile scores representing their interests in each cluster.

The Vocational Interest Inventory, or VII (Lunneborg, 1981), produces scores on eight of Roe's occupational clusters: service, outdoor, business contact, science, organization, general culture, technical, and arts and entertainment. These scores make the application of Roe's 1954 classification quite simple, even though students and adults may find the lack of criterion basing less than satisfying (Krumboltz, 1988). Finally, the Vocational Preference Inventory, or VPI (Holland, 1985c), still receives use, especially in research studies and when separate sex norms are preferred. The eighth revision of the VPI is a one hundred and sixty-item inventory in a "yes," "no," and "indifferent" response format that generates the six Holland type scales and four supplemental scales (self-control, masculinity, status, and infrequency).

Stability, Validity, and Treatment Utility of Homogeneous Hand- or Machine-Scored Interest Inventories.   The UNIACT manual provides stability data on large samples over intervals of six weeks, two and a half years, and four years. Generally, these scales are quite stable. The COPS shows evidence of internal consistency and one-week stability at a high level using large samples, as well as moderate levels of stability over a one-year period, although not as high as other inventories in this class. The VPI has moderate to high stability over a two-week period, with small samples in which reliability coefficients ranging from the high .50s to the high .80s for adult women. Because these

Figure 5-4 World of Work Map (Second Edition). The location of a Job Family on the map shows how much it involves working with DATA, IDEAS, PEOPLE, and THINGS. Arrows by a Job Family show that work tasks often heavily involve both PEOPLE and THINGS (↔) or DATA and IDEAS (↕). Although each Job Family is shown as a single point, the jobs in a family vary in their locations. Most jobs, however, are located near the point shown for the Job Family. (Source: Copyright © 1958 by American College Testing [ACT]. All rights reserved. Printed by permission of ACT.)

homogeneous scales are shorter than their criterion-based counterparts, one would not expect the same level of internal consistency nor reliability that is found in the longer inventories.

These homogeneous scales do appear to be good estimates of the theoretical constructs that they purport to measure. Scale intercorrelations are low, and the scales appear to be independent. Correlations with same-named scales from other established inventories is very good. The correlations between the UNIACT and the VPI, for example, are moderate, in spite of the sex-fair item technology. These correlations are sufficiently varied, however, to suggest that each inventory measures something slightly different,

---

BUSINESS CONTACT JOB CLUSTER

A. MARKETING AND SALES JOB FAMILY
Sales workers in stores; route drivers (milk, etc.); buyers; travel agents; sales workers who visit customers (real estate and insurance agents; stock brokers; farm products, office, and medical supplies sales workers)

B. MANAGEMENT AND PLANNING JOB FAMILY
Store, motel, restaurant, and agribusiness managers; office supervisors; purchasing agents; managers in large businesses; recreation/parks managers; medical records administrators; urban planners

---

BUSINESS OPERATIONS JOB CLUSTER

C. RECORDS AND COMMUNICATIONS
Office, library, hotel, and postal clerks; receptionists; computer tape librarians; office, medical, and legal secretaries; court reporters; medical record technicians

D. FINANCIAL TRANSACTIONS
Bookkeepers; accountants; grocery check-out clerks; bank tellers; ticket agents; insurance underwriters; financial analysts

E. STORAGE AND DISPATCHING
Shipping and receiving clerks; mail carriers; truck, cab, and airline dispatchers; cargo agents; air traffic controllers

F. BUSINESS MACHINE/COMPUTER OPERATION
Computer console, printer, etc., operators; office machine operators; typists; word-processing equipment operators; statistical clerks

---

TECHNICAL JOB CLUSTER

G. VEHICLE OPERATION AND REPAIR
Bus, truck, and cab drivers; auto, bus, and airplane mechanics; forklift operators; merchant marine officers; airplane pilots

H. CONSTRUCTION AND MAINTENANCE
Carpenters; electricians; painters; custodians (janitors); bricklayers; sheet metal workers; bulldozer and crane operators; building inspectors

I. AGRICULTURE AND NATURAL RESOURCES
Farmers; foresters; ranchers; landscape gardeners; tree surgeons; plant nursery workers; pet shop attendants

J. CRAFTS AND RELATED SERVICES
Cooks; meatcutters; bakers; shoe repairers; piano/organ tuners; tailors; jewelers

K. HOME/BUSINESS EQUIPMENT REPAIR
Repairers of TV sets, appliances, typewriters, telephones, heating systems, photocopiers, etc.

L. INDUSTRIAL EQUIPMENT OPERATION AND REPAIR
Machinists; printers; sewing machine operators; welders; industrial machinery repairers; production painters; laborers and machine operators in factories, mines, etc.; firefighters

---

SCIENCE JOB CLUSTER

M. ENGINEERING AND OTHER APPLIED TECHNOLOGIES
Engineers and engineering technicians in various fields; biological and chemical lab technicians; computer programmers; computer service technicians; drafters; surveyors; technical illustrators; food technologists

N. MEDICAL SPECIALTIES AND TECHNOLOGIES
Dental hygienists; EEG and EKG technicians; opticians; prosthetics technicians; X-ray technologists; medical technologists; dentists; optometrists; pharmacists; veterinarians

O. NATURAL SCIENCES AND MATHEMATICS
Agronomists; biologists; chemists; ecologists; geographers; geologists; horticulturists; mathematicians; physicists; soil scientists

P. SOCIAL SCIENCES
Marketing research analysts; anthropologists; economists; political scientists; psychologists; sociologists

---

ARTS JOB CLUSTER

Q. APPLIED ARTS (VISUAL)
Floral designers; merchandise displayers; commercial artists; fashion designers; photographers; interior designers; architects; landscape architects

R. CREATIVE/PERFORMING ARTS
Entertainers (comedians, etc.); actors/actresses; dancers; musicians; singers; composers; writers; art, music, etc. teachers

S. APPLIED ARTS (WRITTEN AND SPOKEN)
Advertising copywriters; disk jockeys; legal assistants; advertising account executives; interpreters; reporters; public relations workers; lawyers; librarians; technical writers

---

SOCIAL SERVICE JOB CLUSTER

T. GENERAL HEALTH CARE
Nursing aides; orderlies; dental assistants; licensed practical nurses; physical therapy assistants; registered nurses; dieticians; occupational therapists; physicians; speech pathologists

U. EDUCATION AND RELATED SERVICES
Teacher aides; preschool teachers; athletic coaches; college teachers;* guidance/career/etc., counselors; elementary and secondary school teachers; special education teachers

V. SOCIAL AND GOVERNMENT SERVICES
Security guards; recreation leaders; police officers; health/safety/food/etc. inspectors; child welfare workers; home economists; rehabilitation counselors; sanitarians; social workers

W. PERSONAL/CUSTOMER SERVICES
Grocery baggers; bellhops; flight attendants (stewards, stewardesses); waitresses and waiters; cosmetologists (beauticians); barbers; butlers and maids

Figure 5-4   (continued)

and may contribute its unique understanding of the client's interests when interpreted by a skilled clinician.

Among this group of inventories, the UNIACT has the greatest treatment utility. A recent series of thoughtful studies by Prediger and his colleagues (Prediger, 1987b; Prediger & Noeth, 1979; Prediger & Swaney, 1986) has convincingly demonstrated the treatment utility of several of the ACT Career Planning components. One study (Prediger & Noeth, 1979) used ACT Career Planning materials with four hundred ninth-grade girls and followed the initial treatment with a second intervention nine weeks later. The subjects reported more exploratory activity, and greater congruence of measured

The Career Clusters

1 SCIENCE, PROFESSIONAL (A) occupations involve responsibility for the planning and conducting of research. They include collecting and applying systematic accumulation of knowledge in the related branches of mathematical, medical, life and physical sciences.

Related courses of study:
SCIENCE – Anatomy, Anthropology, Astronomy, Biology, Chemistry, Geography, Oceanography, Physics, Psychology, Science (General, Life and Physical), Zoology
MATHEMATICS – Algebra, Calculus, Data Processing Math, Geometry, Trigonometry
LANGUAGE – French, German, Latin

SAMPLE OCCUPATIONS

Medical-Life Science
- •●AGRONOMIST (040.061 010)**
- •ANATOMIST (041.061 010)
- •ANESTHESIOLOGIST (070.101 010)
- •ANTHROPOLOGIST (055.067 010)
- •AUDIOLOGIST (076.101 010)
- •BACTERIOLOGIST (041.061 058)
- •BIOCHEMIST (041.061 026)
- •BIOLOGIST (041.061 030)
- •BIOMEDICAL ENGINEER (019.061 010)
- •BOTANIST (041.061 038)
- •ECOLOGIST
- •EMBRYOLOGIST
- •ENTOMOLOGIST (041.061 046)
  FLIGHT SURGEON (070.101 030)
- •GENETICIST (041.061 050)
- •HEALTH PHYSICIST (079.021 010)
  HISTOPATHOLOGIST (041.061 054)

- •MARINE BIOLOGIST (041.061 022)
- •MICROBIOLOGIST (041.061 058)
  MYCOLOGIST (041.061 062)
  NEUROLOGIST (070.101 050)
- •ORAL SURGEON (072.101 018)
  PALEONTOLOGIST (024.061 042)
  PARASITOLOGIST (041.061 070)
  PATHOLOGIST (070.061 010)
- •PHARMACOLOGIST (041.061 074)
  PHYSIOLOGIST (041.061 078)
- •●PSYCHOLOGIST, EXPERIMENTAL (045.061 018)
- •RADIOLOGIST (070.101 090)
  RESEARCH DIETITIAN (077.061 010)
  SURGEON (070.101 094)
  UROLOGIST (070.101 098)
- •●VETERINARIAN (073.101 010)
- •ZOOLOGIST (041.061 090)

Mathematical Science
- •ACTUARY (020.167 010)
  COMPUTER ENGINEER (020.062 010)
  DEMOGRAPHER (020.167 026)
- •●FINANCIAL ANALYST (020.167 014)
- •FINANCIAL ECONOMIST (050.067 010)
  INFORMATION SCIENTIST (109.067 010)
  MATHEMATICAL TECHNICIAN (020.162 010)
- •MATHEMATICIAN (020.067 014)
  OPERATIONS RESEARCH ANALYST (020.067 018)
  PHYSICIST, THEORETICAL (023.067 010)
- •PROGRAMER, ENGINEERING & SCI (020.167 022)
  PROGRAMER, PROCESS CONTROL (020.187 014)
- •●STATISTICIAN, APPLIED (020.167 026)
  STATISTICIAN, MATH (020.067 022)
  STATISTICIAN, PHYSICAL SCIENCE (020.167 026)
- •SYSTEMS ANALYST (012.167 066)
  WEIGHT-ANALYST (020.187 018)

Physical Science
- •●ARCHEOLOGIST (055.067 018)
- •ASTRONOMER (021.067 010)
- •CHEMIST (022.061 010)
- •CHEMIST, WATER-PURIFY (022.281 014)
- •CLIMATOLOGIST
- •GEOGRAPHER (029.067 010)
- •●GEOLOGIST (024.061 018)
  GEOPHYSICIST (024.061 030)
  HYDROLOGIST (024.061 034)
- •METEOROLOGIST (025.062 010)
- •OCEANOGRAPHER (024.061 018)
  PETROLOGIST (024.061 046)
- •PHARMACIST (074.161 010)
- •●PHYSICIST (023.061 014)
  PHYSICIST, NUCLEAR (023.061 014)
  REACTOR OPERATOR, RESEARCH (015.362 026)
- •SOIL SCIENTIST (040.061 058)

Some skills and abilities needed in these jobs
- Use logic or scientific thinking to deal with many different kinds of problems
- Make decisions based on information that can be measured or verified
- Learn and use knowledge about how living things function, how plants and animals are classified, how to use laboratory and scientific equipment
- Understand and use instructions that use words, numbers, diagrams, or chemical formulas
- Do things which require you to be very accurate

- Use non-verbal symbols (such as numbers) to express ideas or solve problems
- Understand and express complex, technical and scientific information
- Understand and use advanced math and statistics
- Use computer technology to solve problems or process large amounts of information
- Make decisions using your own judgments
- Deal with things that are known and things which frequently are not easy to recognize or understand

Suggested activities to get experience
- Join biology, chemistry, math, language, lapidary or chess clubs
- Use a microscope or chemistry set; learn all uses of a calculator
- Enter science fairs; read science magazines
- Take a part-time job in a drug store or laboratory
- Collect rocks and gems; learn to recognize different ores
- Have an aquarium with tropical fish or a salt water aquarium
- Work as a veterinarian's helper
- Do volunteer work at an ecology center
- Watch TV weather shows and learn symbols
- Learn to identify and grow different plants

(For more information, see DOT, Vol. 2 (1965), pages 294, 375, 418, 466, 468, 473.) Work Groups: *Scientific*, Physical Sciences, Life Sciences and Medical Sciences. *Leading · Influencing*, Mathematics and Statistics and Social Research.

2 SCIENCE, SKILLED (H) occupations involve observing and classifying facts in assisting in laboratory research and applying this information in the fields of medicine and life and physical sciences.

Clusters defined by Sample Occupations

SAMPLE OCCUPATIONS

Medical-Life Science
AMPOULE EXAMINER (559.687 010)**
- •●BIOLOGICAL AIDE (049.384 010)
- •CORONER (188.161 010)
  CYTOTECHNOLOGIST (078.281 010)
- •DENTAL ASSISTANT (079.371 010)
- •DENTAL HYGIENIST (078.361 010)
- •DENTAL LAB TECHNICIAN (712.381 018)
  DIALYSIS TECHNICIAN (078.362 014)
- •ELECTROCARDIOGRAPH TECH (078.362 018)
- •ELECTROENCEPHALO TECH (078.362 022)
- •EMBALMER (338.371 014)
  INDUSTRIAL HYGIENIST (079.161 010)
  INDUSTRIAL SAFETY INSPECTOR (168.264 014)
  INDUSTRIAL WASTE INSPECTOR (168.267 054)
- •INHALATION THERAPIST (RESP.) (079.361 010)
- •LABORATORY ASSISTANT (078.687 010)

  LAB. EQUIPMENT CLEANER (381.687 022)
- •●LABORATORY TECHNICIAN (073.361 010)
- •MEDICAL ASSISTANT (079.367 010)
- •MEDICAL LAB ASSISTANT (078.381 010)
- •MEDICAL TECHNOLOGIST (078.361 014)
  MICROBIOLOGY TECHNOLOGIST (078.261 014)
  NUCLEAR MEDICAL TECHNOLOGIST (078.361 018)
  OPTICIAN, DISPENSING (713.361 014)
- •OPTOMECHANICAL TECHNICIAN (007.161 030)
- •RADIATION MONITOR (199.167 010)
  RADIOGRAPHER (199.361 010)
  RADIOLOGIC TECHNICIAN (078.362 026)
- •SURGICAL TECHNICIAN (079.374 022)
  TABLET TESTER (559.667 010)
  TISSUE TECHNOLOGIST (078.361 030)
- •X RAY TECHNOLOGIST (078.362 026)

Physical Science
ASSA   (010 161 018)
- •CHE   (010.161 018)
- •CRIMINALIST (029.281 010)
  DECONTAMINATOR (199.384 010)
- •FINGERPRINT CLASSIFIER (375.387 010)
- •FOOD & DRUG INSPECTOR (168.267 042)
  FOOD TESTER (029.361 014)
  FORMULATION TEST OPERATOR (930.261 014)
  GLASS INSPECTOR (579.687 022)
  INSTRUMENT INSPECTOR (711.281 010)
  INSTRUMENT INSPECTOR (722.381 010)
- •LABORATORY TESTER (029.261 010)
- •LAND SURVEY TECHNICIAN (869.567 010)
  LASER TECHNICIAN (019.181 010)
  MECHANICAL INSPECTOR (549.261 010)
  METER INSPECTOR (710.384 022)

- •PEST CONTROLLER (389.684 010)
- •PHARMACY HELPER (074.381 010)
  PHOTOGRAMMETRIST (018.261 026)
- •POLLUTION-CONTROL TECH. (029.261 014)
  QUALITY CONTROL COORDINATOR (168.167 066)
  SCIENTIFIC HELPER (199.364 014)
- •SURVEYOR, LAND (018.167 018)
  ULTRASOUND TECHNOLOGIST (078.364 010)
- •WASTE TREATMENT OPERATOR (955.382 010)
- •WASTE WATER TREATMENT-PLANT OP (955.362 010)
- •WATER TREATMENT PLANT OPER (954.382 014)
- •WEATHER OBSERVER (025.267 014)

Some skills and abilities needed in these jobs
- Use eyes, hands and fingers to operate and adjust delicate equipment and handle gauges or measuring tools
- Follow technical instructions which may be verbal, written or in the form of charts or drawings
- Do work that requires being very precise or accurate
- Avoid errors in record keeping
- Use mathematics to keep records, take inventory, estimate quantities or schedule the flow of materials
- Use math skills to count, measure or keep inspection records
- Use measuring and testing equipment

- Make decisions based on standards that can be measured or checked
- Recognize slight differences in the shape, color or texture of things
- Do the same thing over and over according to a set procedure
- Keep records and make reports
- Learn all about the product, materials or structure you may inspect or test
- Understand and use scientific and technical language and symbols

Suggested activities to get experience
- Join biology, chemistry, math or language clubs
- Enter science fairs; read science magazines
- Use a microscope or chemistry set
- Take a part-time job in a drug store or laboratory
- Learn to use gauges, calipers and micrometers
- Collect rocks and gems; make charts and graphs
- Have an aquarium with tropical fish or have a salt water aquarium
- Do volunteer work at an ecology center

(See DOT, Vol. 2 (1965), pages 271, 312, 322, 385, 413, 418, 477.) Work Groups: *Scientific*, Laboratory Technology. *Mechanical*, Material Control and Quality Control. *Industrial*, Quality Control.

1 & 2 SCIENCE, COLLEGE MAJORS:

Medical-Life			Mathematical Science		Physical	
Aquatic Biology	Dietetics	Paleontology	Actuarial	Mathematics	Archaeology	Oceanography
Agronomy	Ecology	Parasitology	Science	Meteorology	Astronomy	Optical Sciences
Anatomy	Entomology	Pharmacology	Astronomy	Operational	Atmospheric Sciences	Pharmacy
Anthropology	Genetics	Physiology	Basic Scientific	Research	Chemistry	Physics
Bacteriology	Immunology	Psychology	Research	Planetary	Earth Sciences	Planetary Sciences
Biochemistry	Marine Biology	Radiological	Computer	Science	Geography	Plant Genetics
Biology	Medicine	Sciences	Science	Physics	Geology	Radiology
Botany	Microbiology	Silviculture	Economics	Statistics	Hydrology	Soil Science
Chiropractic Medicine	Mortuary Science	Veterinary Medicine	Information	Systems	Metallurgy	Solar Energy
Dentistry	Mycology	Zoology	Science	Analysis	Meteorology	Water Sciences

• Occupations with a (•) may be looked up in the COPSystem *Career Briefs Kit* alphabetically within clusters.
† Occupations in *italics* may be looked up in the *Occupational Outlook Handbook* (1980-81 or 1982-83), in the DOT Index or the Alphabetical Index.
** The number in parentheses is the *Dictionary of Occupational Titles* (DOT) code. For a complete description of this code, see DOT, Fourth Edition (1977), page XVI. These occupations may be looked up in DOT, Volume 1 (1965), alphabetically. Use the nine-digit code to find titles in DOT, Fourth Edition (1977). Almost all occupations listed above may be looked up alphabetically in the COPSystem *Career Cluster Booklets*.
* Occupations preceded by a (*) indicate occupations which are available in the VIEW program.

4

Figure 5-5 Sample page from the COPS Self-Interpretation Profile and Guide. (Source: R. R. Knapp and L. Knapp, *Manual for the Career Occupational Preference System* [San Diego, CA: Educational and Industrial Testing Service, 1990], p. 4. Reprinted by permission.)

and expressed interests. Studies of the treatment utility of the COPS remain to be done. A good base of evidence attests to the treatment utility of the VPI, although it is not nearly as voluminous as for the SDS.

The following homogeneous interest inventories have been discussed in this section:

Unisex Edition of the ACT Interest Inventory, or UNIACT (American College Testing Program, 1988)

California Occupational Preference System, or COPS (Knapp & Knapp, 1980; 1984)

Vocational Interest Inventory, or VII (Lunneborg, 1981)

Vocational Preference Inventory, or VPI (Holland, 1985c)

Class 5: Career Maturity Inventories

The career maturity inventories are unique in their direct emergence from Super's (1957) developmental stage theory, which guided their construction and validation. Super's extraordinary Career Pattern Study (see Super & Overstreet, 1960) generated several of these instruments, which appear to be the study's most lasting contribution to the field. The career maturity inventories reviewed here are useful for research and, to a degree, as assessment devices in interventions or workshops, but have not achieved either the popularity or the widespread use of interest inventories. Nonetheless, as a group they constitute one of the most persistent attempts to produce a construct-valid measurement device in the history of vocational psychology. Westbrook (1983) chronicled the more-than-thirty-year struggle to measure career maturity. He summarized the evidence of the internal consistency, the median of which ranged from .61 to .91, test-retest stability, which averaged .71, and construct validity of the various career maturity inventories, as well as their reliability and validity.

The most recent of the many efforts to assess career maturity is the Adult Career Concerns Inventory, or ACCI (Super, Thompson, & Lindeman, 1988). The ACCI, the newest of the adult career maturity inventories, is also constructed around the model of adult career adaptability, although only scant reliability and validity data, preliminary norms, and no evidence of treatment utility are provided in the manual.

Even though career maturity is clearly the most popular outcome measure in career intervention treatment studies (Spokane & Oliver, 1983), it is not a routinely used treatment component. As Mehrens and Lehmann (1985) pointed out, clients seldom need information about their developmental level. There is thus little evidence of the treatment utility of career maturity measures, and their principal use may be in outcome studies and research.

The Career Maturity Inventory, or CMI (Crites, 1978), the standard in the field for many years, contains an attitude scale with five subscales (defensiveness, involvement, independence, orientation, and compromise), and a competence scale with five subscales (self-appraisal, occupational information, goal selection, planning, and problem solving). Reviews suggest that there is adequate evidence for the reliability and validity of the attitude scale, but that high scale intercorrelations for both the attitude and competence tests, and weak factorial structures indicate the unidimensional nature of existing career maturity measures (Kapes & Mastie, 1988; Westbrook, 1983). This unidimensionality of career maturity appears to be true not only for the measures generated from Super's theory, but also for more recent measures developed by Westbrook and Parry-Hill (1973) and Gribbons and Lohnes (1982). If the cognitive vocational maturity described by Westbrook (1983) is also heavily correlated with intelligence scores, then a reframing of the career maturity construct along more behavioral and less cognitive lines may be indicated if the multidimensionality is to be retained. This reframing should study behaviors across diverse career situations until a clear set of common situations is distilled, along with the constructive behaviors required for mastering the problems presented in those situations.

The Career Development Inventory, or CDI (Thompson, Lindeman, Super, Jordaan, & Myers, 1984), which is based upon the Career Pattern Study, contains five subscales (career planning, career exploration, decision making, world of work information, and knowledge of preferred occupational group). A factor analysis by Savickas (1975) yielded three scale scores (planning orientation, resources for exploration, and decision making) which have alpha coefficients of .91, .83, and .61, respectively. Thompson et al. provide a technical manual that offers evidence of the CDI's validity and reliability, and some suggested treatment uses, but no direct empirical data on its treatment utility.

The Career Adjustment and Development Inventory, or CADI (Crites, 1982), contains six fifteen-item scales that tap a "graded series of career-developmental tasks which calibrate an individual's progress and maturation" (p. 23) in the establishment and early maintenance stages of Super's (1957) developmental theory (organizational adaptability, position performance, work habits and attitudes, co-worker relationships, advancement, and career choice and plans). In addition, it has open-ended items that are scored on three levels of career adjustment: integrative, adjustive, and nonadjustive. Crites provides evidence of internal consistency in the mid .80s.

Stability, Validity, and Treatment Utility of Career Maturity Inventories. Since the evidence for the construct validity and stability of these career maturity measures is quite substantial, it is difficult to understand why these inventories are not more extensively used as interventions. One possible explanation was offered by N. E. Betz (1988), who argued that the high degree to which career maturity is related to intelligence and middle-class values limits the extent to which the concept can be related to career experiences in the way that Super's developmental theory suggests. The term *maturity* also has a certain pejorative tone that may restrict its routine use. The newer instruments, such as the Career Decision Scale (Osipow, 1987b), that do not use this term seem to be increasing in popularity, even though it can be asserted that they are measuring much the same construct. The applicability of these measures is also limited because, except for the ACCI and the CADI, they were all developed for a restricted adolescent population. In addition, clients appear to be more interested in the *content* of their career choice than in the *process* of that choice. Although the diagnostic utility of the career maturity inventories should be considerable for the professional counselor, the client's insistence upon and demand for interest inventories is dominant. Clearly, however, maturity inventories might be better used if the authors paid more attention to their counseling use and clinical utility. Numerous studies have employed measures of career maturity to evaluate the outcomes of career interventions, but very few if any have ascertained the direct clinical utility of receiving a career maturity measure in conjunction with an intervention.

The following are among the inventories developed to measure career maturity:

Adult Career Concerns Inventory, or ACCI (Super et al., 1988)

Career Maturity Inventory, or CMI (Crites, 1978)

Career Development Inventory, or CDI (Thompson et al., 1984)

Career Adjustment and Development Inventory, or CADI (Crites, 1982)

Cognitive Vocational Maturity Test, or CVMT (Westbrook & Parry-Hill, 1973)

Class 6: Decisional Status Inventories

The decisional status inventories form a relatively new class of instruments that emerged from the large base of studies of career decision making during the 1960s and 1970s (Phillips & Pazienza, 1988; Slaney, 1988). These studies were catalyzed by a theoretical paper (Goodstein, 1972) that differentiated indecision (a temporary state of affairs) from indecisiveness (a traitlike quality), and by a monograph on career development (Tiedeman & Ohara, 1963) that viewed career choice as a decisional process that required the continuous differentiation of the self and integration of the ego in the face of reality constraints.

Tiedeman and Ohara's (1963) monograph cleared the way for work on decisional status that was closely related to ego status. Tiedeman's main protégé, Harren (1978; 1980) used his mentor's theory to develop a model of the career development of college student and inventory called the Assessment of Career Decision Making (ACDM). Harren's instrument was based upon a widely appreciated variation of Tiedeman's career decision-making model that Harren (1980) himself had developed. In addition to incorporating Tiedeman's stages of decision making (awareness, planning, commitment, and implementation), Harren added the important dimension of decision-maker styles (rational, intuitive, and dependent). Harren (1978) then constructed an instrument to measure these three styles and the four stages. He further argued that situational anxiety resulted in avoidance when it was too high and a lack of incentive for constructive behavior when it was too low. He stated that the mastery of three developmental tasks—autonomy, interpersonal maturity, and sense of purpose—were necessary for adequate career decision making.

Following Harren's untimely death, the work on the ACDM was carried on by his colleagues, and a manual was eventually published (Buck & Daniels, 1985). This version of the ACDM contains ninety-four items, which measure the three styles, some content from two of Tiedeman's four stages (unfortunately the original awareness and implementation stage scales were deleted), and some aspects of the developmental tasks that Harren had discussed in his college student model (1980). An interpretive counselor report is generated from the scannable answer sheet, and the interpretive report discusses the student's style pattern and scale scores. A group summary identifies the style preferred by each individual student, and provides group means and standard deviations. The group report also identifies students who are likely to have decision-making problems, who may need individual counseling, or who have no chosen majors or occupations.

The ACDM manual summarizes the research conducted on the scales and data on a small (N = 264) normative sample of high school and college students. Internal consistency ranges from .49 to .86, but the factor analyses and internal consistencies for the intuitive scale suggest that it may not be a very pure measure of the construct. Thus although the ACDM did make the important contribution of describing and measuring the intuitive style of decision making, it is this scale that appears to be the weakest psychometrically. The extensive research base using the scales is well reported in the manual, and the ACDM enjoys a reasonable level of use in research studies. The inventory has been used to assess overall the outcome of career interventions, but there have been no studies of the impact of the instrument itself on a client.

The Career Decision Scale, or CDS (Osipow, Carney, Winer, Yanico, & Koschier, 1976) is perhaps the most heuristic decisional status inventory. It has become a useful clinical and research tool that has been employed in a large number and variety of studies. The most practical and controversial research outcome from CDS was the factor-analytic work investigating the underlying structure of career indecision. Several factor analyses, summarized by Osipow (1987b), suggested four factors underlying the scale: lack of structure, external barriers, approach-approach conflicts, and personal conflicts (see below). Osipow noted that several additional factor-analytic studies of the CDS yielded inconsistent if not unstable findings about its factor structure, a problem that Slaney (1985) attributed to the truncated nature of the original items. A recent review and reanalysis of seven factor-analytic studies of the CDS, however, suggested that its factor structure is quite stable and that a methodological quirk probably accounts for any inconsistencies among the studies (Shimizu, Vondracek, Schulenberg, & Hostetler, 1988). Shimizu et al. argued convincingly that an oblique rather than an orthogonal rotation of the factors derived from the CDS consistently results in a similar four-factor structure:

1. A general lack of structure, including indecision, confusion, discouragement, and lack of experience and information
2. Confirmation and support for a decision under consideration
3. Approach-approach conflict
4. Internal and external barriers

Osipow's (1987) work depicts indecision as a complex problem that can lead to improved treatment outcomes by utilizing preintervention diagnosis and differential treatment.

Another popular inventory of decisional status, My Vocational Situation, or MVS (Holland, Daiger, & Power, 1980a), was developed as a rapid assessment tool from which three apriori subscales (identity, information, and barriers) were extracted. Unlike earlier intrapsychic (Rounds & Tinsley, 1984) classification systems, the MVS assigns intrapsychic decision-making problems to only one of these three subscales: identity. Unfortunately, this is the only scale that shows sufficient internal consistency to be useful, a deficiency that can be traced to the small number of items on the information and barriers scales. The identity scale was correlated with the perceived need for career assistance in the expected direction (− .23 for females, − .29 for males). Recent studies suggest that the MVS is useful in the assessment of intervention outcomes and in research on the correlates and process of indecision (Slaney, 1988).

The Career Exploration Survey, or CES (Stumpf & Colarelli, 1980; Stumpf, Colarelli, & Hartman, 1983), is one of the more pragmatic career outcome measures in use today. Table 5-1 summarizes the various subscales in the inventory, which measure items such as the extent of exploration, reactions to exploration, and beliefs about that exploration.

Stability, Validity, and Treatment Utility of Decisional Status Inventories. Because these measures of decisional status are brief, diagnostic scales, as a group, they do suffer from stability problems. However, the scales fare well

Table 5-1   Dimensions of Career Exploration

Exploration Process

Environment Exploration. The extent of career exploration regarding occupations, jobs, and organizations within the last 3 months.

Self-Exploration. The extent of career exploration involving self-assessment and retrospection within the last 3 months.

Number of Occupations Considered. The number of different occupational areas on which one is acquiring information.

Intended-Systematic Exploration. The extent to which one acquires information on oneself and the environment in an intended or systematic manner (e.g., experimented with different career activities).

Frequency. The average number of times per week that one seeks career information over a 2-month period.

Amount of Information. The amount of information acquired on occupations, jobs, organizations, and oneself.

Focus. How sure one feels in his/her preference for a particular occupation, job, and organization.

Reactions to Exploration

Satisfaction with Information. The satisfaction one feels with the information obtained regarding occupations, jobs, and organizations relative to one's interests, abilities, and needs.

Explorational Stress. The amount of undesirable stress, relative to other significant life events, with which one has to contend, felt as a function of the career exploration process.

Decisional Stress. The amount of undesirable stress, relative to other significant life events, with which one has to contend, felt as a function of the career decision making process.

Beliefs

Employment Outlook. How favorable the employment possibilities look in one's career area.

Certainty of Career Exploration Outcomes. The degree of certainty one feels that he/she will attain a desired position.

External Search Instrumentality. The probability that exploring the environment for career opportunities will lead to obtaining career goals.

Internal Search Instrumentality. The probability that reflection on past career behavior and retrospection will lead to obtaining career goals.

Method Instrumentality. The probability that being intended and systematic in one's career exploration will lead to obtaining career goals.

Importance of Obtaining Preferred Position. The degree of importance placed on obtaining one's career preference.

Source: S. A. Stumpf, S. M. Colarelli, and K. Hartman, "Development of the Career Exploration Survey (CES)," *Journal of Vocational Behavior* 22 (1983): 194. Reproduced with permission of the Academic Press and the authors.

as outcome measures when used in career intervention studies, and the evidence is accumulating for their relationship to other variables (Osipow, 1987b). No direct evidence of their treatment utility could be found.

Decisional status is a new area of inquiry that may suffer technically in comparison to measures of career maturity, and have fewer problems of culture bias, and implied value judgments. Some rapprochement between these two areas of measurement—career maturity and decisional status— would be useful, and might lead to a realization that different decisional strategies, attitudes, behaviors, and emotions are probably appropriate in different decisional situations. These situations are most likely developmentally ordered, and require different complexes of behavior to be properly mastered.

The decisional status inventories discussed in this section are as follows:

Assessment of Career Decision Making, or ACDM (Harren, 1978; Buck & Daniels, 1985)

Career Decision Scale, or CDS (Osipow et al., 1976)

My Vocational Situation, or MVS (Holland et al., 1980a)

Career Exploration Survey, or CES (Stumpf & Colarelli, 1980; Stumpf et al., 1983)

Class 7: Measures of Personal Agency

Three measures currently under development constitute the newest domain in career measurement: personal agency, which is also called perceived self-efficacy. Personal agency is directly related to an individual's tendency to "behave in ways that created rather than simply responded to educational and career opportunities" (N. E. Betz & Hackett, 1987: p. 299). The term *agency* is believed to be "related to terms like proaction, initiative, assertiveness, and persistence" (N. E. Betz & Hackett, 1987: p. 300). The emergence of this new measurement domain has been spurred by the steady and cogent theory-based research work of N. E. Betz and Hackett, and in part by the frustration generated by the history of the attempts to measure career maturity and decisional status.

Several of the measures discussed here are specific scales designed to measure self-efficacy in a small career-related area or subpopulation (e.g., academic self-efficacy or mathematics and science careers [N. E. Betz & Hackett, 1981, 1983; Lent, Brown, & Larkin, 1984]; community college students [Rotberg, Brown, & Ware, 1987]). These measures are very much in the formative stages, and there is a proliferation of newcomers, only one or two of which will survive the initial development. Because perceived self-efficacy offers a clearly focused construct that can be easily measured and tested in future research studies, the "survivors" may become quite popular. Although reasonable validity, reliability, and utility data for these measures are unavailable, they are discussed here because of their importance. However, the exclusive use of these new self-efficacy measures in research or outcome evaluation, without attention to their treatment utility, could lead to yet another dead end in the search for career status measures.

It is no accident that some of the same authors concerned with decisional status and career maturity are now developing self-efficacy measures (N. E. Betz & Hackett, 1987; Krumboltz, 1988; Osipow & Rooney, in press). N. E. Betz and Hackett led the way (N. E. Betz & Hackett, 1981; Hackett & Betz, 1981) in the measurement and study of career self-efficacy. Their joint work has gradually become one of the most heuristic and influential recent contributions of the theory and research of career psychology. The original measure used in this research, the Career Self-Efficacy Scale (N. E. Betz & Hackett, 1981), employed two measures: one of the self-efficacy of educational requirements, and the second of self-efficacy with respect to job duties. Self-efficacy has generally been found to account for significant proportions of the variance in the traditionality of job choices (N. E. Betz & Hackett, 1983; Hackett, 1985); more recent measures of competence and of the level and strength of perceived self-efficacy (N. E. Betz & Hackett, 1987; Lent et al., 1984) now constitute a second generation of self-efficacy measures for which traditional indices of psychometric quality are forthcoming. The number of studies in this area is now so large that it requires a major critical review that is beyond the scope of this brief discussion. How this area of interest can continue to relate to career choice specifically and personality theory generally is an issue that must be faced in the near future.

In related work, Krumboltz (1988) has produced the Career Beliefs Inventory, a 122-item scale with sections subparts assessing career status, flexibility, motivation, and preferences. Dubbed "beliefs" by Krumboltz, these subparts purportedly measure willingness to consider different options, change directions, and relocate, openness to persuasion, and time urgency (flexibility section); risk taking, responsibility taking, and failure tolerance (motivation section); and satisfaction, openness, and work orientation (preferences section). Many of the items, however, seem to tap a generalized self-efficacy in a very useful way, and a factor-analysis should yield the true scalar understructure of this interesting new entry into the field of career measures. At the present, reliability and validity data are being collected for the early version of Krumboltz's scale.

Another new measure, the Activities Survey by Osipow and Rooney (in press), is based on skills statements derived from the forty-four worker-trait categories in the Dictionary of Occupational Titles (U. S. Department of Labor, 1977). The result is a listing of the DOT categories that reflects the concentration or diffusion of skill-based self-efficacies. Early factor analyses suggest four factors and appropriate differences in self-efficacy by gender, indecision status, and course enrollment. More data are presently being collected and analyzed.

Measures of personal agency discussed in this section include the following:

Career Self-Efficacy Scale (N. E. Betz & Hackett, 1981)

Career Beliefs Inventory (Krumboltz, 1988)

Activities Survey (Osipow & Rooney, in press)

Class 8: Vocational Card Sorts

In a landmark presidential address to Division 17 (counseling psychology) of the American Psychological Association, Tyler (1961) questioned whether traditional measurement methods were capable of tapping unique aspects of individual choices. She suggested using a card sort composed of occupational titles to analyze choice patterns according to the number of positive and negative sorting categories, the number of items in each, and any other aspects of the pattern that could be measured. Tyler struggled with the problem of the reliability and validity of the card sort method, an issue that still exists today. Slowly, and informally, Tyler's vocational card sort has been passed from counselor to counselor, spawning clones and imitators with various levels of adherence to and embellishment of her original choice patterns thesis. Although the card sorts were originally intended as structured interview or projective devices, they are also now used to ascertain Holland type or most preferred occupation. Several versions of card sorts are available (Dewey, 1974; Dolliver, 1967; Tyler, 1961), and reviews extol their clinical utility if not their psychometric properties (Dolliver, 1981; Slaney & Slaney, in press).

Most of the newer card sorts, however, have strayed from Tyler's original intent, which the following quote from Tyler (personal communication, 1980) expresses:

> I have come to think of this and the sorting of other sorts of content not as tests, but as interview aids that enable less verbal counseling clients to become more aware of their own motivations. Thus I now consider the psychometric properties less important than I did at first. . . . I think we need techniques that show how the individual's experience is organized rather than how much of any trait he or she possesses . . . if research on the shape of individuality is to be advanced.

The use of a card sort to establish a three-letter Holland code is not in the spirit of Tyler's original paper; these codes are more accurately provided by the SDS. The card sort instead is an interview technique for use with less-verbal clients or the vocational equivalent of a projective technique.

Technique 5–1 is a description of the Tyler Vocational Card Sort as it is typically practiced. Figure 5-6 is a sample construct map that resulted from a client's sorting of the "Would Choose" stimulus cards, and Figure 5-7 is a sample map that documents the joint attempt of the client and the counselor to label the "Would Not Choose" constructs and depict their relationships in two-dimensional space.

A descriptive review of the methodology (Dolliver, 1981) covered five types of card sorts. Although a small amount of evidence concerning their

Technique 5-1

Tyler Vocational Card Sort
A Structured Interview Technique

Purposes

1. To identify and clarify the major constructs used in student evaluations of an occupation.
2. To identify blocks interfering with career exploration.
3. To identify individual patterns and preferences and encourage less-verbal clients to express them.

Background and Development

The Tyler Vocational Card Sort (TVCS), a card sorting exercise using occupational titles as cues, was proposed originally as a method for assessing individual differences in the subject structuring of the occupational world (Tyler, 1961). As work progressed, two practical implications seemed clear: (1) the TVCS elicited rich, complex material that differentiated among individuals rather than groups; and (2) it had promise as a part of the counseling process as well as in assessment programs.

Although Tyler continued to use the TVCS as a research instrument, Dolliver (1967) employed it as a structured interview technique. Dolliver focused on the reasons clients gave for making choices and provided a rationale linking the TVCS with Kelly's *Psychology of Personal Constructs*, thus lending theoretical credibility. Simmons demonstrated that the TVCS added to counseling by identifying problems interfering with career selection.

The TVCS appears to have value as a counseling technique because it offers students a means for communicating their view of the occupational structure. The students not only sort the cards in various ways but are asked to report their reasons for the groupings. They are encouraged to write out occupational titles on blank cards and add them to the deck, thus giving them an opportunity to effect both content and structure. The counselor can assist them in identifying and clarifying preferences among occupational titles, reasons for choices, and work values inferred from choices and reasons. Occupational titles provide cues that may elicit further discussions about broadening the range of occupational goals under consideration or obtaining accurate occupational information.

Materials

1. A *pack* of fifty 3-by-5-inch cards with an occupational title printed on each.
2. *Five blank* 3-by-5-inch cards on which the students may write their current occupational preferences.
3. Three 4-by-6-inch note cards to *label the groupings*: "Might Choose," "Would Not Choose," and "In Question."
4. An *instructional sheet* to which the counselor can refer for an outline of the instructions.
5. A *recording sheet* upon which the counselor can record the students' sorting distribution and significant comments.

Procedure

1. Make an introduction such as the following to the student:

   "This exercise is called a vocational card sort. It is not a test. It is an activity designed to assist you to clarify your thoughts about planning for an occupation. The purpose is to identify and discuss your choices regarding several areas of work.

   This pack contains 50 cards with the name of an occupation printed on each one. I will ask you to arrange the cards in various ways and we can discuss it as you proceed.

   I will be writing down some of your comments for our future use."

2. The student is given the pack of cards and asked to sort them into three groups:

   a. The first group ("Might Choose") is identified as: "Occupations you might actually choose, or that have some specific appeal to you, or that have possibilities for a person like you."

   b. The second group ("Would Not Choose") is identified by repeating the description above in negative terms: "Occupations you would not choose, or that do not have some specific appeal to you, or that do not seem to have possibilities for a person like you."

   c. The third group ("In Question") is identified as: "Those occupations about which you are indifferent, uncertain, or in question."

3. Remove all materials except the "Would Not Choose" stack.

4. The student is shown the sheet used to record the comments about the "Might Choose" occupations, and is asked, "Is this a summary of what you said? Do you wish to add or change anything? Do these statements represent your way of evaluating an occupation?"

5. Finally, the student may be asked, "What are your reactions to this exercise?"

What to Look for:

1. The reasons for sorting in groups can be considered as conscious statements about work values. Patterns of values about work satisfactions may also be noted. Patterns of work situations that are consciously avoided could be discussed.

2. The number of smaller piles may suggest how "tight" the student's category system is. A large number of piles suggests that the student categorizes occupations under a large number of rubrics, thus making the process of eliminating of alternatives more difficult. A small number of piles suggests that the student makes few distinctions among occupations and may need to consider more dimensions about occupations.

3. The balance between the number of "Might Choose" and "Would Not Choose" cards may provide some clues as to the number of occupational alternatives the student still considers. Usually students place more cards in the "Would Not Choose" stack.

Source: Counseling and Consultation Services, Ohio State University. Reprinted by permission.

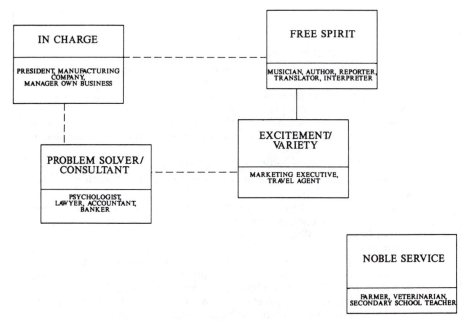

Note: Size of cell indicates salience of construct for client. Top portion of cell contains construct as labelled by client, and bottom portion of cell contains representative stimulus cards used to formulate the construct.

Figure 5-6   Sample Construct Map of a Client's Sorting of "Would Choose" Stimulus Cards.

stability, validity, and treatment utility is now emerging, a technical review would be premature and, if one believes Tyler, inappropriate. The most popular card sorts include:

> Occusort (L. K. Jones, 1979)
>
> Non-Sexist Vocational Card Sort (Dewey, 1974)
>
> Vocational Exploration and Insight Kit, or VEIK (Holland and Associates, 1977)

Class 9: Measures of Personal Style, Values, and Needs

To the extent that career choices are rational and logical, measures of ability and interests make sense in career interventions. If career choices are emotionally driven (Fletcher, 1966), however, the domain of personal values and needs may be an important adjunct in a career intervention. Individuals differ in the degree to which they endorse various values, including the importance attached to work (Zytowski, 1988). The inventories covered in this section measure a range of personal needs, styles, and interests that are judged to be predictive of satisfaction and success in managerial positions. Values

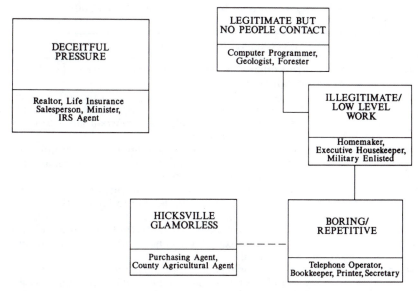

Note: Size of cell indicates salience of construct for client. Top portion of cell contains construct as labelled by client, and bottom portion of cell contains representative stimulus cards used to formulate the construct.

Figure 5-7   Sample Construct Map of a Client's Sorting of "Would Not Choose" Stimulus Cards.

are also the basis for the assessment and interaction package in the SIGI-Plus computer system covered in Chapter 6.

Some of the inventories in this section originally conceived for non-psychological purposes (e.g., managerial development) may offer little information that is relevant to psychometric properties. Some have no reliability or validity data, and still others have no manual. These inventories are not generally used in assessment centers to predict managerial success in the manner shown by Bray and Grant (1966) or more recently by a large Japanese study (Wakabayashi & Graen, 1984). Clients consider these instruments to be among the most helpful they receive, which poses an ethical problem for the counselor. Can a face-valid inventory with no traditional psychometric evidence be used with any confidence in career interventions? No easy answer exists for this question. The personal style, values and needs measures are described below along with currently available evidence.

The Minnesota Importance Questionnaire, or MIQ (Rounds, Henly, Dawis, Lofquist, & Weiss, 1981), measures twenty needs or requirements related to job satisfaction (see Table 5-2). Developed across a number of years in association with the Minnesota Work Adjustment Project, the MIQ is used with the Minnesota Occupation Classification System, or MOCS II (Dawis, Lofquist, Henly, & Rounds, 1979), and represents one of the only adult work roles measures with substantial empirical underpinning.

Table 5-2   Ten of the Twenty Vocational Needs and Their Work-Related
Reinforcers

VOCATIONAL NEED	WORK-RELATED REINFORCERS
Ability utilization	Tasks that allow the exercise of self-perceived skills and talents
Achievement	Tasks that are productive of pride in the accomplishment thereof
Activity	Tasks that call for a relatively constant and sustained level of energy investment
Advancement	Work environment in which there is an opportunity for fair evaluation of and consequent advancement for work-related excellence
Authority	Tasks that include power to decide the methods by which a job is performed and to impose those decisions on co-workers
Company policies and practices	Work environment characterized by explicit and definitive guidelines consistently disseminated and practiced
Compensation	Tasks providing compensation based upon quantity and quality of work performed, and comparable to compensation paid to others for performance of similar tasks
Co-workers	Work environment in which employees are interested in and responsive to friendly interpersonal gestures and relationships
Creativity	Tasks that are amenable to innovations independently conceived and performed by the worker
Independence	Work environment in which the individual works alone

Source: J. B. Rounds, Jr., G. A. Henly, R. V. Dowis, L. H. Lofquist, and D. J. Weiss, *Manual for the Minnesota Importance Questionnaire: A Measure of Vocational Needs and Values* (Minneapolis, MN: University of Minnesota, 1981), p. 5. Reprinted with permission.

The MIQ is perhaps the most underutilized and underappreciated inventory of its kind on the market. Its basis on nearly twenty-five years of studies of occupational needs and specific reinforcer patterns for different occupations (e.g., Borgen, Weiss, Tinsley, Dawis, & Lofquist, 1972) has been virtually ignored by career counselors. In part, this problem is exacerbated by the great difficulty encountered when trying to acquire the test itself and any supporting documentation from the University of Minnesota.

A new inventory under development called the Campbell Work Orientations Inventory (Campbell, 1986) contains five interlocking scales that measure the following components of work orientation:

1. working attitudes
2. working preferences
3. working skills
4. self description
5. observer description

Although scale characteristics and psychometric data are not yet available, this comprehensive battery should be useful in managerial training and development.

The Managerial Style Questionnaire (MSQ) (McBer, 1981) and the Management Skills Profile (MSP) (Personnel Decisions, Inc., 1986) are both general measures of managerial style for use with executive populations.

The Level I Life Style Inventory, or LSI (Human Synergistics, 1989), was very well received by clients and is supported by some psychometric evidence. The LSI is based upon a clocklike circumplex that classifies personal styles as constructive (achievement, self-actualizing, or humanistic-encouraging), passive-defensive (approval, conventional, dependent, or avoidance), or aggressive-defensive (oppositional, power, competitive, or perfectionistic). Successive versions of the LSI have relied increasingly on traditional psychometric evidence for their claims (see Cook, Lafferty, & Rousseau, 1983).

The Hall Occupational Orientation Inventory, or HOOI (Hall & Tarrier, 1976), contains ten need value scales, the three job characteristics scales from the DOT, and eight worker-trait scales; a developmental model of careers is also presented in the manual.

Two tests of personal values have been developed by Super and Nevill. The Salience Inventory, or SI (Nevill & Super, 1986), measures the importance of work using the roles from Super's Life-Career Rainbow (1980), including studying, working, community service, home and family, and leisure (Zytowski, 1988). The Values Scale, or VS (Super & Nevill, 1986), measures the full range of values affecting behavior. It contains twenty-one five-item scales representing the values in Super's developmental model (Harmon, 1988).

Stability, Validity, and Treatment Utility of Measures of Personal Style, Values, and Needs.   The least is known about this group of inventories. The MIQ is probably the most completely validated of the inventories, but is receiving little practical use and thus is not likely to generate more attention. The LSI has widespread practical application, and a factor analysis by R. A. Cooke and Rousseau (1983) found three factors consistent with its life-styles model. Other studies by R. A. Cooke, Rousseau, and Lafferty (1987) and R. A. Cooke and Lafferty (1981) confirmed this finding, and provided evidence of convergent validity through the expert ratings of managers and of internal consistency. As such traditional psychometric evidence for the LSI accumulates, this sophisticated simulation exercise is becoming more significant as a research and counseling instrument. The counselor's manual for the HOOI, however, contains no traditional evidence of validity and reliability, and the inventory, no matter how face-valid, cannot be properly evaluated for psychometric adequacy. While internally consistent, the SI suf-

fers from a certain degree of instability, with test-retest correlations ranging from .37 to .67 (Zytowski, 1988). Like the SI, the VS also shows evidence
of internal consistency (median = .78), and may suffer from similar instability
problems (Harmon, 1988). Both instruments appear to be promising addi-
tions to the measurement values, style, and needs. The number of well-
designed studies evaluating these inventories is growing and may soon form
a critical mass sufficient to judge them as a group. There is, however, no
evidence for the treatment utility of any of these instruments.

Examples of measures of personal style, values, and needs include the
following:

Management Skills Profile, or MSP (Personnel Decisions Inc., 1986)

Managerial Style Questionnaire, or MSQ (McBer & Co., 1981)

Minnesota Importance Questionnaire, or MIQ (Rounds et al., 1981)

Level I Life Styles Inventory, or LSI (Human Synergistics, 1989)

Campbell Work Orientations Inventory, or CWOI (Campbell, 1986)

Hall Occupational Orientation Inventory, or HOOI (Hall & Tarrier,
    1976)

Salience Inventory, or SI (Nevill & Super, 1986)

Values Scale, or VS (Super & Nevill, 1986)

Class 10: Work Sample Batteries

Work sample batteries are controlled examples of specific tasks required for
the performance of an occupation (e.g., fine-finger dexterity, eye-hand coordination, or upper body range of motion). The client completes these work
tasks under simulated working conditions demanding speed and accuracy.
Work samples are especially useful with rehabilitation clients whose physical
disability could limit their performance. They are also useful for observing
work style and manner of approach to work tasks. Several work samples are
generally packaged together, which means they can be very expensive and
may require an entire testing room for storage of the work stations.

Overviews of the role of general assessment strategies in vocational
rehabilitation are available (Power, 1984), and Botterbusch's (1987) unusually
thorough review of twenty-one work sample systems serves as a handy
reference for anyone considering work sampling as a part of a career assessment program. Although many of the systems reviewed by Botterbusch are
designed for special populations (e.g., blind, injured, or special needs), three
representative systems that can be used with a general adult population are
the VALPAR Component Work Samples (VALPAR International Corporation, 1974), the Micro-TOWER System (ICD, 1967), and the McCarron-Dial
System, or MDS (McCarron & Dial, 1986). Each has a history of use, norms,
and evidence of psychometric properties, although rarely clinical utility. The

VALPAR system, for example, contains nineteen well designed work samples, but little evidence of validity or reliability (Botterbusch, 1987). The Micro-TOWER contains thirteen work samples, a substantial norm base, and evidence of validity and reliability (Botterbusch, 1987). The MDS, originally designed for special needs populations, measures five traits (verbal-spatial-cognitive, sensory, fine and gross motor, emotional, and integrative-coping); has an extensive evidential base, including test-retest reliabilities in the .80–.90 range; and construct and predictive validity (Botterbusch, 1987; Peterson, 1988).

Stability, Validity, and Treatment Utility of Work Sample Batteries. Although fascinating pictures of work behavior can be generated using work samples, these assessment devices may be prohibitively expensive, and because of their cost and the need for individual administration, are not well studied. The evidence for them is generally weaker than for other ability assessments, and they serve more as screening devices for establishing employability than as intervention tools for counseling.

The work sample batteries discussed in this section were as follows:

VALPAR Component Work Samples (Valpar International Corporation, 1974)

Micro-TOWER System (ICD, 1967)

McCarron-Dial System, or MDS (McCarron & Dial, 1986)

Class 11: Ability Assessments

This class of assessment instruments contains multiple aptitude and ability batteries as well as tests for specific jobs. Some of them are now available in computer-enhanced versions that have reduced the number of items required to test each subject by adapting the difficulty level of the items to the subjects' ability level (Anastasi, 1988; Borgen, 1988). Although there are a host of tests of specific abilities (e.g., mechanical comprehension), the ability inventories described here are designed to assess the full range of general and specific abilities. The Multidimensional Aptitude Battery, or MAB (Jackson, 1984), which by name alone might seem to be part of this group, is really an intelligence test similar to the WAIS. Although its manual contains an excellent, concise discussion of the problems of general versus specific intelligence, the MAB does not test work-related aptitude.

The Armed Services Vocational Aptitude Battery, or ASVAB (U.S. Department of Defense, 1985a), is a controversial measure, fraught with early technical problems that raised questions about its internal consistency and predictive and treatment utility (Walsh & Betz, 1985). Because the ASVAB is offered for free to school systems as a recruiting tool, these questions are serious, and the Department of Defense appears to be taking steps to rectify these problems. A major longitudinal study (Anastasi, 1988) now testing its predictive validity, and new materials, including an interest inventory, are being designed to enhance counseling applicability.

The ASVAB provides composites of its ten subtests in two areas—academic composites (see Figure 5-8 and occupational composites (see Figure 5-9)—that should be predictive of success in specific occupational groupings. Prediger (1987b) noted that the ASVB is given to over 1.3 million high school students each year, and that educational groups could be differentiated using the ASVAB. Unfortunately, no data were reported on client reactions to the ASVAB, which might shed some light on its treatment utility.

The Differential Aptitude Tests, or DAT (Bennett, Seashore, & Wesman, 1982; 1984), generate a verbal and numerical reasoning score, and subscores for abstract reasoning, clerical speed and accuracy, mechanical reasoning, space relations, spelling, and language usage. In addition, there is a direct measurement career planning questionnaire on which the respondent endorses occupations from eighteen academic areas and twenty occupational groupings (Super, 1984). The DAT, originally designed for use with grades

Figure 5-8   The ASVAB Academic Composites. (Source: U.S. Department of Defense, *Technical Supplement to the Counselor's Manual for the Armed Services Vocational Aptitude Battery Form 14* [North Chicago, IL: U.S. Military Entrance Processing Command, 1985], p. 4.)

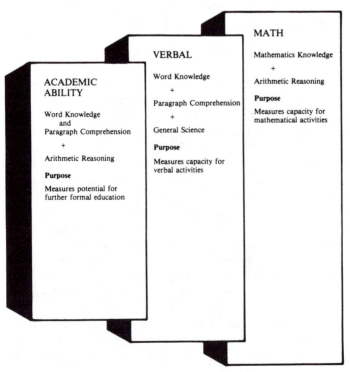

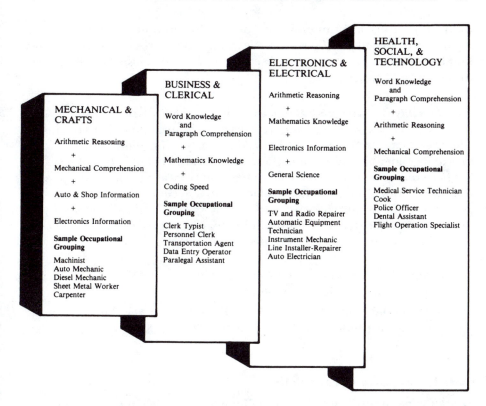

Figure 5-9   The ASVAB Occupational Composites. (Source: U.S. Department of Defense, *Technical Supplement to the Counselor's Manual for the Armed Services Vocational Aptitude Battery Form 14* [North Chicago, IL: U.S. Military Entrance Processing Command, 1985], p. 5.)

eight to twelve, was normed on over 61,000 public and parochial school students in sixty-four school districts in thirty-two states by grade level. Parallel form reliability data are adequate, with extensive evidence of both test-retest reliability and scale independence (Bennett et al., 1984). Anastasi (1988) called the validity evidence, which consists of thousands of correlations between the DAT and academic and performance criteria, "overwhelming." There is an adaptive version available for use on a microcomputer (Anastasi, 1988).

The General Aptitude Test Battery, or GATB (U.S. Employment Service, 1979), contains twelve subtests that are clustered to measure nine aptitudes: intelligence, verbal aptitude, numerical aptitude, spatial aptitude, form perception, clerical perception, motor coordination, finger dexterity, and manual dexterity. Test administration requires a simple pegboard and a screw assembly apparatus in addition to the booklets. Cutoff scores are calculated for sixty occupational aptitude groups. The GATB is now available in a desktop computer-assisted format, and can be used with the AIM, an indirect measurement interest inventory. Free training that certifies a counselor to give the GATB is available in most states from the United States Employment Service. Expanded research is now linking the GATB directly to the DOT (Anastasi, 1988).

Stability, Validity, and Treatment Utility of Ability Assessments. Ability tests received mixed reviews with respect to stability and predictive validity. The argument also rages over the wisdom of specific ability tests, and the race and gender bias inherent in these inventories. Very little recent research has been done on the incremental value of ability measurement in the prediction of vocational success and satisfaction, but accumulating evidence suggests that such comprehensive testing may greatly expand our ability to predict and ultimately to counsel individuals concerning career choice.

Three ability batteries were discussed in this section:

Armed Services Vocational Aptitude Battery, or ASVAB-14 (U.S. Department of Defense, 1989)

Differential Aptitude Tests, or DAT (Bennett et al., 1982; 1984)

General Aptitude Test Battery, or GATB (U.S. Employment Service, 1979)

Class 12: Measures of Personality

Several general measures of personality may be useful in career interventions. Indeed, the overlap between career development and personality may be substantial, and counselors increasingly view career counseling as life and personal style counseling with a career focus, in which a wide range of life issues and concerns are discussed. This overlap between career and personality is especially important with adult clients. However, measures of personality, even when properly constructed and evaluated for stability and validity, may not present adequate evidence for predicting or stimulating career choice, because an inventory validated for one purpose may not be valid for another. For example, Martin and Bartol (1986) recently evaluated the Myers-Briggs Type Indicator, or MBTI (I. B. Myers & McCaulley, 1985), the most popular general measure of personality for use in career counseling, for its ability to predict area of concentration among business students. The MBTI, when compared to the Holland Vocational Preference Inventory (Holland, 1985c), was found to be little better than chance alone in predicting business concentration. Presently, a considerable number of studies are using the MBTI in career and vocational situations, although no convincing evidence for such applications yet exists.

Similar criticisms can be levied at the 16 PF Career Development Profile, or 16 PF (Walter, 1985), which generates information about the respondent's problem-solving patterns, patterns for coping with stressful conditions, patterns of interpersonal interaction, and patterns of career, occupational, and avocational interests. The only empirical evidence for the profile shows uncomfortably weak correlations with measures of the Holland types (Wholeben, 1988).

The FIRO Awareness Scales (Shutz, 1978) and the California Psychological Inventory, or CPI (Gough, 1987, which is a normal version of the MMPI, are also commonly used in career practice. The achievement-via-conformity and achievement-via-independence scales of the CPI are particularly well suited to vocational style assessment. Two recent innovations in the CPI are a scale to measure work orientations (Gough, 1985) and one to measure managerial style (Gough, 1984). The FIRO Awareness Scales, especially the FIRO-B, measure expressed and wanted behavior in three areas: inclusion, control, and affection. Adequate evidence of internal consistency and stability are available for the FIRO and the CPI, and the scales are useful in assessing personal style around career issues, although no specific studies of their career effectiveness have yet been done.

Stability, Validity, and Treatment Utility of Measures of Personality.   As a group, the personality measures have demonstrated excellent stability and validity. At present, it appears that they may be useful in clarifying personal style, even though they have not been found to have predictive validity for career choice. Problems may arise in counseling when the client is presented a range of job options based on the MBTI or the 16PF that are not similar to each other in ways that clients can understand. Interest and ability inventories are far superior predictors of eventual career choice than are personality measures. Perhaps their use should be limited to clarifying interpersonal or intrapersonal aspects of work behavior, rather than predicting career choice. The statement in the MBTI manual that "when the SCII and the MBTI are used together, the SCII points to specific careers of interests, and the MBTI shows the reasons why the careers are attractive" (I. B. Myers & McCaulley, 1985, p. 87), is neither particularly clear nor based upon adequate evidence. The manual does contain some interesting correlations between the MBTI and the SCII and the KOIS, but clear predictive evidence has not been presented. No empirical evidence exists for the treatment utility of personality inventories when used in career interventions.

The following personality inventories were discussed in this section:

Myers-Briggs Type Indicator (I. B. Myers & McCaulley, 1985)
Sixteen Personal Career Development Profile (Walter, 1985)
FIRO Awareness Scales (Shutz, 1978)
California Psychological Inventory, or CPI (Gough, 1987)

Class 13: Measures of Work Environment

Measurement of the nature and quality of the work environment, and individuals' reactions to it has been a constant subject for vocational psychology since the early studies of worker productivity (Roethlisberger & Dickson, 1939). Thousands of studies of the organizational influences on job satisfaction have been reviewed (Crites, 1969; Locke, 1976), and have recently given way to research on the effects of work tasks on job involvement, and finally to measures of the psychological nature of work environments and especially their stress-inducing qualities. In this section we shall discuss three such measures that represent a cross-section of these instruments.

The earliest of these inventories, the Maslach Burnout Inventory, or MBI (Maslach & Jackson, 1981), yields scores for emotional exhaustion, depersonalization, and lack of personal accomplishment. Evidence of stability and validity are presented in the manual, which suggests that the measure seems to tap the global emotional reactions to working conditions. Although there is no evidence of its treatment utility, the MBI has been used extensively in correlational studies and as an outcome measure for interventions (Higgins, 1986). Clients, especially those in human service professions, may benefit from recognizing the level of burnout they are experiencing and acting to alleviate the problem.

The Work Environment Scale, or WES (Moos, 1986), measures three major dimensions of the social climate in work environments: relationship, which is defined as involvement, peer cohesion, and supervisor support; personal growth, which is defined as autonomy, task orientation, and work pressure; and system maintenance and system change, which is defined by clarity, control, innovation, and physical comfort. Norms are presented for more than three-thousand employees, and although internal consistency coefficients are not high, they are adequate for all subscales. One-month test-retest reliability ranges from .69 to .83, which is moderate. A number of studies by Moos and Billings (e.g., Billings & Moos, 1982) suggest that the WES is not only an excellent research tool, but may also have useful clinical and interpersonal applications.

Finally, the Occupational Stress Inventory, or OSI (Osipow & Spokane, 1987), is a three-part generic measure of perceived occupationally induced role stress, personal strain, and coping resources. The OSI has fourteen subscales, six that measure role stress (overload, insufficiency, ambiguity, boundary, and responsibility), four that measure personal strain (vocational, psychological, interpersonal, and physical), and four that measure personal coping resources (recreation, self-care, social supports, and rational cognitive). The OSI can be hand-scored, and is now available in an optical scanner format that generates a client report and a professional report. Two-week test-retest reliability in the .88 to .90 range as well as substantial evidence of internal consistency is presented for the three subinventories. Studies of the validity and use of the OSI as an outcome measure are beginning to appear in the literature, although no evidence for treatment utility exists.

Stability, Validity, and Treatment Utility of Measures of Work Environment.
Measures of work environment are a relatively new phenomenon in the field of career intervention, and their evidential base is still developing. As a group, they seem internally consistent, although more subject to temporal instability than other career measures. Their subscales are often uncomfortably intercorrelated, and very little if any evidence for treatment utility is presented. Nonetheless, clients seem to appreciate the information that they yield, and it may be that a change in coping strategy in the work environment, especially in relation to one's supervisor, is a more viable option for many clients than is a work change.

Three measures of work environment were discussed in this section:

Maslach Burnout Inventory, or MBI (Maslach & Jackson, 1981)

Work Environment Scale, or WES (Moos, 1986)

Occupational Stress Inventory, or OSI (Osipow & Spokane, 1987)

THE USE AND INTERPRETATION OF CAREER INVENTORIES

Several recent articles have provided guidelines for the effective use of tests (Anastasi, 1985b; Mehrens & Lehmann, 1985; Tinsley & Fretz, 1984) and career inventories (Prediger & Garfield, 1988; Tinsley & Bradley, 1986). A number of general principles have emerged from these discussions, which, while not supported by empirical studies, are practical and clear. Tinsley and Bradley (1986), for example, provide two such guidelines for using tests in career counseling:

1. Test interpretation should be part of an ongoing process, and requires the same level of therapeutic support as any other counseling intervention.
2. Tests should be considered to be standardized structured interviews that are more efficient and valid than unstructured interviews.

The authors of these articles seem to agree that the client must understand the meaning of the scores, be familiar with the construct they measure (Mehrens & Lehmann, 1985), and integrate the results with other information gathered in counseling. In using interest inventories, for example, it is important to distinguish between criterion-based and homogeneous inventories, both in the counselor's mind and in the client's understanding.

Knowing that one is being compared to a reference group of employed adults is crucial to the interpretation of a criterion-based inventory. Clients are generally more confused about the meaning of tests that have complex construction and scoring, and will need careful help in interpreting multiscore batteries (Anastasi, 1985b), but will readily understand the criterion-based inventories. Some counselor preparation is required prior to test interpretation, and the client should also be told what to expect in order to minimize possible defensive reactions to negative information (Tinsley & Bradley, 1986; Tinsley & Fretz, 1984). A thorough check list of the basic concepts a counselor should master for the effective use of tests is presented in Appendix E. One of the particularly important concepts involves providing bridges between the statistical results and the clinical situations. Goldman (1971) described various types of statistical and clinical bridges as follows:

Statistical Bridges

1. The norm bridge, or the comparison between a client's scores and some normative sample, as is done with measures of decisional status.
2. The discriminant bridge, or the comparison between the client's scores and multiple samples, as is done on criterion-based interest inventories.
3. The regression bridge, or the correlation between a client's test score and actual performance or satisfaction, as is done with ability and work sample measures.

Clinical Bridges

1. The client model, or the construction and testing of a hypothetical model of the client's situation through inference from test data.
2. The theoretical model, or the comparison of the client's situation with theoretical models of human behavior.

The clearer these bridges are to both the client and the counselor, the better the client will be able to use and absorb the information yielded by the inventory.

The Point of Introduction of a Test or Inventory

Figure 5-10 depicts three positions in the intervention process where tests are commonly introduced. (For a complete depiction of the career intervention process upon which this figure is based, see Table 2-4.) In the first location (A), which appears late in the intervention process, after activation but prior to completion, tests are employed after clients have clarified their interests and goals, and while final options for exploration are being generated. When used at this juncture, tests confirm or narrow the options being considered. The tests are preceded by nontest explorations to clarify the prob-

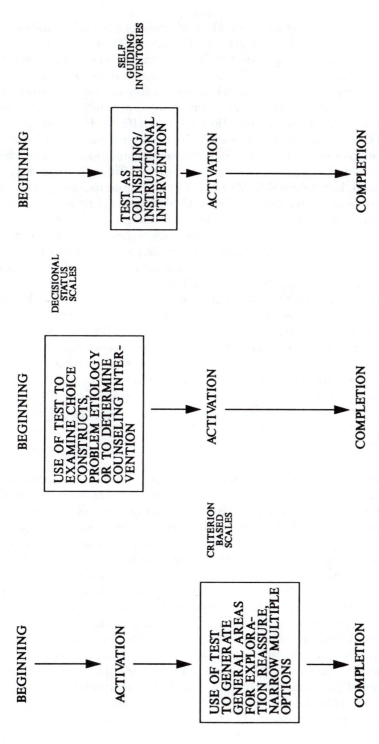

Figure 5-10 Three Major Positions in Which Tests are Employed in the Intervention Process.

145

lem facing the client and the general parameters of the client's decisional process. Criterion-based inventories such as the SCII or the JVIS are appropriate at this point, after a solid foundation has been built for evaluating the specific alternatives generated by the instruments inventory.

In the second position (B), which is found at the beginning of the intervention, tests may be used as an exploratory simulation either to clarify choice constructs, as with card sorts, or to illuminate the client's decisional process as with decisional status inventories. It is usually unwise to introduce a criterion-based or even a homogeneous interest inventory so early in an intervention. Unfortunately, the early use of highly specific inventories may be more common than is desirable. Many career and counseling centers routinely assign the SCII to all entering clients who state career concerns as their principal focus. Experience suggests, however, that giving a criterion-based test given so early in the process prematurely limits the exploration of career options. Such a practice may also reinforce the client's belief that career intervention involves only taking and interpreting an interest inventory ("Give me one of those tests that tells me what I should do").

In the third position (C), which appears just prior to activation, the tests themselves are the counseling intervention or a major component of the intervention. Tests that are self-guiding or that convey large amounts of instructional content, such as the SDS when used in its complete form (SDS plus guides), or the ACT VIESA, can be used at this time to obtain information about the world of work, to enhance self-knowledge, and to provide an exploratory experience.

SUMMARY

In this chapter, the large array of instruments available for use in career interventions was arranged in the following thirteen classes, according to the content and measurement assumptions underlying their construction, and the population for which they were appropriate: (1) criterion-based interest inventories for college-bound clients; (2) criterion-based interest inventories for noncollege-bound clients; (3) homogeneous self-guiding interest inventories; (4) homogeneous hand- or machine-scored interest inventories; (5) career maturity inventories; (6) decisional status inventories; (7) measures of personal agency; (8) vocational card sorts: (9) measures of personal style, values, and needs; (10) work sample batteries; (11) ability assessments; (12) measures of personality; and (13) measures of work environment. The content, stability, validity, and treatment utility of these various career measures were discussed, as were their application to different developmental problems. Although many of these instruments meet traditional psychometric strictures, very little evidence exists for their treatment utility. The number, quality, and variety of career measures is quite remarkable. The professional counselor is constrained only by habit or unfamiliarity from using a wide range of these inventories in everyday career intervention practice. Competent interpretation of the inventories requires the bridging of test findings with the real world of the client, as well as their proper placement in the intervention process.

6

Groups, Structured Workshops, Classes, and Brief Alternative Interventions

This chapter discusses the creative application of career intervention principles in formats that depart from more traditional individual counseling, including the wide array of group strategies, such as structured groups working with a limited amount of time and ongoing therapeutic groups with a career focus, instructional or curricular interventions, workshops, and brief alternative interventions. As Lunneborg (1983) noted, the boundary between career planning and life planning is increasingly blurred. This is a healthy development fueled in part by the large numbers of women returning to the labor market (Lassalle & Spokane, 1987) and in part by a softening of the roles of men and woman in American society. Oliver (1975) supported the blending of career and life-style planning when she argued that career counseling for women should consider overall life plans and career choice processes: "It is too narrow an approach to emphasize the content of a career choice . . . and neglect . . . the process involved in making that choice" (p. 434).

The interventions covered in this chapter range from the most fleeting encounter with the topic of career development to the most intensive semester-long classes devoted entirely to career concerns. These interventions can be visualized along the continuum of counselor involvement and client investment shown in Chapter 1 (see Figure 1-3). As long as a counseling or instructional intervention includes career material or concerns, it can be considered to be a career intervention. Such interventions may include a blend of therapeutic and didactic intervention components, but the underlying processes that contribute to client progress are essentially the same (see Chapter 3). An edited volume by Reardon and Burck (1975), now in its second edition (Burck and Reardon, 1984), extensively describes many of these strategies, and together the two volumes constitute an excellent reference source for the full range of career interventions.

Martin and Hiebert (1985) argued that all counseling involves instruction, which they define as the "active, creative effort on the part of counselors that effectively facilitates learning outcomes desired by clients" (p. 5). Career counseling, whether individual or alternative, should contain the basic five instrumental elements that Martin and Hiebert described: general goals, preassessment, objectives, instructional activities, and evaluation. The dyadic encounter of individual counseling is a unique instance of instruction in that the counselor, an intentional and purposeful professional (Martin & Hiebert, 1985) influences the level of interpersonal support and challenge provided. Martin and Hiebert have asserted that this instructional underpinning ties career counseling to the vast literatures in instructional psychology (Glasser & Bassock, 1989) and social cognition (Sherman, Judd, & Park, 1989), which study the process by which information (in this case about the world of work) is stored and used to make judgments that then translate to behavior.

GROUP CAREER INTERVENTIONS

Group career interventions were the first alternative to individual counseling. As early as 1955, D. P. Hoyt predicted that the demand for counseling services would outstrip the available supply of individual counseling hours and that the solution would be "dealing with clients in groups" (p. 26). Hoyt found the effects of counseling groups on vocational certainty, satisfaction, and realism to be comparable to those in individual counseling.

Since Hoyt's study, groups have assumed a routine place in the offerings of most career and counseling centers. Recent research (Kivlighan, Johnson, & Fretz, 1987; Kivlighan, Hageseth, Tipton, & McGovern, 1981) has infused new vigor into this area of practice. As Lunneborg (1983) noted, nearly all career groups rely on a leader, in contrast with the leaderless approaches of many community-oriented self-help groups. Lunneborg further observed that group career interventions do vary in the degree to which they focus on a specific structured format versus a general process orientation to career exploration. Thus it seems sensible to divide the discussion of group interventions into two sections: structured and unstructured groups.

Structured Career Groups

In 1972 a career counselor packaged a structured career group intervention in a small zippered kit. Called the Vocational Exploration Group, or VEG (Daane, 1972), this kit became a popular, replicable intervention in counseling practice and research studies. Four controlled evaluations of the VEG provided evidence for its effectiveness (Bergland & Lundquist, 1975; Johnson, Johnson, & Yates, 1981; Powers, 1978; Yates, Johnson, & Johnson,

1979). For example, Bergland and Lundquist (1975) used the VEG with sixty Mexican-American high school students. Using the outcome measure included in the kit, they found large differences between the students who received the VEG and those who did not on their ability to differentiate jobs using skills, interests, and satisfiers. Powers (1978) used the VEG with former drug abusers, and found moderate treatment gains on career maturity and clarity of career plans. Although the differences were not as large as those found by Bergland and Lundquist, Powers's outcome measure (Career Maturity Inventory (Crites, 1978) was more stringent. A study by Yates et al. (1979), which also used the VEG with the CMI as the outcome measure, produced results that were nearly the same as Powers's and that were maintained over a six-month follow-up period (Johnson et al., 1981). Although the VEG is a highly structured career intervention with clear and specific goals, it places little emphasis on input and social support from individuals other than the group leader. The intervention was, however, successful with a variety of minority subgroups not often included in outcome studies.

A second example of a structured group intervention, the Job Club (Azrin & Besalel, 1980), is based upon sound principles of behavior modification applied to the job-finding situation. This highly specific but open-ended intervention is designed to promote job-seeking and -finding behaviors as directly and efficiently as possible. The Job Club includes all of the ingredients found in those career interventions that produce consistent gains (see Chapter 3). There is heavy use of member and counselor social support and reinforcement, large doses of constructive behavior promotion, information giving, and a cognitive structure for understanding the job-finding process. The thirty-three activities in the Job Club are detailed in its manual (Azrin & Besalel, 1980), and include a "buddy system," telephone contacts, and interview training. The list of appendices from the Job Club manual (see Table 6-1) provides an excellent sketch of this comprehensive intervention program. Its helpful and complete selection of forms for use with participants is a unique contribution to the practice of structured group career interventions. Outcome evaluations of the Job Club technique are discussed in Chapter 9, but in general this is a well-designed, forceful, and carefully evaluated strategy.

In contrast with the VEG and Job Club findings, a general, comprehensively structured group intervention (Pavalk & Kammer, 1985) for juvenile offenders who participated in eight two-hour group sessions revealed no significant treatment outcomes for either black or white subjects. Because the group's pretest levels of career maturity were a full standard deviation below the mean for college students, this result is surprising. It is possible that the motivation level of the juvenile offenders was simply too low to result in a beneficial outcome. Pavalk and Kammer's study does represent one of the few failures of structured group career intervention.

Table 6-1   Appendices in the Job Club Manual

1. Program Introduction Letter
2. Background Information Form
3. Daily Outline of Activities: First Day Chart
4. Daily Outline of Activities: Second Day Chart
5. Daily Outline of Activities: Third Day Chart
6. Daily Outline of Activities: Fourth Day Chart
7. Daily Outline of Activities: Fifth Day Chart
8. Daily Outline of Activities: Chart for Second Week and All Other Days
9. Counselor-Job Seekers Agreement
10. Job Seeker Information Form
11. Family Support Letter
12. Group Progress Chart
13. Reminder List of Relatives
14. Reminder List of Former Co-Workers
15. Reminder List of Classmates and School Acquaintances
16. Reminder List of Friends and Acquaintances
17. Reminder List of Contacts for Newcomers
18. Office Leads List
19. Former Successful Job Club Members
20. Response to a Help Wanted Ad
21. Examples of Job Wanted Ads
22. Jobs Lead Log
23. Sample Statements: Why You Are Looking for a Job
24. Sample Statements: Special Qualities of a Contact Being Asked for Help
25. Sample Statements: Job Seeker's Skills
26. Sample Statements: How a Contact Can Help
27. Telephone Reminder List for Calling Friends
28. Job Leads You Have Heard About
29. Sample Letter: Requesting Assistance in Finding a Job
30. Sample Letter: Responding to a Help Wanted Ad
31. Sample Letter: Cover Letter to Accompany Résumé
32. Sample Letter: Contacting Employer Who Cannot Be Reached By Telephone
33. Request for Interview Checklist
34. Buddy's Telephone Checklist
35. Places to Go/Things to Do Schedule
36. Sample Completed Résumé
37. Hobbies and Interests
38. Job Skills Categories
39. Sample Application for Employment
40. Written Request for a Letter of Recommendation
41. Open Letter of Recommendation
42. Appropriate Responses to Typical Interview Questions
43. After Interview Checklist
44. Sample Letter to Newly Hired Members
45. Second Follow-Up Letter to Previous Job Club Members
46. Tips on How to Relocate

Source: N. H. Azrin and V. A. Besalel, *Job Club Counselor's Manual: A Behavioral Approach to Vocational Counseling* (Baltimore: University Park Press, 1980).

Unstructured Career Groups

In contrast with the specialized approach of structured career groups, a more process-oriented, ongoing intervention is found in unstructured career groups, whose participants discuss their career concerns in small groups of eight to ten individuals. While these groups may have some modest structure (e.g., completion of an interest inventory), the goal is to probe the emotional, interpersonal, and intrapsychic issues the members are facing in an effort to clarify their personal identity and decidedness. Typically, clients are initially identified as undecided, may receive a few sessions of individual counseling, and then are referred to an ongoing group for undecided clients. The group may replace individual career counseling or serve as an adjunct to such treatment. Unstructured career groups are likely to increase in popularity as the boundary between personal and career counseling erodes (Spokane, in press-a).

Since most of the published work on group career counseling refers to structured groups, process-oriented groups are still only vaguely described. Butcher (1982) noted that although most structured career groups resemble guidance more than group counseling, true group intervention should stimulate "a dynamic interaction between members with the objective of exploring internal experiences and feelings" (p. 202). Butcher argued that since clients differ in their readiness for career planning, a developmental, sequential process that moves from readiness to action will insure that more clients will make use of structured career content. The group process model, according to Butcher, encourages the development of the self-concept and provides a forum for testing a vocational identity before implementation is undertaken. This process underscores Herr's (in press) assertion that career counselors should increasingly incorporate *intrapsychic* dynamics in their interventions. Indeed, there is some evidence that career groups are more effective in reducing personal or intrapsychic indecision than specific career indecision (Cooper, 1986). Morrill and Forrest (1970) argued that counseling practice overemphasizes assisting the client who faces a specific decision or needs information at the expense of helping the client to acquire self-identity and direction through the ongoing process of career development.

Enhancing the Effectiveness of Group Career Interventions

The evidence on the effectiveness of group career interventions has been mixed. The reanalysis of several studies suggested that group interventions of six to seven sessions are about as effective as individual interventions of one to two sessions (Oliver & Spokane, 1988; Spokane & Oliver, 1983). Since most of this research has involved *structured* approaches, however, these data do not speak to the effectiveness of unstructured groups. Kivlighan et al.

(1981) offered one reason why groups may appear less effective than individual counseling when they found the the group participants' personality type (task oriented versus group oriented) played a major role in the outcome magnitude of a group treatment. When client personality was not considered, there were no significant outcome differences between group and individual treatments. When client personality type was considered, however, significant treatment differences emerged. Although these findings have not been convincingly replicated, they do suggest more differences between group and individual career counseling than is evident from current data.

Several steps might be taken to improve the rather unimpressive outcomes that are typical of group interventions. First and perhaps most importantly, some efforts must be made to control group dropout, which frequently runs as high as 50 percent. There are good explanations for this dropout. Repeated studies have shown that anxiety about career concerns is high. At some point in the process, groups that offer prepackaged material will encounter this anxiety, which, if unattended, will result in high dropout. Attempts should be made to personalize the group process for each participant. In addition, it now seems that nonsocial, shy, or withdrawn individuals will not fare well in group interventions. In these cases, care must be taken to supplement group with individual counseling, or to screen members for appropriateness before the group begins. Pre-intervention assessment may also be useful in identifying those individuals who will benefit most from a group intervention rather than indiscriminant assignment of all clients to groups in an effort to save professional time.

The group interventions summarized in this section are unfortunately naïve with respect to their ties to the contemporary research literature. Indeed, far too high a proportion of studies on group counseling generally and group career counseling specifically are still conducted at the level of treatment documentation, that is, comparing a group treatment with a traditional modality or one structured group treatment with another. Only a handful of studies attempt analysis of the complex interpersonal processes involved in group treatment (for a review of this work, see Bednar & Kaul, 1978). One good example of such an analytical study (Subich & Coursol, 1985) showed that precounseling expectations may affect the client's preference for and progress in group versus individual treatment.

WORKSHOPS AND SEMINARS

Workshops, or structured interventions lasting from one or two hours to a day or two, have been a mainstay of most career centers since the early 1970s. The Colorado Life Planning Workshop (Thomas, 1972) was a novel and creative approach to career assistance that served as the model for many of these efforts. This workshop consists of an intensive, systematic reevaluation of career goals that includes a career life line, some fantasy work, and a clever exercise called role stripping, in which the participant sheds current life roles one at a time and then reassumes only those desired. The life line, a developmental exercise aimed at long-term planning, has probably received more use in structured career interventions than any other (see Technique 6-1).

There have been several careful evaluations of the Colorado model career workshops. Mencke and Cochran (1974), for example, used a sophisticated Solomon four-group design to evaluate the effects of a five-hour Colorado Life Planning Workshop on college students. Randomly assigned workshop participants made post intervention choices that were significantly more congruent with their interests. They also reported more information seeking and a narrowing of the range of alternatives they were considering. Narrowing can be beneficial in some cases but detrimental in others. Generally, a narrowing of alternatives was associated with greater identity and focus, especially when the alternatives are more congruent with measured interests, as they were in Mencke and Cochran's study.

In a related controlled study, Knickerbocker and Davidshofer (1978) conducted a Life Planning Workshop of indeterminant length with college students and staff. Treatment subjects made moderate gains on feeling and reactivity and on a general measure of attitudinal outcomes (awareness that others had similar concerns, confidence in forming goals, personal problem-solving competence, and personal confidence) developed for the workshop. Apparently, the gains were not related to the verbal interaction during the workshop but rather to quite personal or intrapsychic factors. This conclusion is consistent with the experiential and self-actualizing atmosphere generated in workshops that follow the Colorado model.

Ganster and Lovell (1978) evaluated a five-session, fifteen-hour career seminar that included the Self-Directed Search, or SDS (Holland, 1985b), a discussion of Holland's theory, an examination of work values and socially supportive allies, exposure to the Dictionary of Occupational Titles, or DOT (U.S. Department of Labor, 1977), and information about careers. Treatment subjects showed significant gains on both the attitude and competency scales of the Career Maturity Inventory (Crites, 1978). Although treatment and control conditions were not randonly assigned in this study, its findings were consistent with those of others testing workshop interventions.

One advantage of the workshop approach is the possibility of tailoring the content for a specific focus. For example, O'Neil, Ohlde, Barke, Gelwick, and Garfield (1980) exposed sixty midwestern college women to a workshop designed to increase the number of nontraditional sex-role options they were considering. The workshop did produce some loosening of stereotypes, but dropouts, and there were a very large number, were not included in the outcomes. Similarly, Robbins, Mullison, Boggs, Riedesel, and

---

Technique 6-1

Career Lifeline

Purpose: The purpose of the Career Lifeline is to catalyze the client's thinking about the developmental nature of careers. The lifeline assists the client in reviewing critical decisions or events in his or her personal career and emphasizes the need for planning for the future.

Group size: The lifeline is most effective when participants are divided into small groups (generally no more than eight people) and have an opportunity to review their personal lifeline with other group members. It is advisable to have a facilitator available for the small groups, and the number of groups can be unlimited.

Time required: Approximately 45 minutes—10 minutes to draw the lifeline, 3-5 minutes per participant to present and discuss the personal lifeline, and 10 minutes to discuss the differences among individual lifelines in the constructs used to analyze the lifeline.

Materials: One sheet of paper, at least $8\frac{1}{2} \times 11$, a pencil, and masking tape.

Process: Each participant is asked to draw a personal career lifeline that represents the high and low points in his or her career and life thus far, including a projection into the future. The lifeline is then labeled with those significant events on or below the line that affected the career or that represent high and low points in the career.

Each participant then presents his or her lifeline to the small group, explaining both the events that affected the line, and the future as the participant sees it. Following these presentations, the facilitator notes differences among the participants in the nature of the factors affecting the lifeline (e.g., family influences, financial considerations, spousal considerations, etc.).

As a variation, the lifeline can be drawn using best and worst decisions to mark the highs and lows. As a second variation, soft metal wire can also be used to construct the line, and the participant simply explains the bends to the group.

Jacobson (1985), studying individuals who registered for but did not attend a career workshop, found that 45 percent had either forgotten or felt discouraged, 38 percent reported environmental problems such as scheduling or transportation, and 17 percent said they had already met personal goals. Those who had forgotten or were discouraged reported lower self-esteem and fewer information-seeking behaviors than participants, whereas those who had met their goals reported substantially better beginning scores on a variety of measures than attenders. This study suggested that some of the high rates of dropout in career workshops may be due to low self-esteem, a finding supported by Zager (1982). Paricipants should therefore be contacted more vigorously to encourage their attendance. On the other hand, some dropouts may have made a reasoned decision not to attend, improved their career situation on their own, or been inappropriate participants from the start. It seems clear, however, that workshops and structured groups will have high dropout rates throughout their course, and that we know relatively little about this problem and even less about how to deal with it.

Finally, comparing three, two-hour workshop sessions in which interpersonal interaction was minimal with a workshop of identical length in which group process and self-disclosure were encouraged, Robbins and Tucker (1986) found that participants with unstable goals benefited more from the interactional than the noninteractional workshop, as shown by higher posttest career maturity and information seeking. This supports Butcher's (1982) argument that clients with low readiness may benefit from more process-oriented interventions, and strengthens Fretz's (1981) and Kivlighan et al.'s (1981) assertion of the importance of personality and precounseling diagnosis in the differential outcome of group career interventions. Generally, most participants preferred the interactional workshops, which, as in many such treatments, may simply reflect the fact that artificially manipulated treatments are rarely convincing to our increasingly sophisticated research subjects.

INSTRUCTIONALLY BASED CAREER INTERVENTIONS

Any discussion of instructionally based career intervention strategies must examine the prolific work of the U.S. Office of Career Education, its director, Kenneth Hoyt, and its philosophical adviser, Sidney Marland (Marland, 1974). The Education Amendments of 1974 established the office and provided more than $30 million to fund its first three years of operation (U.S. Office of Career Education, 1978). Under the influence of Donald Super, David Tiedeman, and Eli Ginzberg, the practical application of developmental career theories because the principal focus of the office. Instructional curricular intervention was the logical extension of this developmental approach to career selection (Healy, 1982). As director, Hoyt believed it was his job to infuse career skills into the general curriculum of American schools. In one of the clearest statements of these efforts, Hoyt (1977) outlined what was to become a dramatic shift in the way career interventions were conceptualized and delivered. His influence is still felt, even though the virtual dismantling of the Office of Career Education brought an abrupt end to many of these efforts.

Hoyt (1977) argued for a change "FROM an assumption that . . . a general education alone is the best preparation for work TO an assumption that ... both general education and a set of specific marketable vocational skills are increasingly necessary for entry into the world of paid employment" (p. 1). He also popularized the idea that the career education effort must be supported by the business and industrial community. The popular career classes now offered in community and junior colleges, universities, and some school systems are the direct outgrowth of this movement.

In their review of the research studies on career education interventions, Baker and Popowicz (1983) used meta-analysis, or the statistical reanalysis of data from eighteen empirical studies, to evaluate the effectiveness of proactive career intervention at the K–12 level. Although no attempt was made to separate strategies of intervention (e.g., curricular infusion), the results did suggest moderate effects (Effect Size [ES] = .50) for K–12 interventions generally. The lack of high-quality empirical studies testing career education outcomes was troublesome for Hoyt as well as for the field. There were so few studies because the technical problems of evaluating the effects of the career curriculum as compared to the effects of the general education curriculum were many and difficult to resolve. Brickell (1976) chronicled the frustrations of the Appalachian Educational Laboratory (AEL) in trying to develop measures to tap the outcomes of classroom interventions, which were not sensitive to traditional measures derived from developmental theory. Among the curricular studies investigated by Baker and Popowicz, only a handful (three or four reflected the original intent expressed by Hoyt (1977).

From Career Education to Classroom Instruction

Because curricular infusion effects were so difficult to separate from general educational outcomes, the question of what constituted a reasonable outcome in such interventions was ambiguous. An incisive review (Osipow, 1982) and an entire volume (Krumboltz & Hamel, 1982) have recently been devoted to clarifying the outcome problem. Although infusion is still done in many classrooms, usually in the form of speakers, or a career unit or day, most instructional interventions now take the form of freestanding, credit-bearing career classes lasting a semester or more. These programs are especially popular in community and junior colleges and in four-year colleges and universities. Enough evidence has now accumulated to insure the effectiveness of such direct classroom instructions; in fact reviews (Oliver & Spokane, 1988; Spokane & Oliver, 1983) have found them to be by far the most effective of the interventions surveyed. Classroom interventions were also the most time intensive, however, requiring thirteen to fifteen weeks to complete.

Of the seven classroom intervention outcome studies reviewed by Oliver and Spokane (1988), Barker's (1979; 1981) evaluation of the AEL's Career Planning and Decision-Making Course is particularly noteworthy. This complete and standardized instructional package has six course goals: applying decision-making concepts, forming an occupational preference, integrating self and work knowledge, forming goals and plans, implementing plans, and understanding the continual career development process (Barker, 1981). The program has a detailed professional manual with instructional guides. An overview chart shows which sessions are devoted each goal (see Table 6-2).

Barker field-tested fifteen experimental and fifteen control classes, using the Assessment of Career Decision Making, or using the ACDM (Harren, 1978), as the prepost measure of decisional status. Average gains for subjects who had received the AEL course were very large across the semester. Both students and their instructors reported high levels of satisfaction with the course. Earlier, however, Carey and Weber (1979) had studied the effect of CPDMC in a single school system. They found no evidence of its effectiveness, and argued that the outcome measures employed with the course had been too soft. Yet although the evidence has been mixed, Barker's evaluation stands as a reasonable test with an established and relevant outcome measure.

Rayman, Bernard, Holland, and Barnett (1983) evaluated twenty-two sections of an eleven-week career decision-making course using the Vocational Identity Scale, or VI (Holland, Daiger, & Power, 1980a). Large gains in identity were found overall, but the impact of the course varied considerably across sections. Johnson et al. (1981) also found prepost gains by using the VI. Participants in a semester-long career course rated talking to employed people about careers, taking the SDS, and using the *Occupational*

Table 6-2   Overview of the AEL's Career Planning and Decision-Making Course

SUBJECT	ACTIVITIES	TIME
Introduction	Discussion	½ class period
Goal identification	Career goals Goal focus chart	1 class period
Career information	Self-information Occupational information Organizing occupational information Using the center information system	2½ class periods
Career exploration	Expressed interest Work activities Work situations School subjects Aptitudes Other factors Occupational exploration	14½ class periods
Summary	Discussion Summary chart	1 class period

Source: Career Information System: A.E.L. career decision-making program. Charleston, W.V.: Appalachian Educational Laboratory, 1979, p. 73. Reprinted by permission.

Outlook Handbook (U.S. Department of Labor, 1989) as the most helpful components of the class.

Other studies have also found dramatic gains for such courses using outcomes such as career maturity (Babcock & Kaufman, 1976; Carey & Weber, 1979; C. W. Smith, 1981) and locus of control (Bartsch & Hackett, 1979). Babcock and Kaufman compared walk-in counselees, no-treatment controls, and participants in a seven-week, fourteen-hour process-oriented intervention that emphasized values clarification. Very sizeable outcomes were found when class participants were compared with controls on self-knowledge and planfulness. Bartsch and Hackett evaluated a two-credit intensive course involving 1,500 hours of class contact. Self-direction and personal responsibility for choice were emphasized in the course, and locus of control was an outcome measure. Participants became significantly more internal in their locus of control, spent more time thinking about their career choices, and could articulate their choices more clearly. The class intervention studied by C. W. Smith consisted of twenty one-hour sessions that involved either a highly structured didactic program of twenty steps or an individualized workbook approach that allowed for great individual flexibility. Career maturity was enhanced in both treatment groups and deteriorated in the control group. Compared to a control condition, the highly structured approach was significantly more effective, whereas the less-structured, more-individualized approach was less effective.

More recently, Lent, Larkin, and Hasegawa (1986) evaluated a ten-week career course using the Career Decision Scale, or CDS (Osipow, Carney, Winer, Yanico, & Koschier 1976), a measure of self-knowledge, and a measure of information seeking. The average gains were comparable to or larger (ES = 1.33–2.85) than those found previously. Remer, O'Neill and Gohs (1984) and Varvil-Weld and Fretz (1984) used multiple outcome measures and sophisticated designs with similarly positive findings. Remer et al. (1984) designed a course to build skills among clients that would help them to overcome barriers to the implementation of their choices. This long, credit-bearing course (2.5 hours per week for sixteen weeks) was analyzed using a sophisticated design and multiple outcome measures, as suggested by Oliver (1979). The only weaknesses in the analysis were the failure to use random assignment and the use of unreliable gain scores. Nonetheless, large gains were found on decidedness, identity, and decisional style; dropout was minimal.

At times, however, the use of multiple outcome measures can be carried too far. Authors such as Remer et al. (1984), for example, should justify the use of each measure and limit the inclusion of gratuitous measures, which are employed simply so the researchers can say that multiple measures were used. In addition, the measures should tap different domains of client reaction (e.g., cognitive, behavioral, and emotional), and the effects of the interventions on these domains should be analyzed and related to theory. For example, Varvil-Weld and Fretz (1984) used multiple measures to study the outcomes of a ten-week, twenty-session career course. The measures were selected to evaluate appropriateness of choice, but included both unintrusive and behavioral measures of appropriateness exploration and satisfaction. Because the effects of career courses have been replicated sufficiently, their benefits to clients, are no longer questioned. That these classroom interventions are more intensive and therefore more costly is also clear. Future analytic studies may clarify the processes by which these courses work their uniformly helpful outcomes, but it may be that the combination of gain factors discussed in Chapter 3 is simply greater in these treatments than in most others.

BRIEF ALTERNATIVE CAREER INTERVENTIONS

Computer-Assisted Career Interventions

Many clients expect computer assistance to be a routine component in a career intervention. A special issue of the *Counseling Psychologist*, with guest editors Roger Myers and Peter Cairo (1983), sheds much light on the use of the computer in counseling. Whereas interest inventories once reigned alone, computers now provide technical structure and information comparable or superior to that offered by the inventories. For example, Bowlsbey (1983) proposed a model of career decision making whose core is the collection of data about occupations. Although several intervention strategies (e.g., courses, groups, printed self-help materials, telephone inquiries and one-to-one counseling) may be useful in the search for and evaluation of such data, the computer is the ideal data file—complete, accurate, and with easily retrieved information, a wide array of complexity, and a capacity for localization. Bowlsbey argued that in its brief history, computer intervention has witnessed an "astounding progression" in size, cost, and independence from the frustrating time-sharing problems of hardware. Whereas once only large school districts could afford computer-assisted career guidance systems, they can now be installed in "community counseling agencies, libraries, shopping malls, business and industry, prisons and homes" (Bowlsbey, 1983, p. 13).

The potential for computer intervention, when properly administered, is nearly limitless. For example, videodisk technology promises to be able to make more than one hundred thousand pictorial representations of jobs from computer data (Bowlsbey, 1983). Artificial intelligence applications will soon show to which aspects of information the client attends, which aspects are most influential, and the nature and veracity of the client's information and preferences about careers. We will soon be able to study and remediate the client's cognitive processes about career preference and choice in ways never before possible. However, for the moment our fascination with the technical capabilities of these machines may have impeded our ability to use and evaluate them properly (Cairo, 1983).

In one of the first carefully controlled studies of computer interventions, Melhus, Hershenson, and Vermillion (1973) compared a computer-assisted intervention and individual counseling with high- and low counseling-readiness clients; readiness was ascertained by a measure of educational development. Low-readiness students who saw a counselor showed more beneficial changes in occupational plans than those in the high-readiness group who saw a counselor. Melhus et al. concluded that since readiness was a factor in the differential effectiveness of career treatments, the more costly dyadic counseling might be reserved for more serious cases. R. A. Myers, Lindeman, Thompson, and Patrick (1975) compared the effects of a computer-based occupational exploration system on vocational maturity. In twelve experimental schools, 376 male and 415 female tenth-graders used the system, and were compared with a matched control group of 1,453 male and female tenth-graders. Three subscales (planning orientation, resources for exploration, and information and decision making) of the Career Development Inventory (Thompson, Lindeman, Super, Jordaan, & Myers, 1984) were the outcome measures. The study revealed small but significant gains in career maturity for the treated subjects; the longer the time spent with the computer, the higher the gains. Although this study used an early version of computer software and hardware, and only a single outcome measure, it provided the first hard (i.e., controlled) evidence of the effects of computer-assisted career interventions.

Pilato and Myers (1975) used computer-generated interest inventory feedback about the accuracy of self-knowledge, and found that the combination of a classification scheme and computer-generated feedback had a modest effect on the appropriateness of field choices. Likewise, Maola and Kane (1976) compared an hour-per-week computer-based occupational information system with a similar counselor-based system. Both the systems were significantly superior to a no-treatment control, but the effects of the computer system were twice as large. Cochran, Hoffman, Strand, and Warren (1977) evaluated a three-hour interaction with the black-and-white early edition of SIGI, a computerized career guidance package. Treatment subjects showed modest gains in vocational decision making and locus of control. Pyle and Stripling (1977) also used SIGI in a comparison with group counseling. Although they used no control group and only a self-report evaluation of the computer treatment, Pyle and Stripling showed, as others have, that computer-assisted interventions are generally enjoyable and informative for most users. More recently, Pinder and Fitzgerald (1984) compared a computer program with a no-treatment control condition, and also found that the computer treatment resulted in significant gains in career decision status. The use of parallel materials in both the treatment and control groups in this study is an advance over earlier computer studies, in which the hardware and software were fairly crude, and care was not taken to equate the time in treatment or the "fascination quotient" of the presentation medium, which gave the edge to the computer system.

More definitive studies of computer-assisted interventions will reveal how computers can be most effectively mixed with other strategies, and when a computer intervention alone is sufficient. The use of multiple measures with demonstrated validity will also improve these studies. Designs pitting the computer against the counselor or the SDS are reminiscent of the fable of John Henry and the steam engine: Both did the job, but the steam engine broke, and John Henry died. Anyone contemplating beginning a new computer study would first do well to read Rounds and Tinsley's (1984) description of advanced designs. Simple prepost designs comparing a single computer-assisted strategy against a no-treatment control group will advance knowledge very little, nor will studies that compare multiple interventions but employ only a single or a homemade outcome measure.

Three recent studies, which unfortunately have not made their way through traditional journal and review outlets, approximate the comprehensive evaluation designs necessary to increase our knowledge about the effectiveness of computer-assisted career interventions.

One carefully controlled outcome study (Garis & Harris-Bowlsbey, 1984) randomly assigned college students to either DISCOVER alone (an average of four modules), dyadic counseling alone (an average of 1.8 sessions), or a combination of DISCOVER and dyadic counseling (an average of 4½ hour modules and 2.3 sessions), and compared these three interventions to a wait-list control condition. Two measures designed for use with DISCOVER, a behavioral log, and the Career Development Inventory (CDI) (Super et al., 1981) were employed as outcome measures. Analysis of covariance using pretest scores as covariates revealed significant differences among all three groups (DISCOVER alone, counseling alone, DISCOVER plus counseling) on a survey designed for use with DISCOVER, confidence and progress in planning, analysis of behavioral log reports of library use and career resource contacts, the career planning, and career exploration scales of the CDI; but oddly, not on the work information or knowledge of preferred occupation scales. Indeed, the treated groups seemed somewhat worse following treatment on the knowledge of preferred occupation subscale. The findings from this study were generally positive, though the one instrument of known validity and reliability produced mixed outcomes. Garis and Harris-Bowlsbey (1984) produced a good example of a brief intervention outcome study which confirms that computer assisted interventions are effective on a stand alone basis or in combination with other career interventions. More intensive interventions of longer duration and greater frequency would probably demonstrate more consistently beneficial outcomes, but it should come as no surprise that three interventions of roughly equal duration should produce comparable findings. We must now study ways to improve the potency of these treatments and to employ blocking variables as Kivlighan et al. (1981) did in studies of group interventions. It is possible that such an attribute-treatment-interaction study using computer interventions would have produced differential effects for one treatment over another. An unpublished study by Marin (1984) used random assignment, and compared a computer-only treatment, a computer-plus-counselor treatment, and a deferred treatment control. Marin, who employed the CDS and the Assessment of Career Decision Making, or ACDM (Harren, 1980), as outcome measures, found that the computer-plus-counselor intervention was significantly more effective than the computer alone, and that both were more effective than the control. No blocking or attribute-treatment interactions were found for the ACDM decisional styles.

A second study, by Shahnasarian and Peterson (1986), employed multiple outcome measures and a cognitive structuring intervention along with DISCOVER. Unfortunately, this otherwise clever study did not include a no-treatment control group, and its failure to find significant group differences is probably due to the lack of a no-treatment anchor for the analysis of variance.

Although the future of computer-assisted career interventions holds great promise, until now their applications have been crude, and the outcome data from controlled studies suggest that their effects are modest (ES = .50–.60 [Oliver & Spokane, 1988]). The present generation of computer-assisted interventions is approaching sufficiency as stand-alone treatments, but their modest effects are sometimes offset by the expense of the hardware and software and the need for attentive counselor support during the process. For the present, they should be considered to be valuable adjuncts to career intervention, which may become increasingly complete with advances in software and reductions in cost. An implementation model by Sampson, Shahnasarian, and Maddox (1984) has described the four stages in the successful implementation of a computer guidance systems for adults: planning, staff training, trial, and operation-evaluation-refinement (see Table 6-3).

The Kellog Foundation has funded several projects on computer applications, including the work by James Sampson and Robert Reardon at Florida State University, and by Cynthia Johnson at Columbia University. The Clearinghouse for Computer-Assisted Guidance Systems at Florida State is an active and effective source of information, programs, and research on computer career interventions. In particular, the bibliographies, abstracts, and technical reports published by the center are an invaluable resource for counselors. The major career intervention software systems in use today are summarized below. Much of this material is drawn from an excellent new guide to counseling software edited by Walz and Bleuer (1989) that reviews software in three areas: (1) career selection and job readiness, (2) résumé writing, and (3) job search (Sampson, 1989); this excellent

Table 6-3   Implementation Model for Computer Guidance Systems for Adults

Planning Phase

Selection of computer applications
1. Evaluation of existing client needs
2. Evaluation of the effectiveness of present services in meeting client needs
3. Identification of unmet needs
4. Identification of computer software that may assist in meeting client needs
5. Evaluation of computer software in terms of:
   a. Potential to assist in meeting client needs
   b. Congruence with existing program goals
6. Selection of computer software
7. Selection of computer hardware
8. Assessment of potential need for external consultants

Program development in counseling and human development

9. Integration of computer applications with existing services (including individual, group, and curricular approaches)
10. Delineation of staff roles in terms of
    a. Counselor intervention strategies
    b. Management of computer application
    c. Clerical support
11. Development of an evaluation strategy
12. Identification of data needed for a program evaluation
13. Delineation of operating procedures
    a. Scheduling counselor and computer appointments
    b. Maintaining confidentiality of all client data
    c. Collecting data related to program evaluation
    d. Maintaining computer hardware
14. Selecting a location for the computer hardware that
    a. Maximizes security
    b. Minimizes environmental problems related to dust, temperature, humidity, and visual and auditory distractions
15. Development of a strategy for institutional and public relations

Staff Training Phase

Development of a strategy for staff training that includes
1. Review of program and computer application needs
2. Presentation of an overview of the application
3. Orientation to computer hardware and software
4. Completion of the application by each staff member
5. Review of all staff roles
6. Review of operational procedures
7. Review of case studies for purpose of integration

Source: J. P. Sampson, Jr., M. Shahnasarian, and E. N. Maddox, *Implementing Computer-Assisted Career Guidance and Other Computer Applications for the Adult Learner* (Ann Arbor: ERIC/CAPS, 1984), p. 36. Reprinted with permission of the Journal of Counseling and Development.

resource also reviews testing software. Bridges's (1989) brief but thorough discussion of the trends in software for career counseling in the same volume suggests that as a group these software programs have some good qualities, such as the ability to move freely among modules in a package, handy printouts, advance organizers to make the material more easily understood and absorbed, and attractive graphics and design. Among their weak points Bridges mentioned some redundancy in assessment items, technical problems, and programs that were ineffective or simply not worth the effort required to complete them. Although there are far too many computer systems on the market to mention here, a few of the better and more comprehensive examples will be described:

DISCOVER.   DISCOVER (American College Testing Program, 1987), which comes in three versions (for college students and adults, for high school students, and for junior high school students, uses American College Testing's World-of-Work Map (see Figure 5-4) and the UNIACT inventory (ACT, 1988) (see Chapter 5) to provide information about hundreds of occupations and thousands of colleges and universities. This classic system, developed by JoAnn Harris Bowlsbey, the "dean" of computer-assisted career systems, is one of the most comprehensive and widely available examples available. It is also the one with the most evaluation and research data.

SIGI Plus.   This system, developed by Martin Katz and marketed by the Educational Testing Service, uses values as the principal focus of the job selection. It has eight sections that allow an individual to create a personalized list of occupational choices and receive information about those jobs. The entire program takes about three hours to complete (Walz & Bleuer, 1989).

Career Point.   A relatively new entry designed for use in business and industry, Career Point (Conceptual Systems Inc., 1989) combines the SDS, the Work Environment Scale (Moos, 1986), and the Myers-Briggs Type Indicator (I. B. Myers & McCaulley, 1985) with excellent graphics and the potential to customize all of the jobs in a work organization. Although there are no outcome studies of Career Point, the SDS feature is an excellent addition to a career software package. A recent professional manual describes the content of Career Point and Figure 6-1 is a model of the Career Point.

Other Brief Alternative Career Interventions

The number and variety of brief alternative noncomputer-assisted career interventions is limited only by the professional's imagination. They can range from a brightly colored sticker placed on student exams, to a pamphlet mailed to first-year college students discussing services at a career center, to a careful reading of Bolles's classic *What Color Is Your Parachute?* (1988). Two others are outlined below.

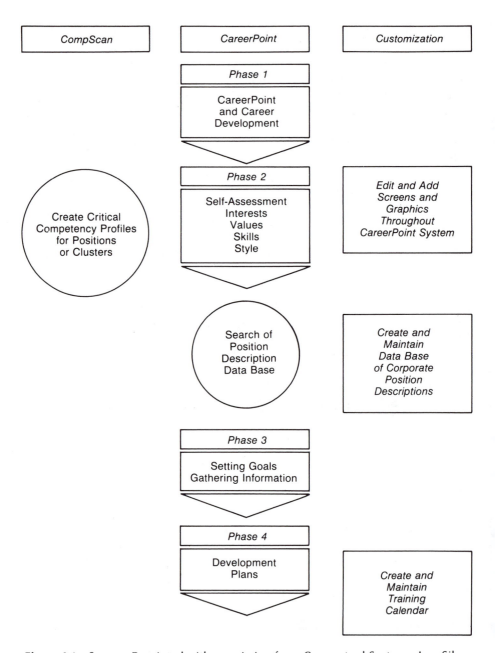

Figure 6-1 Source: Reprinted with permission from Conceptual Systems, Inc, Silver Spring, MD.

The Work Station.   The typical career center in business, industry, and universities is now organized into work stations, after an innovative model designed by Zandy Leibowitz as director of the career development center at Goddard Space Flight Center. The work station has become very popular among professionals and clients alike, and is an easy way to organize a complete set of counselor-free career interventions. In addition to work stations, most centers also contain lending libraries of readings, computer programs, and photocopies of articles of interest to the population served. A work station known as Assessing My Environment, which was developed for the Career Development Center at the U.S. Department of Labor (DOL) using Leibowitz's model, is depicted in Table 6-4. Other work stations at this DOL

Table 6-4   Work Station B: Assessing My Environment

Box 1:	Introduction to the station
	What's included in this station?
	How do I use this station?
Box 2:	Summary work sheet
Box 3:	DOL history
	Mandate information
	Organizational charts
Box 4:	Work-force profiles
Box 5:	DOL positions/titles listed by Holland code or occupational interest
	Identify act positions
	Specify x118 series
	Outside positions
	x118 for DOL MAP jobs
	CP
	Resource sheet
Box 6:	Career mobility programs
	Upward mobility
	Mentor
	Weld
	College advanced placement
	Resource sheet
Box 7:	Training opportunities and alternatives
	CJT
	Education
	CALC
	Non-credit courses
	DOL Academy
	List of local schools and colleges and phone numbers
	Resource sheet
Box 8:	Gathering career information
	Informational interviewing
	Summary sheet
	Sources of career information
	Resource sheet

Source: U.S. Department of Labor, Career Development Center, 1988.

center included Self-Assessment, Taking Action, and one for the Career Point computer program.

The activities in the work stations are designed to be self-guiding with periodic assistance or supervision from a counselor. Typically, the SDS is a part of the self-assessment station, and the Occupational Stress Inventory, or OSI (Osipow & Spokane, 1987) is increasingly used to assess levels of stress, strain, and coping. These work stations are very popular interventions that, in combination with briefings and outreach to management and employees, draw potential clients into a career center who subsequently request additional services.

Self-Help Books.   There are dozens of self-help books aimed at career concerns, and virtually all contain essential elements of career intervention such as the following:

1. Self-assessment, usually of interests and skills derived from life experiences
2. Job-finding assistance, including résumé writing and interview skills
3. Action planning, including sections on establishing short-term and long-term goals and overcoming barriers to implementation.

Many of these self-help books are aimed at a market successfully tapped by Bolles (1988), but with added sophistication and detail (Birnbach, 1988; Borchard, Kelly, & Weaver, 1988; Carney & Wells, 1987; Figler, 1979; Kennedy & Larramore, 1988; Lock, 1988; Otto, 1984; Shertzer, 1981). The recent poll completed by the National Career Development Association (1988) suggests the widespread public need for career assistance. These user-friendly, "over-the-counter" career interventions thus address an important societal need that could not possibly be met through traditional means.

Bolles's classic self-help book, which is updated annually, is skill-based and thorough, and has an excellent section on how to find additional professional help if needed. Shertzer's (1981) book contains a comprehensive blend of didactic material and worksheets for college students. Borchard et al.'s (1988) work, now in its fourth edition, offers an assessment of skills, thinking styles, and interests based upon Holland's (1985b) system. This volume emerged from a very successful instructional intervention at Prince Georges Community College in suburban Maryland, where Borchard is director of career development. Likewise, Carney and Wells's (1987) self-help book, probably the most seasoned and thorough of the lot, was the product of years of career interventions at the counseling center at Ohio State University. Their publication contains a variant of the SDS, and a college majors finder with a clear and easy-to-use format. An unusual new entry by Birnbach (1988) reviews the inside details of dozens of companies. Otto's (1984) excellent resource for parents is a useful way to conceptualize the process of helping a child to implement a college or career search.

Some Cautions Concerning Brief
Alternative Interventions

The broadening of the concept of career counseling to include counselor-free interventions produced a striking change in the way career services were delivered. Lunneborg (1983) attributed this shift toward self-help to the prohibitive cost of one-on-one counseling, client preferences for an array of services, and the diversion of counselor time to personal social concerns. Lunneborg noted that individual career counseling is not so much "out-of-date" as it is "out of the question" (p. 52). The SDS advanced this self-assistance movement substantially during the 1970s. At one time it was believed that self-help devices were as effective as counselors, but more recent evidence suggests that they are shorter than other approaches, less expensive, and less potent (Oliver & Spokane, 1988; Spokane & Oliver, 1983). Their modest outcomes, however, are reasonable considering the minimal investment required of the counselor and the client. Spokane (in press-b) reviewed the studies of self-guided interventions, and concluded that self-assistance was most effective with clients who are high in identity and low in indecision, or in other words, those least in need of counseling. In addition, substantial research suggests that career intervention with self-guided inventories results in the client acquiring one additional option that would not otherwise be considered. Finally, it appears that more task-oriented individuals will benefit most from these self-help procedures, presumably because they will persist until they complete the intervention. Mahalik and Kivlighan (1988), for example, found that those classified as realistic according to the Holland code were able to reduce their depression more in response to a self-help intervention than were those classified as enterprising, who were more likely to drop out of treatment. Mahalik and Kivlighan suggested that the realistic type's preference for objects and things (i.e., their orientation) is more compatible with a self-help intervention than with one that requires intensive interactions with a counselor or group.

Rosen (1987), however, has warned of the dangers in the unrestrained use of self-assistance. Rosen noted that it was George Miller (1969) who, in an American Psychological Association (APA) presidential address, urged that psychology be "given away" to the public. Miller further urged psychologists to acknowledge their social responsibility "to learn how to help people help themselves" (Rosen, 1987, p. 46). Although this is a noble goal that Rosen and an APA task force saw as very beneficial, it has not been realized. Rosen cautioned that the "do-it-yourself" movement in psychology has become a commercial enterprise in which psychologists are more interested in marketing products and profits than in meeting societal needs or insuring the quality of the services they deliver. He observed that rather than "giving psychology away," as Miller had suggested, we were simply "finding new ways to sell it." Rosen noted that therapist-designed treatments may not be applied correctly when self-administered, and that some self-help efforts may actually make matters worse. He also argued that wholesale misdiagnosis may be taking place, which results in the indiscriminant use of self-help interventions, especially when exaggerated claims are made for their effectiveness. Rosen urged the establishment of strict professional standards for self-help interventions, including the insistence upon evidence to support any claims of effectiveness; an APA task force has made recommendations for such standards. Rosen's caveats are well taken, and the future of the self-assistance movement in career development may depend on the profession's ability to address some of the concerns he has raised.

Career intervention is one of the most appropriate areas for the use of self-help psychology. Fortunately, no negative outcomes have been found in research studies of career self-assistance, but little is known about misdiagnoses or outcomes when the interventions are truly used without counselor observation or follow-through. The formulation of guidelines for the content of career self-help materials would be very useful. Such standards should include: (1) a direct link to a valid occupational classification system, (2) referral information for those needing additional assistance, (3) a cognitive framework for utilizing the information provided, and (4) accurate statements about the benefits and limits of the intervention derived from controlled trials or outcome evaluations. The best current materials contain most of the elements that such standards would require.

There is very little question that alternatives to individual intervention (groups, workshops, classes, and self-help) are the fastest growing segment of career counseling. These new interventions show repeated evidence of beneficial outcomes, and should become even more potent as research continues.

SUMMARY

A wide array of brief career interventions that do not require a dyadic interaction between a counselor and a single client, yet are supported by consistent outcome evidence, are now available. The general client process across the course of these interventions seems similar to that involved in dyadic, individual career counseling. Group interventions can be structured or unstructured, but suffer from unusually high dropout rates. Workshops and seminars are one-shot, time-limited strategies that are more condensed and time intensive than groups. Career education has given way to very successful classroom interventions of a semester or more that have an instructional underpinning in addition to the traditional therapeutic base underlying dyadic career counseling. Computer interventions are increasing in sophistication, but convincing outcome evidence has yet to be generated. Self-guided career interventions seem to be growing in popularity, even though they are less powerful than other interventions.

7

Prevention and Consultation in Career Practice

As the field of vocational psychology and career development matures, the demand for indirect services such as prevention and consultation appears to be increasing, and to be spreading to a wider adult audience beyond the student populations typically served. The skills and background required to implement these consultative interventions are often largely the same as those that are effective in individual counseling, although at times they are different from or even diametrically opposed to those required in one-on-one interventions. Thus while certain counselors are skilled or comfortable in both domains, considerable specialization has occurred, with some preferring therapeutic interventions and others favoring consultative modes.

PREVENTION IN CAREER PRACTICE

The field of preventive psychology presumes that many predictable psychological disorders can be averted by "developing interventions designed to short-circuit negative psychological sequelae for those who have experienced risk-augmenting life situations or stressful life events" (Cowen, 1984, p. 485). Psychologists began to define prevention as one of their professional goals when the demand for psychological services increased and the negative effects of mental disorders became clearer. Rather than treat each individual with a full-blown disorder (tertiary treatment), prevention psychologists insist that many disorders can be entirely prevented (primary prevention) or at least minimized by early identification and intervention (secondary prevention) (Klein & Goldston, 1976). Primary prevention involves the following steps: (1) "reducing new instances of the disorder"; (2) "reducing irritants to dysfunction before they exact their toll"; and (3) "building psychological health" (Cowen, 1978a, p. 8). G. Caplan (1964) has written that

> primary prevention ... involves lowering the rate of new cases of mental disorder in a population over a certain period by counteracting harmful circumstances before they have had a chance to produce illness. It does not seek to prevent a specific person from becoming sick. Instead it seeks to reduce the risk for a whole population so that, although some may become ill, their numbers will be reduced" (p. 26).

The creativity and variety of applications of preventive psychology to mental health problems are impressive (Murphy & Frank, 1979). Cowen (1982), for example, compared findings from studies of psychological assistance given by hairdressers, divorce lawyers, industrial supervisors, and bartenders, and found that these informal helpers handled a variety of serious psychological concerns and felt that they did a good job doing so.

Promoting Career Competence

One emphasis in the prevention literature is on the promotion of healthy behaviors that, although not designed to prevent any specific psychological disorder, might ward off problems among large segments of the population. Albee's (1982) definition of primary prevention as "the reduction of unnecessary stress, including powerlessness, and the enhancement of social competence, self-esteem and support networks" (p. 1043) highlights the role of the promotion of competence in reducing psychopathology. More to the point, Albee argued that although the loss of one's job is stressful, even the threat of losing one's job is equally stressful. Competence-building approaches to social and community intervention typically teach a specific set of personal and/or social skills, and relate the acquisition of those skills to important mental health outcomes (Gesten & Jason, 1987). To qualify as a preventive intervention, a competence-building strategy must show that the development of a specific skill will lower the levels of a subsequent disorder in at-risk populations. Bloom (1977) wrote that competency building is the most compelling construct for integrating mental health and community interventions. This emphasis on competence has recently been carefully extended to career problems (Herr, in press; Herr & Cramer, 1988).

Applying Prevention to Career Problems

Suppose that 10 percent of the 30,000 employees in a large company or students in a major university decided to pursue career assistance in one year. Could any career center accommodate 3,000 clients with traditional individual, group, or workshop interventions? If each client required the average 3.74 individual sessions assistance with a trained counselor (Oliver & Spokane, 1988), over 9,000 sessions would be required. These figures probably underestimate the service delivery problem in the field of career development. A recent poll commissioned by the National Career Development Association (NCDA, 1988) revealed that 9.7 percent of adults, or nearly 11 million individuals, needed assistance with job selection and changing in the year surveyed. These numbers are consistent with previous studies that revealed that career assistance is usually the most highly subscribed need in surveys conducted in higher education settings. The NCDA poll further suggests that the problem is substantially worse among noncollege and minority populations.

Obviously, we can no longer meet the need for career services with traditional one-on-one and group interventions alone, or even with consultation approaches that attempt to treat groups. Huebner and Corazzini (1984) have noted that counseling psychologists have slowly but steadily moved toward preventive intervention among the various alternatives that are being pursued. The case can be made that the more convincing demonstration of cure or mastery is made by preventing rather than treating a specific disorder (Long, 1986).

A Philosophy of Career Development Versus a Model for Preventing Career Accidents. Developmental theories of careers typically describe how careers evolve and change over longer time spans (Herr & Cramer, 1988), and evoke specific career-related constructs (e.g., career maturity) to account for successful progression through desired stages.

In contrast, primary prevention has as its goal the prevention of the development of a specific disorder through more general psychological means. Whereas developmental career intervention would provide a curriculum to ensure completion of the developmental tasks of a given stage (Healy, 1982), a preventive intervention might identify the devastating effects of unemployment on self-esteem and promote early coping skills in the face of adversity.

Figure 7-1 is a model of the disorders commonly presented by clients who seek career assistance and preventive strategies for approaching these disorders. The disorders are considered to be accidental; some people will be more inclined toward accidents than others, yet random events may also produce accidents. Using logic similar to that cleverly employed by L. S. Gottfredson (1986), it is possible to use career development and counseling studies to estimate the incidence rates of several of these disorders. Whereas Gottfredson argued that membership in certain minority groups generally increased problems of career choice, the model estimates population incidence rates of more specific career disorders as the bases of the design and evaluation of primary prevention efforts designed to lessen the probability and severity of those disorders. Of course, as Gottfredson has carefully documented, membership in a minority group would increase the probability of many of these disorders.

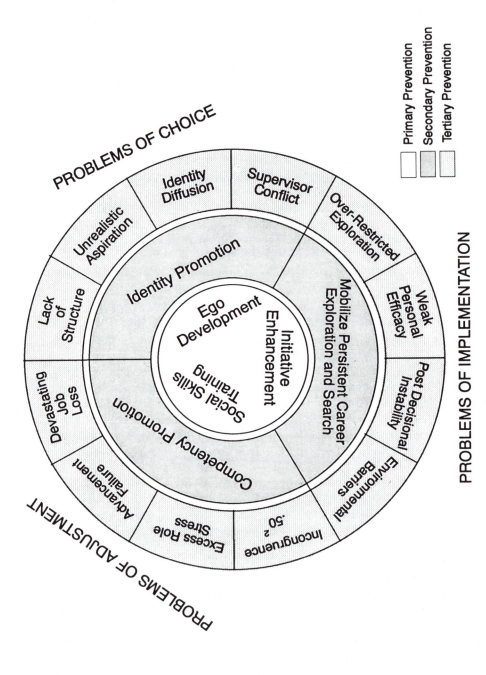

Figure 7-1 A Model of Career Accident Prevention.

174

As an example of the more specific epidemiology approach required to conduct truly preventive studies, it is possible to consult studies of person-environment fit (Spokane, 1985) that suggest that 50 percent of respondents will have incongruent first-letter person and environment Holland codes (.50 on Figure 7-1). Figure 7-1 depicts this incongruence as a specific disorder that has detrimental consequences for career adjustment and well-being (Assouline & Meir, 1987; Spokane, 1985). The ring of secondary strategies on Figure 7-1 indicates that incongruence might be prevented by general training in competently identifying one's interests and correctly classifying the nature of work environments. The innermost ring of the figure shows that some combination of ego development, social skills training, and initiative enhancement could promote competent adjustment and increase the likelihood of congruence.

In Figure 7-1, the outer ring of general problems—of choice, implementation, and adjustment—resembles those described in the problem-focused assessment section in Chapter 5. These adult career problem categories were first detailed by R. E. Campbell and Cellini (1981). The second ring of specific problems includes a series of common disorders that can have devastating career results if left untreated. Secondary prevention (the middle ring in Figure 7-1) of these problems can be achieved by promoting competence and identity formulation, and then mobilizing constructive client behaviors. Primary prevention (the innermost ring on Figure 7-1) of these problems can include the development of ego, social skills training, and initiative enhancement.

Evaluating Preventive Interventions.   The evidence on the effectiveness of preventive interventions is somewhat uneven. The true test of such an intervention, of course, is its impact on the incidence and severity of specific, predictable disorders in the treated versus the control group. A study by Lindquist and Lowe (1978), for example, drew on the campus ecology model (Huebner and Corazzini, 1984) and applied preventive methods in a college student population. Although the fact that participation in the study was voluntary badly confounded motivation with intervention outcome, neither a written interactive program nor a peer-led group was effective in reducing the dropout rate. The weak outcomes that Lindquist and Lowe found starkly contrast with the substantial effect sizes uncovered by Baker, Swisher, Nadenichek, and Popowicz (1984) in a meta-analysis of primary prevention strategies. Their reanalysis of forty preventive counseling studies resulted in an effect size even higher than that found in individual psychotherapy (M. L. Smith, Glass & Miller, 1980). It is debatable, however, how many of Baker et al.'s set of studies would have been considered primary or even secondary prevention if strict inclusion rules had been used. Few of the studies used base-line rates of disorder, and most were secondary or tertiary treatment studies conducted after a disorder had been identified (e.g., Yates, Johnson, & Johnson, 1979). The content of the studies was also quite broad, whereas a review of career prevention studies in particular would have been more germane to this discussion; however, such a review (and the studies) do not exist. Thus we have little empirical evidence for the effectiveness of career prevention efforts.

In sum, the identification of base rates for specific career disorders opens the possibility that these disorders might be addressed through primary prevention rather than after-the-fact intervention. Once a base rate has been calculated for any sample, an intervention can be evaluated with respect to its effect on the prevalence and severity of that disorder in that population. Base-rate data might be extracted from research studies for each of the disorders or accidents depicted in Figure 7-1 using a technique similar to that employed by L. S. Gottfredson (1986). These data could then be used to evaluate an intervention with college students or adolescents who were followed through the developmental point at which such problems could be expected to occur, and the incidence and severity of the disorders in the treated groups could be compared to those in the untreated groups.

Intergenerational Interactions and Career Choice

Primary social groups have long been understood to effect a wide range of human behaviors. Parental influence, for example, is a substantial predictor of general vocational development, and may have a complex effect on both the level and field of attainment, and decisional process (Lopez & Andrews, 1987; Schulenberg, Vondracek, & Crouter, 1984). Parents, regardless of background, are generally concerned about the vocational progress of their children. But most parents fear that the direct exercise of their influence at key decision times will cause rebellion in an adolescent and have the effect opposite to that desired. Conventional wisdom dictates that a laissez-faire approach to parental career intervention will have more beneficial outcomes for an adolescent who is struggling to achieve an independent identity.

In a refreshing departure from this acquiescent parental strategy, Ginzberg (1984) advised "against parents' adopting a withholding or neutral attitude toward the occupational choice determination of their children" (p. 183). Ginzberg argued that parents who refrained from expressing their feelings about their child's career would be unable to hide their anxieties and would be depriving a child of the opportunity to discuss their career concerns constructively. Children who had no such opportunities would find career decision making more, not less, difficult.

J. V. Miller (1985) offered a model of the relationship between career and family. She observed that career planning is too frequently considered to be an individual undertaking, with few people systematically considering family influences in the decision process. Difficulty in combining career and family roles appears to be a problem for men as well as women, although a higher proportion of men reported such conflicts (NCDA, 1988). Miller is not specific about how to work with families in career interventions, but did suggest that families could progress in developmental career stages much as individuals do. Evans and Bartolome (1984) interviewed twenty-two male managers and their wives, and found most reported a negative spillover of work emotions into family life. The authors concluded that work plays a very significant role early in a manager's career, whereas family plays an increasingly important role later in a career. Managers between the ages of thirty-five and forty-two experienced a new sensitivity to their private lives, and many started to spend more time with their families on weekends. This developmental interplay is the kind of stage theory Miller alluded to, and while it probably does not hold for women returning to the labor force in midlife, it seems reasonable for many traditional career patterns.

A group of researchers at the University of British Columbia, led by Richard A. Young and Larry Cochran, is making substantial strides in studies of career development (Young, 1983) and the family. Recent work by Palmer and Cochran (1988), for example, showed that parents can act as agents of career development for their children. In their study forty families with tenth- and eleventh-grade children completed the four-week Partners program, a self-administered parent-child career intervention. Pre- and post-comparisons between the treatment group (twenty families) and the control group (twenty families) on career maturity (Super et al., 1987), and quality of parent-child relationship revealed that the treated children showed significant gains in overall career orientation, moving from the thirtieth percentile to between the sixtieth and seventieth percentile. In posttreatment interviews, parents reported feeling closer to their children and having better understanding of their plight. Overall, there was a marked strengthening in the parent-child bond around career issues. The authors concluded that parents can serve as an important source of continuous support, even when counselors or teachers change or are unavailable.

Munson and Manzi (1982) similarly proposed that young people learn about careers at home by watching, listening, assisting, participating, and performing, a model that resembles Krumboltz's (1976) social learning theory, which holds that individuals acquire their work orientations and attitudes through direct experience and observation. Friesen (1986) argued that psychological and sociological approaches to careers could be compatible if the interaction between the individual and the social structures they inhabit were the focus of inquiry. The developmental contextual approach of Vondracek and his colleagues (Vondracek & Schulenberg, 1986; Vondracek, Lerner, & Schulenberg, 1983) depicts these person-environment interactions as the central theoretical focus.

As Lopez and Andrews (1987) noted, little is known about the influence of family interactions on career decision making. Much of the void was probably created by studies of Roe's (1956) theory that could not confirm any long-term effects of parenting styles on eventual vocational choices. Oddly,

Lopez and Andrews appear to believe that a more distant parental role, although unlikely in most families, will lead to better adolescent career choices, presumably because less conflict and more individuation will arise. They characterized the indecisive youngsters and their parents as "involved in a series of tiresome, repetitive interactions over the subject of career decision-making" (p. 305). They suggested that during career decisions both parents and children must display novel behaviors, which cannot be mobilized if there is overinvolvement by the parents.

Otto (1984) reviewed evidence that suggested a very different conclusion from that formed by Lopez and Andrews. Declaring that adolescence is "a period of continuing strong ties between parents and children" (p. 15), Otto summarized data from studies that showed that most young people have very strong and positive emotional ties to their parents. Otto argued that it is one of the "great tragedies of our time" (p. 15) that we so underestimate the beneficial influence of parents on their children's careers. Indeed, there was as much difference between the adolescents themselves as between adolescents and their parents. Surveys have continued to show that parents are the most significant influence on adolescents' career choice (NCDA, 1988).

The Family as a Social Support Buffer During Career Decisions.   Families have traditionally served as competence-training grounds for young children, but, as Murphy and Frank (1979) observed, there are now fewer children in each family, and thus correspondingly fewer opportunities for older children to observe younger siblings and learn child-rearing skills to use when they have their own children. Natural protective devices that traditionally assisted families have weakened. A study of the buffering effects of work and family support on stress (Billings & Moos, 1982) revealed that social support had a significant ameliorative effect on stress, especially for men; similar studies by Osipow and Spokane (1984) and Osipow and Davis (1988) confirmed this finding. Families provide this social support in several ways. First, they offer the financial resources that pay for education and vocational expenses. Second, families provide for the transmission of values and interests, and for the inheritance of traits or dispositions that most likely help an individual in the pursuit of certain careers. Exciting breakthroughs in genetic psychology in the last decade, for example, suggest that a specific chromosome can be assigned to some mental disorders, such as Alzheimer's disease and bipolar depression (Loehlin, Willerman, & Horn, 1988). The scientific community generally agrees that we have overestimated the environmental and underestimated the genetic contribution to many psychological traits (Bouchard, 1983). Koshland (1987) concluded that part of the brain is "hard-wired" and part is malleable under environmental influences. The relative weight placed on the inheritability of traits, especially abilities in areas such as music or athletics, is increasing after a period of decreased attention. Moderate genetic contributions to personality, temperament, and ability are routinely found (Loehlin et al., 1988).

Although the idea that occupational interests might be genetically determined is difficult for most career psychologists to accept, two studies suggest that this may, to a certain extent, be true (Grotevant, Scarr, & Weinberg, 1977; Vandenberg & Stafford, 1967). Vandenberg and Stafford studied 124 pairs of fraternal twins (50 percent of the same genes) and identical twins (exactly the same genes). Since identical twins develop from the same egg, any differences between them are attributed to environmental influences. Differences between fraternal twins are considered to be a combination of genetic and environmental effects. Vandenberg and Stafford found differences between fraternal and identical twins on nine interest scales, and concluded that genetic influences on interests probably work indirectly through temperament, personality, and aptitude.

Similarly, Grotevant et al. studied 223 biological and adoptive families using the Strong-Campbell Interest Inventory, or SCII (Hansen & Campbell, 1985). Whereas biological families were similar in interests, adoptive families were found to be unrelated. Their study supported previous work on the heritability of interests, and added that the "patterning" of interests was probably as heritable as separate interests. Grotevant et al. found that only the investigative and artistic Holland themes correlated with intelligence, which thus argued against the notion that the heritability of interests is simply an artifact of the heritability of aptitudes. The authors concluded, as did Vandenberg and Stafford (1967), that temperament probably influences an individual's prework activities and thereby moderates genetic influences. Any discussion of the impact of family on careers must consider the possibility that several specific interests, and even the pattern of general interests, may be genetically influenced. Heritability may be stronger in mathematics, science, artistic, musical, and athletic ability, since they overlap with aptitude inheritance.

The third type of family influence on careers rests in its role as a forum for the discussion of aspirations and the construction of exploratory experiences. Maternal encouragement, which plays a significant part in the transmission of aspirations, may be given in diverse ways, including having quiet one-on-one discussions, providing role models (Krumboltz, 1976), and offering specific job leads or contacts (Becker, 1977). Repeated studies have suggested that parents are the resource most often consulted by adolescents in their job search (Otto, 1984). The family intervention programs reviewed by Palmer and Cochran (1988) reinforced the importance of the family as a setting for the exploration and crystallization of interests and values. Another recent study (Young, Friesen, & Pearson, 1988) used a critical incident technique based upon a model of activities, relations, and roles to examine the nature of parental influence on children's careers. Their comprehensive research elicited more than 1,500 incidents from 207 parents that reflected the parents' attempts to facilitate their children's career development. Table 7-1 shows twenty-four categories of incidents in a subsample from Young et al. The most frequently reported general categories of parental activities were structuring the environment (22.8 percent of parents) and providing instrumental support (16.6 percent).

Several substantial differences were found in the parental interventions used with boys and girls: Boys were given more information, challenging, and interest than were girls. This study reinforces the belief that parents and

Table 7-1   Frequency of Incidents for the Joint Parent Activities Category

PARENT JOINT ACTIVITY	TOTAL N = 837		FATHER INCIDENTS N = 293		MOTHER INCIDENTS N = 544	
	f	%	f	%	f	%
Gives information	241	28.8	113	38.6	128	23.5
Advises, suggests	246	29.4	89	30.4	157	28.9
Requests information	108	12.9	34	11.6	74	13.6
Develops alternatives	61	7.3	28	9.6	33	6.1
Demonstrates	21	2.5	12	4.1	9	1.7
Sets expectations	167	20.0	67	22.9	100	18.4
Gives feedback	168	20.1	57	19.5	111	20.4
Teaches	72	8.6	29	9.9	43	7.9
Challenges ideas, actions	107	12.8	37	12.6	70	12.9
Rejects ideas, actions	80	9.6	35	11.9	45	8.3
Creates novel environment	39	4.7	20	6.8	19	3.5
Incorporates other ideas	28	3.3	9	3.1	19	3.5
Initiates compromise	14	1.7	4	1.4	10	1.8
Sets personal limits	23	2.7	12	4.1	11	2.0
Sets limits	108	12.9	53	18.1	55	10.1
Shows interest	132	15.8	41	14.0	91	16.7
Communicates values	72	8.6	35	11.9	37	6.8
Encourages	165	19.7	53	18.1	112	20.6
Dialogues	147	17.6	45	15.4	102	18.8
Allows freedom	132	15.8	44	15.0	88	16.2
Joins in ventures	75	9.0	27	9.2	48	8.8
Models behavior	57	6.8	20	6.8	37	6.8
Takes over	16	1.9	5	1.7	11	2.0
Monitors	57	6.8	27	9.2	30	5.5

NOTE: Percentages refer to the total number of incidents in each subcategory over the total number of incidents for the column. f = frequency

Source: R. A. Young, J. D. Friesen, and H. M. Pearson, "Activities and Interpersonal Relations as Dimensions of Parental Behavior in the Career Development of Adolescents," *Youth and Society* 20 (1988): 38. Reprinted by permission.

children do interact around career choice, but that many of these interactions may be stereotyped, an observation made earlier by Birk (1979) in a module for parents and children.

A final way in which families may interact on career issues is in the intergenerational support and transmission of career values and other, everyday assistance. For example, a grandmother may provide day care while a young mother continues her career, or a son may act as a sounding board for a father approaching retirement who is considering a second career. The interactions across generations may not always be positive, however. L. S. Gottfredson (1986) has argued that having abilities and aspirations that are either higher or lower than those of one's immediate social group may put an individual at risk for subsequent choice problems. The family thus is the potential source of stress around career issues, but can be very effective in both treating and preventing career problems if it is considered and included in career interventions. Although career discussions may engender considerable anxiety in parents and children alike, systematic attempts to intervene both within and across generations to help parents and children support and assist one another during career transitions appear to be quite effective and deserve much future attention. Such an approach, however, presumes the following:

1. Parents and children will be experiencing career concerns simultaneously and should be seen together in interventions whenever possible.
2. Children will learn from close participation in parental career decisions and should not be shielded from them. Adolescent and adult children will benefit particularly and may contribute to successful parental outcomes.
3. Measures of family process should be included in studies of career intervention, and models of career development theory should pay more attention to parental and familial variables.

CONSULTATION IN CAREER PRACTICE

Career consultation can be conducted by professionals from either outside or within the organization or work unit. In either case, the consultant is seen as an "independent outsider" (Schein, 1987) who offers some special expertise. The goal of many consultations is to influence organizational processes or events to move toward stated goals (Schein, 1987). Schein argued that a good consultant, like a good manager, must help subordinates, peers, and managers to achieve set goals and accomplish tasks. Gallesich (1982) suggested five basic models of consultations, many of which are employed in career consultations in schools, organizations, and groups:

Education and Training Consultations: These approaches, which are largely cognitive or skill based, include lectures, media presentations, structured laboratory experiences, measurement and behavior feedback, and small group discussions. Career education employed these models almost exclusively by infusing career material into school curricula (see Chapter 6). The most common vehicle for an education and training consultation is the workshop technique.

Clinical and Mental Health Consultations: These approaches, called doctor-patient consultations by Schein (1987), are derived from the pioneering work of psychiatrist Gerald Caplan (1964) who classified consultations as either problem focused or target focused. Mental health approaches sometimes involve crisis intervention, and frequently include intensive interactions with key individuals or those with serious problems under the assumption that beneficial effects would spread to others in the organization. Individual career counseling is now common in many large organizations, and the overlap between career problems and mental health concerns is one of the most active topics in career psychology.

Behavioral Consultations: Typically these approaches use principles of behavior modification to intervene in organizations by identifying a problem through a needs assessment and base-line data collection, establishing concrete performance goals, and using reinforcement to increase desired behaviors. The classic but controversial Hawthorne study at Western Electric (Roethlisberger & Dickson, 1939), in which alterations in plant lighting resulted in unintended improvements in industrial output even among control groups, is a good example of an organizational intervention that involved learning. As G. D. Gottfredson (personal communication, 1989) noted, in the Hawthorne case, productivity was a function of clearly specified goals and group norms for behavior and output. Numerous studies of ward behavior in psychiatric hospitals have also used behavioral intervention models.

Organizational Consultations: These sociopsychological approaches have a rich history in the work of Warren Bennis, Chris Argyris, and Edgar Schein.

Schein (1987) described three consultation models: purchase of expertise, doctor-patient, and process. In the purchase-of-expertise model, the client organization appears to know what the problem is, what help is needed and where to find that assistance. The success of this model depends on whether the organization has correctly diagnosed the problem, has identified an appropriate consultant, and has fully communicated the nature of the problem to the consultant. The doctor-patient consultation is based on the notion that although the client organization is experiencing some distress or dysfunction, it is unable to diagnose the problem with any confidence. A consultant is engaged to assess the problem and locate "sick" areas. A prescription is then offered, which in many cases is left to the client to administer after the consultant leaves. By contrast, process consultation is an ongoing pattern of diagnosis and intervention. The client participates in the diagnostic process, and the goals are shared by the client and the consultant. Conditions are arranged to facilitate the accurate perception of an organizational problem and the development of a solution that depends heavily on input by the client and follow-through by both the client and the consultant.

Because of emotional and interpersonal impact of an organizational consultation, a consultant must learn how to intervene while still "saving face" for the client. Schein described a three-stage model of the change a process consultation should elicit. In the first stage, there is an unfreezing of attitudes and the creation of motivation for change. In the second stage, cognitive restructuring helps the client to see circumstances more productively, and in the third stage, a "refreezing," occurs as the new view of the organization is integrated fully into existing schemas. The process consultant, according to Schein, employs ten types of interventions:

Listening actively and with interest
Forcing historical restructuring
Forcing concretization
Forcing process emphasis
Asking diagnostic questions and probing
Engaging in process management and agenda setting
Providing feedback
Making content suggestions and recommendations
Supplying structure management
Offering conceptual inputs

Program Consultations: In these approaches internal programs are designed and evaluated. An unusually clear and comprehensive presentation of the content and process of program development was offered by Herr and Cramer (1988), who outlined and gave examples of a five-stage model of career program development:

1. *Program Rationale and Philosophy:* This crucial step in any systematic intervention involves gathering data and reviewing the needs of the target population. A formal needs assessment occurs in this stage. Herr and Cramer's description of the detailed steps in such an assessment is one of the clearest guides available (see Table 7-2). Developmental career theory is especially useful for program planning in organizations and schools. Herr and Cramer offered career maturity and the mastery of developmental tasks appropriate to one's stage as key philosophical concepts for use in developing programmatic interventions.

Table 7-2   Stages in Planning for and Implementing a Career Guidance Program

STAGE 1	STAGE 2	STAGE 3
1. Develop a program philosophy	1. Specify program rationale	1. Select alternative program processes
1.1 Review research and theory pertinent to career guidance and career development	1.1 Describe theoretical and philosophical basis for program	2. Relate program processes to program goals or specific behavioral objectives
1.2 State assumptions	2. Specify program goals	3. Identify resources necessary to implement various program processes
1.3 Define concepts	3. Specify student or client behavioral objectives	4. Identify personnel (teachers, counselors, administrators, community representatives, parents) who have contributions to make to various program processes
2. Collect comprehensive data on what consumers (students, adults) and others (parents, teachers, administrators, community representatives) believe should be program priorities		
3. Collect data on the current program—goals, resources, etc.		
4. Identify where students or other clients currently stand on their career development		
5. Determine discrepancies between what current program is and what it should be		

Source: E. L. Herr and S. H. Cramer, *Career Guidance and Counseling Through the Life Span*, 3rd ed. (Glenview, IL: Scott, Foresman, 1988), p. 190. Reprinted by permission.

2. *Program Goals and Performance Objectives:* After program goals are agreed upon, detailed behavioral objectives are formulated. The desired outcomes must be observable and easily evaluated. Herr and Cramer (1988) provide a wealth of examples of program goals and objectives.

3. *Intervention Activities:* Activities are identified that will insure that the performance objectives are met. For a sample program goal, performance

STAGE 4	STAGE 5
1. Describe evaluation procedures	1. Identify milestones (critical events) which must occur for program implementation
1.1 Summative evaluation to assess whether total program goals are being met	
1.2 Formative evaluation to assess whether program elements are contributing effectively to program goals	1.1 When staff in-service will occur
	1.2 When information about the program must be prepared and sent to consumers
1.3 Identify evaluative data to be secured, from whom, and by whom	1.3 When materials and resources for the program must be ordered
1.4 Build or secure data-collection instruments	1.4 When base-line data on participants will be collected
1.5 Decide on the form of data analysis and who will be responsible	1.5 When program will be introduced
1.6 Identify persons or groups to whom evaluative data will be provided and in what form	

objectives, intervention activity, and evaluative criterion consistent with Herr and Cramer's framework, see Table 7-3.

4. *Evaluation Plan:* An evaluation design is developed to establish criteria for effective performance, select measures of the criteria, collect data, and feed that data back to the system for use in reforming or fine-tuning the program and in determining its overall effectiveness.

Table 7-3 Sample Program Goal, Performance Objectives, Intervention Activity, and Evaluative Criterion for a Client in a Job-Loss Transition

PROGRAM GOAL	PERFORMANCE OBJECTIVES	INTERVENTION ACTIVITY	EVALUATIVE CRITERION
Persistently mobilize constructive career behaviors, attitudes, and emotions	Engage in daily contacts with potential employers	Participate in telephone bank and letter writing as part of Job Club (Azrin and Besalel, 1980)	Record calls and keep copies of letters
	Discuss feelings and frustrations associated with negative responses to job search	Attend daily group sessions with fellow job seekers	Attend all group sessions

5. *Time Lines:* Time lines and milestones in the effective implementation of the program are anticipated so that progress can be monitored continuously and the program can be adjusted as necessary to keep it on track.

The Nature of Career Consultation

Although there is a substantial literature on what career consultation programs *should* include (APGA, undated), there is very little data on current career development practice in organizations and schools. Empirical studies of programmatic and curricular career interventions have been very slow to accumulate, as Baker and Popwicz (1983) observed. The design and outcome measurement problems in such studies are legion (Brickell, 1976). One exception is the study of forty companies by Gutteridge and Otte (1983), which revealed that thirty-one of the companies conducted career planning seminars and that twenty-eight provided individual career counseling. A variety of other career interventions were employed, including job posting, workbooks and inventories, a career resource center, and discussions with supervisors. Such programs were started because of pressure from top management, a desire to promote employees from within, employee interest, or EEO pressure. Gutteridge and Otte concluded that career intervention programs in industry were proceeding at a remarkable rate. They also made a number of very clear recommendations that make this brief book one of the most useful resources for corporate career programming.

Generally, career consultations are of the purchase-of-expertise model detailed by Schein (1987), the program development model, or the organizational development model described by Gallesich (1982). Leibowitz, Farren and Kaye (1988) recently provided a generalized model for the implementation of career programs in government, corporate, and industrial set-

Table 7-4   Steps and Tasks in Establishing a Career Development System

Step 1. Needs: Defining the Present System

Establish roles and responsibilities of employees, managers, and the organization
Identify needs; establish target groups
Establish cultural parameters; determine organizational receptivity, support, and commitment to career development
Assess human resource structures; consider possible links
Determine prior attempts at solving the problem or need
Establish mission/philosophy of program
Design and implement needs assessment to confirm/collect more data
Establish indicators of success

Step 2. Vision: Determining New Directions and Possibilities

Create a long-term philosophy
Establish vision/objectives of the program
Design interventions for employees, managers, and the organization
Organize and make available career information needed to support the program

Step 3. Action Plan: Deciding on Practical First Steps

Assess and obtain support from top management
Create a pilot program
Assess resources and competencies
Establish an advisory group
Involve advisory group in data gathering, program design, implementation, evaluation, and monitoring

Step 4. Result: Maintaining the Change

Create long-term formalized approaches
Publicize the program
Evaluate and redesign the program and its components
Consider future trends and directions for the program

Source: Z. B. Leibowitz, C. Farren, and B. L. Kaye, *Designing Career Development Systems* (San Francisco: Jossey-Bass, 1988), p. 273. Reprinted with permission.

tings, and some of the material would be useful in educational settings as well (see Table 7-4). The first step in their model is to assess the present system in the organization. The second step is to formulate the philosophy and objectives of the program. The important third step, during which an action plan is developed, is to establish an advisory board of key employees whose investment and involvement in the program will provide valuable feedback to the consultant as well as credibility in the eyes of the other employees and management. Finally, the fourth step is to maintain and evaluate the ongoing program. Figure 7-2 is a handy work sheet for the consultant that is designed to construct modules for the consultation steps, and to develop goals and objectives for each module.

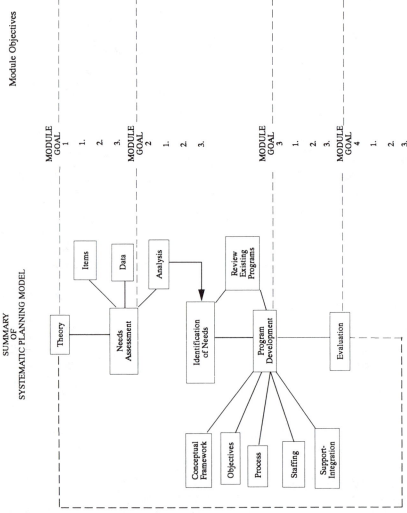

Figure 7-2 Work Sheet for Constructing Consultation Modules. (Source: Adapted from Z. B. Leibowitz and N. K. Schlossberg, *Designing Career Development Progams for Business and Industry* [College Park, MD: National Consortium on Competency-Based Staff Development and U.S. Department of Health, Education, and Welfare, 1979], p. 112.)

   Consultative approaches to career intervention represent a useful and exciting addition to the counselor's skill base. The overlap between career consultation and industrial-organization consultation may sometimes be problematic, even though the goals, assumptions, and content of the two approaches are different. The success of both, however, depends on the degree to which organizational changes are made to support the consultation (Goldstein, 1980). A great many consultations have a short-lived effect or none at all due to the lack of such organizational support and follow-through.

SUMMARY

Prevention and consultation are emerging areas of career practice that require divergent views about the causes and remediation of career difficulties, and somewhat different skills from the counselor. The promotion of career competence is the principal organizing construct of prevention, and parental interactions are seen as crucial in promoting this competence.

8

The Client as Personal Information Scientist

This chapter presents some of the clinical and psychological issues involved in career search and information seeking, with an emphasis not upon commercially available sources of information but instead upon the client's acquisition of information from diverse sources. The dry, often vacuous descriptions of career information sources found in some textbooks do not explain the complex psychological process whereby an individual filters and integrates environmental information for use in career decisions. The promotion or mobilization of an effective search and information processing is a fascinating and vital part of any career intervention. The study of career search and information overlaps to a degree with ongoing work in industrial-organizational psychology on recruitment and job preview (Meglino, DeNisis, Youngblood, & Williams, 1988; Reilly, Brown, Blood, & Malatesta, 1981; Wanous, 1973), and provides a natural linkage between counseling psychology and industrial psychology. Rapidly developing theory and research in social cognition also provide fresh perspectives on this core area of career psychology.

THE LAMINATION OF INFORMATION AND BARRIERS AROUND OCCUPATIONS

Occupations and professions develop protective mechanisms to limit the number of new recruits and aspirants. Bucher (1976) provided an unusually clear and concise perspective on the constraints that prevent an individual from gaining entry to or information about specific occupations. One form of constraint is pervasive, and affects an individual's development without that person's immediate awareness; the second form of constraint includes those sudden or random events that an individual may be aware of but have little power to control. The pervasive constraints include one's position in society, which result in the unconscious formation of a world view peculiar to that position, and which may act to limit one's aspirations and horizons simply through the lack of consideration of different life possibilities. For example, according to Bucher, the poor ghetto child may be less likely than the upper middle class child to aspire to a career in science.

Secondly, there are certain opportunity structures, which Bucher (1979) defined as "range of life chances or options available to the individual" (p. 117), that are associated with one's position in society. These structures interact with position constraints to limit the range of choices open to an individual. For example, Bucher described one common problem in vocational counseling in which the son or daughter of an upwardly mobile professional family chooses a job in the skilled crafts. The opportunities and barriers operating when an upper middle class child aspires to a nonprofessional occupation are similar to those when a lower class child aspires to a high-level position. Finally, Bucher noted that most occupations project auras or images of what might be required for entry that often discourage minority or disadvantaged applicants from aspiring or applying to those professions.

In addition to the pervasive constraints that limit access to jobs, certain specific barriers further restrict access. Most occupations have inside channels of communication, such as trade journals or professional societies, that are designed to slow entry to their ranks. One's access—or lack of access—to the flow of information on the inside of an occupation also determines one's ability to acquire a job in that field. Frequently, there is a socialization system (usually called an "old boy" network) that controls exposure to the experiences that provide the opportunity to test and improve one's skills in order to advance to the higher ranks in an occupation (McCall, Lombardo, and Morrison, 1988).

One of the major tasks in career intervention is to help the client penetrate the layers of constraints surrounding an occupation by positioning the client inside the flow of accurate information around that profession (Pavalko, 1976). The systematic study of how information affects decision making and which aspects of that information are crucial has lagged far behind the development of new media and technology for presenting occupational information. However, four long-range programs of research on the problem of the effects of career information on career decision making are beginning to improve our understanding of the process of acquiring such information. The first, a twenty-year research program by Krumboltz and his colleagues, attempted to promote information seeking through model reinforcement. The second, by Bodden (1970) and his co-workers, studied the role of cognitive complexity in reactions to career information. The third, a more recent variation of Bodden's original work by Neimeyer and associates, focused on the differentiation and integration of cognitive vocational structures. The final program of research used principles of social cognition to view the career client as a personal hypothesis tester who examines occupations in the face of information encountered (Blustein & Strohmer, 1987).

Promoting Career Information Seeking

In an unusually vigorous series of studies, Krumboltz and his associates (Krumboltz & Schroeder, 1965, Ryan & Krumboltz, 1964; Thoresen, Hosford, & Krumboltz, 1970; Thoresen & Krumboltz, 1968; Thoresen, Krumboltz, & Varenhorst, 1967) used direct counselor reinforcement of interview responses or treatments employing audiotaped models being reinforced to promote the frequency and variety of information-seeking behavior (ISB) both inside and outside of the counseling interview. In the first of these studies, Ryan and Krumboltz (1964) reinforced decision or deliberation responses during a twenty-minute interview. The reinforced responses significantly increased in frequency in both the decision and deliberation groups when compared to a nonreinforced control. Subsequent work by Krumboltz and Schroeder (1965) compared reinforcement counseling, model reinforcement counseling, and a no-treatment control group. The reinforced groups engaged in significantly more ISB than the controls. Direct reinforcement increased ISB more for females than for males, whereas model reinforcement produced the opposite result.

Thoresen et al. (1967) used an improved design to examine the differential effects of sex-pairings on the promotion of ISB. This study replicated the gender difference in model reinforcement (males responded more), but it may simply be that the male model, who engaged in athletics, was more attractive than the female model, who was a speech therapist. Pursuing this problem further, Thoresen and Krumboltz (1968) found that high-success athletic models who were reinforced for ISB on an audiotape were most effective in promoting ISB among subjects who heard the tape. Thoresen et al. (1970) varied the level of success (attractiveness) of the model on the tape but found no significantly different effects for the highly successful model, although the results were in the hypothesized direction. Related studies (Hoffman, Spokane, & Magoon, 1981; Krivatsy & Magoon, 1976) found increases in ISB following brief inventory feedback, and Kivlighan, Hageseth, Tipton, and McGovern (1981) found gains in ISB following individual or group intervention.

It seems quite clear from these findings that nearly any career intervention, regardless of how brief or artificial, will stimulate a modest increase in information seeking. Perhaps the term *focused exploratory behavior* would be a better label for what was stimulated in these studies. R. A. Myers (1971; 1986) classified information seeking as an instrumental outcome behavior, and wondered why it continued to be so popular as an outcome measure considering that few attempts were made to verify the accuracy of the client's self-report of the information seeking, and that any exploratory behavior was assumed to be beneficial, regardless of its content. Although Krumboltz and his colleagues were more concerned with the properties of the model as a stimulus for exploratory behavior, later investigators have simply used ISB as an outcome measure, without paying attention to the nature or content of the exploration that results. In this respect Myers's advice is well taken: We have already demonstrated that career intervention will result in increases in exploratory behavior, and that these increases will result in beneficial client outcomes (Grotevant, Scarr, & Weinberg, 1977). What is needed is a more analytic look at the data and its effects on the client's cognitive process (Myers, 1986). Krumboltz's (1983) most recent work, for example, suggested that private belief systems may delimit exploration and consideration of options at a level that is not entirely conscious to the client nor open to the counselor. More sophisticated, recently developed measures of exploration (Stumpf, Colarelli, & Hartman, 1983) are instrumental outcomes that can be tied to very specific treatment components, and contain both behavioral and cognitive elements. New work in computer-assisted intervention offers a unique way to study which aspects of information are attended to and which are absorbed during exploration.

Cognitive Complexity and Career Information

A later and more analytic line of research on career information by Bodden (1970) and his associates at Texas Tech University attempted to assess the impact of controlled information presentations on the client's cognitive state. In an unusually heuristic doctoral dissertation and several subsequent papers with his colleagues, Bodden outlined a model of the relationship between cognitive complexity and career information. Arguing that cognitive complexity should lead to finer judgments among stimuli and information about jobs, and therefore greater appropriateness, Bodden (1970) used a variant of Kelly's Role Construct Rep Test to measure complexity, a measure of realism based upon ability and a congruence measure based upon Holland's (1985a) theory of person-environment fit to assess appropriateness. No significant relationship between complexity and appropriateness was found in this first study, although there was some evidence that complexity was related to congruence as measured in Holland's theory. A subsequent study (Bodden & Klein, 1972), however, confirmed the relationship between cognitive complexity and congruence. Furthermore, complexity was found to be independent of Holland type. Bodden and Klein (1973) later found a significant relationship between cognitive complexity and the affective stimulus value of occupations. When judging negatively valued occupations, subjects tended to be more cognitively complex than when judging positively valued occupations. In a subsequent correlational study, Winer, Cesari, Haase, and Bodden (1979) found that a measure of cognitive complexity was related to career maturity.

Bodden and James (1976) shifted the research tactics of the Texas Tech group from a correlational to an experimental mode. They either presented subjects with information on the twelve occupations that are included on Bodden's (1970) cognitive differentiation grid, or relegated them to a control group that received no information. Unexpectedly, reading the information significantly *reduced* complexity and differentiation, a finding that Bodden was hard-pressed to explain and interpreted as a refutation of his model. He suggested that clients may actually "tighten" their construct system and use new information selectively to bolster their current views of the world of work (Bodden & James, 1976). The findings from these studies challenged the conventional wisdom that information was uniformly beneficial in career intervention and suggested a more complex view of information processing, which meant that "the practicing counselor should be wary of the possibility that his [*sic*] clients may distort new information in such a way as to fit preconceived ways of viewing the world of work" (Bodden & James, 1976, p. 282).

In a replication and extension of Bodden and James (1976) with a markedly improved design, Haase, Reed, Winer, and Bodden (1979) presented subjects with either positive, negative, or mixed information about the twelve occupations on the cognitive differentiation grid. They found that any negative information moderated the simplifying effects of information on complexity; that is, mixed or negative information resulted in less simplification than positive information alone.

Two final entries in this important series of research studies (Cesari, Winer, & Piper, 1984; Cesari, Winer, Zychlinski & Laird, 1982) examined differences in cognitive complexity between career decided and undecided students following exposure to occupational information. In both studies, no differences were found between decided and undecided students, although the simplification effects found in Haase et al. (1979) were replicated.

The Differentiation and Integration of Cognitive Structures

A series of studies by Neimeyer and associates at the University of Florida documented the differentiation, integration, and development of cognitive vocational structures. In a study early in this series, Neimeyer, Nevill, Probert, and Fukuyama (1985) used the cognitive differentiation grid to estimate the level of differentiation and integration, and found that more integrated cognitive schemas were associated with more effective decision making, but that lower levels of integration were associated with increased exploration. A second study (Neimeyer & Ebben, 1985) again used the grid to measure cognitive complexity and compared the effects of four self-directing vocational interventions: (1) the Self-Directed Search (Holland, 1985b); (2) an occupational information treatment; (3) a computer intervention; and (4) an attention control. This carefully designed study unearthed a wealth of information about the role of complexity and information in career intervention. Across all treatments, subjects decreased in complexity, with an associated increase in positivity. The presentation of positive information reduced complexity, but the authors suggested that this reduction might be short-lived. They offered the interesting notion of curvilinear relationship between complexity and information that explains why information may both decrease and increase complexity.

A subsequent study by Nevill, Neimeyer, Probert, and Fukuyama (1986) found that cognitive schemas became better organized over time, and work by Neimeyer and Metzler (1987) using a cross-sectional design showed that differentiation and integration increased as procedures to assess vocational identity became more specific. Finally, Neimeyer, Brown, Metzler, Hagans, and Tanguy (1989) compared a standard with a personalized cognitive grid and confirmed the finding that women demonstrated higher levels of integration but lower levels of differentiation than men, which seems consistent with L. S. Gottfredson's (1981) belief that acceptable careers are circumscribed by gender early in life.

Analytic research efforts such as those described above are rare in vocational behavior and thus deserve careful scrutiny. Taken together, these studies suggest that although a complex set of personal constructs related to occupations is associated with career maturity and congruence, the presentation of information in its most common form—uniformly positive—may bolster and reinforce overly simplistic views of the world of work. Positive information may therefore result not only in premature career choices, but also, if overdone, the rejection of career options. Furthermore, because various vocational interventions convey information differently, this aspect of the treatment may have a greater effect on the success or failure of the intervention than does the mode of the intervention (e.g., individual or group) (Neimeyer & Ebben, 1985).

To illustrate, studies by Osipow (1962) and Spokane and Spokane (1981) suggested that although exposure to minimal positive information resulted in positive attitude changes toward an occupation, information that was presented *too* positively actually produced the opposite effect: a blocking or rejection of the occupation. This conclusion is supported by a long history of research on realistic preview in industrial-organizational psychology (Wanous, 1973) that concluded that balanced or realistic information about a job was more likely to lead to beneficial organizational outcomes (e.g., stability and satisfaction) than unrealistically positive previews. A recent study of the realistic preview effect by Meglino et al. (1988) presented subjects with either an enhanced preview, a reduced preview designed to lower overly optimistic job expectations, or no preview at all. Some subjects received both the enhanced and reduced previews. Those who were given the combined previews (positive and negative information) had significant less job turn-over than those who had received the negative preview, but any preview resulted in some lessening of turnover compared to no preview. Further-more, subjects' attitudes toward the occupation after five weeks were related to the preview in expected ways. Because this study was conducted with women in the Army rather than in analogue fashion, the results strengthen the idea that balanced information is important to career choice. Meta-analytic evidence (Breaugh, 1983; Reilly et al., 1981) confirms that realistic job previews are somewhat more effective, especially when self-selection is controlled for (Miceli, 1985), but that no convincing explanation for this ef-fect has yet been offered. We have much to learn about information processing.

Personal Hypothesis Testing and Career Information

In a recent paper, Blustein and Strohmer (1987) applied principles of social cognition to the problem of career information in a natural extension of earlier information-seeking and cognitive complexity research. The authors argued that individuals will favor information and hypotheses that confirm their existing personal beliefs. This confirmatory bias seems to hold across a variety of life situations and decisions. Blustein and Strohmer noted that it is unbiased hypothesis testing or the undistorted evaluation of vocational options that leads to high-quality decision making. Janis and Mann (1977) also considered the unbiased consideration of negative (disconfirmatory) in-put to be the hallmark of a high-quality personal decision. Such a conclu-sion is quite consistent with the work of Haase et al. (1979) and Neimeyer et al. (1989), who found that negative or mixed information led to greater complexity, whereas positive information led to greater cognitive simplici-ty. Since complexity has been significantly related to congruence, it can be argued that negative information improves the quality of the decision and thus leads to greater congruence.

Blustein and Strohmer (1987) conducted two experiments to test the notion that career decisions are instances of personal hypothesis testing. In the first experiment, it was theorized that hypotheses that were directly rele-vant to an individual's career plans would generate confirmatory bias, whereas those that were unrelated to personal plans would lead to the unbiased consideration of new information. Subjects were accordingly pre-sented with "objective" information about occupations that was either rele-vant or irrelevant to their personal career plans, and their responses were rated for evidence of confirmatory bias. Subjects who were given the rele-vant information exhibited considerably more confirmatory bias than those who received irrelevant information. In the second substudy, a bogus in-terest inventory was used to simulate expert input. Again subjects were inclined to consider information that confirmed the match between the occupation under consideration and their personal attributes (e.g., skills, interests, and personality). The authors suggested that this confirming process may be an example of the subjects attempting to reduce cognitive dissonance by ignoring or discounting disconfirming information in an effort to bolster an option already chosen on some conscious or internal level.

Blustein and Strohmer's (1987) study opened a large area of research on the role of social cognition in career search and information. Social cognition theory holds that values, needs, and expectancies affect the way individuals perceive the social environment. These perceptions differ from what would result from a simple analysis of the information received (Higgins & Bargh, 1987). Further, the theory also argues that people may not use rational strategies to weigh the available evidence or to use it to inform their decisions. Research in social cognition has repeatedly demonstrated that in experimental studies individuals go well beyond the data presented during the experiment, even to the point of "remembering" an abstract version of data that they never received (Higgins & Bargh, 1987). Certain features of the data will also influence its salience. For example, Higgins and Bargh concluded that the framework used to process information markedly affects how it is encoded and retrieved, a conclusion supported by Holland, Magoon, and Spokane (1981), who argued that a cognitive framework was an important part of a successful career intervention. This framework is probably most effective when it is a personally derived rather than a counselor-supplied explanation, but some framework is generally better than none (Hoffman & Teglasi, 1982). Considering how prone individuals are to accepting confirming versions of information, Higgins and Bargh have posed the question, "Do people never seek the truth?" (p. 397).

It is increasingly clear that the simple presentation of positive or confirming information about career options, without the benefit of a well-constructed cognitive framework for organizing that information, portrays the problem of career information in its least flattering and ineffective manner. Certain aspects of career information will be more salient and influential than others, and the absorption of information presented in career interventions is affected as much by certain characteristics of the perceiver as by the qualities of the information. This was noted some time ago by Samler (1961), who observed that it was the psychosocial or human side of occupational information that was attended to in counseling, not the detailed data about jobs (e.g., salary). Samler observed that it was the occasional photograph in the Dictionary of Occupational Titles that received the most notice from clients, and it is the pictorial content of information that has received the most criticism from minorities and women wishing to rectify imbalances in occupational participation rates. Likewise, Fletcher (1966) argued that vocational interests were compilations of concepts that each had a feeling or affect tone that was considered when making a career decision. A few studies have identified which aspects of information will be salient for which people. Heilman (1979), for example, showed that the sexual composition of a field will have a clear and differential effect on its attractiveness for male and female high school students. Females expressed more interest in and estimated their chances to be better when the ratio of women to men was rising. Male subjects, on the other hand, were less interested in an occupation as the ratio of men to women became more favorable. Likewise, Norman and Bessemer (1968) found that subjects clung to familiar notions about occupations even in the face of new or conflicting information about their prestige; simple descriptive information, however, did eradicate some prestige effects. Spokane and Spokane (1981) found that positive descriptions and pictorial representations of a reinforced model for participating in an occupation were effective in increasing positive reactions to an occupation, except when that information was unrealistically positive or imbalanced. Biggers (1971) found that most subjects used two or three categories of information to evaluate an occupation, and that the type of work was by far the most commonly used category. Biggers, in this early effort, made no attempt to study respondent characteristics.

A CONTINUUM OF CAREER-RELATED INFORMATION

Rusalem (1954) argued that the presentation of occupational information was more than a simple collection of facts, for it also involved the client's selective perception, which was influenced by the client's feelings about an occupation as well as the client's self-concept. Rusalem further noted that the closer the individual was to the occupation, the more helpful information about it would be. Occupational information can reside in sources very close to the individual (e.g., parents, a personal book) or very much of a distance (e.g., a job site).

Figure 8-1 presents a continuum of vocational information sources, from those most proximal (or closest) to the client to those most distal (or farthest) from the client. Most exploratory experiences begin with proximal information but must proceed to more distal experiences. An examination of Figure 8-1 shows that the most proximal information may come from naïve or informal assessments by the client rather than actual information about occupations. Other proximal and easily gathered data can be derived from interest inventories administered in the counseling sessions, information supplied by the counselor, or a computer-assisted exploration. More distal information may be drawn from simulated experiences such as work samples or job experience kits (Krumboltz, 1971), or from discussions or conversations with friends or family members. The most distal, complex, and usually accurate information is gathered when the client moves out into the world of work for a "shadowing" experience, a cooperative arrangement, internship, or trial job. For example, Heitzmann, Schmidt, and Hurley (1986) described a program in which students could make regular on-site visits to

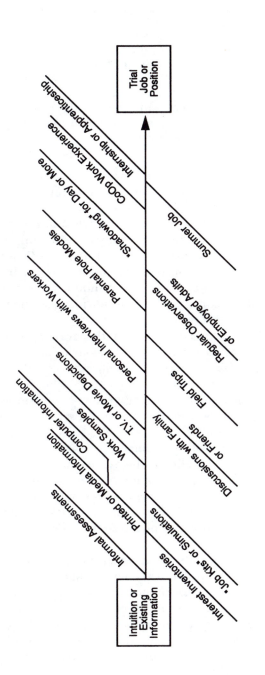

Figure 8-1 Continuum of Vocational Information Sources (from Proximal at the Left to Distal at the Right).

a company. Typically in career counseling, it is desirable to mobilize the client to search for distal information and to bring that information back to the counseling session for evaluation.

Mobilizing the Effective Acquisition of Relevant Information

The research in the three areas of career information discussed above—information seeking, cognitive complexity and social cognition—suggest the following applications to counseling practice:

1. Counselors should encourage clients to integrate negative or disconfirming information about every option under consideration. The client's and perhaps the counselor's tendency will be to ignore such information in favor of more confirming input. Some evaluation of the underlying constructs (and their appropriateness) that the client is using to evaluate occupations should result from the consideration of this disconfirming information. There are methods of reviewing personal constructs (e.g., the Tyler Vocational Card Sort; see Tyler, 1961), but an effort should be made to uncover and challenge any hidden constructs or private rules that may be affecting a client's exploration (see Krumboltz, 1983).

2. Exploration should be focused upon options that are congruent with the client's interest and abilities, as well as those that may be at the leading or growing edge of the client's zone of "acceptable" alternatives. The broader the exploration, the more likely a congruent outcome will be. A blend of exploratory strategies in which some sweeping review of possibilities is followed by a more in-depth and focused search is the most common model of exploration (Gati & Tikotzi, 1989).

3. Exploration should begin with proximal information and become increasingly distal. Counselors should discuss the exclusionary nature of information systems around occupations and anticipate any constraints that may be operating to limit the client's access to accurate information. Counselors should not try to supply the client with information, but rather should mobilize the client to explore and penetrate to inside levels of an occupation.

4. Exploration and information seeking entail both behavioral and cognitive aspects, and should be considered as complex phenomena during counseling. Information based upon the counselor's experience or taken from some readily available commercial source should not be presented until and unless the client has clearly expressed an interest in and readiness for this information. Rather, the contextual and individual factors involved in the decision will probably dictate the nature of the client's exploratory behavior (Blustein & Phillips, 1988).

THE SOURCES AND METHODS OF A JOB SEARCH

A job search overlaps with an information search, but is distinguished by its goal and its temporal position. The goal of a job search is to secure a paid position of employment, and this search usually occurs following some interim career decision. The results of the search may influence or alter an interim decision, but do not normally precede it unless the information search never occurs. In such cases the client may move directly to the job search without any preliminary information search or solely on the basis of proximal or personal information. A job search is characterized by exposure to the reality of the marketplace, the rigors of which may cause an individual to return to an earlier decision stage to reconsider options. It is during the job search that imagination meets reality, a time that Tiedeman (Tiedeman and Ohara, 1963) captured so well in his differentiation between anticipation and implementation. Client behaviors in the face of job search are an important arena for future research in career behavior.

Data provided by the U.S. Department of Labor on job search strategies spawned a number of studies on the frequency and effectiveness of these various formal and informal search methods. Becker (1977), in a lucid technical report on job search, maintained that the specific behaviors of individual job seekers and recruiting employers are the most important unit of analysis in the job search process. Becker (1977) identified the following sources of information that are used to find a job:

applying directly to an employer without suggestions or referrals by anyone,

asking relatives about jobs where they work,

asking relatives about jobs elsewhere,

asking friends about jobs where they work,

asking friends about jobs elsewhere,

checking with the state employment service,

checking with private employment agencies,

answering ads in a local newspaper,

answering ads in a newspaper from outside the local area,

placing ads in a local newspaper,

checking with a labor union hiring hall,

taking a civil service test or filing an application for a government job,

contacting an organization, such as a community action group such as the Urban League, Welfare Agency, etc.,

contacting a school placement officer,

asking a teacher or professor for job leads,

answering ads in professional or trade journals,

placing ads in professional or trade journals,

using any other method to find a job. (pp. 26–27)

Becker argued that informal or personal sources of information were not only more frequently used but also more effective during the search process. Most young people appeared to grab the first job they encountered, even though many of them did not mount anything resembling an effective search. Table 8-1 summarizes the percentage of young women using each job search method and the percentage who found a job using each method. More recent data (U.S. Department of Labor, 1985) suggest that, if anything, informal sources of information are being utilized more heavily than in previous years.

Allen and Keaveny (1979) noted that most of the research on job search has been conducted by economists. As a result, although personality factors are viewed as contributing to job search strategy, little else is known other than the repeated observation that most individuals rely on informal sources for job leads (Granovanter, 1974). Allen and Keaveny found that graduates of two-year colleges who had used informal sources were more likely to be working in blue-collar occupations, whereas those who had used formal sources were more likely to be employed in white-collar occupations. This study reflected the fact that hiring in engineering and accounting traditionally proceeds through formal means, whereas hiring in nonprofessional areas and in the social sciences and humanities is more often done informally.

Effective Search Behaviors

In an unusual study of the wisdom of assertive job-seeking behaviors, Cianni-Surridge and Horan (1983) asked three hundred corporate college representatives to rank a list of sixteen assertive job search behaviors. Their ratings suggested that small companies rewarded assertive behaviors, including conducting informational interviews, sending a follow-up letter after an interview, making periodic follow-up telephone calls, and sending a second letter if a first inquiry receives no response, more than medium-sized companies. Generally, the smaller the company, the higher the rating given to assertive job search behaviors. Asking for names of employees or requesting a second interview, however, were not highly rated. There are thus some risks associated with such overly or inappropriately assertive behaviors, challenging the myth that they are universally beneficial.

In a similar vein, Latham (1986) examined upper-level college students' views of the most effective job search strategies. A factor analysis of the strategies revealed eight factors that were then subjected to a cluster analysis, from which four clusters or types of searchers emerged: moderates, who found all strategies moderately helpful: agency avoiders, who gave poor

Table 8-1 Job Search and Selected Job-Finding Methods Among Females, 1973

	TEEN-AGE GIRLS, 16-19		WOMEN, 20-24		ALL FEMALES	
	Proportion Finding Job by This Method	Proportion Using This Method	Proportion Finding Job by This Method	Proportion Using This Method	Proportion Finding Job by This Method	Proportion Using This Method
Direct application to employer	30.9%	62.8%	33.1%	64.8%	34.6%	64.4%
Ask friends about jobs where they worked	15.3%	59.7%	7.8%	50.1%	10.7%	47.2%
Ask friends about jobs elsewhere	3.1%	44.9%	4.9%	42.4%	4.8%	36.6%
Ask relative about jobs where they work	10.4%	37.7%	4.6%	27.5%	5.1%	25.1%
Ask relatives about jobs elsewhere	3.5%	33.5%	2.1%	31.1%	1.7%	23.9%
Answer ads in local newspaper	12.2%	40.8%	13.0%	51.0%	14.5%	47.5%
Check with private agency	7.7%	18.1%	10.2%	30.2%	7.9%	22.4%
State employment	3.1%	24.3%	5.6%	31.2%	5.2%	29.2%
School placement	3.0%	12.5%	5.2%	21.2%	2.8%	13.0%
Civil service test	2.4%	12.0%	2.7%	20.1%	2.8%	15.2%
Ask teachers	3.1%	18.8%	2.3%	16.8%	1.6%	11.8%

Source: Adapted from H. J. Becker, *How Young People Find Jobs*, Tech. Rep. No. 241 (Baltimore: Johns Hopkins University, Center for Social Organization of Schools, 1977), p. 52. Reprinted by permission.

ratings to formal school or community employment agencies; optimists, who gave high ratings to all strategies; and formal job seekers, who assigned high ratings to the use of résumés and classified ads.

Taylor (1985) found that self-concept crystallization and occupational knowledge affected students' ability to sell their job qualifications, even though neither variable was substantially related to overall job satisfaction. More importantly, however, Taylor found that increased exposure to job information was a significant predictor of occupational knowledge.

COMPREHENSIVE PROGRAMS FOR PROMOTING AN EFFECTIVE JOB SEARCH

Teaching Interview Skills

One of the most popular and effective techniques for teaching and promoting job search skills is mock interview workshops with live or videotape feedback of interview behaviors. For example, Hollandsworth, Dressel, and Stevens (1977) compared a four-hour, behaviorally based interview workshop with discussion and no-treatment control conditions, and found a combination of behavioral and discussion interventions to be the most effective in lowering anxiety about interviews and in improving ratings of verbal and nonverbal interview skills. Similarly, Speas (1979) compared modeling and role-playing interventions for promoting interview skills. Ratings of videotaped segments of subjects' postintervention interview behaviors revealed that a combination of modeling, role playing, and videotape feedback were the most effective in promoting verbal and nonverbal interview skills. In contrast, Austin and Grant (1981) found significant benefits for every one of the five interventions used to promote interview skills but no differential effectiveness for combination interventions. McGovern, Jones, Warwick, and Jackson (1981) showed that highly verbal candidates were more likely to be hired than less verbal ones, but that a poor visual presentation (e.g., poor eye contact or distracting body movements) resulted in lower hire ratings for less verbal clients.

One of the most thorough, ongoing programs of systematic research on the behaviors associated with an effective job search has been conducted by Stumpf and Colarelli (1980; 1981) using an instrument called the Career Exploration Survey (Stumpf, Colarelli, & Hartman, 1983). Stumpf and Colarelli (1980) found that four dimensions characterized the exploratory behavior of college seniors:

1. Intended-systematic exploration
2. Environment-oriented exploration
3. Self-oriented exploration
4. Degree of focus

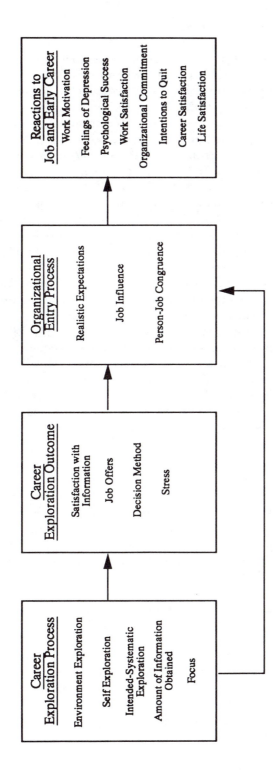

Figure 8-2 A Process Model of the Effects of Career Exploration on Organizational Entry and Career-Related Outcomes. (Source: S. A. Stumpf "The Effects of Exploration on Organizational Entry and Career-Related Outcomes," Unpublished manuscript. New York University, 1981:24.) Reprinted with permission.

These dimensions reflected psychological processes that were more useful than the formal-informal categories employed in descriptive studies. Apparently, individuals receive and assimilate environmental data to fit existing cognitive schemata (Stumpf & Colarelli, 1980).

Stumpf's (1981) path analysis provided a clear model of the effects of career exploration, on organizational entry and career-related outcomes (see Figure 8-2). Stumpf found very strong correlations between respondents' level of environmental exploration and the level ($r = .53$; $p > .01$) and focus ($r = .57$; $p > .01$) of information derived. Extent of exploration was also significantly correlated with person-environment congruence in the same manner found by Grotevant et al. (1986). The more extensive the exploration process, the more positive the organization entry process; in other words, there will be more realistic job expectations, greater selection of positions with an opportunity for influence, and closer person-job fit (Stumpf, 1980). Specifically, individuals with a positive entry experience reported "more work motivation, less depression, greater feelings of personal success, more work, career, and life satisfactions, more commitment to the organization, and fewer intentions to leave the organization" (Stumpf, 1981, p. 15). This line of research and reasoning about career exploration and subsequent well-being offer great promise for the clear specification of constructive behavior sequences and the examination of what individuals actually do when faced with difficult career situations. The relationship of the quality of the career decision to subsequent personal and vocational adjustment may well be the most important agenda for our field in the next decade.

The Job Club

In one of the few carefully evaluated attempts to promote effective job search strategy, Azrin and his colleagues applied behavioral principles to the problem, with quite remarkable results. In a recent manual, Azrin and Besalel (1980) described the Job Club, which specifies those behaviors necessary to mount and sustain a successful job search. The program is a unique combination of active social support from peers in the club, and the promotion of persistent and repeated contacts with employers using telephone banks, letters, and interviews. A series of papers (Azrin, Besalel, Wisotzek, McMorrow, & Bechtel, 1982; Azrin, Flores, & Kaplan, 1975; Azrin & Philip, 1979; Azrin, Philip, Thienes-Hontos, & Besalel, 1980; 1981; Jones & Azrin, 1973) provided evaluative data using the Job Club with the most intransigent of unemployed workers. For example, Jones and Azrin viewed the role of social factors in job finding as an exchange of social reinforcers. A survey of 120 jobs revealed that two-thirds of the job leads had come from friends or relatives. An information-reward procedure that was used to motivate community residents to publicize job openings increased job leads tenfold.

In the first test of the full Job Club procedure, Azrin et al. (1975)

matched treatment and control subjects, and conducted at least a five-session program of group meetings, a "buddy" system, family support, and a motivational intervention to overcome discouragement, as well as various strategies for finding and pursuing job leads. The average Job Club participant started work in fourteen days, compared with fifty-three days for the matched control group. Ninety percent of the participants had jobs after two months, compared with 55 percent of the controls. Participants also earned an average of $2.73 per hour, compared with $2.01 for the *no-treatment* controls. The cost of the program was only $20 per client, not including professional time. Although Azrin et al. included in their calculations only those participants who did not drop out before five sessions, thus confounding client motivation with treatment success, the results are still quite remarkable.

In a second study, Azrin and Philip (1979) compared the Job Club procedure with a standard rehabilitation program to promote job seeking. Figure 8-3 depicts the percent of clients obtaining full employment during the six months following the program; only four of the eighty participants did not secure a job within that time.

In a larger-scale study, Azrin et al. (1980), randomly assigned one-thousand welfare clients from minority and at risk populations to either a Job Club or the usual services as a control. After twelve months, 80 percent of the Job Club participants had jobs, compared with 59 percent of the controls. Costs per placement were $167, but again it was difficult to know how dropouts were treated. Nonetheless, success of this magnitude with nontraditional clients is virtually unprecedented in the field of career intervention. Another study (Azrin et al., 1982) further documented the effectiveness of the Job Club. Data of this magnitude and thoroughness are rare indeed.

THE CLINICAL APPLICATION OF JOB SEARCH METHODS

In spite of the evidence favoring a highly structured job search, most clients will initially avoid systematic methods and rely on informal approaches. This is so in part because of time pressure to implement a decision and in part because of the anxiety (and therefore avoidance) that the initiation of the search generates. Informal methods have a firm place among search techniques, but through avoidance behavior may be used to the exclusion of other methods, as the following excerpt from a case illustrates. The client, Donna, is very unhappy in her present job in retail sales administration; she has extensive, successful writing and presentation background, and feels a great sense of urgency about leaving. We had narrowed alternatives to several traveling sales positions. The job under consideration during the session from which this excerpt was taken was in pharmaceutical sales. As the passage illustrates, having to write even a simple cover letter produced enough anxiety to cause Donna to avoid the task. Thus we composed the letter during the session:

COUNSELOR   Do you have access to a typewriter?
CLIENT   I have a friend who does word processing. When you send stuff out for this pharmaceutical job, do you have to send out a cover letter?
COUNSELOR   Yes.
CLIENT   That's a problem, I haven't spoken to you about writing them.
COUNSELOR   Well, let's write a cover letter after we've finished this, O.K.?
CLIENT   I hate to write; well, eventually I'll have to get into this. I know what I want to say in my head, but what gets down on paper just doesn't mesh.

Even though Donna knew she had to engage in an aggressive job search, she avoided any structured behaviors, instead favoring informal sources (e.g., friends and acquaintances), where the possibility for rejection or failure seemed lower. Indeed, in spite of vigorous attempts to persuade her to do otherwise, Donna accepted a job on a tip from a friend that had little relationship to the areas we had discussed during our sessions.

In summary, although informal methods are the most commonly used search strategies, they are by no means universally effective. Highly assertive methods, which are appropriate in some situations, are also inappropri-

Figure 8-3 Percentage of Clients who Obtained Employment in the Six Months After the First Day of Job Club Counseling. (Source: N. H. Azrin and R. A. Philip, "The Job Club Method for the Job Handicapped: A Comparative Outcome Study," *Rehabilitation Counseling Bulletin* 23 [1979]:149. Copyright © 1979 by the American Association for Counseling and Development. Reproduced by permission.)

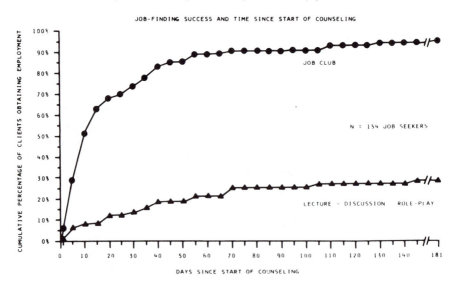

ate in others. Perhaps the best technique is a hybrid search composed of formal and informal methods, but with a careful analysis of the barriers and problems in the market one is trying to enter. This analysis is the element of success in Azrin's Job Club: a careful study of the behaviors likely to lead to a successful job search and a systematic intervention to insure a high rate of those behaviors.

FUTURE POSSIBILITIES IN THE STUDY OF CAREER INFORMATION RETRIEVAL

The proportion of professional effort devoted to problems in career information acquisition and processing, and to subsequent search behaviors is very small, considering their importance to the quality of clients' decisions. There are many more studies of counseling techniques and interventions, yet comparatively few on basic processes such as search and information. There are a few bright lights on the horizon, however. If clients do act as personal scientists in formulating and testing career-relevant hypotheses (Blustein & Strohmer, 1987), then it should be possible to study the process by which they form and evaluate their options. Further, a recent book by Vondracek, Lerner, and Schulenberg (1986) drew heavily on the work of J. J. and E. J. Gibson on the psychology of perception. J. J. Gibson (1966) argued that the visual world is scanned for information and that to an extent visual systems had to be self-guided to "home in" on visual information. An individual's perceptual field (environment) becomes increasingly differentiated as that person learns what to attend to and what to ignore. Each object in the perceptual field has a certain affordance—or whatever the perceiver presumes the environment will offer, good or bad—associated with it that links the perception to the action that follows it (E. J. Gibson, 1988). Perceiving, according to E. J. Gibson, is "active, a process of obtaining information about the world. We don't simply see, we look" (p. 5). The environment makes demands upon an individual that require action for survival. The individual must draw information from the array presented and use it to shape insights and to direct actions toward survival. In career decision making, much the same situation pertains. To the degree that career choice influences survival, much is at stake in these decisions. Developing a science of career information is an essential next step in the survival of a scientific approach to career intervention.

SUMMARY

Several seemingly disparate programs of empirical research—information-seeking, cognitive complexity, differentiation and integration of cognitive structures, personal hypothesis testing, and realistic preview—all portray the information-gathering and retrieval process as a complex person-environment transaction with a quasiscientific basis, rather than a simple assimilation of commercially available sources of information. Recommendations to promote information retrieval have been discussed, as well as the few formal approaches to information and job search that now exist.

9

Evaluating Career
Interventions

This chapter discusses the evaluation of the complete array of career intervention programs and services described in this book. The evaluation of career intervention differs from research on vocational behavior in several ways. Although both evaluation and research contribute important information to career professionals, research involves the testing of hypotheses drawn from theory, with the goals of the increased control over and prediction of behavior, and a high level of rigor and precision (Burck & Peterson, 1975). Evaluation, on the other hand, provides information for assessing stated intervention goals and objectives, and for making decisions about the provision of career services. According to one definition, "evaluation is always undertaken with reference to some intentional action that is designed to influence one or more people, change personal/social relationships, or alter a material situation" (Reicken, 1977, p. 394). Evaluations contain four types of elements: (1) scientific-technical; (2) administrative-managerial; (3) political-social; and (4) ethical. The paramount concern of evaluation is that at the very least individuals should not be worse than they were before the intervention; that is, they should not deteriorate (Reicken, 1977).

As recently as ten years ago, the distinction between evaluation and research in career psychology was a simple one to make. Field studies assessing the impact of an intervention were considered to be evaluations, and developmental or differential studies testing a theory were considered to be research. At that time, evaluation studies were done in natural settings (Gelso, 1979b) and sacrificed rigor for relevance (Goldman, 1976), whereas research studies were done in contrived settings, such as laboratories or analogues, where maximum rigor was sought. In contrast, evaluation and research are now converging, and distinctions between them are less important. Field research, process studies, and case studies are increasingly popular, whereas correlational designs are yielding decreasing returns in some areas of study (Spokane, 1985). Research on career intervention closely resembles evaluation when it compares the efficacy of several treatments, or studies an aspect of the treatment in order to increase its potency. One remaining contemporary boundary between evaluation and research, however, lies in the analytic study of the gain process (see Chapter 3), and in the study of complex interactions between treatments and client characteristics (Fretz, 1981). Such studies contribute to our understanding of not only specific treatments and their outcomes, but also of the psychological processes involved in career selection. Thus, process studies can be considered to be either research or evaluation.

Rounds and Tinsley (1984) have stated that we are unlikely to understand career intervention until we restrict our definition of the process to dyadic or group interactions between a counselor and a client. The underlying question in the dispute over the definition of career counseling is whether parallel intervention and client gain processes are involved in traditional and alternative interventions. This book takes the position that the processes are essentially similar, but that the mix is weighted for different interventions. Thus we might have slightly varied outcome expectations for workshops than for individual counseling based on the blend of processes (client and counselor) in the intervention.

WHY EVALUATE CAREER INTERVENTIONS?

Perloff and Perloff (1977) described two historical bases of the mental health evaluation movement. The first is the concern in a democratic society for the general welfare of individuals, and the shared desire to improve "economic and educational opportunities, decrease illness and environmental blight, and to make people happier, healthier, and more hopeful about their futures" (Perloff & Perloff, 1977, p. 379). Although Perloff and Perloff argued that there may be less of this humanitarian motive for evaluating mental health programs and services than might be desirable, most federal programs are designed with this belief in mind.

A second reason for evaluating mental health programs and services derives from the consumer movement, and has been called *accountability*. Various consumer groups (e.g., school boards, state legislatures, and third-party payers) have led the campaign for accountability in the counseling field, insisting on evidence of its effectiveness (Herr, 1976). Cost has been an important aspect of such accountability (Krumboltz, 1974). Because the vast sums of federal money that had been devoted to mental health programs during the 1950s and 1960s diminished sharply in 1970s and 1980s just as the service needs were expanding, the efficient use of available funds was a serious concern for mental health professionals (Coursey, 1977).

There are thus many reasons for evaluating mental health interventions in general and career interventions in particular. These efforts, however, are not nearly as thorough as similar evaluations in the medical community. The FDA approval process for a new drug, for example, requires sufficient evidence of the drug's effectiveness from controlled studies *prior* to its release. Where would career intervention stand in a controlled approval process? What is a reasonable outcome for a career intervention?

WHAT WE CAN EXPECT FROM A CAREER INTERVENTION

In the past fifteen years, several comprehensive and penetrating reviews of career development theory and interventions have increased our general understanding of the overall effectiveness of career interventions (Baker & Popowicz, 1983; Fretz, 1981; Holland, Magoon, & Spokane, 1981; Krumboltz, Becker-Haven, & Burnett, 1979; Lunneborg, 1983; R. A. Myers, 1971, 1986; Spokane and Oliver, 1983; Osipow, 1982, 1987c; Pickering & Vacc, 1984; Rounds & Tinsley, 1984; Savickas, in press; Spokane & Oliver, 1983; Super & Hall, 1978; Watts & Kidd, 1978). In addition, numerous annual reviews of the career development literature, many of which included studies of career intervention, have been published in the *Journal of Vocational Behavior* (Bartol, 1981; E. L. Betz, 1977; Borgen, Layton, Veehnhuizen & Johnson, 1985; Fitzgerald & Rounds, 1989; Garbin & Stover, 1980; Greenhaus & Parasuraman, 1986; Muchinsky, 1983; Osipow, 1976; Phillips, Cairo, Blustein, & Myers, 1988; Slaney & Russell, 1987; Tinsley & Heesacker, 1984; Walsh, 1979; Zytowski, 1978). Each of these reviews has had a slightly different interpretation of the literature, although there is considerable overlap among their conclusions. Although a detailed discussion of the hundreds of studies covered in these articles is beyond the scope of this book, a distillation of the reviews does suggest the following general observations that may help guide the practicing counselor:

The General Potency of Career Interventions

1. The results of nearly one hundred controlled empirical studies, conducted with a variety of clients and using the full range of career intervention techniques, strategies, and programs, demonstrate moderate but robust beneficial effects on a wide array of vocational outcome variables (Baker & Popowicz, 1983; R. A. Myers, 1986; Oliver & Spokane, 1988; Osipow, 1982; Pickering & Vacc, 1984; Rounds & Tinsley, 1984; Spokane & Oliver, 1983).

2. Longer (at least ten sessions), more comprehensive interventions, although requiring much more time from the client and the counselor, will have roughly twice the beneficial effects of briefer interventions (Baker & Popowicz, 1983; Oliver & Spokane, 1988; Phillips, Friedlander, Kost, Specterman, & Robbins, 1988).

3. Long-term effects of career interventions have been demonstrated for up to six months after treatment, with little loss of potency (Azrin, Philip, Thienes-Hontos, & Besalel, 1981; R. A. Myers, 1971; Johnson, Johnson, & Yates, 1981), although "booster" treatments have not been tried. R. A. Myers (1971) suggested that the follow-up period most appropriate for a career intervention is the time at which the next career decision must be faced, but assigned no time interval to that next point.

Differential Effects of Career Intervention Strategies

4. Individual counseling, although much more costly than other approaches, is the most efficient intervention in terms of amount of gain per hour of effort (Oliver & Spokane, 1988).

5. Inventories and self-assessment devices are still the most sought-after and effective intervention strategies in the counselor's armamentarium, with computer-assisted interpretations enhancing their effects with written information and media presentations (Fretz, 1981; Kirschner, 1988; Phillips et al., 1988; Wiggins, 1987).

6. Job-seeking self-presentation skills can be effectively learned using role plays, role models, and group discussions (R. A. Myers, 1986).

Specificity of Career Intervention Outcomes

7. Typically, one can expect an average of one standard deviation of gain following a career intervention on measures of career maturity, decisional status, appropriateness of choice, and information-seeking behavior (Krumboltz et al., 1979; Spokane & Oliver, 1983).

8. On the average, clients will seriously consider one additional career option following a career intervention (Fretz & Leong, 1982).

Deterioration Effects

9. The teaching of cognitively oriented decision strategies to intuitive deciders (Harren, 1980) is the only intervention that has been found to produce consistently ineffective and/or harmful outcomes (Holland et al., 1981).

Individual Differences in Career Intervention Outcomes

10. Individuals who are low in self-esteem and social skills, who are high in indecision and low in vocational identity, or who have unrealistic aspirations will have better outcomes in individual counseling than in self-guided or group interventions (R. A. Myers, 1986).

11. Special groups (e.g., gifted or minority individuals) will have better outcomes with more structured as opposed to more vague and diffuse career interventions (Savickas, in press).

Such reviews of the literature and controlled studies increase our confidence in career interventions as currently practiced, and suggest that evaluation and research can now be directed at the discovery of the process underlying interventions and of ways to strengthen the already considerable effects demonstrated in career intervention outcome studies. There is no need to fear evaluation or research, either in following one's own clients after a suitable period or in allowing others to study one's techniques. The number of analytic studies of intervention outcomes is tapering off, in part because of the difficulty in conducting such studies and in part because easily conceived prepost studies are no longer very helpful. Counselors and researchers will thus have to work together on field studies if further progress is to be made.

WHAT WE SHOULD BE EVALUATING VERSUS WHAT WE HAVE BEEN EVALUATING

In his scathing review of the state of counseling research, Goldman (1976) argued that most of this work had very little to offer practitioners (Myers, 1989), a charge that was echoed by Krumboltz et al. (1979) and countered by Gelso (1979b), who called for methodological pluralism along the rigor-relevance dimension.

Relevance of Measures

Career counseling outcome research has generally used measures that were developed from longitudinal or large-scale theoretical studies of the general population (e.g., career maturity [Super], person-environment congruence [Holland], or information-seeking [Krumboltz]) because they had established records of reliability and validity. Nonetheless, these measures have only tangential relevance to a client faced with a career decision. R. A. Myers (1986; 1989) suggested suspending studies using information seeking as an outcome until the relevance of the measure could be improved. Another common outcome measure, career maturity, while useful to developmental theorists, has very little utility for clients under pressure to make a career decision. Treatment satisfaction, a seeming improvement, actually has very little relation to the client's ability to make improved career decisions. In cases in which a relevant outcome measure has been employed, it frequently has been homemade, and without demonstrated reliability or validity (Spokane & Oliver, 1983). The use of multiple outcome measures (Oliver, 1979) is an improvement only if their relevance and psychometric quality are firmly established.

In a candid, tongue-in-cheek article on the problems in designing relevant outcome measures entitled "Needed: Instruments as Good as Our Eyes," Brickell (1976) chronicled a four-year attempt to verify the positive outcomes that a team of skilled observers had found for a certain career intervention. Brickell began by writing multiple-choice items, which were administered to six thousand students; no difference between treated and untreated students was found. The observers were sent out to the field sites again, however, and again found beneficial outcomes. Finally, the evaluators went back to the classes to observe the students' outcomes directly rather than employing teacher ratings of student progress. If an observer witnessed any learning about careers in the classroom, an item was written to reflect what was seen, sometimes right on the spot. The evaluators went from school to school, writing more than one thousand usable items while discarding hundreds of others. The items were compiled into grade-level tests that were administered to twelve thousand students.

The result was a set of sensible, significant differences in program effectiveness that took nearly five years to find. Brickell's final assessment was a goal-free, theory-free field test that had maximum relevance to actual student learning but minimum relation to program goals and career development theory. Traditional program evaluation methods had not worked because the theories were not relevant to the learning that was taking place; nor were the objectives written to reflect the actual outcomes. Brickell's refreshing account of this case is must reading for anyone seeking to implement and evaluate a career intervention.

Relevance of Interventions

Career intervention outcome studies have used such distorted caricatures or analogues of actual career counseling that it is difficult to draw conclusions from their findings. Twenty-minute test interpretations or one-shot workshops on cognitive decision making conducted out of the counseling context tell us very little about how to improve the quality of client career decisions. Fortunately, actual subjects are now more frequently used in such studies, and natural career interventions are more common (Phillips, Cairo, et al., 1988). While it is true that analogue research studies may illuminate the complex processes involved in counseling through laboratory control, studies evaluating (rather than researching) actual interventions have been far too few. Naturalistic studies are difficult and expensive to conduct, but essential to progress in the field of career intervention.

TOWARD MEANINGFUL CAREER
INTERVENTION OUTCOMES

Are different outcome criteria appropriate for different types of career interventions and client presenting problems? Certainly, counseling with a high school graduate in search of a first job will be evaluated differently from counseling with a mature adult with a high level of perceived incongruence. Does this difference mean, then, that no common outcome standard can be applied to all interventions? Reviews of the career literature often presume that interventions can be roughly compared using a common metric not only within studies but across them as well. Career intervention outcome studies, however, reveal that evaluations of developmentally oriented interventions rely heavily on outcome measures of career maturity and decisional status, whereas traditional counseling studies most often use information seeking or appropriateness of choice as outcome measures (Watts & Kidd, 1978). In fact, even a meta-analytic review strategy that converts various outcome measures to a common metric may, when comparing treatments across studies, face the problem that different interventions (e.g., class versus individual) may employ systematically different outcome measures. If, for example, it is true that studies of developmentally oriented interventions employ career maturity measures more often than individual counseling interventions, reviews of the entire set of developmental interventions would generally yield more favorable outcomes than a series of studies that used an unobtrusive measure (Webb, Campbell, Schwartz, Sechrest & Grove, 1981) of appropriateness of realism—a more difficult outcome to affect.

A single measure for evaluating all interventions would be very cumbersome, although a set of brief scales is certainly possible. A standard outcome battery composed of existing measures with demonstrated validity and reliability, and employed by every study is desirable, although very unlikely. One feasible alternative to multiple, specific outcomes is Goal Attainment Scaling, or GAS (Kiersok & Sherman, 1968), which may be used to evaluate those goals agreed upon either by the counselor and the client, or an agency or program at both the beginning and end of an intervention. When used as an outcome measure GAS has no demonstrated reliability or validity, since it must be created anew for each application. GAS has been used in career counseling studies (Hoffman, Spokane, & Magoon, 1981), to create a self-guided outcome sheet (see Figure 9-1), but a review of studies using GAS (Cytrynbaum, Ginath, Birdwell, & Brandt, 1979) showed only modest inter-rater reliability, and very little construct or content validity. Furthermore, proper use of GAS appears to need the intensive negotiation of the goals and their perceived outcomes between the client and the counselor. Thus the technique is far from a perfect answer to the outcome problem in career interventions.

Several authors (Fretz, 1981; R. A. Myers, 1986; Oliver, 1979) have suggested using multiple measures that cut across a common set of outcome domains. The result of Oliver's suggestion, however, was often the unsystematic selection of several measures without much thought about why they were chosen. Her four classes of outcomes build on Myer's (1981) earlier classifications and have been recently revised (Oliver & Spokane, 1988):

Career Decision Making
Accuracy of self-knowledge
Appropriateness of choice
Instrumental behaviors
Attitudes toward choice
Other characteristics of choice

GOAL SHEET

	EXAMPLE	Goal #1	Goal #2	Goal #3
Much less than the expected level of outcome	DISCOVER NEW CAREER OPTIONS TO EXPLORE DISCOVER NO * NEW CAREER OPTIONS TO EXPLORE			
Somewhat less than the expected level of outcome	DISCOVER ONE NEW CAREER OPTION TO EXPLORE			
Expected level of outcome	DISCOVER TWO NEW CAREER OPTIONS TO EXPLORE			
Somewhat more than the expected level of outcome	DISCOVER THREE NEW CAREER OPTIONS TO EXPLORE			
Much more than the expected level of outcome	DISCOVER SEVERAL NEW CAREER OPTIONS TO EXPLORE			

GOALS   OUTCOMES

Figure 9-1   Self-Guided Vocational Goal Attainment Outcome Sheet.

Effective Role Functioning
Performance variables
Adjustment variables

Counseling Evaluation
Satisfaction
Effectiveness
Helpfulness

Miscellaneous Measures

Choosing a representative from each of these classes is sensible, although there are no guidelines governing the selection process. Many specific outcome measures can be classified using Oliver's system, but no single set of scales or measure has been compiled to measure the most important outcomes in career intervention. The rating scales in Figure 9-1 tap many of these outcomes as well as those on promoting gain specified in Chapter 3, and might be used by counselors, clients, or parents (with minor wording changes) to evaluate the effectiveness of an intervention, or to assess their personal level of career functioning.

Figure 9-2 Multidimensional Rating Scales for Evaluating Career Intervention Outcomes

Persistent Search and Exploratory Behavior

1. The client appears easily discouraged in the face of career-related rejections.

1	2	3	4	5	6	7
yes			sometimes			no

2. The client consistently makes phone calls, writes letters, and follows through on job contacts.

1	2	3	4	5	6	7
yes			sometimes			no

3. The client actively unearths possible career options.

1	2	3	4	5	6	7
yes			sometimes			no

Information

4. The client has sufficient information about the career options under consideration.

1	2	3	4	5	6	7
yes			somewhat			no

5. The client needs more information about a particular career option.

1	2	3	4	5	6	7
yes			somewhat			no

(continued on next page)

Figure 9-2 (continued)

6. The client considers negative or disconfirming information about the career options under consideration.

1	2	3	4	5	6	7
no			somewhat			yes

7. The client's level of career information is sufficient in depth and complexity.

1	2	3	4	5	6	7
yes			somewhat			no

8. The client's career information comes from sources close to the jobs themselves.

1	2	3	4	5	6	7
yes			somewhat			no

Realism

9. The career options under consideration appear realistic given the client's ability and skills level.

1	2	3	4	5	6	7
yes			somewhat realistic			no

10. The career options under consideration appear realistic considering the client's level of motivation and personal adjustment.

1	2	3	4	5	6	7
yes			somewhat realistic			no

11. The career options under consideration appear realistic considering the client's level of education.

1	2	3	4	5	6	7
yes			somewhat realistic			no

12. The client is "undershooting" career options with respect to occupational level.

1	2	3	4	5	6	7
no			somewhat			yes

13. The client is overestimating career options with respect to occupational level.

1	2	3	4	5	6	7
no			somewhat			yes

Barriers

14. The client faces financial barriers in implementing the career options under consideration.

1	2	3	4	5	6	7
no			minor barriers			yes

15. Primary child-care responsibilities will present a barrier for the client in implementing the career options under consideration.

1	2	3	4	5	6	7
no			minor barrier			yes

Hope and Morale

16. The client expresses hope that a reasonably fitting career option can be found.

1	2	3	4	5	6	7
no			somewhat			yes

(continued on next page)

Figure 9-2 (continued)

17. The client expresses hope about successfully implementing one of the career options under consideration.

1	2	3	4	5	6	7
yes			somewhat			no

18. The client seems happy about the outcome of counseling.

1	2	3	4	5	6	7
no			somewhat			yes

Activity Level

19. The client maintains a high level of constructive career-related activity.

1	2	3	4	5	6	7
no			sometimes			yes

20. The client makes many phone calls, writes letters, or conducts frequent personal interviews about career options.

1	2	3	4	5	6	7
yes			sometimes			no

21. The client misses sessions, does not complete homework assignments, or does not follow through on agreements.

1	2	3	4	5	6	7
yes			sometimes			no

22. The client is simply unable to get moving.

1	2	3	4	5	6	7
yes			somewhat			no

Congruence

23. The career options under consideration are a reasonable fit with the client's measured interests.

1	2	3	4	5	6	7
yes			somewhat			no

24. The client perceives the career options under consideration to be a reasonable fit with his or her expressed interests.

1	2	3	4	5	6	7
yes			somewhat			no

Cognitive Framework

25. The client has acquired a cognitive framework for understanding self, career, and his or her role in career choice.

1	2	3	4	5	6	7
yes			somewhat			no

26. The cognitive framework acquired by the client is scientifically and theoretically accurate and valid.

1	2	3	4	5	6	7
no			somewhat			yes

27. The client appears confused about how to make a career choice.

1	2	3	4	5	6	7
yes			somewhat confused			no

(continued on next page)

Figure 9-2 (continued)

Commitment and Predicament Appreciation

28. The client fully appreciates the nature of the career problem he or she faces at this time.

1	2	3	4	5	6	7
no			somewhat			yes

29. The client indicates a willingness to commit the time and energy necessary to make a career choice.

1	2	3	4	5	6	7
yes			somewhat willing			no

30. The client indicates a willingness to commit to implementing one of the career options under consideration.

1	2	3	4	5	6	7
no			somewhat willing			yes

Goals and Options

31. The client expresses clear long-term career goals.

1	2	3	4	5	6	7
no			somewhat			yes

32. The client expresses clear short-term career goals.

1	2	3	4	5	6	7
no			somewhat			yes

33. The client has a contingency plan for implementing career goals.

1	2	3	4	5	6	7
no			somewhat			yes

34. The client is considering a reasonable number of career options.

1	2	3	4	5	6	7
yes			somewhat reasonable			no

35. The client expresses certainty that the career options under consideration are appropriate.

1	2	3	4	5	6	7
yes			somewhat certain			no

Decisional Status

36. Making a career decision is still an agonizing and difficult process for the client.

1	2	3	4	5	6	7
no			somewhat			yes

37. The client has a conflict about his or her career choice with a significant other.

1	2	3	4	5	6	7
no			some conflict			yes

38. The client's career choice is blocked or delayed by some external constraint.

1	2	3	4	5	6	7
yes			somewhat			no

(continued on next page)

Figure 9-2 (continued)

39. The client has too many attractive career options from which to choose.

1	2	3	4	5	6	7
yes			somewhat			no

Decisional Process

40. The client feels pressured to make a career decision.

1	2	3	4	5	6	7
no			somewhat			yes

41. The client's present career situation is acceptable even if no alternative can be found.

1	2	3	4	5	6	7
no			somewhat			yes

42. The client thoroughly canvased all available career alternatives.

1	2	3	4	5	6	7
no			somewhat			yes

43. The client thoroughly considered the negative consequences of the available career options.

1	2	3	4	5	6	7
yes			somewhat			no

Anxiety

44. *The client appears anxious about the career decision he or she faces.*

1	2	3	4	5	6	7
no			somewhat			yes

45. *The client's anxiety level appears to be increasing.*

1	2	3	4	5	6	7
yes			somewhat			no

46. *A specific intervention designed to reduce the client's anxiety level would be helpful at this point.*

1	2	3	4	5	6	7
yes			somewhat helpful			no

Performance

47. The client's work and educational performance has improved.

1	2	3	4	5	6	7
no			somewhat			yes

Although the items on these scales have been derived from clinical experience, they are a blend of theory-based and goal-based items. They are not designed specifically from actual client behaviors, as Brickell (1976) did in his study, but they are certainly closer to what Brickell suggests than are traditional outcome measures. The set of scales described above might be revised to include more items written from direct observation of client behavior from video or audiotapes, and should reflect what clients actually do in the face of a career decision, rather than what they would like to do, report having done, or wish they could do (Pervin, 1987). A blend of client self-report, which may be more reliable than previously believed (R. A. Myers, 1986), and counselor observation, which is the method employed in these scales, may be the most effective evaluative strategy. Of course, no evidence of their validity or reliability is available, and they should be viewed more as an evaluative aide than as a psychometrically sound instrument.

WHAT TO DO WHEN THERE ARE NO SIGNIFICANT RESULTS

As indicated (Spokane & Oliver, 1983), most career intervention outcome studies have been single-shot affairs, done for doctoral dissertations or master's theses, with no follow-up, or single studies by experienced researchers. The seasoned researcher who evaluates career interventions in a series of studies is a rare professional. When nonsignificant results are found in controlled outcome studies, it is usually presumed that the intervention is at fault. But as Brickell (1976) appropriately noted, this is only one of four possible conclusions the evaluator might draw:

1. No beneficial career outcomes occurred, and the outcome measures correctly identified the nonsignificant outcomes.
2. There were beneficial outcomes, but the measures employed were irrelevant to the outcomes, and thus did not detect them.
3. No beneficial outcomes were detected, but the fault is in the intervention, which was either too brief, too artificial, or too general to achieve the desired result.
4. There was no effect, but the methodology was at fault (e.g., improper control group, low power, poorly trained counselors, or high dropout rates).

More than the usual single effort is needed to arrive at one of the final three explanations for a negative (no-benefit) outcome. Because they require follow-up studies, which are rare, penetrating outcome studies have been very slow to accumulate (Spokane & Oliver, 1983). Until we have a body of literature on improving unsuccessful outcomes, when an evaluation is conducted and career interventions are found to be unsuccessful, any of the following strategies can be employed to increase the effectiveness of the counselor or the program. These corrective steps require some courage on the counselor's part, as well as a scientific rather than a defensive attitude:

1. *Intensify the intervention:* This may include a longer intervention, a different mix of strategies and techniques, or one based upon individual counseling, but some evidence exists to support the delivery of a more intensive intervention after a brief intervention has failed (Bernard & Rayman, 1982).

2. *Review the goals, objectives, and outcome measures:* Make sure that the intervention is appropriate to the client's problem. If no goals or objectives are available for a group or workshop, write them yourself, and see that they really capture the essence of the intervention.

3. *Review the client's needs and problems:* An assessment of this kind might include using focus groups of clients or participants who are questioned about the problems they are facing and the appropriateness of the intervention process for those problems.

4. *Institute treatment plans:* Career treatment plans, such as the example shown in Figure 9-3, should contain treatment goals, some discussion of assessment devices, and recommendations for intervention strategies and techniques.

5. *Engage a peer consultant:* Present several cases or groups to this consultant, who reviews tapes and sessions, and evaluates data in an effort to improve treatment potency. (See Appendix F for the Case Presentation Form.)

6. *Establish an advisory board:* This board should represent the client population from which your cases are drawn: if a school or college, the board should be composed of students and faculty from all grades; if an industrial or governmental organization, employees and management should be represented; if a practice setting, a selection of clients should be represented.

7. *Contact dropouts:* Complete this step especially if your dropout rate is over 30 percent. Dropouts will frequently be quite candid about why they left, and this information can be valuable in revising intervention strategies.

EVALUATING THE FULL RANGE OF CAREER INTERVENTIONS

A volume edited by Krumboltz and Hamel (1982) contained an informative set of articles on career program evaluation. An effective evaluation-accountability model, according to Krumboltz (1974), must accomplish several outcomes: (1) define the counselor's role and the goals of counseling; (2) chart observable behavior as the outcome; (3) state costs; (4) promote professional effectiveness rather than assigning blame; (5) tolerate failures; (6)

INDIVIDUAL CAREER INTERVENTION PLAN

Client's Name: _____

Date of Birth: _____

Soc. Sec.#: _____

COUNSELOR: _____

PRESENT JOB TITLE: _____

DIAGNOSIS

DSM III-R CODE AXIS I _____
(If Appropriate) AXIS II _____
                  AXIS III _____
                  AXIS IV _____
                  AXIS V _____

Holland Code □ □ □
              1st 2nd 3rd

PRESENTING CONCERNS:

REFERRAL TYPE

□ SELF   □ FAMILY MEMBER   □ SUPERVISOR   □ PROFESSIONAL   □ OTHER

CAREER OBJECTIVES	INTERVENTION GOALS

SHORT TERM
1.
2.
3.
4.

LONG TERM
1.
2.
3.
4.

FAMILY CONSIDERATIONS: _____

ACTIVITY PLAN

INTERVENTION STRATEGIES & TECHNIQUES

TYPE	# OF SESSIONS
INDIVIDUAL COUNSELING	□
STRUCTURED GROUP COUNSELING	□
UNSTRUCTURED GROUP COUNSELING	□
COMPUTER INTERVENTION	□
CLASS	□
RESUME WRITING	□
INTERVIEW SKILLS	□
JOB CLUB	□
STRESS MANAGEMENT	□
OTHER _____	□

226

Assessment Procedures (Circle All Applicable)

INTEREST MEASURES

Criterion Based (College)	SCII KUDER DD ECO OTHER _____
Criterion Based (Non College)	CAI MVII OTHER _____
Homogeneous (Self-Guiding)	SDS IDEAS HARRINGTON-O'SHEA OTHER _____
Homogeneous (Hand/Machine)	VPI JVIS UNIACT COPS OVIS VII OTHER _____

DECISION-MAKING MEASURES

Decisional Status	CDS MVS ACDM OTHER _____
Career Maturity	CMI CDI ACCI CVMT OTHER _____
Goal Setting	GAS OTHER _____

WORKPLACE MEASURES

Job Satisfaction/Involvement	JSB JDI JI OTHER _____
Managerial Style	MIQ MSQ LILS MSB OTHER _____

PERSONALITY MEASURES

General	NEO EPPS ACL POI FIRO-B MBTI _____
	CPI OPI 16 PF MMPI OTHER _____

ABILITY MEASURES

Batteries	GATB ASVAB DAT ECO OTHER _____
Specific Tests	SPECIFY _____

OTHER MEASURES

Card Sort	SPECIFY _____
Work Values	AVL HOOI WVI MIQ CWO OTHER _____
Work Environment	OSI RCAS WES OTHER _____
Work Samples	VALPAR TOWER SPECIFY _____

Figure 9-3 Sample Career Treatment Plan.

seek input from all concerned parties; and (7) be open to periodic revision. Before undertaking an evaluation, however, the following basic data must be available:

1. *Client attitudes, knowledge, behavior, and emotion:* These domains are tapped by the rating scales in Figure 9-2.

2. *Client attributes:* What is the profile of the client population (e.g., demographics and family background)? How do clients differ from nonclients in this population? What is the epidemiology of career problems in this population? Does the intervention reduce the prevalence of further predictable problems?

3. *Diagnostic categories:* What are the most common diagnoses for clients served in the program? Have the diagnostic impressions changed over time?

4. *Referral sources:* Who is referring the clients for intervention? What are the reasons for the referral? Do these referral sources have any impressions about the service rendered?

5. *Costs:* The cost effectiveness of vocational interventions can be estimated by calculating the time, materials, and personnel necessary to achieve a desired outcome. The costs can be calculated as cost per counselor or client hour invested, or by total program costs, which can be amortized over a longer period if career resources or computer equipment is purchased.

6. *Service utilization:* Are the clients receiving the services they need? What percentage of the potential clientele is taking advantage of the various services? How much counseling time (i.e., number and kind of sessions) is being used by the average client? Do clients return for repeat services? What is the average length of treatment upon repeat visits?

7. *Extra-treatment support:* Where are clients receiving outside help and support? How effective are these interventions?

8. *Staff-professional activities:* In what activities and with which clients are staff members spending most of their time?

9. *Unobtrusive measures:* Such measures, which can include tallies of information usage, records data, and other information derived from data not collected directly from the client, are very useful in establishing outcomes that are free from the bias and reactivity often associated with self-reports.

Special Considerations in Evaluating Individual Interventions

The collection of individual client data and ratings by the counselor (see Figure 9-2) may be sufficient for a superficial evaluation of individual career interventions. Follow-up data on graduation rates, employment stability, use of counseling services (Spokane, 1979), and the ability to make an improved career decision (R. A. Myers, 1971) are all important aspects of such an evaluation. In addition, the cost effectiveness in terms of counselor time, testing expenses, and resource center usage, and the utilization rates among the population in question should be considered. In other words, how many clients actually use the available counselor time? Some estimates suggest that a small proportion of a given population (usually 20 percent) will utilize most clinical time (generally 80 percent).

Finally, process measures, especially of the working alliance, and/or counselor evaluation may be important in evaluating intervention effectiveness.

Special Considerations in Evaluating Group Interventions

There is some disagreement among evaluation specialists about the unit of analysis in group interventions. Whereas studies of group interventions have generally presumed that each individual within the group should be considered as a separate subject, many specialists suggest that the group as a whole should be aggregated and treated as a single subject. When the group is the unit of analysis the degrees of freedom and power are vastly reduced, which means that many more groups must be studied than are typically required in career intervention research and evaluation. As an example, two counseling groups with ten participants each would be treated as only two subjects, rather than twenty. In either case, multiple groups should be evaluated in any careful evaluation of group interventions. The success of the group as a whole can be as important an outcome as the behavior of the individuals within the group.

Also, in evaluating group interventions, it is important to consider whether participants have received individual counseling during intake or at some previous time, and whether the group is viewed as a supplement to individual intervention or as the only intervention. If clients are receiving several intervention modalities simultaneously, it may be difficult to establish the contribution of each. Dropout rates are generally high in group interventions. Care must be taken to document this figure and to include dropouts in the final sample. Ongoing groups occasionally allow temporary membership so that individuals may enter and leave freely. It should also be remembered that the availability of the group is frequently a more salient determinant of referral for intervention than client diagnostic status. Also, as indicated, some individuals do not benefit from group interventions.

Finally, group process factors (e.g., cohesion and leader style) may be important indicators of the success of a career group. Some groups may take on a very different tone than others, and the tone may be more responsible for derived benefits than any particular treatment content. The level of structure (structured versus unstructured) in the group should also be assessed, and an attempt should be made to determine whether the groups being evaluated were actually similar in tone and process.

Special Considerations in Evaluating Classroom Interventions

Since classroom interventions involve large groups, multiple classes should always be evaluated. Tone and process questions may also be important. In addition, classroom interventions last longer than any other interventions (Oliver & Spokane, 1988) and thus more susceptible to the influences of time (T. D. Cook & Campbell, 1979). Also, the possibility that subjects received additional assistance is quite large; the interim measurement of outcomes may reduce this problem somewhat. If multiple instructors or guest lecturers are employed, their contributions should be assessed separately.

Special Considerations in Evaluating Computer-Assisted Interventions

The evidence suggests that the length of time a client spends on the computer is an important determinant of the benefit derived. In addition, some individuals will derive more benefit from computer interventions than others, making individual differences a factor in evaluations. As with group interventions, computer interventions are sometimes used as stand-alone treatments and at other times as adjuncts to a comprehensive intervention package, which makes their evaluation more difficult.

The price of hardware, software, and annual maintenance fees must be figured into the costs of computer-assisted interventions. The initial costs of purchase, however, may be offset over time if a large number of clients use the system; computers are also decreasing in price, as are the microcomputers required to operate them. Evaluation of these systems has frequently been conducted in terms of user satisfaction rather than client outcomes, but more rigorous studies are now beginning to appear.

SUMMARY

Evaluation is distinct from research. Career interventions are evaluated to promote the welfare of individuals and to insure the accountability of the counseling profession in times of decreasing resources. A variety of interventions have been repeatedly found to be moderately effective, but evaluative efforts suffer from problems of irrelevance. A preliminary set of multidimensional rating scales has been suggested in the hope that more evaluations will incorporate similar outcomes. Special considerations in evaluating diverse interventions were also discussed.

10

The Professional Context of Career Intervention

It is unnerving that so little has been written about the professional context of career intervention, but this chapter will attempt to address some of the issues that counselors face, including the following: How does a person become a competent career intervention specialist? What skills and experiences are necessary? How should career counselors spend their time? Is counselor training and supervision in career intervention different than in personal or social intervention? What didactic courses should an aspiring career counselor complete?

TRAINING AND SUPERVISION IN CAREER INTERVENTION

For a time, the content of the psychotherapy session was judged to be private, too secret for study or discussion (Matarazzo & Patterson, 1986). As a consequence, very little was written about the conduct of psychotherapy until Rogers (1957) employed audiotapes to study the process directly. After Rogers, two distinct research thrusts developed. The first, as illustrated by Truax and Carkhuff (1967), led to simple, prescriptive methods for teaching counseling skills. Matarazzo's discussion of the teaching and learning of psychotherapeutic skills was the first prominent review to acknowledge these methods, which became known as the therapy skills approach. The work of Kagan and Krathwohl (1967) on interpersonal process recall and of Ivey (1971) on microcounseling also focused on the "painless" acquisition of basic counseling skills. The second research thrust concentrated on describing the therapy process, arguing that a complete understanding of both the client's and the counselor's perspectives would promote more effective interventions, regardless of the theory they employed (Goldfried, 1980). This process approach spawned extensive studies of the client and the counselor (Hill, 1989) as well as an equally extensive effort to build a model of the dynamics between the counselor and the supervisor (Russell, Crimmings, & Lent, 1984). Research on the psychotherapy process is now the dominant concern in the counseling literature (Hill, 1989), with the study of the supervision process a rapidly growing complement to this work.

If career counseling is judged to be largely or wholly similar to psychotherapy (Rounds & Tinsley, 1984), then career counseling supervision strategy should be similar to its psychotherapeutic counterpart as well. However, because career intervention is distinct from psychotherapy in some important ways, there should be separate literature on training and supervision in career intervention. Unfortunately, no such literature exists. Indeed, only one of the seven most current texts on career counseling had even a single reference to supervision in its index. Career counselors appear even more reluctant to subject themselves and their practices to careful scrutiny than were psychotherapists. Those career counselors who favor models that concentrate on the dyadic interaction probably rely on the vast and growing literature on psychotherapy supervision to guide their efforts. Those who favor a broad interpretation of career intervention may consider the process of intervention to be education rather than therapy, and thus draw upon instructional psychology research; they likely find little need for training and supervision research. However, both therapeutic and instructional models are needed if we are to understand how to train for the full array of career interventions.

There is very little specific research or models of career supervision, even though beginning counselors often find career counseling to be their most technical and difficult assignment. In this section we shall review some of the work on psychotherapy training and supervision as it applys to career counseling and intervention; discuss the unique requirements of training in career intervention; and examine treatment planning, course construction, and case supervision.

Career interventions range from the most counselor intensive and therapeutically oriented individual interventions to the more educationally oriented and less counselor intensive alternative interventions, such as self-help materials. As we pay increased attention to the underlying processes of career intervention, we may find that the same processes are involved in both types of interventions. On the other hand, quite different sequences may be operating. A solid grounding in principles of educational psychology, instructional design, and human development is necessary for successful educative or preventive programs; this material may also be helpful in structuring dyadic interventions. A thorough understanding of counselor intentions and client reactions in therapy is the essence of effective career counseling, and may be equally useful for designing therapeutic as well as classroom interventions.

Supervising Therapeutic Interventions

What material from the burgeoning literature on counseling and psycho-therapy supervision can be applied to career intervention? Much of the early work on counseling supervision focused on the provision of adequate core counseling conditions (Rogers, 1957); later work emphasized the acquisition of specific interpersonal skills (Ivey, 1971). Both approaches demonstrated that specific counseling skills could be isolated and learned. Although there is still some controversy about whether such skills are either necessary or sufficient to beneficial outcomes (Gelso, 1979b), it seems apparent that their absence may produce no gain or even harmful results.

Two models of the stages of counselor supervision (Loganbill, Hardy, & Delworth, 1982; Stoltenberg, 1981) have generated considerable research and discussion; a comparison of their stages appears in Table 10-1.

Table 10-1   Two Models of the Stages of Counselor Supervision

STAGE	LOGANBILL ET AL., 1982	STOLTENBERG, 1982
1	Stagnation	Dependency
2	Confusion	Dependency-autonomy conflict
3	Integration	Conditional dependency
4	—	Master counselor

Kell and Mueller's (1966) book on supervision—*Conflict*—was aptly named. Close supervision of professional work has always generated a certain amount of self-consciousness if not illogical resentment. Thus it is no surprise that both Loganbill et al. (1982) and Stoltenberg (1981) characterize the counselor-in-training during first stage of supervision as lacking in awareness, and being immobile and dependent upon the supervisor for direction and basic instruction. Both models then move to a second stage in which the counselor gains increasing awareness coupled with a growing independence that is sometimes characterized by ambivalence or doubt about the efficacy of counseling interventions. In the final stages the counselor-in-training begins to integrate the values, skills, and attitudes of the experienced counselor, and the supervisory relationship becomes more collegial and less didactic.

Research reveals two or three basic dimensions of the complex supervision process that may affect the quality of the supervision and indirectly of the counseling. Ellis and Dell (1986) used multidimensional scaling to analyze supervisory roles, and found that they had a three-dimensional structure that differed along cognitive versus emotional and support versus nonsupport dimensions. The authors concluded that developmental models generally did not account for differences between cognitively or emotionally oriented supervisors, and should make greater use of the challenge-support dichotomy in which the supervisee makes the greatest progress in response to supervision challenges when sufficient emotional support is available. This notion confirms the conflictual nature of supervision described by Kell and Mueller (1966), and implies that the resolution of the conflict results in counselor gain.

In an unusually thoughtful study of self-presentation in supervision, Ward, Friedlander, Schoen, and Klein (1985) argued that supervisees wanting to create a favorable impression on a supervisor might be defensive, taking credit for any client improvement but denying responsibility for any failure. Defensive supervisees might also use a tactic called counterdefensiveness to accept responsibility for failures and deny credit for success.

Worthington (1984) found that the following ten supervisor behaviors were significantly correlated with supervisee satisfaction:

1. Encouraging counselor independence in a supportive atmosphere.
2. Offering help with infrequently taught skills, including live observation, co-counseling intake interview training, and case handling.
3. Being task oriented.
4. Focusing on the supervisory relationship to demonstrate counseling skills.
5. Providing feedback, especially positive feedback.
6. Displaying personal interest in the supervisee, especially when using role playing or addressing defensiveness.
7. Establishing and negotiating goals.
8. Showing respect for supervisee, including the use of the supervisee's name.
9. Providing support while teaching, including labeling behavior and assisting in the development of self-confidence.
10. Establishing rapport with the supervisee, which was related to satisfaction, competence, and impact.

Worthington found generally that support and encouragement were helpful during the early stages of supervision. Supervisors who provided acceptance and support, and who taught conceptualizing and intervention skills were clearly the most effective.

Changes in Supervisory Relationships with Time and Experience. Recent studies suggested that different supervisor behaviors are effective at different levels of training and experience (Heppner & Roehlke, 1984; Miars et al., 1983). For example, Heppner and Roehlke found that supervisees rated supervision as more effective when their supervisors combined support and specific skills training in a progressive fashion, moving from intake skills to alternative conceptualization skills and finally to an examination of the supervisee's personal concerns about the counseling process. Beginning students were more often concerned with issues of support and self-awareness, whereas more advanced students were more defensive and concerned with personal issues.

Miars et al. (1983) found that listening to tapes, directive instruction, and support were viewed as significantly more important with beginning supervisees, whereas collaboration, personal development, and issues of client resistance and transference were more important with more advanced trainees.

Supervising Instructional Interventions

Although the literature on the supervision of *therapeutic* interventions is now very large, there is almost no comparable literature on the supervision of *instructional* interventions. Yalom (1985), in his classic volume on group psychotherapy, argued that an optimum ratio for group supervision is one hour of supervision for every group session conducted. This ratio seems reasonable in group career interventions such as classes or workshops. An excellent model for the supervision of classroom interventions with multiple sections and instructors, is in use at the University of Maryland. The Counseling Department, which offers credit for the career course, and the Career Development Center collaborate to train and supervise the instructors for the class. The instructors take a basic course in career development, and a senior graduate student holds a seminar for the instructors once each week. In the past this seminar has carried graduate credit, and focuses on the problems of planning and delivering classroom career interventions, using the assessment devices in the workbook, and sharing experiences and difficulties. A structured intervention model developed by the center is used as the basis for each class, and separate but interlocking manuals have been developed for instructors and class participants (University of Maryland Career Development Center, 1989).

Improving Instructional Interventions

Contemporary instructional psychology is based upon the premise that the simple presentation of material is insufficient to optimize learning. Instead, what is needed are strategies to allow learners to assemble and assimilate knowledge that they construct themselves (Resnick, 1981): "They transform what they receive from instruction and create and construct knowledge in their own minds" (Pintrich, Cross, Kozma, & McKeachie, 1986, p. 613). Recent findings in instructional design suggest that whatever the nature of the instruction, it should enhance the already present learning structures in an individual.

Mayer's (1979) work on advanced cognitive organizers is a good example of a contribution from instructional psychology to the interpretation of career inventories. Mayer found that it is especially important to preface presentation of new material with a clear explanation or system for understanding that information. Asking questions about forthcoming material before the presentation increases the likelihood that the material will be retained. In the career domain, Holland, Magoon, and Spokane (1981) argued that formulating clear organizing ideas can increase the amount of information the client derives from an inventory. In a direct test of that proposition, Fogg (1983) showed that providing a cognitive framework (UMAPS depicting all university majors according to Holland's system) (Jacoby, Rue, & Allen, 1984) for understanding the Self Directed Search (Holland, 1985b) improved the client's ability to absorb the information presented in the inventory. Subjects who received this cognitive framework also seemed to need less additional information *after* the intervention.

In a similar vein, Resnick (1983) argued that learners bring naïve personal theories or models about how the world operates to the science classroom. Effective science instruction must first unearth and debunk these naïve theories to make room for scientifically accurate replacements. Likewise, problem-solving interventions use concrete examples to teach general principles of problem solving, and the more explicit the thought processes are made, the more effective the instruction will be. To be effective, positive feedback (praise) must be specific and accurate, not global (Pintrich et al., 1986). It appears that the careful review and repeated checking of previously learned material presented in small steps, with clear feedback and lots of practice, result in increased learning (Pintrich et al., 1986).

In summary, although there is no current literature on the supervision of career intervention, some of the work on psychotherapy supervision has implications for this field. First and foremost, direct, supervised experience, preferably with audio- or videotape, is essential to effective supervision. Basic counseling skills of establishing rapport and a working alliance probably improve the quality of most career interventions. There may be a few differences in the supervision of individual versus group or class interventions, but it seems clear that novice counselors will have strong feelings about being supervised and about their supervisor. Sufficient time and regular contacts (at least one hour of supervision per intervention session) will increase the chances of a complete supervision experience in which the counselor moves from dependency and confusion to independent judgment and performance.

THE COUNSELOR'S ROLE IN CAREER INTERVENTION

Counselors in different settings will spend their time in different ways. The counselor's training, personality, and temperament, and the goals of the supervisor and the institution may also affect the distribution of activities that a particular counselor undertakes. The contemporary career counselor must be capable of a good deal more than traditional individual or group counseling. In recognition of this broadening role, the National Vocational Guidance Association, or NVGA (now the National Career Development Association, or NCDA), formed a task force to study and consider the skills needed to be an effective vocational counselor. The result was a matrix of counselor competencies that broadens the role of the career professional to include planning and design, and the implementation and evaluation of interventions (see Table 1-2). The schema also specifies that the broadened role may include a certain amount of knowledge, expertise, leadership, management, and indirect as well as direct service provision. The matrix suggests the need for more comprehensive course work and practical training for career counselors, who now generally take only a single career course at the master's level and perhaps an additional course at the doctoral level. In many instances the career counselor-in-training will see no actual career clients nor receive any direct supervision on career cases. Even though supervision is provided on personal and social cases in most counselor training programs, specialized career supervision is recommended, in addition to broad training in consultation, groups, and program evaluation.

In traditional career practice, the counselor works with individuals and small groups, administers assessments, disseminates information, conducts career awareness experiences, and operates resource centers. While these direct services are still valued, the broader view of the role of the career counselor in intervention encompasses all of the other activities in Table 1-2. In addition to providing direct and indirect career services, counselors may be called upon to exercise leadership and to possess management skills. For example, a career counselor in a higher education setting may be called upon to develop and evaluate a special unit during parents' orientation about career choice, or to design a career intervention for a special group, such as college athletes, whose needs may be different from other students.

The more innovative areas of career intervention practice are the indirect services, which include designing activities in school and work settings to facilitate career development; consulting with teachers, parents, and managers; and disseminating information to the public.

Settings for Professional Practice

In 1988, the NCDA published a resource document that described the six subspecialties of professional career counseling, which were organized according to the predominant settings in which counselors practice:

1. Career counselors in private and public practice, who are involved in the direct provision and evaluation of career assistance.
2. Human resources or career development specialists in organizational settings, who provide career-related services (e.g., job analyses or employee career development, preretirement, and out-placement

counseling) to or in consultation with the organization and its employees.

3. Job placement counselors in public settings, who act as brokers between employers and clients, and teach and evaluate job-seeking skills.

4. Career or employment search consultants in private settings, who offer search assistance, résumé writing, interviewing and negotiating skills, and support during a job search.

5. Employment agents in private settings, who actually locate and secure jobs for a client for a fee.

6. Cooperative education instructors in educational settings, who assist students and act as liaisons with employers during the education-to-work transition.

It is clear from this NCDA paper that career intervention is now practiced in a wider variety of settings and by a more diverse array of professionals than has ever been the case (Holland et al., 1981).

Professional Support for Career Counselors

As the professional role of the career counselor is becoming increasingly defined and socialized, the practicing counselor has several resources to turn to for help, information, and support:

Professional Associations.   A growing number of career professionals are affiliated with several professional associations. This diversity enriches and expands the practice of career intervention, but may cause some temporary confusion as roles and professional boundaries soften. Professional meetings and conventions sponsored by the following associations are stimulating ways to expand one's professional knowledge:

1. The *American Association for Counseling and Development (AACD)* is the umbrella organization under which many career counselors operate. The AACD has many members who conduct career interventions, although career counselors are affiliated with three principal career-related divisions: The first, and oldest, is the NCDA, which serves a broad range of counselors who identify with career development as their professional role. The second, the American College Personnel Association (ACPA), has an active group of college counselors who identify with career intervention, as does the third, the National Employment Counselors Association (NECA). Many states now also have local affiliates, such as the Maryland Career Development Association (MCDA). Many professionals belong to independent regional associations as well, such as the MidAtlantic Career Counselors Association (MACA).

Two suborganizations of the AACD (NCCC, NBCC) are engaged in granting credentials to career counselors. An examination administered by the National Board of Certified Counselors is required for national certification. Receiving the title "National Certified Career Counselor" indicates that the counselor has a graduate degree, supervised experience, and a specialized knowledge base.

2. The *American Society for Training and Development (ASTD)* has recently captured the attention of the increasing numbers of career counselors working in organizational settings. The ASTD has an annual meeting that focuses on the provision of high-quality training, consultation and practice in organizational settings.

3. The *American Educational Research Association (AERA)* has a counseling division (Division E) that includes career development and counseling. Papers presented at the AERA convention, and articles in AERA journals are occasionally of interest to career counselors, and more frequently to those conducting research on career development and intervention.

4. Division 17, or the Division of Counseling Psychology, of the *American Psychological Association (APA)* is reviving its long history of work in career psychology and practice. A special interest group of the division, entitled Vocational Psychology and Career Intervention, now has a membership directory and publishes a periodic newsletter. Several presentations at the APA's annual convention will also be of interest to career counselors. Division 14 of the APA, the Division of Industrial-Organizational Psychology, also presents papers of interest and publishes a divisional newsletter called TIP.

Publications. The number of periodicals, magazines, newsletters, and journals that either only or often publish articles of interest to career professionals is now quite large. Some of the more useful are listed below:

American Educational Research Journal
American Sociological Review
Career Development Quarterly
Educational Researcher
Harvard Business Review
Journal of Applied Psychology
Journal of Career Development
Journal of College Placement
Journal of College Student Development
Journal of Counseling and Development
Journal of Employment Counseling
Journal of Occupational Behavior
Journal of Vocational Behavior

Measurement and Evaluation in Counseling and Development
Occupational Sociology
Occupational Outlook Quarterly
Organizational Behavior and Human Performance
Personnel Psychology
Review of Educational Research
Training and Development Journal
Wall Street Journal

Funding for Career Development and Intervention. Many federal, state, and agencies as well as private industries fund career projects, and/or provide grants for the improvement of career service delivery. For further information, the interested professional should contact these funding sources, and if possible make a visit. Wise (1982) has listed the following possible sources of federal funds for career intervention projects:

1. The *National Institute of Education (NIE)* sponsors basic and applied studies on the relationship between education and work, but does not fund demonstration projects. Contact the National Institute of Education, Department of Education, Washington, DC 20208.
2. The *Employment and Training Administration (ETA)* supports employment, unemployment, and transitions between school and work. It also sponsors demonstration projects dealing with job-related needs. Contact the Office of Research and Development, Employment and Training Administration, Department of Education, Patrick Henry Building, Room 9100, 601 D Street NW, Washington, DC 20213.
3. The *Office of Vocational and Adult Education (OVAE),* especially its Division of National Vocational Programs, administers discretionary research programs on a variety of youth and adult programs, and questions of worker productivity and training. Contact the Division of National Vocational Programs, Office of Vocational and Adult Education, Department of Education, Room 5052, FOB-3, Washington, DC 20202.
4. The *Office of Special Education (OSE)* sponsors research on education of the handicapped and especially on youth employment. For a list of priorities, contact the Research Projects Branch, Office of Special Education, Department of Education, Donohoe Building, Room 3165, Washington, DC 20202.
5. The *Office of Career Education (OCE)* administers grants to states. Contact the Office of Career Education, Department of Education, Room 3100, FOB-3, Washington, DC 20202.

6. The *Fund for the Improvement of Postsecondary Education (FIPSE)* provides seed money for education projects, including those related to work, for one to three years. Contact the Fund for the Improvement of Postsecondary Education, Department of Education, 400 Maryland Avenue SW, Room 3123, FOB-6, Washington, DC 20202.

Another possible source of funding is *The Women's Educational Equity Act Program (WEEAP)*, Department of Education, 1100 Donohoe Building, 400 Maryland Avenue SW, Washington, DC 20202.

Didactic Training for Career Intervention.   The broader the definition of career intervention, the broader the training for its practice becomes. Disciplines other than counseling (e.g., family development and business) can train career practitioners as long as a curriculum with certain basic components is provided. There is also no reason why such training could not occur at the undergraduate level. In general, however, most career intervention specialists are trained at the master's level, either in counseling programs in colleges of education, or in human resource management programs in colleges of business. It is not unusual for individuals with an undergraduate background in engineering, sciences, psychology, or liberal arts to pursue a graduate degree in school, rehabilitation, community, or college student personnel counseling with an emphasis on career counseling. In addition, many career professionals receive doctorates in counseling psychology, counselor education, or business, and then focus on career development and intervention as a part of their training.

HOW TO SELECT A GRADUATE PROGRAM IN CAREER INTERVENTION.   In selecting a graduate program in career intervention, a prospective student should do the following:

1. Ensure that the department has established solid relationships with intervention sites in business, industry, and career development centers. Ask to see a list of the on-site supervisors and then check their qualifications. Make your interest in career intervention known early in your training or, even, before you apply.
2. Check to see that more than one course on career development is offered, if not within the department, then at least in the college of business, or in the psychology or sociology departments.
3. Verify that the career development courses are taught by faculty with interest, experience, and, most importantly, published contributions to career intervention and development. Ask to see faculty curricula vitae.

4. Ask to be assigned to an adviser with career development interests, and work with that person on research and consultations, and as a teaching assistant.

5. Look for articles that interest you in the journals listed in this chapter. Call or write to the author or authors, and ask if they are part of a graduate faculty, or where they did their graduate work. Or, better yet, ask to work with that person directly.

6. Check the list of APA-approved counseling psychology programs and the list of Council for the Accreditation of Counseling and Related Educational Programs (CACREP) approved master's and doctoral programs that must adhere to at least minimal standards. Do not, however, place much faith in program brochures, catalogues, or bulletins issued by the programs themselves.

7. Attend one or two professional conferences, and see who is most active. Ask to talk with them for a moment, or attend a social hour and introduce yourself.

8. If you apply to a program, ask for an interview. If interviews are ordinarily not granted, visit the school on your own and check with some current students to see if any have an interest in career intervention. Visit the counseling center and the career development center, as they may be likely training sites.

A graduate curriculum in career intervention should include the following components, which may also be presented as a specialty in a general graduate or undergraduate program in counseling, business, social work, family development, education, or psychology:

1. *Structure of the world of work:* Familiarity with the job classification systems used to analyze the world of work and with the social and economic barriers to job implementation, is a must. The latter can be taught from the perspective of sociology, economic theory, or social psychology, and should include the problems facing special groups.

2. *Measurement and assessment:* Since the client will expect and benefit from the judicious use of career inventories, a counselor must have a thorough grounding in psychometrics, including the specifics of test construction, validation, scoring, and interpretation as they apply to the measurement of interests, abilities, and personality. The difference between criterion-based and homogeneous scales should also be discussed. Finally, training in recognizing serious pathology and in distinguishing career concerns from more severe problems is recommended.

3. *Basic interviewing skills:* Instruction and practice in basic counsel-

ing and interviewing skills paired with supervised practice is the most fundamental element in the preparation for career intervention.

4. *Supervised practice:* There should be at least a semester of work with actual *career* clients under direct supervision. In addition, the development of treatment plans should be covered. The treatment plan shown in Figure 9-3 is an example of the type that should be implemented with each client, or group. Finally, some practice in presenting cases for discussion by professional colleagues is necessary.

5. *Career development theory:* Didactic exposure to theories of career development, including developmental, structural, and social theories, is important. A course on programs and principles, and an advanced seminar in career development theory or assessment should be taken. These courses can be taught from a sociological, psychological, or educational perspective.

6. *Bias and multicultural issues:* A career counselor must be exposed to the effects of bias, both sexual and cultural, on career choice and decision making, and on measurement.

7. *Computers and career information:* Instruction should cover computer-assisted career interventions and programs, and the computerization of career information. Other, alternative sources of career information should also be discussed.

8. *Program evaluation:* Principles of program design and evaluation, such as the formulation of goals and objectives and the evaluation of intervention outcomes, must be thoroughly understood.

9. *Consultation, prevention, and instruction:* Familiarity with the principles and practices of consultation and prevention, and the basics of instructional psychology is crucial.

10. *Group and organizational process and practice:* Study should include the psychology and sociology of group and organizational process, including the family process. The benefits and problems of interventions with groups and organizations must also be examined.

THE PRAGMATICS, ETHICS, AND LEGAL ISSUES IN CAREER PRACTICE

The ethical code of the National Board for Certified Counselors has been reworded and adapted for career counselors by the National Career Development Association (see Appendix C). These standards cover the general responsibilities of a professional career counselor, and the ethics of the counseling relationship, testing and evaluation, research and publication, consulting, and private practice. Although this statement, when used in conjunction with the APA's ethical standards, is reasonably complete, some common ethical conflicts that the career counselor may face deserve additional discussion.

Pressure to See as Many Clients as Possible

Many career professionals face intense pressure from their superiors to serve large numbers of clients, which in some cases results in "head counting" without much attention to the level of service needed by a particular client. While it is necessary to respond to institutional needs (alternate intervention can often be used to do this efficiently), the client's needs should dictate the length and intensity of the intervention.

Indiscriminate Testing

The inappropriate or indiscriminate use of psychological tests is another common source of ethical complaints. Only those tests that are necessary for a complete evaluation should be used, and no more. A list of these procedures and their cost should be presented to the client.

Informational Interviews

It is not uncommon to use established business or government contacts to set up informational interviews for a client. I view this as priming the "exploratory pump," for usually it must be done only once or twice to stimulate the client's self-directing exploratory activity. Whenever I discuss my client with an outside party, I first obtain a written release from the client. I will, once a release is signed, give the contact my client's name and ask the client to call to arrange for the informational interview. In a number of cases, a job offer has resulted from such meetings, even though that is not their purpose.

Exaggerated Claims of Effectiveness

Although the evidence for the effectiveness of career intervention is convincing, no client can be guaranteed a positive outcome, and some may have a negative one. I make no promises, but I may describe the findings from career intervention outcome research to reassure the client and to provide a common expectation for a reasonable outcome. I am careful not to encourage blind faith in the intervention process, and to remind clients that their work and commitment are important predictors of a positive outcome.

Client Follow-Up

If a client misses more than one session without notifying me, I usually assume that the client is experiencing some emotion barrier that may cause the person to drop out of the intervention. In these cases, I call the client directly for a discussion, but I do *not* notify a supervisor if the intervention is on-site. After an intervention has been completed, I will occasionally call a client to see how things are going. Also, I send my clients holiday greeting cards, which are greatly appreciated. While this practice is generally not encouraged in psychotherapy practice, I find it useful in career intervention practice. I very frequently receive lengthy letters in response, most of them quite positive.

Note Taking and Record Keeping

I write brief postsession notes, and retain copies of all client test results and interpretations, correspondence, and reports for an indefinite period, because court precedent has changed the liability limits from seven years after treatment to seven years after the client realizes that harm may have been done.

When the Client Is the Organization but Individuals Are Counseled

When a career counselor is hired by an organization, a potential ethical conflict arises if the counselor is asked to evaluate an individual within that organization for outplacement, promotion, career consultation, or work-related psychological problems. My personal view, which may differ with that of my industrial-organizational psychology colleagues, is that the ethical standards apply to the individual case *first* and then to the organization; that is, I consider my client to be the individual, and the confidentiality accorded to that individual by legal precedent, if not by law, is the confidentiality I uphold. I will never discuss an individual client with the employer that had referred that person to me, even if the employer is paying for the services, unless the client has, in writing, specifically released me to do so. I may agree to release grouped test data from an intervention if I feel that the confidentiality of the respondents can be protected, and if the individuals know in advance that the information may be released to the employer.

Referral

Every career intervention office should have available for clients a list of male and female, and minority psychological and psychiatric professionals, some of whom provide sliding-scale or free services, to whom serious problems can be referred. Career professionals should practice only within the limits of their training and should be prepared to recognize serious pathology (see Chapter 11).

Fee Setting

Perhaps the most common complaint of ethical violations is that of being billed for counselor services that were never rendered. Although this fraudulent practice must be distinguished from the issue of fee setting, a fair amount of criticism has been directed at the practice of charging exorbitant amounts for placement counseling or assistance without reguard to the services being rendered. On the other hand, fee setting is problematic because career counselors in independent practice are probably inclined to charge too little for their services. Fees, of course, must be adjusted for the cost of overhead (e.g., office space and nonprofessional salaries). The costs of practice in Washington, D.C., for example, may be very different from the costs of practicing in a small midwestern town. To a degree, then, the market will adjust the fees one charges. Career counselors are professionals, and can expect to make an adequate living. Although exact fees have not been attached, the following are some of the services for which counselors may bill:

1. *Career consultation:* Billed by the fifty-minute hour. Group counseling is generally billed at a rate of about half the hourly rate for a ninety-minute group.

2. *Testing and scoring:* Billed for each test administered. The fee is a function of the cost of the test and the scoring fee, and the counselor's time needed to interpret the results. If the test is scored on the counselor's computer, a small charge may be added to help cover the cost of the equipment. A reasonable overhead and profit margin should also be added.

3. *Organizational consultation:* Billed by the day or half-day at a rate consistent with the counselor's experience and expertise. One day equals eight to ten hours of work. Preparation days can be billed if they are used to gather materials for the consultation.

4. *On-site counseling:* Billed by the standard hourly rate plus travel time at the same rate.

5. *Program or manuscript or evaluation:* Billed at the standard hourly rate plus any expenses. Occasionally, a flat rate for a project can be negotiated.

6. *Supervision for novice counselors:* Billed at the standard hourly rate.

7. *Videotape feedback and mock interviews:* Billed at the hourly rate plus a charge to help defray the cost of the equipment.

8. *Report writing, résumé preparation, expert testimony, and other professional activities:* Billed at the standard hourly rate.

It is generally better to ask for payment at the time the service is rendered, although many of my clients, especially those who are young or in-between jobs, carry a balance on which I require a modest but regular payment. It is occasionally necessary and certainly proper to pursue collection channels if an outstanding bill remains uncollected after repeated notification.

Third-Party Reimbursement

Some career counselors are also licensed psychologists or social workers who are eligible for reimbursement from third-party insurers. Whereas career interventions are not ordinarily reimbursible, there is a very delicate line between career counseling and psychotherapy with a career focus. There are often complicating factors accompanying the career concern that render the career therapy indistinguishable from psychotherapy. Indeed, it is increasingly difficult to support Crites's (1981) position that career counseling begins where psychotherapy leaves off. Significant levels of psychic distress, depression, or anxiety may call for a blended approach to career intervention, or they may be a signal for a referral. A client with a career concern accompanied by work inhibition, or the inability to work due to stress or serious adjustment problems is certainly a candidate for psychotherapy. Of course, competent career professionals will know the limits of their training and refer cases that exceed the limits of that training. As a safeguard, however, I always carry malpractice insurance through the APA. Malpractice insurance for counselors is also available through the American Association of Counseling and Development (AACD).

Other Ethical and Legal Issues

During my seventeen years as a practicing career counselor, I have encountered nearly every possible ethical legal issue one can imagine, including whether to warn a person of a client's intention to harm him or her (*Tarasoff v. Regents of California,* 1976), to report child abuse, and to release of information to the police. The research literature (Hinkeldey & Spokane, 1986) suggests that most counselors are poorly informed about legal precedents and may use some instinctual ethical standards to direct their behavior in such situations, which, I argue is a dangerous way to handle an ethical-legal conflict. One instead can call the APA or the AACD for advice, consult with a supervisor or colleague, or seek legal counsel; any of these measures is better than relying on instinct. Every career center should have a written policy for dealing with such situations, and these documents should be reviewed by a competent lawyer. The standards endorsed by the NCDA (Appendix C) are helpful in regard to the ethical basis of practice, but not necessarily the legal basis.

Professional Renewal

Although career counselors are not certified, nor are they licensed in most states unless they qualify for generic counselor licensing, professional renewal is an important ethical obligation as well as good common sense. Renewal includes attending professional meetings, workshops, and occasional courses; reading books and journals, and periodically reviewing and evaluating one's practices. One excellent means of renewal is to form a small group with like-minded professionals, who read the same book and then meet to discuss its implications for their practices. Waterman (1987) discussed the general problem of worker renewal and suggested twelve steps in the process, including examining one's attitudes about one's role, taking responsibility for change, and thinking creatively about how to work more efficiently.

SUMMARY

Professional issues in career intervention have received less attention than is warranted, given the level of activity and the diversity of settings in which career intervention is practiced. In this chapter, the supervision of therapeutic and instructional career interventions, the counselor's complex role, the professional support available to career counselors in an increasingly wide range of practice settings, and professional organizations and publications were all described. The essential elements of a graduate curriculum to prepare career professionals were outlined, and ethical and practical issues were discussed.

11

Epilogue

This chapter will examine several important problems in career intervention that require a perspective drawn from earlier chapters yet did not fit comfortably into any of the areas previously discussed.

THE INTERPLAY BETWEEN CAREER CONCERNS AND MENTAL HEALTH PROBLEMS

This volume presents a model of career intervention that maintains that there is a degree of overlap but some definite separation between psychotherapy and career counseling, although this view is certainly not shared by many scholars and practitioners (Blustein, 1987; Rounds & Tinsley, 1984). The historical separation between career and personal domains in counseling psychology facilitated both large-scale studies of career development as a distinct domain of psychological development and pragmatic interventions into career problems. The blending of career and psychopathology threatens the integrity of this work and thus, however alluring, should be approached with caution. It is, furthermore, not entirely clear that work induces psychopathology, nor that career adjustment and mental health adjustment are continuously related when an individual is not experiencing a transition or a serious stressor (Spokane, in press-a). While there is considerable evidence that severe psychopathology interferes grossly with work performance, it does not suggest that improvements in personal adjustment lead to corresponding increments in work performance (Neff, 1985). Some individuals with marked pathology can manage work tasks quite well, often at high levels. Work and personality are undoubtedly related (Borgen, 1986), but future research is needed to show the extent of relationship between individual mental health and characteristics of the work environment. Unfortunately, very little mental health research has been conducted in work settings. One exception was Repetti's (1987) study, which clarified the relationship between mental health status, and the individual and aggregate social climate reported by nonmanagement bank employees. Participants completed measures of depression, anxiety, and self-esteem, and the social environment was measured using a composite survey, which was factor-analyzed to yield measures of the individual and aggregate social environment, including co-worker and supervisor support. Both perceptions of the environment predicted substantial variance in depression and anxiety scores, but small proportions of self-esteem variance. Importantly, individual perceptions of the work environment mediated aggregate influences. This finding, which was achieved using an independent measure of the social environment and controlling for respondent bias, confirmed previous evidence on the buffering effects of personal coping skills (Osipow & Davis, 1988), family support (Billings & Moos, 1982), and supervisor support (Ganster, Fusillier, & Mayes, 1986).

Osipow (1979) called attention to counseling psychologists' tendency to concentrate on adult clients, and termed the blend of vocational development and mental health a perfect marriage that resulted in an offspring known as occupational mental health. The mental and physical risks from exposure to work-place stress are increasingly clear, and include depression, spousal abuse, anxiety, and coronary disease (Osipow & Spokane, 1984). Herr (in press) confirmed the linkages among career counseling, career theory, and mental health:

> The workplace becomes an environment in which both positive and negative, healthy and unhealthy, good and bad outcomes are stimulated; a context in which conflicts, thwarted aspirations, and emotional distress from one's life outside the workplace can be brought into the workplace to filter and shape one's life as a worker. (p. 4)

Herr reviewed the mental health consequences of prolonged unemployment, problematic work relationships, and stressful work conditions, and argued that career counseling should be viewed as a mental health modality. Herr concluded by suggesting a preventive approach to work mental health based on the development of personal competence around work issues.

Suppose that there is an interactive relationship between career concerns and psychopathology. What strategy should be employed by a career counselor who suspects serious pathology? If all professionals who provide career assistance had similar backgrounds and preparation, this would be an easy question to answer. Of course, diversity is the reality among career professionals, and recognizing one's professional limits may not always be a simple matter. However, two cardinal rules must apply when a career counselor is faced with a client with overt pathology or any other condition with which the counselor is unfamiliar (e.g., gender or cross-cultural issues). First and foremost, if one has received no training in the problem at hand, a referral may be appropriate. Second, if a professional is confused, feels unprepared, or is unable to understand the problem, a referral should be considered. In some cases the counselor may be unable to recognize overt pathology in a client, although one could argue that psychopathology is sufficiently common to merit the training of every career professional, counselor or not, to identify its presence in a client.

At the most basic level, clients who are not oriented in all three spheres—person, place, and time—and do not know where they are, who they are, or what the date is, should be helped to find immediate mental health assistance. In fact, any two of these confusion signs is probably indicative of serious pathology requiring attention at once. There are also several other, less serious mental health problems that may be seen in career clients.

The Depressed Career Client

Depression, the most common mental health problem, is present to some degree in many adult clients and in some adolescents, and is often misdiagnosed. Brown (1985) noted that clients with depression or psychosomatic ailments have traditionally been referred for psychotherapy or personal counseling rather than career counseling, under the presumption (Crites, 1981) that career counseling begins where psychotherapy leaves off. Adherents of this referral view postpone career intervention until a reasonable level of mental health is reestablished (Brown, 1985). But, as Brown observed, some mental health problems may be caused by problems at work and, if properly diagnosed, could be resolved with a career intervention. Clients with intrapsychic problems can be separated from those with work-induced psychopathology.

Clients with mild to moderate depression (Beck, 1967) can certainly been seen for career intervention, and, if the provider is not a mental health counselor, psychologist, clinical social worker, or other professional trained in dealing with depression, adjunctive treatment can be arranged coincident with career intervention. When seen in career intervention, however, depressed clients are prone to paralysis of the will and supression of responses on interest inventories. Pietromonaco and Rook (1987), for example, examined the decision style of depressed persons, and found that they weighted risk factors more heavily and expressed greater reluctance to implement target actions than their nondepressed counterparts. The authors concluded that depressed individuals appraised common life situations in such a way as to "promote their social isolation, and thereby perpetuate their depression" (p. 399), while at the same time protecting their fragile self-esteem and emotional sensitivity. Since an active stance is so important to the successful negotiation of many career situations, depression may pose a considerable stumbling block during an intervention. If, as the career intervention proceeds, it becomes clear that the client is unable to mobilize persistently constructive behaviors (see Chapters 2 and 3), a referral may become necessary. Certainly, if there are indications that the depression is worsening or if signs of suicidal ideation are evident, career intervention should be deferred until adequate functioning is restored. I have frequently seen clients at the end of a hospitalization for major depression, and successful career intervention is often the ingredient that insures their continuous and successful recovery (Neff, 1985). Depression that can be linked to a specific cause or set of causes (i.e., reactive depression), such as job loss or death of a spouse, is more likely to be brief and responsive to treatment (Beck, 1967). Ordinarily, if such a depression is acute and severe, it is unlikely that much career progress will be made until the symptoms lessen. Depression can also be chronic or endogenous. An individual with mild to moderate endogenous depression may respond to a career intervention if the depression is under control (i.e., through therapy or medication or both).

Beck (1967) has described the major symptoms which are common to mild, moderate, and severe depression in varying degrees, which include the following:

Emotional Manifestations
Dejected mood
Negative feelings toward self
Reduction in gratification
Loss of emotional attachments
Crying spells
Loss of mirth response

Cognitive Manifestations
Low self-evaluation
Negative expectations
Self-blame and self-criticism
Indecisiveness
Distortion of body image

Motivational Manifestations
Paralysis of the will
Avoidance, escapist, and withdrawal wishes
Suicidal wishes
Increased dependency

Vegetative and Physical Symptoms

Loss of appetite

Sleep disturbance

Loss of libido

Fatigability

Delusions

Delusions of worthlessness

Crime and punishment delusions

Nihilistic delusions

Somatic delusions

Delusion of poverty

Hallucinations

Beck (1967) provides specific levels of each symptom that are characteristic in mild, moderate or severe disorder.

The Obsessive-Compulsive Career Client

The best description of any set of types of human behavior and personality I have seen is Shapiro's (1965) rich discussion of neurotic styles. Two of Shapiro's types have been especially prominent in my practice: obsessive-compulsive and hysterical. Although these are clinical labels, they offer an unusually clear picture of the characteristic mode of functioning in these types, their "ways of thinking and perceiving, ways of experiencing emotion, modes of subjective experience in general, and modes of activity" (Shapiro, 1965, p. 1). Shapiro's descriptions are appropriate for career interventions not because they can be used for diagnostic labeling, but because they provide a window into the ordinary reactions of complex humans in so far as there is any consistency in behavior, emotions, and attitudes.

According to Shapiro, the obsessive-compulsive style, the clearest and most widely studied style, is marked primarily by a tense, rigid, characteristically intellectual style of thinking and/or behaving. Such individuals harbor intense opinions and points of view, and discussions with them are frustrating because there is a sense that no real contact has been made, and that the obsessive-compulsive individual is not open to new information or experience. Indeed, these people may actually have a rigid posture or interpersonal manner to match this thinking style, and usually have a very sharp focus of attention. When faced with a problem, they show a lack of flexibility and an overattention to detail. If presented with a career counseling exercise such as a decision matrix or asked to list their skills, these individuals will often produce endless lists of requirements for an ideal job without reaching any closure; these written lists are a reliable indication of the obsessive-compulsive style.

There are, of course, many positive aspects to the obsessive style; since attention to detail is an important part of any scientific, technical, or numeric occupation, obsessive individuals will excel in such occupations. They will also be able to concentrate on an isolated problem and persist until it is solved. Consistent with the models presented in Chapters 2 and 3, the obsessive will grasp a cognitive structure easily as long as it is not discordant with the detailed structure already in place in the client's mind. Just as often, unfortunately, during a career intervention an obsessive-compulsive individual will become "stuck" or suspended between two or more options, persevering unproductively. As anxiety about an impending choice or a commitment to a serious course of action escalates, the obsessive-compulsive individual may retrench further into the less productive aspects of the style. The client will do all the homework, complete any lists or exercises presented, and appear, for a time, to be making excellent progress. If uninterrupted, however, this pattern can lead to a lack of direct, constructive action toward a career goal.

Shapiro described the obsessive as the "overseer" of his or her own life, often burdened by intense "shoulds" or internally imposed demands, unable to relax, and often having a very sparse social and recreational life. In career interventions, it is unwise to pressure the obsessive-compulsive individual with further demands. Rather, one should try to uncover the emotional valences around the options being considered (Fletcher, 1966), rather than the intellectual pros and cons of that option.

The Hysterical Career Client

Once one moves beyond the pejorative connotations of the word *hysterical*, aspects of this common style, studied early by Freud, can be seen in many clients. Its main feature, according to Shapiro (1965), is the tendency to repress, forget, or fail to attend to detail—the diametric opposite of the obsessive-compulsive style. Shapiro suggested that in many cases the hysteric may not observe the details while an event is occurring, and therefore may be unable to retrieve the details afterward. The hysteric operates on the basis of global, diffuse impressions, often exaggerated, such as, "I despise my boss," or "It's the worst job in the world." Horowitz (1977) added the hysterical features of fluid emotions, attention-seeking behaviors, drifting, dramatic lives, and the tendency toward incomplete statements about personal feelings or ideas.

The hysteric may also lack the ability to conduct sustained intellectual undertakings. Although the style may be creative and even charming, the career counselor may find that the hysterical client finds it difficult to concentrate on the details and content of specific options. The client may also be unable to acquire a clear and accurate organizing system for understanding self, the world of work, and the relationship between the two. The hysteric works on hunches and waits for inspirations (Shapiro, 1965). The hallmarks of quality decision making reviewed in Chapter 5, such as being open to disconfirming information once a preliminary decision has been made, are quite foreign to the hysteric. Shapiro noted that hysterics are often "remarkably deficient in knowledge" (p. 115).

In place of the detailed, factual, subjective world of the obsessive-compulsive, the hysteric lives in a romantic, almost fantastical world of intense pleasure and relationships. Often hysterics will have vague complaints about life being dull or a job being a bad fit because their current world is not sufficiently colorful or emotionally charged to suit them (Shapiro, 1965). The theatrical nature of their personality demands more emotional stimulation than the typical job and, in some cases, the average life can provide. The theatrical nature of the hysteric produces a serious problem in some cases, however, when the naïve counselor repeatedly confronts, provokes, or evokes emotional material (Weiner, 1982), and thus unwittingly unleashes a hysterical, emotional spiral in the form of a diatribe or outburst, usually directed at a close friend, family member, or spouse, that can dominate an entire session, group, or workshop. Once triggered, such a spiral is hard to control, and a less evocative stance is a good preventive measure in working with the hysterical client (Weiner, 1982). What is desired is to mix the hysterical emotion with detail, information, fact, and intellect rather than eliciting further emotion. Thus during a career intervention with a hysteric it is preferable to focus on content, work sheets, and assignments rather than unearthing emotional reactions. In this respect the strategy is opposite to that employed with the obsessive-compulsive client. The emotions experienced by the hysteric are often shallow and superficial, lacking in the sustained, thoughtful reaction desired for optimal outcome. A negative reaction to a supervisor, for example, may have this ephemeral quality.

The anxiety that builds during an intervention will be expressed directly and overtly, often in exaggerated fashion, and may dominate the intervention unless it can be managed and reduced to workable levels. Conflicts with others over a career option will be frequent, and the hysterical client may forget or repress much of the content of individual, group, or workshop sessions, and material may have to be repeatedly reintroduced to ensure its assimilation. Follow-through will be a problem for the hysterical career client, and the counselor must take special care to see that the client explores options carefully, writes letters where appropriate during implementation, and attends all of the sessions. The counselor's focus must be calm, clear, and simple, since the client may be prone to overreaction and emotional exhaustion.

An individual client may display a combination of styles, or "overtones" of one style on another. This is most common with a hysteric (especially the men) who uses an obsessive overlay to maintain control over their inner world; this is a successful strategy until the obsessive overlay breaks down, and the client is viewed as having "lost it." Actually what is seen as "losing it" is simply the normally hysterical style breaking through in the absence of the obsessive overlay.

Interacting with Clients with Psychopathology

If, as this volume suggests, career interventions are more structured and goal directed than psychotherapy, one has to decide how to handle psychopathology, and the intensive dynamics between the counselor and the client that develop over longer interventions. As a rule, I do not attempt to alter an individual's pathological style in career intervention except when it interferes directly with the focus of the work.

There is, however, an exception to this rule. Casserly (1982) alleged that some clients find the experience of making a difficult career decision so anxiety producing and so full of failure possibilities that the responsibility for the decision becomes unbearable. These clients may then attempt to shift the responsibility to the counselor, who, wishing to be helpful and expert, readily assumes this task by overstructuring or overcontrolling the sessions. The result is a collusive relationship in which the counselor, not the client, is principally responsible for the success or failure of the intervention. Gelso (1979a), in a thoughtful paper on gratification in psychotherapy, argued that overgratifying a client's infantile wishes, when there is no serious crisis, may slow therapeutic movement. Overgratification is a common pitfall in career interventions. While a certain level of therapeutic conditions seems desirable and expected (although neither necessary nor sufficient), too much of a good thing may lead the client to believe that the counselor will do all the difficult work, which is a very untenable position for the counselor. Horowitz (1977) observed that the hysterical is likely to become involved in relationships in which they assume a childlike stance in relation to a powerful caretaker, thus making them more susceptible to the collusive relationship described by Casserly (1982).

EDUCATION, TRAINING, AND RESTRICTIVE LABOR MARKETS AS CONSIDERATIONS IN CAREER INTERVENTION

I admit to experiencing an uncomfortable mix of feelings of ignorance and dismay while writing this section. I recently moved from relatively recession-proof Washington, D.C., which is a large metropolitan area dominated by the federal government, which provides job security to its employees—to the Lehigh Valley of Pennsylvania, which is surrounded on three sides by mountains and on the east by New Jersey's industrial corridor. Heavy industries, some of which have declined in recent years, have dominated its employment patterns, and to an extent the morale and thinking about careers of its inhabitants. New high-tech, postindustrial companies are arriving, but it will take some years for this transition to be complete. The reduced operations of Bethlehem Steel have had a profound effect on the career psychology of this area. Although I am a psychologist and educator at heart, the contrast between Washington, D.C., and the Lehigh Valley has further sharpened my sensitivity to the external constraints that mediate career selection. Sociological perspectives on career choice that emphasize structural barriers, labor demand, and market forces (Hotchkiss & Borow, 1984) account for substantially more of the variance in career selection than do psychological approaches. Nonetheless, these sociological approaches are *descriptive* rather than *prescriptive*, and whereas psychological variables account for less variance in career selection, the effectiveness of prescriptive career interventions suggests that participants in well-designed programs may overcome some socioeconomic constraints on status attainment (Azrin, Philip, Thienes-Hontos, & Besalel, 1981; L. S. Gottfredson, 1981, 1986). These constraints however, are real and powerful, and should not be underestimated.

Open access to education and training, and a strong demand for labor are essential if successful career interventions and orderly career development are to occur (Ginzberg, 1984). Devastating disruptions have been rare in the United States's continuously expanding economy (Ginzberg, 1984), and opportunities for women and minorities are increasing. In a postindustrial economy, however, dominated by higher levels of technology, education and training are key elements in career choice (Herr, 1984), and a variety of life transitions may serve as triggers to further education or training (Aslanian & Brickell, 1980). Employability skills may be general (e.g., affective competencies, task discipline, or career planning) and specific (e.g., technical skill) (Herr, 1984). Education and training occur both before employment, in elementary, junior high, and high schools, area vocational and technical schools, proprietary and trade schools, community and junior colleges and universities, and the armed forces (Herr, 1984), and on the job. Although many jobs require no formal training, most industries, the government, and other large employers are heavily involved in training. One insurance corporation, for example, runs an intensive training program for entry-level minority employees who might otherwise never qualify for those jobs.

Herr (1984) noted that we have no strong national policy or program for job training, even though we continue to collect and analyze data on labor force and employment patterns, trends, and projections (Lassalle & Spokane, 1987; Su, 1985; U.S. Department of Labor, 1986). Since engaging in training and education can interfere with income potential and therefore family financial responsibilities, access to training and education is less open than it might appear, especially for adults. In a number of cases, self-employment seems to be a better alternative than additional education and training. Further, many individuals are either unable or unwilling to relocate, although career professionals often overlook this obvious alternative. It is possible, of course, to commute a long distance for a job. Career professionals can work for the establishment or relocation of employers into their geographic area, but a complete exposure to and knowledge of the education, training, and employment possibilities in one's region seems indispensible.

A grant project to establish a career development center for employees of the U.S. Department of Labor (DOL) in Washington, D.C., took the following steps to address the problem of education, training, and labor market constraints:

1. All counseling staff, including practicum students, received extensive briefings on the federal employment system, including procedures for applying for jobs within and between agencies, and to outside industries. All necessary forms were acquired.

2. The extensive training and educational opportunities offered by the DOL were made available to staff and clients in an on-line data base and calendar.

3. All clients completed an individual development plan that included training and education requirements, and plans for garnering support from supervisors for release time and/or tuition costs if external training were requested.

4. A complete set of catalogues and applications from community colleges, four-year colleges and universities, and proprietary schools was acquired so that employees could apply with a minimum of effort. The admissions offices of each of these institutions was contacted to facilitate applications from DOL clients.

5. A complete set of job descriptions in the DOL in particular and in the federal government in general was collected for use in counseling.

6. U-MAPS (Jacoby, Rue, & Allen, 1984), which included telephone numbers and the names of contact persons, were constructed for DOL jobs and training opportunities.

7. A customized version of Career Point (Conceptual Systems Inc., 1989) was obtained into which all DOL job opportunities were entered and classified by Holland type for linkage to the Self-Directed Search (Holland, 1985b).

This strong emphasis on training was a central focus of the center's activities, and underscored our belief that even in a major metropolitan area such as Washington, where a full range of job opportunities was available and training was easily accessible, overcoming the constraints imposed by education, training, and the labor market constraints is possible, but requires direct, concerted effort and attention.

SUMMARY

This final chapter, or epilogue, contains discussions of several issues which do not fit comfortably in other areas of this volume on career intervention. These final issues include the interplay between mental health and career concerns, which were historically separate and are now converging, and especially depression which is a common ancillary problem during career intervention. Clients may present distinct personality styles which may include obsessive compulsive (overattention to detail), and the hysterical style (inattention to detail and overuse of global impression). The author's recent experience underscores the pervasive effects of labor market constraints upon career implementation, and the need for aggressive action to ensure adequate training.

References

Albee, G. W. (1982). Preventing psychopathology and promoting human potential. *American Psychologist, 37,* 1043–1050.

Allen, R. E., & Keavenly, T. J. (1979). The relative effectiveness of alternative job sources. *Journal of Vocational Behavior, 16,* 18–22.

American College Testing Program. (1987). *DISCOVER.* Iowa City: Author:

American College Testing Program. (1988). *Interim psychometric handbook for the 3rd edition ACT Career Planning Program.* Iowa City: Author.

Anastasi, A. (1985a). Mental measurement: Some emerging trends. In J. V. Mitchell, Jr. (Ed.), *Mental measurements yearbook* (9th ed., pp. xxiii–xxix). Lincoln: University of Nebraska Press.

Anastasi, A. (1985b). Testing the test: Interpreting results from multiscore batteries. *Journal of Counseling and Development, 64,* 84–86.

Anastasi, A. (1988). *Psychological testing* (6th ed.). New York: Macmillan.

Andberg, M. A., & Johansson, C. B. (1987). *ECO: Exploring Career Options.* Minnetonka, MN: National Computer Systems.

Apostac, R. A., & Miller, J. G. (1959). A manual for the use of a set of diagnostic categories. Columbia University of Missouri Testing and Counseling Service. Rep No. 21.

Aranya, N., Barak, A., & Amernic, J. (1981). A test of Holland's theory in a population of accountants. *Journal of Vocational Behavior, 19,* 15–24.

Aslanian, C. B., & Brickell, H. M. (1980). *Americans in transition: Life changes as reasons for adult learning.* New York: College Entrance Examination Board.

Assouline, M., & Meir, E. I. (1987). Meta-analysis of the relationship between congruence and well-being measures. *Journal of Vocational Behavior, 31,* 319–332.

Astin, A. W. (1964). Distribution of students among higher educational institutions. *Journal of Educational Psychology, 55,* 276–287.

Astin, A. W., & Panos, R. J. (1969). *The educational and vocational development of college students.* Washington, DC: American Council on Education.

Austin, M. F., & Grant, T. N. (1981). Interview training for college students disadvantaged in the labor market: Comparison of five instructional techniques. *Journal of Counseling Psychology, 28,* 72–75.

Azrin, N. H., & Besalel, V. A. (1980). *Job Club counselor's manual: A behavioral approach to vocational counseling.* Baltimore: University Park Press.

Azrin, N. H., Besalel, V. A., Wisotzek, I., McMorrow, M., & Bechtel, R. (1982). Behavioral supervision versus informational counseling of job seeking in the job club. *Rehabilitation Counseling Bulletin, 25,* 212–218.

Azrin, N. H., Flores, T., & Kaplan, S. J. (1975). Job-finding club: A group-assisted program for obtaining employment. *Behaviour Research and Therapy, 13,* 17–27.

Azrin, N. H., & Phillip, R. A. (1979). The job club method for the job handicapped: A comparative outcome study. *Rehabilitation Counseling Bulletin, 23,* 144–155.

Azrin, N. H., Philip, R. A., Thienes-Hontos, P., & Besalel, V. A. (1980). Comparative evaluation of the job club program with welfare recipients. *Journal of Vocational Behavior, 16,* 133–145.

Azrin, N. H., Philip, R. A., Thienes-Hontos, P., & Besalel, V. A. (1981). Follow-up on welfare benefits received by job club clients. *Journal of Vocational Behavior, 18,* 253–254.

Babcock, R. J., & Kaufman, M. A. (1976). Effectiveness of a career course. *Vocational Guidance Quarterly, 24,* 261–266.

Baker, S. B., & Popowicz, C. L. (1983). Meta-analysis as a strategy for evaluating effects of career education interventions. *Vocational Guidance Quarterly, 31,* 178–186.

Baker, S. B., Swisher, J. D., Nadenichek, P. E., & Popowicz, C. L. (1984). Measured effects of primary prevention strategies. *Personnel and Guidance Journal, 62,* 459–464.

Barak, A., & Friedkes, R. (1981). The mediating effects of career indecision subtypes on career-counseling effectiveness. *Journal of Vocational Behavior, 20,* 120–128.

Barker, S. B. (1979). *Career planning and decision-making course for college students.* Charleston, WV: Appalachia Educational Laboratory.

Barker, S. B. (1981). An evaluation of the effectiveness of a college career guidance course. *Journal of College Student Personnel, 22,* 354–358.

Barlow, D. H. (1988). *Anxiety and its disorders: The nature and treatment of anxiety and panic.* New York: Guilford.

Bartol, K. M. (1981). Vocational behavior and career development, 1980: A review. *Journal of Vocational Behavior, 19,* 123–162.

Bartsch, K., & Hackett, G. (1979). Effect of a decision-making course on locus of control, conceptualization, and career planning. *Journal of College Student Personnel, 20,* 230–235.

Baumgardner, S. R. (1977). Vocational planning: The great swindle. *Personnel and Guidance Journal, 56,* 17–22.

Beck, A. T. (1967). *Depression.* Philadelphia: University of Pennsylvania Press.

Beck, A. T. (1976). *Cognitive therapy and the emotional disorders.* New York: International Universities Press.

Becker, H. J. (1977). *How young people find jobs* (Tech. Rep.). Baltimore: Johns Hopkins University, Center for Social Organization of Schools.

Bednar, R. L., & Kaul, T. J. (1978). Experiential group research: Current perspectives. In S. L. Garfield & A. E. Bergin (Eds.), *Handbook of psychotherapy and behavior change: An empirical analysis* (2nd ed., pp. 169–815). New York: Wiley.

Bennett, G. K., Seashore, H. G., & Wesman, A. G. (1982). *Differential Aptitude Tests: Administrators handbook.* San Antonio, TX: Psychological Corporation.

Bennett, G. K., Seashore, H. G., & Wesman, A. G. (1984). *Differential Aptitude Tests: Technical supplement.* San Antonio, TX: Psychological Corporation.

Berezin, A. G. (1957). The development and use of a system of diagnostic categories in counseling. *Dissertation Abstracts International, 17,* 3087 (University Microfilms No. 57-4916).

Berger-Gross, V., Kahn, M. W., & Weare, C. R. (1983). The role of anxiety in the career decision making of liberal arts students. *Journal of Vocational Behavior, 22,* 312–323.

Bergland, B. W., & Lundquist, G. W. (1975). The Vocational Exploration Group and minority youth: An experimental outcome study. *Journal of Vocational Behavior, 7,* 289–296.

Bernard, C. B., & Rayman, J. R. (1982, March). *The winners and losers: A follow-up.* Paper presented at the meeting of the National Vocational Guidance Association, Detroit.

Betz, E. L. (1977). Vocational behavior and career development, 1976: A review. *Journal of Vocational Behavior, 11,* 129–152.

Betz, N. E. (1988). The assessment of career development and maturity. In W. B. Walsh & S. H. Osipow (Eds.), *Career decision making* (pp. 77–136). Hillsdale, NJ: Lawrence Erlbaum.

Betz, N. E., & Hackett, G. (1981). The relationship of career-related self-efficacy expectations to perceived career options in college women and men. *Journal of Counseling Psychology, 28,* 399–410.

Betz, N. E., & Hackett, G. (1983). The relationship of mathematics self-efficacy expectations to the selection of science-based college majors. *Journal of Vocational Behavior, 23,* 329–345.

Betz, N. E., & Hackett, G. (1987). Concept of agency in educational and career development. *Journal of Counseling Psychology, 34,* 299–308.

Biggers, J. I. (1971). The use of information in vocational decision making. *Vocational Guidance Quarterly, 19,* 171–176.

Billings, A., & Moos, R. H. (1982). Work stress and the stress-buffering roles of work and family resources. *Journal of Occupational Behavior, 3,* 215–232.

Binet, A. (1903). *L'étude expérimentale de l'intelligence.* Paris: Schleicher.

Birk, J. M. (1979). *Helping parents to help adolescents in career exploration.* College Park, MD: National Consortium on Competency-Based Staff Development.

Birnbach, L. (1988). *Going to work: A unique guided tour through corporate America.* New York: Villard.

Bishop, J. B. (1979). Combining counseling and career services: Conflicts and choices. *Personnel and Guidance Journal, 57,* 550–553.

Bixler, R. H., & Bixler, V. H. (1945). Clinical counseling in vocational guidance. *Journal of Clinical Psychology, 1,* 186–192.

Bloom, B. L. (1977). *Community mental health: A general introduction.* Monterey, CA: Brooks/Cole.

Blustein, D. L. (1987). Integrating career counseling and psychotherapy: A comprehensive treatment strategy. *Psychotherapy, 24,* 794–799.

Blustein, D. L. (1988). The relationship between motivational processes and career exploration. *Journal of Vocational Behavior, 32,* 345–357.

Blustein, D. L., Ellis, M. V., & Devenis, L. E. (in press). The development and validation of a two-dimensional model of the commitment to career choices. *Journal of Vocational Behavior.*

Blustein, D. L., & Phillips, S. D. (1988). Individual and contextual factors in career exploration. *Journal of Vocational Behavior, 33,* 203–216.

Blustein, D. L., & Strohmer, D. C. (1987). Vocational hypothesis testing in career decision making. *Journal of Vocational Behavior, 31,* 45–62.

Bodden, J. L. (1970). Cognitive complexity as a factor in appropriate vocational choice. *Journal of Counseling Psychology, 17,* 364–368.

Bodden, J. L., & James, L. E. (1976). Influence of occupational information giving on cognitive complexity. *Journal of Counseling Psychology, 23,* 280–282.

Bodden, J. L., & Klein, A. J. (1972). Cognitive complexity and appropriate vocational choice: Another look. *Journal of Counseling Psychology, 19,* 257–258.

Bodden, J. L., & Klein, A. J. (1973). Cognitive differentiation and affective stimulus value in vocational judgments. *Journal of Vocational Behavior, 3*, 75–79.

Bolles, R. N. (1988). *What color is your parachute? A practical manual for job-hunters and career changers.* Berkeley, CA: Ten Speed Press.

Borchard, D. C., Kelly, J., & Weaver, N. P. (1988). *Your career: Choices, chances, changes* (4th ed.). Dubuque, IA: Kendall-Hunt.

Bordin, E. S. (1946). Diagnosis in counseling and psychotherapy. *Educational and Psychological Measurement, 66*, 169–184.

Bordin, E. S. (1986). The effectiveness of psychotherapy: An introduction. *American Journal of Orthopsychiatry, 56*, 500.

Borgen, F. H. (1984). Counseling psychology. *Annual Review of Psychology, 35*, 579–604.

Borgen, F. H. (1986). New approaches to the assessment of interests, In W. B. Walsh & S. H. Osipow (Eds.), *Advances in vocational psychology: Vol. 1. The assessment of interests* (pp. 83–125). Hillsdale, NJ: Lawrence Erlbaum.

Borgen, F. H. (1988). Strong-Campbell Interest Inventory. In J. T. Kapes & M. M. Mastie (Eds.), *A counselor's guide to career assessment instruments* (2nd ed.), pp. 121–126). Alexandria, VA: National Career Development Association.

Borgen, F. H., Layton, W. L., Veehnhuizen, D. L., & Johnson, D. J. (1985). Vocational behavior and career development 1984: A review. *Journal of Vocational Behavior, 27*, 218–269.

Borgen, F. H., & Seling, M. J. (1978). Expressed and inventoried interests revisited: Perspicacity in the person. *Journal of Counseling Psychology, 25*, 536–543.

Borgen, F. H., Weiss, D. J., Tinsley, H. E. A., Dawis, R. V., & Lofquist, L. H. (1972). *Occupational reinforcer patterns I.* Minneapolis: Vocational Psychology Research, Department of Psychology.

Botterbusch, K. F. (1987). *Vocational assessment and evaluation systems: A comparison.* Menomonie, WI: University of Wisconsin, Stout. Materials Development Center, Stout Vocational Rehabilitation Institute.

Bouchard, T. J., Jr. (1983). Do environmental similarities explain the similarity in intelligence of identical twins reared apart? *Intelligence, 7*, 175–184.

Bowlsbey, J. H. (1983). The computer and the decider. *The Counseling Psychologist, 11*(4), 4–14.

Brandt, J. D. (1977). Model for the delivery of career development programs by college counseling centers. *Journal of Counseling Psychology, 24*, 494–502.

Bray, D. W., & Grant, D. L. (1966). The assessment center as the measurement of potential for business management. *Psychological Monographs, 80*(625), No. 17, 2.

Breaugh, J. A. (1983). Realistic job previews: A critical appraisal and future research directions. *Academy of Management Review, 8*, 612–619.

Brickell, H. M. (1976). Needed: Instruments as good as our eyes. *Journal of Career Education, 2*, 56–66.

Bridges, M. P. (1989). Software for career counseling. In G. R. Walz & J. C. Bleuer (Eds.), *Counseling software guide* (pp. 15–18). Alexandria, VA: American Association for Counseling and Development.

Brown, D. (1985). Career counseling: Before, after, or instead of personal counseling? *Vocational Guidance Quarterly, 33*, 197–201.

Brunstein, J. C., & Olbrich, E. (1985). Personal helplessness and action control: Analysis of achievement-related cognitions, self-assessments, and performance. *Journal of Personality and Social Psychology, 48*, 1540–1551.

Bucher, R. (1976). Social-structural constraints in career decision-making occupational hurdles. In J. D. Krumboltz, A. M. Mitchell, & G. B. Jones (Eds.), *Social learning and career decision making* (pp. 116–133). Cranston, RI: Carrol Press.

Buck, J. N., & Daniels, M. H. (1985). *Assessment of Career Decision Making (ACDM) manual.* Los Angeles: Western Psychological Services.

Burck, H. D. (1978). Evaluating programs: Models and strategies. In L. Goldman (Ed.), *Research methods for counselors* (pp. 177–197). New York: Wiley.

Burck, H. D., & Peterson, G. W. (1975). Needed; More evaluation, not research. *Personnel and Guidance Journal, 53,* 563–569.

Burck, H. D., & Reardon, R. C. (Eds.). (1984). *Career development interventions.* Springfield, IL: Charles C. Thomas.

Butcher, E. (1982). Changing by choice: A process model for group career counseling. *Vocational Guidance Quarterly, 30,* 200–209.

Byrne, R. H. (1958). Proposed revisions of the Bordin-Pepinsky diagnostic constructs. *Journal of Counseling Psychology, 5,* 184–187.

Cairo, P. C. (1983). Counseling in industry: A selected review of the literature. *Personnel Psychology, 36,* 1–18.

Campbell, D. P. (1973). Give me one of those interest tests so I can see what I should be. In *Measurement for self-understanding and personal development.* Invitational conference on testing problems, Educational Testing Service, Princeton.

Campbell, D. P. (1986). *Campbell work orientations.* Greensboro, NC: Center for Creative Leadership.

Campbell, R. E., & Cellini, J. V. (1981). A diagnostic taxonomy of adult career problems. *Journal of Vocational Behavior, 19,* 175–190.

Campbell, R. E., Cellini, J. V., Shaltry, P. E., Long, A. E., & Pinkos, D. (1979). *A diagnostic taxonomy of adult career problems.* Columbus, OH: National Center for Research in Vocational Education.

Caplan, G. (1964). *Principles of preventive psychiatry.* New York: Basic Books.

Caplan, R. D. (1987). Person-environment fit theory and organizations: Commensurate dimensions, time perspectives, and mechanisms. *Journal of Vocational Behavior, 31,* 248–267.

Carey, M. A., & Weber, L. J. (1979). Evaluating an experienced-based career education program. *Vocational Guidance Quarterly, 27,* 216–222.

Carney, C. G., & Wells, C. F. (1987). *Career planning: Skills to build your future* (2nd ed.). Monterey, CA: Brooks-Cole.

Casserly, M. (1982). Effects of differentially structured career counseling on the decision quality of subjects with varying cognitive styles. Unpublished doctoral dissertation, University of Maryland, College Park.

Cesari, J. P., Winer, J. L., & Piper, K. R. (1984). Vocational decision status and the effect of four types of occupational information on cognitive complexity. *Journal of Vocational Behavior, 25,* 215–224.

Cesari, J. P., Winer, J. L., Zychlinski, F., & Laird, I. O. (1982). Influence of occupational information-giving on cognitive complexity in decided versus undecided students. *Journal of Vocational Behavior, 21,* 224–230.

Cianni-Surridge, M., & Horan, J. J. (1983). On the wisdom of assertive job-seeking behavior. *Journal of Counseling Psychology, 30,* 209–214.

Clark, K. E. (1961). *The vocational interests of non-professional men.* Minneapolis: University of Minnesota Press.

Clark, K. E., & Campbell. D. P. (1965). *Minnesota Vocational Interest Inventory.* New York: Psychological Corporation.

Cochran, D. J., Hoffman, S., Strand, K. H., & Warren, P. (1977). Effects of client/computer interaction in career decision-making processes. *Journal of Counseling Psychology, 24,* 308–312.

Conceptual Systems Inc. (1989). *Career Point: A computer-based career development system for organizations.* Silver Spring, MD: Author.

Cook, R. A., & Lafferty, J. C. (1981). *Level I: Life Styles Inventory—An instrument for assessing and changing the self-concept of organizational members.* Plymouth, MI: Human Synergistics.

Cook, R. A., Lafferty, J. C., & Rousseau, D. M. (1987). Thinking and behavioral styles: Consistency between self-descriptions and descriptions by others. *Educational and Psychological Measurement, 47,* 815–823.

Cook, R. A., & Rousseau, D. M. (1983). The factor structure of Level I: Life Styles Inventory. *Educational and Psychological Measurement, 43,* 449–457.

Cook, T. D., & Campbell, D. T. (1979). *Quasi-experimentation.* New York: Rand McNally.

Cooper, S. E. (1986). The effects of group and individual vocational counseling on career indecision and personal indecisiveness. *Journal of College Student Personnel, 27,* 39–42.

Coursey, R. D. (1977). Introduction: The need, history, definition, and limits of program evaluation. In R. Coursey (Ed.), *Program evaluation for mental health: Methods, strategies, participants* (pp. 1–8). New York: Grune & Stratton.

Cowen, E. L. (1978a). Demystifying primary prevention. In D. G. Forgays (Ed.), *Primary prevention of psychopathology: Vol. 2. Environmental influences* (pp. 7–24). Hanover, NH: University Press of New England.

Cowen, E. L. (1978b). Some problems in community program evaluation research. *Journal of Consulting and Clinical Psychology, 46,* 792–805.

Cowen, E. L. (1984). A general structural model for primary prevention program development in mental health. *Personnel and Guidance Journal, 62,* 485–490.

Cowen, E. L. (1982). Help is where you find it: Four informal helping groups. *American Psychologist, 37,* 385–395.

Crites, J. O. (1961). A model for the measurement of vocational maturity. *Journal of Counseling Psychology, 8,* 255–259.

Crites, J. O. (1969). *Vocational psychology.* New York: McGraw-Hill.

Crites, J. O. (1978). *Theory and research handbook for the Career Maturity Inventory.* Monterrey, CA: CTB/McGraw Hill.

Crites, J. O. (1981). *Career counseling: Models, methods, and materials.* New York: McGraw-Hill.

Crites, J. O. (1982). Testing for career adjustment and development. *Training and Development Journal, 36,* 20–29.

Cytrynbaum, S., Ginath, Y., Birdwell, J., & Brandt, L. (1979). Goal attainment scaling: A critical review. *Evaluation Quarterly, 3,* 5–40.

Daane, C. J. (1972). *Vocational Exploration Group.* Tempe, AZ: Studies for Urban Man.

Dawis, R. V. (1987). Scale construction. *Journal of Counseling Psychology, 34,* 481–489.

Dawis, R. V., Lofquist, L. H., Henley, G. A., & Rounds, J. B., Jr. (1979). *Minnesota Occupational Classification System II (MOCS II) L. Minneapolis:* Vocational Psychology Work Adjustment Project.

Deci, E. L., & Ryan, R. M. (1985). *Intrinsic motivation and self-determination in human behavior.* New York: Plenum.

Dewey, C. R. (1974). Exploring interests: A non-sexist method. *Personnel and Guidance Journal, 52,* 311–315.

Dolliver, R. H. (1967). An adaptation of the Tyler Vocational Card Sort. *Personnel and Guidance Journal, 45,* 916–920.

Dolliver, R. H. (1981). Test review of the occupational/vocational card sorts. *Measurement and Evaluation in Guidance, 14,* 168–174.

Dolliver, R. H., & Nelson, R. E. (1975). Assumptions regarding vocational counseling. *Vocational Guidance Quarterly, 24,* 12–19.

Dorn, F. J. (in press). Integrating career counseling and social influence theory. In W. B. Walsh & S. H. Osipow (Eds.), *Career counseling: Contemporary topics in vocational psychology,* Hillsdale, NJ: Lawrence Erlbaum.

Ellis, M. V., & Dell, D. M. (1986). Dimensionality of supervisor roles: Supervisors' perceptions of supervision. *Journal of Counseling Psychology, 33,* 282–291.

Elton, C. F., & Rose, H. A. (1967). Personality characteristics of students who transfer out of engineering. *Personnel and Guidance Journal, 45,* 911–915.

Evans, P., & Bartolome, F. (1984). The changing picture of the relationship between career and family. *Journal of Occupational Behavior, 5,* 9–21.

Farmer, H. S. (1985). Model of career and achievement motivation for women and men. *Journal of Counseling Psychology, 32,* 363–390.

Fassinger, R. E., 1985. A causal model of college women's career choice [Monograph]. *Journal of Vocational Behavior, 27,* 123–153.

Figler, H. (1979). *The complete job search handbook.* New York: Holt, Rinehart & Winston.

Figler, H. (1984, Spring). A new direction for career counseling. *Journal of College Placement,* pp. 48–52.

Fitzgerald, L. F., & Osipow, S. H. (1986). An occupational analysis of counseling psychology: How special is the specialty? *American Psychologist, 41,* 535–544.

Fitzgerald, L. F., & Rounds, J. B. (1989). Vocational behavior, 1988: A critical analysis. *Journal of Vocational Behavior, 35,* 105–163.

Flamer, S. (1986). Editorial—Clinical-career intervention with adults: Low visibility, high need? *Journal of Community Psychology, 14,* 224–227.

Fletcher, F. M. (1966). Concepts, curiosity, and careers. *Journal of Counseling Psychology, 13,* 131–138.

Fogg, N. J. (1983). *Use of advanced cognitive organizers in the interpretation of interest inventory results.* Unpublished master's thesis, University of Maryland, College Park.

Frank, J. D. (1976). Restoration of morale and behavior change. In A. Burton (Ed.), *What makes behavior change possible?* (pp. 73–95). New York: Brunner/Mazel.

Fretz, B. R. (1981). Evaluating the effectiveness of career interventions [Monograph]. *Journal of Counseling Psychology, 28,* 77–90.

Fretz, B. R., & Leong, F. T. L. (1982). Career development status as a predictor of career intervention outcomes. *Journal of Counseling Psychology, 29,* 388–393.

Friesen, J. (1986). The role of the family in vocational development. *International Journal for the Advancement of Counseling, 9,* 87–96.

Fryer, D. (1925). *Vocational self-guidance: Planning your life work.* Philadelphia: J. B. Lippincott.

Fuqua, D. R., & Newman, J. L. (1989, April). *An emergent paradigm shift in career psychology.* Paper presented at the annual meeting of the American Educational Research Association, San Francisco.

Fuqua, D. R., Newman, J. L., & Seaworth, T. B. (1988). Relation of state and trait anxiety to different components of career indecision. *Journal of Counseling Psychology, 35,* 154–188.

Fuqua, D. R., Seaworth, T. B., & Newman, J. L. (1987). The relationship of career indecision and anxiety: A multivariate examination. *Journal of Vocational Behavior, 30,* 175–186.

Gallesich, J. (1982). *The profession and practice of consultation.* San Francisco: Jossey Bass.

Ganster, D. C., Fusilier, M. R., & Mayes, B. T. (1986). Role of social support in the experience of work stress. *Journal of Applied Psychology, 71,* 102–110.

Ganster, D. C., & Lovell, J. E. (1978). An evaluation of a career development seminar using Crites' Career Maturity Inventory. *Journal of Vocational Behavior, 13,* 172–180.

Garbin, A. P., & Stover, R. G. (1980). Vocational behavior and career development, 1979: A review. *Journal of Vocational Behavior, 17,* 125–170.

Garis, J., & Harris-Bowlsbey, J. (1984). *DISCOVER and the Counselor: Their effects upon college student career planning progress.* Research report #85. Iowa City, IA American College Testing Program.

Gati, I. (1986). Making career decisions: A sequential elimination approach. *Journal of Counseling Psychology, 33,* 408–417.

Gati, I., & Tikotzki, Y. (1989). Strategies for collection and processing of occupational information in making career decisions. *Journal of Counseling Psychology, 36,* 430–439.

Gelso, C. J. (1979a). Gratification: A pivotal point in psychotherapy. *Psychotherapy, Theory, Research, and Practice, 16,* 276–281.

Gelso, C. J. (1979b). Research in counseling: Methodological and professional issues. *The Counseling Psychologist, 8,* 7–30.

Gesten, E. L., & Jason, L. A. (1987). Social and community interventions. *Annual Review of Psychology, 38,* 427–460.

Gibson, E. J. (1988). Exploratory behavior in the development of perceiving, acting, and the acquiring of knowledge. *Annual Review of Psychology, 39,* 1–41.

Gibson, J. J. (1966). *The senses considered as perceptual systems.* New York: Houghton Mifflin.

Ginzberg, E. (1984). Career development. In D. Brown & L. Brooks (Eds.), *Career choice and development: Applying contemporary theories to practice* (pp. 169–191). San Francisco: Jossey Bass.

Ginzberg, E., Ginsburg, S. W., Axelrad, S., & Herma, J. L. (1951). *Occupational choice.* New York: Columbia University Press.

Glaser, R., & Bond, L. (Eds.). (1981). Testing: Concepts, policy, practice, and research [Special issue]. *American Psychologist, 36,* 997–1189.

Glasser, R., & Bassock, M. (1989). Learning theory and the study of instruction. *Annual Review of Psychology, 40,* 631–666.

Goldfried, M. R. (1980). Toward the delineation of therapeutic change principles. *American Psychologist, 35,* 991–999.

Goldman, L. (1971). *Using tests in counseling* (2nd ed.), Englewood Cliffs, NJ: Prentice-Hall.

Goldman, L. (1976). A revolution in counseling research. *Journal of Counseling Psychology, 23,* 543–552.

Goldstein, I. L. (1980). Training and organizational psychology, *Professional Psychology, 11,* 421–427.

Goodstein, L. (1972). Behavioral views of counseling. In B. Steffire & W. H. Grant (Eds.), *Theories of counseling* (2nd ed.), pp. 243–286. New York; McGraw-Hill.

Gottfredson, G. D. (1978). Evaluating vocational interventions. *Journal of Vocational Behavior, 13,* 252–254.

Gottfredson, G. D., & Holland, J. L. (1989). *The dictionary of Holland occupational codes* (rev. ed.). Odessa, FL: Psychological Assessment Resources.

Gottfredson, L. S. (1981). Circumscription and compromise: A developmental theory of occupational aspirations. *Journal of Counseling Psychology, 28,* 549–579.

Gottfredson, L. S. (1986). Special groups and the beneficial use of vocational interest inventories. In W. B. Walsh & S. H. Osipow (Eds.), *Advances in vocational assessment: Vol. 1. The assessment of interests* (pp. 127–198). Hillsdale, NJ: Lawrence Erlbaum.

Gottfredson, L. S. (Ed.). (1988). Fairness in employment testing [Special issue]. *Journal of Vocational Behavior, 33,* 225–477.

Gottfredson, L. S., & Becker, H. J. (1981). A challenge to vocational psychology: How important are aspirations in determining male career development? *Journal of Vocational Behavior, 18,* 121–137.

Gottman, J. M., & Leiblum, S. R. (1974). *How to do psychotherapy and how to evaluate it.* New York: Holt, Rinehart & Winston.

Gough, H. (1984). A managerial potential scale for the California Personality Inventory. *Journal of Applied Psychology, 69,* 233–240.

Gough, H. (1985). A work orientation scale for the California Personality Inventory. *Journal of Applied Psychology, 70,* 505–513.

Gough, H. G. (1987). *California Psychological Inventory Administrator's Guide,* Palo Alto, CA: Consulting Psychologists Press.

Granovanter, M. S. (1974). *Getting a job: A study of contacts and careers.* Cambridge: Harvard University Press.

Greenhaus, J. H., & Parasuraman, S. (1986). Vocational and organizational behavior, 1985: A review. *Journal of Vocational Behavior, 29,* 115–176.

Gribbons, W., & Lohnes P. R. (1982). *Careers in theory and experience: A twenty-year longitudinal study.* Albany: State University of New York Press.

Griggs v. Duke Power Co., 401 U.S. 424 (1971).

Grotevant, H. D., Copper, C. R., & Kramer, K. (1986). Exploration as a predictor of congruence in adolescents career choices. *Journal of Vocational Behavior, 29,* 201–215.

Grotevant, H. D., Scarr, S., & Weinberg, R. A. (1977). Patterns of interest similarity in adoptive and biological families. *Journal of Personality and Social Psychology, 35,* 667–676.

Grumer, M. (1949). Aims and scope of vocational counseling. *Journal of Social Casework, 30,* 330–335.

Gutteridge, T. G., & Otte, F. L. (1983). *Organizational career development: State of the practice.* Washington, DC: American Society for Training and Development, ASTD Press.

Gysbers, N. C., & Moore, E. J. (1987). *Career counseling: Skills and techniques for practitioners.* Englewood Cliffs, NJ: Prentice-Hall.

Haase, R. F., Reed, C. F., Winer, J. L., & Bodden, J. L. (1979). Effect of positive, negative, and mixed occupational information on cognitive and affective complexity. *Journal of Vocational Behavior, 15,* 294–302.

Hackett, G. (1985). Role of mathematics self-efficacy in the choice of math-related majors of college women and men: A path analysis. *Journal of Counseling Psychology, 32,* 47–56.

Hackett, G., & Betz, N. E. (1981). A self-efficacy approach to the career development of women. *Journal of Vocational Behavior, 18,* 326–339.

Hall, L. G., & Tarrier, R. B. (1976). *Counselor's manual for the Hall Orientation Inventory* (3rd ed.). Bensenville, IL: Scholastic Testing Service.

Hampl, S. P., Lonborg, S. D., Lassiter, W. L., Williams, D. A., & Schmidt, L. D. (1987). *The process and outcome of initial career counseling sessions.* Unpublished manuscript. Ohio State University, Columbus.

Haney, W. (1981). Validity, vaudeville, and values: A short history of social concerns over standardized testing. *American Psychologist, 36,* 1021–1034.

Hansen, J. C. (1989). *SCII topical reports: Leisure.* Palo Alto, CA: Consulting Psychologists Press.

Hansen, J. C., & Campbell, D. P. (1985). *Manual for the SVIB-SCII* (4th ed.). Stanford, CA: Stanford University Press.

Harmon, L. W. (1988). Values Scale. In J. T. Kapes & M. M. Mastie (Eds.), *A counselor's guide to career assessment instruments* (2nd ed., pp. 156–158). Alexandria, VA: National Career Development Association.

Harren, V. A. (1978). *Assessment of Career Decision Making.* Carbondale: Southern Illinois University, Department of Psychology.

Harren, V. A. (1980). *Assessment of Career Decision Making: Preliminary manual.* Unpublished manuscript, Carbondale: Southern Illinois University, Department of Psychology.

Hayes, S. C., Nelson, R. O., & Jarrett, R. B. (1987). The treatment utility of assessment: A functional approach to evaluating assessment quality. *American Psychologist, 42,* 963–974.

Healy, C. C. (1982). *Career development: Counseling through the life stages.* Boston: Allyn and Bacon.

Heesacker, M., Elliott, T. R., & Howe, L. A. (1988). Does the Holland code predict satisfaction and productivity in clothing factory workers? *Journal of Counseling Psychology, 35,* 144–148.

Heilman, M. E. (1979). High school students' occupational interests as a function of projected sex ratios in male-dominated occupations. *Journal of Applied Psychology, 64,* 275–279.

Heitzmann, D., Schmidt, A. K., & Hurley, F. W. (1986). Career encounters: Career decision making through on-site visits. *Journal of Counseling and Development, 65,* 209–210.

Heppner, P. P., & Roehlke, H. J. (1984). Differences among supervisors at different levels of training: Implications for a developmental model of supervision. *Journal of Counseling Psychology, 31,* 76–90.

Herr, E. L. (1976). Counseling: Accountability, reality, credibility. *Journal of Counseling Services, 1,* 14–23.

Herr, E. L. (1982, April). *Oversight hearings on guidance and counseling.* Testimony presented to R. T. Stafford (Chair), U.S. Senate, Labor and Human Resources Committee, Subcommittee on Education, Arts, and Humanities, Washington, DC.

Herr, E. L. (1984). Links among training, employability, and employment. In N. Gysbers (Ed.), *Designing careers* (pp. 78–105). San Francisco: Jossey Bass.

Herr, E. L. (in press). Career development and mental health. *Journal of Career Development*

Herr, E. L., & Cramer, S. H. (1988). *Career guidance and counseling through the life span* (3rd ed.). Glenview, IL: Scott, Foresman.

Hershenson, D. B., Power, P. W., & Seligman, L. (1989). Mental health counseling theory: Present status and future prospects. *Journal of Mental Health Counseling, 11,* 44–69.

Hershenson, D. B., & Roth, R. M. (1966). A decisional process model of vocational development. *Journal of Counseling Psychology, 13,* 368–370.

Hesketh, B. (1985). In search of a conceptual framework for vocational psychology. *Journal of Counseling and Development, 64,* 26–30.

Hewer, V. H. (1963). What do theories of vocational choice mean to a counselor? *Journal of Counseling Psychology, 10,* 118–125.

Higgins, E. T., & Bargh, J. A. (1987). Social cognition and social perception. *Annual Review of Psychology, 38,* 369–425.

Higgins, N. (1986). Occupational stress and working women: The effectiveness of two stress reduction programs. *Journal of Vocational Behavior, 29,* 66–78.

Hill, C. E. (1989). *Therapist techniques and client outcomes: Eight cases of brief psychotherapy.* Newbury Park, CA: Sage.

Hill, C. E., Carter, J. A., & O'Farrell, M. K. (1983). A case study of the process and outcome of time-limited counseling. *Journal of Counseling Psychology, 30,* 3–18.

Hill, C. E., Helms, J., Spiegel, S. B., & Tichenor, V. (1988). Development of a system for assessing client reactions to therapist interventions. *Journal of Counseling Psychology, 34,* 27–36.

Hill, C. E., & O'Grady, K. E. (1985). List of therapist intentions illustrated in a case study and with therapists of varying theoretical orientations. *Journal of Counseling Psychology, 32,* 3–22.

Hinkeldey, N. S., & Spokane, A. R. (1986). Effects of pressure and legal guideline clarity on counselor decision making in ethical-legal conflict situations. *Journal of Counseling and Development, 64,* 240–245.

Hoffman, M. A., Spokane, A. R., & Magoon, T. M. (1981). Effects of feedback mode on counseling outcomes using the Strong-Campbell Interest Inventory: Does the counselor really matter? *Journal of Counseling Psychology, 28,* 119–125.

Hoffman, M. A., & Teglasi, H. (1982). The role of causal attributions in counseling shy subjects. *Journal of Counseling Psychology, 29,* 132–139.

Holland, J. L. (1984). A celebration of the career point of view [Review of *Handbook of Vocational Psychology*]. *Contemporary Psychology, 29,* 862.

Holland, J. L. (1985a). *Making vocational choices: A theory of vocational personalities and work environments* (2nd ed.). Englewood Cliffs, NJ: Prentice-Hall.

Holland, J. L. (1985b). *The Self-Directed Search: Professional manual.* Odessa, FL: Psychological Assessment Resources.

Holland, J. L. (1985c). *Vocational Preference Inventory: Manual.* Odessa, FL: Psychological Assessment Resources.

Holland, J. L. (1987a). *Manual supplement for the Self-Directed Search.* Odessa, FL: Psychological Assessment Resources.

Holland, J. L. (1987b). *You and your career.* Odessa, FL: Psychological Assessment Resources.

Holland, J. L., Daiger, D. C., & Power, P. G. (1980a). *My Vocational Situation.* Palo Alto, CA: Consulting Psychologists Press.

Holland, J. L., Daiger, D. C., & Power, P. G. (1980b). Some diagnostic scales for research in decision making and personality: Identity, information, and barriers. *Journal of Personality and Social Psychology, 39,* 1191–1200.

Holland, J. L., Magoon, T. M., & Spokane, A. R. (1981). Counseling psychology: Career interventions, research, and theory. *Annual Reviews in Psychology, 32,* 279–305.

Holland, J. L., & Rayman, J. R. (1986). The Self-Directed Search. In W. B. Walsh & S. H. Osipow (Eds.), *Advances in vocational assessment: Vol. 1. The assessment of interests* (pp. 55–82). Hillsdale, NJ: Lawrence Erlbaum.

Holland, J. L., Whitney, D. R., Cole, N. S., & Richards, J. M., Jr. (1969). *An empirical occupational classification derived from a theory of personality and intended for practice and research* (ACT Research Rep. No. 29). Iowa City: American College Testing Program.

Holland and Associates. (1977). *Vocational Exploration and Insight Kit.* Palo Alto, CA: Consulting Psychologists Press.

Hollandsworth, J. G., Dressel, M. E., & Stevens, J. (1977). Use of behavioral versus traditional procedures for increasing job interview skills. *Journal of Counseling Psychology, 24,* 503–510.

Holt, P. A. (1989). Differential effect of status and interest in the process of compromise. *Journal of Counseling Psychology, 36,* 42–47.

Horowitz, M. (1977). The core characteristics of hysterical personality. In M. Horowitz (Ed.), *Hysterical personality* (pp. 3–6). New York: Jason Aronson.

Hotchkiss, L., & Borow, H. (1984). Sociological perspectives on career choice and attainment. In D. Brown & L. Brooks (Eds.), *Career choice and development: Applying contemporary theories to practice* (pp. 137–168). San Francisco: Jossey Bass.

Hoyt, D. P. (1955). An evaluation of group and individual programs in vocational guidance. *Journal of Applied Psychology, 39,* 26–30.

Hoyt, K. (1977). *A primer for career education* (Monographs on Career Education). Washington, DC: U.S. Office of Education.

Huebner, L. A., & Corazzini, J. G. (1984). Environmental assessment and intervention. In S. D. Brown & R. W. Lent (Eds.), *Handbook of counseling psychology* (pp. 579–621). New York: Wiley.

Human Synergistics. (1989). *Life Styles Inventory: Leader's guide.* Plymouth, MI: Author.

Hunter, J. E. (1986). Cognitive ability, cognitive aptitudes, job knowledge, and job performance. *Journal of Vocational Behavior, 29,* 340–362.

Irish, R. K. (1973). Go hire yourself an employer. Garden City, NY: Doubleday.

Ivey, A. (1971). *Microcounseling: Innovations in interviewing training.* Springfield, IL: Charles C. Thomas.

ICD Rehabilitation and Research Center (1967). *Tower Evaluator's Manual.* NY: Author.

Jackson, D. N. (1977, March). An introduction to the Jackson Vocational Interest Survey. In D. Jackson (Chair), *Jackson Vocational Interest Survey.* Symposium conducted at the meeting of the American Personnel and Guidance Association, Dallas.

Jackson, D. N. (1977). *Jackson Vocational Interest Survey (JVIS) Manual.* Port Huron MI: Research Psychologists Press.

Jackson, D. N. (1984). *Multidimensional Aptitude Battery manual.* Port Huron, MI: Research Psychologists Press.

Jackson, D. N. (1986). *Career Directions Inventory manual.* Port Huron, MI: Research Psychologists Press.

Jacoby, B., Rue, P., & Allen, K. (1984). UMAPS: A person-environment approach to helping students make critical choices. *Personnel and Guidance Journal, 62,* 426–428.

Janis, I. L. (Ed.). (1982). *Counseling on personal decisions: Theory and research on short-term helping relationships.* New Haven: Yale University Press.

Janis, I. L. (1983). The role of social support in adherence to stressful decisions. *American Psychologist, 38,* 143–160.

Janis, I. L., & Mann, L. (1977). *Decision making: A psychological analysis of conflict, choice, and commitment.* New York: The Free Press.

Jepsen, D. A., & Dilley, J. S. (1974). Vocational decision-making models: A review and comparative analysis. *Review of Educational Research, 44,* 331–349.

Johansson, C. B. (1980). *Manual for IDEAS: Interest Determination, Exploration, and Assessment System.* Minneapolis: National Computer Systems.

Johansson, C. B. (1982). *Manual for Career Assessment Inventory* (2nd ed.). Minneapolis, MN: National Computer Systems.

Johnson, N., Johnson, J., & Yates, C. (1981). A 6-month follow-up on the effects of the vocational exploration on career maturity. *Journal of Counseling Psychology, 28,* 70–71.

Jones, L. K. (1979). Development and evaluation of an occupational card sort. *Vocational Guidance Quarterly, 12,* 206–213.

Jones, L. K., & Chenery, M. F. (1980). Multiple subtypes among vocationally undecided college students: A model and assessment instrument. *Journal of Counseling Psychology, 27,* 469–477.

Jones, R. J., & Azrin, N. H. (1973). An experimental application of a social reinforcement approach to the problem of job-finding. *Journal of Applied Behavior Analysis, 6,* 345–353.

Kagan, J. (1988). Twentieth-century trends in developmental psychology. In E. R. Hilgard (Ed.), *Fifty years of psychology* (pp. 13–25). Glenview, IL: Scott, Foresman.

Kagan, N., & Krathwohl, D. R. (1967). *Studies in human interaction: Interpersonal process recall stimulated by videotape.* East Lansing: Michigan State University.

Kahneman, D., & Tversky, A. (1984). Choices, values, and frames. *American Psychologist, 39,* 341–350.

Kanfer, F. H., & Saslow, G. (1965). Behavioral analysis: An alternative to diagnostic classification. *Archives of General Psychiatry, 12,* 529–538.

Kapes, J. T., & Mastie, M. M. (Eds.). (1988). *A counselor's guide to career assessment instruments* (2nd ed.). Alexandria, VA: National Career Development Association.

Kell, B. L., & Mueller, W. J. (1966). *Impact and change.* Englewood Cliffs, NJ: Prentice-Hall.

Keller, K. E., Biggs, D. A., & Gysbers, N. C. (1982). Career counseling from a cognitive perspective. *Personnel and Guidance Journal, 60,* 367–371.

Kennedy, J. L., & Larramore, D. D. (1988). *Joyce Lain Kennedy's career book.* Chicago: National Textbook.

Kernis, M. H., Zuckerman, M., Cohen, A., & Spadafora, S. (1982). Persistence following failure: The interactive role of self-awareness and the attribution basis for negative expectancies. *Journal of Personality and Social Psychology, 43,* 1111–1124.

Kerr, B. A., Olson, D. H., Claiborn, C. D., Bauers-Gruenler, S. J., & Paolo, A. M. (1983). Overcoming opposition and resistance: Differential functions of expertness and attractiveness in career counseling. *Journal of Counseling Psychology, 30,* 323–331.

Kiersuk, T., & Sherman, R. (1968). Goal attainment scaling: A general method for evaluating comprehensive community mental health programs. *Community Mental Health Journal, 4,* 443–453.

Kirschner, T. (1988). *Process and outcome of career counseling: A case study.* Unpublished doctoral dissertation, University of Maryland, College Park.

Kivlighan, D. M., Johnson, B., & Fretz, B. R. (1987). Participant's perception of change mechanisms in career counseling groups: The role of emotional components in career problem solving. *Journal of Career Development, 14,* 35–44.

Kivlighan, D. M., Jr., Hageseth, J. A., Tipton, R. M., & McGovern, T. V. (1981). Effects of matching treatment approaches and personality types in group vocational counseling. *Journal of Counseling Psychology, 28,* 315–320.

Klein, D. C., & Goldston, S. E. (Eds.). (1976). Primary prevention: An idea whose time has come. In *Proceedings of the Pilot Conference on Primary Prevention.* Rockville, MD: U.S. Department of Health, Education, and Welfare.

Knapp, L., & Knapp, R. R. (1980). *Manual for the California Occupational Preference System (Form R).* San Diego: Educational and Industrial Testing Service.

Knapp, R. R., & Knapp, L. (1984). *Manual for the COPS Interest Inventory.* San Diego: Educational and Industrial Testing Service.

Knickerbocker, B., & Davidshofer, C. (1978). Attitudinal outcomes of the life planning workshop. *Journal of Counseling Psychology, 25,* 103–109.

Koshland, D. E., Jr. (1987). Nature, nurture, and behavior. *Science, 235,* 1445.

Koslowsky, M., Kluger, A. N., & Yinon, Y. (1988). Predicting behavior: Combining intention with investment. *Journal of Applied Psychology, 73,* 102–106.

Krivatsy, S. E., & Magoon, T. M. (1976). Differential effects of three vocational counseling treatments. *Journal of Counseling Psychology, 43,* 112–118.

Krumboltz, J. D. (1971). *Job experience kits.* Chicago: Science Research Associates.

Krumboltz, J. D. (1974). An accountability model for counselors. *Personnel and Guidance Journal, 52,* 639–646.

Krumboltz, J. D. (1976). A social learning theory of career selection. In J. D. Krumboltz, A. M. Mitchell, & G. B. Jones (Eds.), *Social learning and career decision making* (pp. 19–49). Cranston, RI: Carroll Press.

Krumboltz, J. D. (1983). *Private rules in career decision making* (Special Publication Series No. 38). Columbus, OH: National Center for Research in Vocational Education.

Krumboltz, J. D. (1988). *Career Beliefs Inventory.* Palo Alto, CA: Consulting Psychologists Press.

Krumboltz, J. D., Becker-Haven, J. F., & Burnett, K. F. (1979). Counseling psychology. *Annual Review of Psychology, 30,* 555–602.

Krumboltz,, J. D., & Hamel, D. A. (Eds.). (1982). *Assessing career development.* Palo Alto, CA: Mayfield.

Krumboltz, J. D., Kinnier, R. T., Rude, S. S., Scherba, D. S., & Hamel, D. A. (1986). Teaching a rational approach to career decision making: Who benefits most? *Journal of Vocational Behavior, 29,* 1–6.

Krumboltz, J. D., Mitchell, A. M., & Jones, G. B. (Eds.). (1976a). *Social learning and career decision making*. Cranston, RI: Carroll Press.

Krumboltz, J. D., Mitchell, A. M., & Jones, G. B. (1976b). A social learning theory of career selection. *The Counseling Psychologist, 6,* 71–81.

Krumboltz, J. D., Rude, S. S., Mitchell, L. K., Hamel, D. A., & Kinnier, R. T. (1982). Behaviors associated with "good" and "poor" outcomes in a simulated career decision. *Journal of Vocational Behavior, 21,* 349–358.

Krumboltz, J. D., & Shroeder, W. W. (1965). Promoting career planning through reinforcement. *Personnel and Guidance Journal, 11,* 19–26.

Krumboltz, J. D., & Thoresen, C. E. (1964). The effect of behavioral counseling in groups and individual settings on information-seeking behavior. *Journal of Counseling Psychology, 17,* 324–333.

Kuder, G. F., & Diamond, E. E. (1979). *Occupational Interest Survey: General manual* (3rd ed.). Chicago: Science Research Associates.

Kulik, C. T., Oldham, G. R., & Hackman, J. R. (1987). Work design as an approach to person-environment fit. *Journal of Vocational Behavior, 31,* 278–296.

Lassalle, A., & Spokane, A. R. (1987). Patterns of early labor force participation in American women. *Career Development Quarterly, 36,* 55–65.

Latack, J. C., Josephs, S. L., Roach, B. L., & Levine, M. D. (1987). Carpenter apprentices: Comparison of career transitions for men and women. *Journal of Applied Psychology, 72,* 393–400.

Latham, V. M. (1986, August). *Toward the development of typologies of job seekers*. Paper presented at the meeting of the American Psychological Association, Washington, DC.

Lawler, A. C. (1979). Career exploration with women using the non-sexist vocational card sort and the Self-Directed Search. *Measurement and Evaluation in Guidance, 12,* 87–97.

Leibowitz, Z. B., Farren, C., & Kaye, B. L. (1988). *Designing career development systems*. San Francisco: Jossey Bass.

Leibowitz, Z. B., & Schlossberg, N. K. (1979). *Designing career development programs for business and industry*. College Park, MD: National consortium on Competency-Based Staff Development and U.S. Department of Health, Education, and Welfare.

Leibowitz, Z. B., & Spokane, A. R. (nd.). Circa 1980. *The career connection: A practitioner's guide to career development intervention*. San Jose, CA: Career Concepts.

Lent, R. W., Brown, S. D., & Larkin, K. C. (1984). Relation of self-efficacy expectations to academic achievement and persistence. *Journal of Counseling Psychology, 31,* 356–362.

Lent, R. W., Larkin, K. C., & Hasegawa, C. S. (1986). Effects of a "focused interest" career course approach for college students. *Vocational Guidance Quarterly, 34,* 151–159.

Levinson, D. J., Darrow, C. N., & Klein, E. B., Levinson, M. H., & McKee, B. (1978). *The seasons of a man's life*. New York: Knopf.

Lindquist, C. U., & Lowe, S. R. (1978). A community-oriented evaluation of two prevention programs for college freshman. *Journal of Counseling Psychology, 25,* 53–60.

Lock, R. D. (1988). *Taking charge of your career direction*. Pacific Grove, CA: Brooks/Cole.

Locke, E. L. (1976). The nature and causes of job satisfaction. In M. D. Dunnette (Ed.), *Handbook of industrial and organizational psychology* (pp. 1297–1349). Chicago: Rand McNally.

Loehlin, J. C., Willerman, L., & Horn, J. M. (1988). Human behavior genetics. *Annual Review of Psychology, 39,* 101–133.

Loganbill, C., Hardy, E., & Delworth, U. (1982). Supervision: A conceptual model. *The Counseling Psychologist, 10,* 3–42.

Long, B. B. (1986). The prevention of mental-emotional disabilities. *American Psychologist, 41,* 825–829.

Lopez, F. G., & Andrews, S. (1987). Career indecision: A family systems perspective. *Journal of Counseling and Development, 65,* 304–307.

Lowman, R. L., & Williams, R. E. (1987). Validity of self-ratings of abilities and competencies. *Journal of Vocational Behavior, 31,* 1–13.

Lubin, B., Larsen, R. M., & Matarazzo, J. D. (1984). Patterns of psychological test usage in the United States: 1935–1982. *American Psychologist, 39,* 451–454.

Lucas, M. S. (1983). *Personality characteristics of undecided students.* Unpublished doctoral dissertation, Iowa State University, Ames.

Lucas, M. S., & Epperson, D. L. (1986, August). *Cluster analysis of vocationally undecided students: A replication and validation.* Paper presented at the annual meeting of the American Psychological Association, Washington, DC.

Lucas, M. S., & Epperson, D. L. (1988). Personality types in vocationally undecided students. *Journal of College Student Personnel, 29,* 460–466.

Lunneborg, P. W. (1979). The Vocational Interest Inventory: Development and validation. *Educational and Psychological Measurement, 39,* 445–451.

Lunneborg, P. W. (1981). *Manual for the Vocational Interest Inventory.* Los Angeles: Western Psychological Services.

Lunneborg, P. W. (1983). Career counseling techniques. In W. B. Walsh & S. H. Osipow (Eds.), *Handbook of vocational psychology* (Vol. 2, pp. 41–76). Hillsdale, NJ: Lawrence Erlbaum.

MacAllister, L. W. (1989). *SCII topical reports: Leadership/management style.* Palo Alto, CA: Consulting Psychologists Press.

Magoon, T. M. (1980). The eye of a beholder. *The Counseling Psychologist. 8*(4), 26–28.

Mahalik, J. R., & Kivlighan, D. M. (1988). Self-help for depression: Who succeeds? *Journal of Counseling Psychology, 35,* 237–242.

Mahrer, A. R. (1988). Discovery oriented psychotherapy research: Rationale, aims, and methods. *American Psychologist, 43,* 694–702.

Malett, S. D., Spokane, A. R., & Vance, F. L. (1978). Effects of vocationally relevant information on the expressed and measured interests of freshmen males. *Journal of Counseling Psychology, 25,* 292–298.

Maola, J., & Kane, G. (1976). Comparison of computer-based versus counselor-based occupational information systems with disadvantaged vocational students. *Journal of Counseling Psychology, 23,* 163–165.

Marcia, J. E. (1980). Development and validation of ego-identity status. In R. E. Muss (Ed.), *Adolescent behavior and society: Basic readings* (pp. 237–241). New York: Random House.

Marin, P. (1984). *The differential effectiveness of computer-based career counseling intervention and decision-making style on progress in career decision status.* Unpublished doctoral dissertation, University of Michigan, Ann Arbor.

Markus, H., & Nurius, P. (1986). Possible selves. *American Psychologist, 41,* 954–969.

Marland, S. P., Jr. (1974). *Career education: A proposal for reform.* New York: McGraw-Hill.

Marmor, J. (1976). Common operational factors in diverse approaches to behavior change. In A. Burton (Ed.), *What makes behavior change possible?* (pp. 3–11). New York: Brunner/Mazel.

Martin, D. C., & Bartol, K. M. (1986). Holland's VPI and the Myers-Briggs Type Indicator as predictors of vocational choice among MBAs. *Journal of Vocational Behavior, 29,* 51–65.

Martin, J. (in press). Individual difference in client reactions to counseling and psychotherapy: A challenge for research. *Counseling Psychology Quarterly.*

Martin, J., & Hiebert, B. A. (1985). *Instructional counseling.* Pittsburgh: University of Pittsburgh Press.

Maslach, C., & Jackson, S. E. (1981). *Maslach Burnout Inventory.* Palo Alto, CA: Consulting Psychologists Press.

Matarazzo, R. G., & Patterson, D. R. (1986). Methods of teaching therapeutic skills. In S. L. Garfield & A. E. Bergin (Eds.), *Handbook of psychotherapy and behavior change* (3rd ed., pp. 821–843). New York: Wiley.

Mayer, R. E. (1979). Can advance organizers influence meaningful learning? *Review of Educational Research, 49,* 371–383.

McBer & Co. (1981). *Managerial Style Questionnaire.* Boston: Author.

McCall, M. W., Jr., Lombardo, M. M., & Morrison, A. M. (1988). *The lessons of experience: How successful executives develop on the job.* Greensboro, NC: Center for Creative Leadership.

McCarron, L., & Dial, J. (1986). *McCarron-Dial System (MDS).* Dallas, TX: McCarron-Dial Systems.

McGovern, T. V., Jones, B. W., Warwick, C. L., & Jackson, R. W. (1981). A comparison of job interviewee behavior on four channels of communication. *Journal of Counseling Psychology, 28,* 369–372.

Meehl, P. E. (1954). *Clinical versus statistical prediction: A theoretical analysis and a review of the evidence.* Minneapolis: University of Minnesota Press.

Meglino, B. M., DeNisis, A. S., Youngblood, S. A., & Williams, K. J. (1988). Effects of realistic job previews: A comparison using an enhancement and a reduction preview. *Journal of Applied Psychology, 73,* 259–266.

Mehrens, W. A., & Lehmann, I. J. (1985). Intepreting test scores to clients: What score should one use? *Journal of Counseling and Development, 63,* 317–320.

Meichenbaum, D., & Turk, D. C. (1987). *Facilitating treatment adherence: A practitioner's guidebook.* New York: Plenum.

Meir, E. I. (1989). Integrative elaboration of the congruence theory. *Journal of Vocational Behavior, 35,* 219–230.

Meir, E. I., & Melamed, S. (1986). The accumulation of person-environment congruences and well-being. *Journal of Occupational Behavior, 7,* 315–323.

Melhus, G. E., Hershenson, D. B., & Vermillion, M. E. (1973). Computer assisted versus traditional vocational counseling with high and low readiness clients. *Journal of Vocational Behavior, 3,* 137–144.

Mencke, R. A., & Cochran, D. J. (1974). Impact of a counseling outreach workshop on vocational development. *Journal of Counseling Psychology, 21,* 185–190.

Mendonca, J. D., & Siess, T. F. (1976). Counseling for indecisiveness: Problem-solving and anxiety-management training. *Journal of Counseling Psychology, 23,* 339–347.

Messick, S. (1980). Test validity and the ethics of assessment. *American Psychologist, 35,* 1012–1027.

Meyer, P. M. (1989). *SCII topical reports: Organizational specialty.* Palo Alto, CA: Consulting Psychologists Press.

Miars, R. D., Tracey, T. J., Ray, P. B., Cornfeld, J. L., O'Farrell, M., & Gelso, C. J. (1983). Variation in supervision process across trainee experience levels. *Journal of Counseling Psychology, 30,* 403–412.

Miceli, M. P. (1985). The effects of realistic job previews on newcomer behavior: A laboratory study. *Journal of Vocational Behavior, 26,* 277–289.

Miller, G. A. (1969). Psychology as a means of promoting human welfare. *American Psychologist, 24,* 1063–1075.

Miller, J. V. (1985, September). The family-career connection: A new component for career development programs. *Journal of Career Development,* pp. 8–23.

Miller, M. F. (1982). Interest pattern structure and personality characteristics of clients who seek career information. *Vocational Guidance Quarterly, 31,* 28–35.

Miller, M. J. (1985). Counselor as hypothesis tester: Some implications of research. *Journal of Counseling and Development, 63,* 276–278.

Mitchell, L. K., & Krumboltz, J. D. (1987). The effects of cognitive restructuring and decision-making training on career indecision. *Journal of Counseling and Development, 66,* 171–174.

Moos, R. H. (1986). *Work Environment Scale manual* (2nd ed.). Palo Alto, CA: Consulting Psychologists Press.

Moos, R. H. (1987). Person-environment congruence in work, school, and health care settings. *Journal of Vocational Behavior, 31,* 231–247.

Morgan, J. I., & Skovholt, T. M. (1977). Using inner experience: Fantasy and daydreams in career counseling. *Journal of Counseling Psychology, 24,* 391–397.

Morrill, W. H., & Forrest, D. J. (1970). Dimensions of counseling for career development. *Personnel and Guidance Journal, 49,* 1–6.

Muchinsky, P. M. (1983). Vocational behavior and career development, 1982: A review. *Journal of Vocational Behavior, 23,* 123–178.

Muchinsky, P. M., & Monahan, C. J. (1987). What is person-environment congruence? Supplementary versus complementary models of fit. *Journal of Vocational Behavior, 31,* 268–277.

Munson, H. L., & Manzi, P. A. (1982). Toward a model of work task learning in the home. *Vocational Guidance Quarterly, 31,* 5–13.

Murphy, L. B., & Frank. C. (1979). Prevention: The clinical psychologist. *Annual Review of Psychology, 30,* 173–207.

Myers, I. B., & McCaulley, M. H. (1985). *Manual: A guide to the development and use of the Myers-Briggs Type Indicator.* Palo Alto, CA: Consulting Psychologists Press.

Myers, R. A. (1971). Research on educational and vocational counseling. In A. E. Bergin & S. L. Garfield (Eds.), *Handbook of psychotherapy and behavior change* (pp. 863–891). New York: Wiley.

Myers, R. A. (1986). Research on educational and vocational counseling. In A. E. Bergin & S. L. Garfield (Eds.), *Handbook of psychotherapy and behavior change* (3rd ed., pp. 715–738). New York: Wiley.

Myers, R. A. (1989). *Research on career counseling fifteen years later.* Paper presented at the meeting of the American Psychological Association, Atlanta.

Myers, R. A., & Cairo, P. C. (Eds.). (1983). Computer-assisted counseling [Special issue]. *The Counseling Psychologist, 11,* 3–74.

Myers, R. A., Lindeman, R. H., Thompson, A. S., & Patrick, T. A. (1975). Effects of Educational and Career Exploration System on vocational maturity. *Journal of Vocational Behavior, 6,* 245–254.

National Career Development Association. (1988). *Planning for working in America: Report of a national survey.* Alexandria, VA: Author.

National Career Development Association. (1989). *The professional practice of career counseling and consultation: A resource document.* Alexandria, VA: American Association for Counseling and Development.

Neff, W. S. (1985). *Work and human behavior* (3rd ed.). New York: Aldine.

Neimeyer, G. J., Brown, M. T., Metzler, A. E., Hagans, C., & Tanguy, M. (1989). The impact of sex-role orientation and construct type on vocational differentiation, integration, and conflict. *Journal of Vocational Behavior, 34,* 236–251.

Neimeyer, G. J., & Ebben, R. (1985). The effects of vocational interventions on the complexity and positivity of occupational judgments. *Journal of Vocational Behavior, 27,* 87–97.

Neimeyer, G. J., & Metzler, A. (1987). The development of vocational schemas. *Journal of Vocational Behavior, 30,* 16–32.

Neimeyer, G. J., Nevill, D. D., Probert, B., & Fukuyama, M. (1985). Cognitive structures in vocational development. *Journal of Vocational Behavior, 27,* 191–201.

Nevill, D. D., Neimeyer, G. J., Probert, B., & Fukuyama, M. (1986). Cognitive structures in vocational information processing and decision making. *Journal of Vocational Behavior, 28,* 110–122.

Nevill, D. D., & Super D. E. (1989). *Manual for the Salience Inventory*. (2nd ed.) Palo Alto, CA: Consulting Psychologists Press.

Newman, J. L., Fuqua, D. R., & Seaworth, T. B. (1989). The role of anxiety in career indecision: Implications for diagnosis and treatment. *Career Development Quarterly, 37,* 221–231.

Norman, R. D., & Bessemer, D. W. (1968). Job preferences and preference shifts as functions of job information, familiarity, and prestige. *Journal of Applied Psychology, 52,* 280–285.

Oliver, L. W. (1975). Counseling implications of recent research on women. *Personnel and Guidance Journal, 53,* 430–437.

Oliver, L. W. (1978). *Outcome measures for career counseling research* (Tech. Paper No. 316). Alexandria, VA: Army Research Institute for the Behavioral and Social Sciences.

Oliver, L. W. (1979). Outcome measurement in career counseling research. *Journal of Counseling Psychology, 26,* 217–226.

Oliver, L. W., & Spokane, A. R. (1988). Career counseling outcome: What contributes to client gain? *Journal of Counseling Psychology, 35,* 447–462.

O'Neil, J. M., Ohlde, C., Barke, C., Gelwick, B. P., & Garfield, N. (1980). Research on a workshop to reduce the effects of sexism and sex role socialization on women's career planning. *Journal of Counseling Psychology, 27,* 355–363.

Osipow, S. H. (1962). Perceptions of occupations as a function of titles and descriptions. *Journal of Counseling Psychology, 9,* 106–109.

Osipow, S. H. (1976). Vocational behavior and career development, 1975: A review. *Journal of Vocational Behavior, 9,* 129–145.

Osipow, S. H. (1979). Occupational mental health: Another role for counseling psychologists. *The Counseling Psychologist, 8*(1), 65–70.

Osipow, S. H. (1982). Research in career counseling: An analysis of issues and problems. *The Counseling Psychologist, 10*(4), 27–38.

Osipow, S. H. (1983). *Theories of career development* (3rd ed.). Englewood Cliffs, NJ: Prentice-Hall.

Osipow, S. H. (1987a). Applying person-environment theory to vocational behavior. *Journal of Vocational Behavior, 31,* 333–336.

Osipow, S. H. (1987b). *Career Decision Scale: Manual.* Odessa, FL: Psychological Assessment Resources.

Osipow, S. H. (1987c). Counseling psychology: Theory, research, and practice in career counseling. *Annual Review of Psychology, 38,* 257–278.

Osipow, S. H. (1988). Toward a Clinical Science of Career Counseling. *Contemporary Psychology, 33,* 875–876.

Osipow, S. H., Carney, C. G., & Barak, A. (1976). A scale of educational vocational undecidedness: A typological approach. *Journal of Vocational Behavior, 9,* 233–243.

Osipow, S. H., Carney, C. G., Winer, J. L., Yanico, B., & Koschier, M. (1976). *The Career Decision Scale* (3rd rev. ed.). Odessa, FL: Psychological Assessment Resources.

Osipow, S. H., & Davis, A. S. (1988). The relationship of coping resources to occupational stress and strain. *Journal of Vocational Behavior, 32,* 1–15.

Osipow, S. H., & Rooney, R. A. (in press). *Task Specific Occupational Self-Efficacy Scales (TSOS).* Columbus, OH: Authors.

Osipow, S. H., & Spokane, A. R. (1984). Measuring occupational stress, strain, and coping. In S. Oskamp (Ed.), *Applied Social Psychology Annual Vol. 5.* (pp. 67–86) Beverly Hills: Sage.

Osipow, S. H., & Spokane, A. R. (1987). *Manual for the Occupational Stress Inventory.* Odessa, FL: Psychological Assessment Resources.

Otte, F. L. (1982). Creating successful career development programs. *Training and Development Journal, 36,* 30–37.

Otto, L. B. (1984). *How to help your child choose a career.* New York: M. Evans.

Palmer, S., & Cochran, L. (1988). Parents as agents of career development. *Journal of Counseling Psychology, 35,* 71–76.

Parsons, F. (1909). *Choosing a vocation.* Boston: Houghton Mifflin.

Pavalk, M. F., & Kammer, P. P. (1985). The effects of a career guidance program on the career maturity and self-concept of delinquent youth. *Journal of Vocational Behavior, 26,* 41–54.

Pavalko, R. M. (1976). Commentary. In J. D. Krumboltz, A. M. Mitchell, & G. B. Jones (Eds.), *Social learning and career decision making* (pp. 130–133). Cranston, RI: Carrol press.

Pepinsky, H. B. (1948). The selection and use of diagnostic categories in clinical counseling. *Applied Psychology Monographs, 15.*

Pepinsky, H. B., & Pepinsky, P. N. (1954). *Counseling theory and practice.* New York: Ronald Press.

Perloff, R., & Perloff, E. (1977). Evaluation of psychological service delivery programs: The state of the art. *Professional Psychology, 8,* 379–388.

Pervin, L. A. (1983). The stasis and flow of behavior: Toward a theory of goals. In R. A. Dienstbier (Ed.), *Nebraska symposium on motivation* (pp. 1–55). Lincoln: University of Nebraska Press.

Personnel Decisions Inc. (1986). *Management Skills Profile* (MSP). Minneapolis, MN: Author.

Pervin, L. A. (1987). Person-environment congruence in the light of the person situation controversy. *Journal of Vocational Behavior, 31,* 222–230.

Peterson, M. (1988). McCarron-Dial Evaluation System. In J. T. Kapes & M. M. Mastie (Eds.), *A counselor's guide to career assessment instruments* (2nd ed., pp. 256–259). Alexandria, VA: National Career Development Association.

Phillips, S. D. (1982). The development of career choices: The relationship between patterns of commitment and career outcomes in adulthood. *Journal of Vocational Behavior, 20,* 141–152.

Phillips, S. D., Cairo, P. C., Blustein D. L., & Myers, R. A. (1988). Career development and vocational behavior, 1987: A review. *Journal of Vocational Behavior, 33,* 119–184.

Phillips, S. D., Friedlander, M. L., Kost, P. P., Specterman, R. V., & Robbins, E. S. (1988). *Personal versus vocational focus in career counseling: A retrospective outcome study.* Unpublished manuscript, State University of New York, Albany.

Phillips, S. D., & Pazienza, N. (1988). History and theory of the assessment of development and decision making. In W. B. Walsh & S. H. Osipow (Eds.), *Career decision making* (pp. 1–31). Hillsdale, NJ: Lawrence Erlbaum.

Phillips, S. D., & Strohmer, D. C. (1982). Decision-making style and vocational maturity. *Journal of Vocational Behavior, 20,* 215–222.

Pickering, J. W., & Vacc, N. A. (1984). Effectiveness of career development interventions for college students: A review of published research. *Vocational Guidance Quarterly, 32,* 149–159.

Pietromonaco, P. R., & Rock, K. S. (1987). Decision style in depression: The contribution of perceived risks versus benefits. *Journal of Personality and Social Psychology, 52,* 399–408.

Pilato, G., & Myers, R. A. (1975). The effects of computer-mediated vocational guidance procedures on the appropriateness of vocational preference. *Journal of Vocational Behavior, 6,* 61–72.

Pinder, F. A., & Fitzgerald, P. W. (1984). The effectiveness of a computerized guidance system in promoting career decision making. *Journal of Vocational Behavior, 24,* 123–131.

Pinkney, J. W., & Jacobs, D. (1985). New counselors and personal interest in the task of career counseling. *Journal of Counseling Psychology, 32,* 454–457.

Pintrich, P. R., Cross, D. R., Kozma, R. B., & McKeachie, W. J. (1986). Instructional psychology. *Annual Review of Psychology, 37,* 611–651.

Power, P. W. (1984). *A guide to vocational assessment.* Austin, TX: Pro-ED.

Powers, R. J. (1978). Enhancement of former drug abusers' career development through structured group counseling. *Journal of Counseling Psychology, 25,* 585–587.

Prediger, D. J. (1987a). Ability differences across occupations: More than g. *Journal of Vocational Behavior, 34,* 1–27.

Prediger, D. J. (1987b). *Career counseling validity of the ASVAB job cluster scales used in DISCOVER* (ACT Research Rep. No. 87–2). Iowa City: American College Testing Program.

Prediger, D. J., & Garfield, N. J. (1988). Testing competencies and responsibilities: A checklist for counselors. In J. T. Kapes & M. M. Mastie (Eds.), *A counselor's guide to career assessment instruments* (2nd ed., pp. 49–54). Alexandria, VA: National Career Development Association.

Prediger, D. J., & Noeth, R. J. (1979). Effectiveness of a brief counseling intervention in simulating vocational exploration. *Journal of Vocational Behavior, 14,* 352–368.

Prediger, D. J., & Swaney, K. (1986). Role of counselee experiences in the interpretation of vocational interest scores. *Journal of Counseling and Development, 64,* 440–444.

Prestholdt, P. H., Lane, I. M., & Mathews, R. C. (1987). Nurse turnover as reasoned action: Development of a process model. *Journal of Applied Psychology, 72,* 221–227.

Pryor, R. G. L. (1982). Values, preference, needs, work ethics, and orientations to work: Toward a conceptual and empirical integration. *Journal of Vocational Behavior, 20,* 40–52.

Pryor, R. G. L., & Taylor, N. B. (1986). On combining scores from the interest and value measures for counseling. *Vocational Guidance Quarterly, 34,* 178–187.

Pyle, K. P., & Stripling, R. (1977). Counselor vs. computer in career development. *NASPA Journal, 14,* 38–40.

Raskin, P. M. (1987). *Vocational counseling: A guide for the practitioner.* New York: Teachers College Press.

Rayman, J. R. (1982). *Selecting an interest inventory: A case for the SDS.* Unpublished manuscript, Iowa State University, Ames.

Rayman, J. R., Bernard, C. B., Holland, J. L., & Barnett, D. C. (1983). The effects of a career course on undecided college students. *Journal of Vocational Behavior, 23,* 346–355.

Reardon, R. C., & Burck, H. D. (Eds.). (1975). *Facilitating career development: Strategies for counselors.* Springfield, IL: Charles C. Thomas.

Reicken, H. W. (1977). Principal components of the evaluation process. *Professional Psychology, 8,* 392–410.

Reilly, R. R., Brown, B., Blood, M., & Malatesta, C. Z. (1981). The effects of realistic previews: A study and discussion of the literature. *Personnel Psychology, 34,* 823–834.

Remer, P., O'Neill, C. D., & Gohs, D. E. (1984). Multiple outcome evaluation of a life-career development course. *Journal of Counseling Psychology, 31,* 532–540.

Repetti, R. L. (1987). Individual and common components of the social environment at work and psychological well-being. *Journal of Personality and Social Psychology, 52,* 710–720.

Resnick, L. B. (1981). Instructional psychology. *Annual Review of Psychology, 32,* 659–704.

Resnick, L. B. (1983). Mathematics and science learning: A new conception. *Science, 220,* 477–478.

Robbins, S. B., Mullison, D., Boggs, K., Riedesel, B., & Jacobson, B. (1985). Attrition behavior before career development workshops. *Journal of Counseling Psychology, 32,* 232–238.

Robbins, S. B., & Tucker, K. R., Jr. (1986). Relation of goal instability to self-directed and interactional career counseling workshops. *Journal of Counseling Psychology, 33,* 418–424.

Robinson, F. P. (1950). *Principles and procedures in student counseling,* New York: Harper & Row.

Robinson, F. P. (1963). Modern approaches to counseling diagnosis. *Journal of Counseling Psychology, 10,* 325–333.

Roe, A. (1954). A new classification of occupations. *Journal of Counseling Psychology,* 1, 215–220.

Roe, A. (1956). *The Psychology of Occupations.* New York: Wiley.

Roethliesberger, F. J., & Dickson, W. J. (1939). *Management and the worker.* Cambridge: Harvard University Press.

Rogers, C. R. (1957). The necessary and sufficient conditions of therapeutic personality change. *Journal of Consulting Psychology, 21,* 95–103.

Rosen, D., Holmberg, K., & Holland, J. L. (1987). *The college majors finder.* Odessa, FL: Psychological Assessment Resources.

Rosen, G. M. (1987). Self-help treatment books and the commercialization of psychotherapy. *American Psychologist, 42,* 46–51.

Rotberg, H. L., Brown, D., & Ware, W. B. (1987). Career self-efficacy expectations and perceived range of career options in community college students. *Journal of Counseling Psychology, 34,* 164–170.

Rothbaum, F., Weisz, J. R., & Snyder, S. S. (1983). Changing the world and changing the self: A two-process model of perceived control. *Journal of Personality and Social Psychology, 42,* 5–37.

Rounds, J. B., Jr., Dawis, R. V., & Lofquist, L. H. (1987). Measurement of person-environment fit prediction of satisfaction in the theory of work adjustment. *Journal of Vocational Behavior, 31,* 297–318.

Rounds, J. B., Jr., Henly, G. A., Dawis, R. V., Lofquist, L. H., & Weiss, D. J. (1981). *Manual for the Minnesota Importance Questionnaire: A measure of vocational needs and values.* Minneapolis, MN: University of Minnesota.

Rounds, J. B., Jr., & Tinsley, H. E. A. (1984). Diagnosis and treatment of vocational problems. In S. D. Brown & R. W. Lent (Eds.), *Handbook of counseling psychology* (pp. 137–177). New York: Wiley.

Rusalem, H. (1954). New insights on the role of occupational information in counseling. *Journal of Counseling Psychology, 1,* 84–88.

Russell, R. K., Crimmings, A. M., & Lent, R. W. (1984). Counselor training and supervision: Theory and research. In S. D. Brown & R. W. Lent (Eds.), *Handbook of counseling psychology* (pp. 625–681). New York: Wiley.

Ryan, T. A., & Krumboltz, J. D. (1964). Effect of planned reinforcement counseling on client decision-making behavior. *Journal of Counseling Psychology, 11,* 315–323.

Salomone, P. R. (1982). Difficult cases in career counseling: II—The indecisive client. *Personnel and Guidance Journal, 60,* 496–500.

Salomone, P. R., & McKenna, P. (1982). Difficult career counseling cases: I—Unrealistic vocational aspirations. *Personnel and Guidance Journal, 60,* 283–286.

Salzman, L. (1976). The will to change. In A. Burton (Ed.), *What makes behavior change possible?* (pp. 13–33). New York: Brunner/Mazel.

Samler, J. (1953). Toward a theoretical base for vocational counseling. *Personnel and Guidance Journal, 32,* 34–35.

Samler, J. (1961). Psycho-social aspects of work: A critique of occupational information. *Personnel and Guidance Journal, 39,* 458–465.

Samler, J. (1966). A new psychological specialty: Vocational counseling. *Vocational Guidance Quarterly, 15,* 82–89.

Samler, J. (1968). Vocational counseling: A pattern and a projection. *Vocational Guidance Quarterly, 17,* 2–11.

Sampson, J. P., Jr., (1989). Introduction. In G. R. Walz & J. C. Bleuer (Eds.), *Counseling Software Guide,* (pp. 1–3). Alexandria, VA: American Association for Counseling and Development.

Sampson, J. P., Jr., Shahnasarian, M. & Maddox, E. N. (1984). *Implementing computer-assisted career guidance and other computer applications for the adult learner.* Ann Arbor: ERIC/CAPS.

Sandelands, L. E., Brockner, J., & Glynn, M. A. (1988). If at first you don't succeed, try, try again: Effects of persistence-performance contingencies, ego involvement, and self-esteem on task persistence. *Journal of Applied Psychology, 73,* 208–216.

Savickas, M. L. (1975, August). Consistency of expressed interests as indicators of vocational maturity in college freshmen (doctoral dissertation, Kent State University, August, 1975).

Savickas, M. L. (in press). Annual review: Practice and research in career counseling and development, 1988. *Career Development Quarterly.*

Schein, E. H. (1987). *Process consultation* (Vol. 2). Reading, MA: Addison Wesley.

Schlossberg, N. K. (1983). Exploring the adult years. In A. M. Rogers & C. J. Schreirer (Eds.), *G. Stanley Hall Lecture Series No. 4.* Washington, DC: American Psychological Association.

Schneider, B. (1987). E = f (P, B): The road to a radical approach to person-environment fit. *Journal of Vocational Behavior, 31,* 353–361.

Schulenberg, J. E., Vondracek, F. W., & Crouter, A. C. (1984, February). The influence of the family on vocational development. *Journal of Marriage and the Family,* Feb., pp. 129–141.

Shahnasarian, M., & Peterson, G. W. (1986). *Use of computer-assisted career guidance with prior cognitive structuring* (Tech. Rep. No. 3). Tallahassee: Florida State University, Clearinghouse for Computer-Assisted Guidance Systems.

Shapiro, D. (1965). *Neurotic styles.* New York: Basic Books.

Sherman, S. J., Judd, C. M., & Park, B. (1989). Social cognition. *Annual Review of Psychology, 40,* 281–326.

Shertzer, B. (1981). *Career planning: Freedom to choose.* Boston: Houghton Mifflin.

Shimizu, K., Vondracek, F. W., Schulenberg, J. E., & Hostetler, M. (1988). The factor structure of the Career Decision Scale: Similarities across selected studies. *Journal of Vocational Behavior, 32,* 213–225.

Shutz, W. (1978). *FIRO Awareness Scales manual.* Palo Alto, CA: Consulting Psychologists Press.

Simon, H. (1955). A behavioral model of rational choice. *Quarterly Journal of Economics, 69,* 99–118.

Skinner, B. F. (1987). Whatever happened to psychology as the science of behavior? *American Psychologist, 42,* 780–786.

Skovholt, T. M., Morgan, J. I., & Negron-Cunningham, H. (1989). Mental imagery in career counseling and life planning: A review of research and intervention methods. *Journal of Counseling and Development, 67,* 287–292.

Slaney, R. B. (1980). Expressed vocational choice and vocational indecision. *Journal of Counseling Psychology, 27,* 122–129.

Slaney, R. B. (1983). Influence of career indecision on treatments exploring the vocational interests of college women. *Journal of Counseling Psychology, 30,* 55–63.

Slaney, R. B. (1985). Review of S. H. Osipow, C. G. Carney, J. L. Winer, B. Yanico, & M. Koschier, Career Decision Scale. In D. J. Keyser & R. C. Sweetland (Eds.), *Test Critiques:* Vol. 2 (pp. 138–143). Kansas City, MO: Test Corporation of America.

Slaney, R. B. (1988). The assessment of career decision making. In W. B. Walsh & S. H. Osipow (Eds.), *Career decision making* (pp. 33–76). Hillsdale, NJ: Lawrence Erlbaum.

Slaney, R. B., & Lewis, E. T. (1986). Effects of career exploration and career undecided reentry women: An intervention and follow-up study. *Journal of Vocational Behavior, 28,* 97–109.

Slaney, R. B., Palko-Nonemaker, D., & Alexander, R. (1981). An investigation of two measures of career indecision. *Journal of Vocational Behavior, 18,* 92–103.

Slaney, R. B., & Russell, J. E. A. (1987). Perspectives on vocational behavior, 1986: A review. *Journal of Vocational Behavior, 31,* 111–173.

Slaney, R. B. & McKinnon–Slaney, F. (in press). Use of vocational card sorts in vocational counseling. In C. E. Watkins and V. L. Campbell (Eds.), *Testing in Counseling Practice.* Hillsdale, NJ: Erlbaum.

Smart, J. C., Elton, C. F., & McLaughlin, G. W. (1986). Person-environment congruence and job satisfaction. *Journal of Vocational Behavior, 29,* 216–225.

Smith, C. W. (1981). Cognitive and affective benefits of a career development course. *Journal of Career Education, 8,* 57–66.

Smith, M. L., Glass, G. V., & Miller, T. I. (1980). *The benefits of psychotherapy.* Baltimore: Johns Hopkins University Press.

Speas, C. M. (1979). Job-seeking interview skills training: A comparison of four instructional techniques. *Journal of Counseling Psychology, 26,* 405–412.

Spielberger, C. D., Gorsuch, R. L., Lushene, R. E., Vagg, P. R., & Jacobs, G. A. (1983). *Manual for the State-Trait Anxiety Inventory.* Palo Alto, CA: Consulting Psychologists Press.

Spokane, A. R. (1979). Validity of the Holland themes for college women and men. *Journal of College Student Personnel, 20,* 335–340.

Spokane, A. R. (1985). A review of research on person-environment congruence in Holland's theory of careers [Monograph]. *Journal of Vocational Behavior, 26,* 306–343.

Spokane, A. R. (1987). Conceptual and methodological issues in person-environment fit research. *Journal of Vocational Behavior, 31,* 217–221.

Spokane, A. R. (in press-a). Are there psychological and mental health consequences for difficult career decisions? *Journal of Career Development.*

Spokane, A. R. (in press-b). Self-guided interest inventories: The Self-Directed Search. In E. Watkins & V. Campbell (Eds.), *Testing in couseling practice.* Hillsdale, NJ: Lawrence Erlbaum.

Spokane, A. R., Malett, S. D., & Vance, F. L. (1978). Consistent curricular choice and congruence of subsequent changes. *Journal of Vocational Behavior, 13,* 45–53.

Spokane, A. R., & Oliver, L. W. (1983). The outcomes of vocational intervention. In W. B. Walsh & S. H. Osipow (Eds.), *Handbook of vocational psychology* (Vol. 2, pp. 99–136). Hillsdale, NJ: Lawrence Erlbaum.

Spokane, A. R., & Spokane, R. H. (1981). Effects of information on the occupational preference of a sample of college women. *Journal of Employment Counseling, 18,* 64–72.

Stiles, W. B., & Snow, J. S. (1984). Counseling session impact as viewed by novice counselors and their clients. *Journal of Counseling Psychology, 31,* 3–12.

Stoltenberg, C. (1981). Approaching supervision from a developmental perspective: The counselor complexity model. *Journal of Counseling Psychology, 28,* 59–65.

Stotland, E. (1969). *The psychology of hope: An integration of experimental, clinical, and social approaches.* San Francisco: Jossey Bass.

Strohmer, D. C., (Newman, L. J. (1983). Counselor hypothesis-testing strategies. *Journal of Counseling Psychology, 30,* 557–565.

Strong, S. R. (1978). Social-psychological approach to psychotherapy research. In S. L. Bergin & A. E. Garfield (Eds.), *Handbook of psychotherapy and behavior change: An empirical analysis* (2nd ed., pp. 101–135). New York: Wiley.

Strupp, H. H. (1976). The nature of the therapeutic influence and its basic ingredients. In A. Burton (Ed.), *What makes behavior change possible?* (pp. 96–111). New York: Brunner/Mazel.

Stumpf, S. A. (1980). *Career success, career roles, and job attitudes* (No. 80–51). New York: New York University, Graduate School of Business Administration.

Stumpf, S. A. (1981). Career roles, psychological success, and job attitudes. *Journal of Vocational Behavior, 19,* 98–112.

Stumpf, S. A., & Colarelli, S. M. (1980). Career exploration: Development of dimensions and some preliminary findings. *Psychological Reports, 47,* 979–988.

Stumpf, S. A., & Colarelli, S. M. (1981). *The effects of career education on exploratory behavior and job search outcomes.* Unpublished manuscript, New York University.

Stumpf, S. A., Colarelli, S. M., & Hartman, K. (1983). Development of the Career Exploration Survey (CES). *Journal of Vocational Behavior, 22,* 191–226.

Su, B. W. (1985). The economic outlook to 1995: New assumptions and projections. *Monthly Labor Review, 108(11),* 3–16.

Subich, L., & Coursol, D. H. (1985). Counseling expectations of clients and nonclients for group and individual treatment modes. *Journal of Counseling Psychology, 32,* 245–251.

Super, D. E. (1956). Vocational development: The process of compromise or synthesis. *Journal of Counseling Psychology, 3,* 249–256.

Super, D. E. (1957). *The psychology of careers: An introduction to vocational development.* New York: Harper & Row.

Super, D. E. (1980). A life-span, life-space approach to career development. *Journal of Vocational Behavior, 16,* 282–298.

Super, D. E. (1984). Career and life development. In D. Brown & L. Brooks (Eds.), *Career choice and development: Applying contemporary theories to practice* (pp. 192–234). San Francisco: Jossey Bass.

Super, D. E., & Bohn, M. J., Jr. (1970). *Occupational psychology.* Belmont, CA: Wadsworth.

Super, D. E., Bohn, M. J., Jr. Forrest, D. J., Jordaan, J. P., Lindeman, R. H., & Thompson, A. A. (1971). *Career Development Inventory,* New York: Columbia University, Teachers College.

Super, D. E., & Crites, J. O. (1962). *Appraising vocational fitness by means of psychological tests* (rev. ed.). New York: Harper & Row.

Super, D. E., Crites, J. O., Hummel, R. C., Moser, H. P., Overstreet, P. L., & Warnath, C. F. (1958). *Vocational development: A framework for research.* New York: Columbia University, Teachers College.

Super, D. E., & Hall, D. T. (1978). Career development: Exploration and planning. *Annual Review of Psychology, 29,* 333–372.

Super, D. E., & Nevill, D. D. (1986). *Manual for the Values Scale (VS).* Palo Alto, CA: Consulting Psychologists Press.

Super, D. E., & Overstreet, P. L. (1960). *The vocational maturity of ninth-grade boys.* New York: Teachers College Press.

Super, D. E., Thompson, A. S., & Lindeman, R. H. (1988). *Adult Career Concerns Inventory: Manual for research and exploratory use in counseling.* Palo Alto, CA: Consulting Psychologists Press.

Super, D. E., Thompson, A. S., Lindeman, R. H., Jordaan, J. P., & Myers, R. A. (1983). *Manual for the Career Development Inventory,* Palo Alto, CA: Consulting Psychologists Press.

Swanson, J. L., & Hansen, J. C. (1985). The relationship of the construct of academic comfort to educational level, performance, aspirations, and prediction of college major choices. *Journal of Vocational Behavior, 26,* 1–12.

Tanaka, K., & Ogawa, K. (1986). Personality-environment congruence and attitudes among schoolteachers: A test of Holland's theory. *Hiroshima Forum for Psychology, 11,* 75–81.

Tarasoff v. Regents of California et al., 13 Cal. 3d 177, 17 Cal. 3d 425, 551 P. 2d 334 (1976).

Taylor, M. S. (1985). The roles of occupational knowledge and vocational self-concept crystallization in students' school-to-work transition. *Journal of Counseling Psychology, 32,* 539–550.

Taylor, N. B., & Pryor, R. G. L. (1985). Exploring the process of compromise in career decision making. *Journal of Vocational Behavior, 27,* 171–190.

Thomas, L. E. (1972). *Leader's manual: Life Planning Workshop.* Fort Collins: Colorado State University, University Counseling Center.

Thompson, A. S. (1960). Personality dynamics and vocational counseling. *Personnel and Guidance Journal, 38,* 350–358.

Thompson, A. S., Lindeman, R. H., Super, D. E., Jordaan, J. P., & Meyers, R. A. (1984). *Career Development Inventory: Vol. 2. Technical Manual.* Palo Alto, CA: Consulting Psychologists Press.

Thoresen, C. E., Hosford, R. E., & Krumboltz, J. D. (1970). Determining effective models for counseling clients of varying competencies. *Journal of Counseling Psychology, 17,* 369–375.

Thoresen, C. E., & Krumboltz, J. D. (1968). Similarity of social models and clients in behavioral counseling: Two experimental studies. *Journal of Counseling Psychology, 15,* 393–401.

Thoresen, C. E., Krumboltz, J. D., & Varenhorst, B. (1967). Sex of counselors and models: Effect on client career exploration. *Journal of Counseling Psychology, 14,* 503–508.

Tiedeman, D. V. (1967). Predicament, problem, and psychology: The case for paradox in life and counseling psychology. *Journal of Counseling Psychology, 14,* 1–8.

Tiedeman, D. V., & Miller-Tiedeman, A. (1984). Career decision making: An individualistic perspective. In D. Brown & L. Brooks (Eds.), *Career choice and development: Applying contemporary theories to practice* (pp. 281–310). San Francisco: Jossey Bass.

Tiedeman, D. V., & Ohara, R. P. (1963). *Career development: Choice and adjustment.* New York: College Entrance Examination Board.

Tinsley, H. E. A., & Bradley, R. W. (1986). Testing the test: Test interpretation. *Journal of Counseling and Development, 64,* 462–466.

Tinsley, H. E. A., & Fretz, B. R. (1984). *Test interpretation.* Unpublished manuscript revised with permission by B. R. Fretz, University of Maryland, College Park.

Tinsley, H. E. A., & Heesacker, M. (1984). Vocational behavior and career development, 1983: A review. *Journal of Vocational Behavior, 25,* 139–190.

Truax, C. B., & Carkhuff, R. R. (1967). *Toward effective counseling and psychotherapy: Training and practice.* Chicago: Aldine.

Tversky, A. (1972). Elimination by aspects: A theory of choice. *Psychological Review, 79,* 281–299.

Tyler, L. E. (1961). Research explorations in the realm of choice. *Journal of Counseling Psychology, 8,* 195–201.

Tyler, L. E. (1969). *The work of the counselor* (3rd ed.). New York: Appleton-Century-Crofts.

Tyler, L. E. (1984). Testing the test: What tests don't measure. *Journal of Counseling and Development, 63,* 48–50.

University of Maryland Career Development Center. (1989). *108D Workbook and instructor's manual.* College Park, MD: Author.

U.S. Department of Defense. (1985). *Technical supplement to the counselor's manual for the Armed Services Vocational Aptitude Battery Form 14*, North Chicago, IL: U.S. Military Entrance Processing Command.

U.S. Department of Labor. *Occupational Outlook Handbook*. Washington, DC: Author.

U.S. Department of Labor. (1977). *Dictionary of occupational titles* (4th ed.). Washington, DC: U.S. Government Printing Office.

U.S. Department of Labor. (1985). *Handbook of Labor statistics* (Bureau of Labor Statistics Bulletin No. 2217). Washington, DC: Author.

U.S. Department of Labor. (1986). *Occupational projections and training data* (Bureau of Labor Statistics Bulletin No. 2251). Washington, DC: Author.

U.S. Department of Labor (1988). *Occupational Outlook Handbook* 1988–1989 edition, Washington, DC: U.S. Government Printing Office.

U.S. Employment Service. (1979). The General Aptitude Test Battery (GATB). Washington, DC: Author.

U.S. Office of Career Education. (1978). *Profiles of career education projects*. Washington, DC: Author.

Valpar International Corporation. (1974). *VALPAR Component Work Samples*. Tucson, AZ: Author.

Vandenberg, S. G., & Stafford, R. E. (1967). Hereditary influences on vocational preferences as shown by scores of twins on the Minnesota Vocational Interest Inventory. *Journal of Applied Psychology, 51,* 17–19.

Varvil-Weld, D. C., & Fretz, B. R. (1983). Expectancies and the outcome of a career development intervention. *Journal of Counseling Psychology, 30,* 290–293.

Vondracek, F. W., Lerner, R. M., & Schulenberg, J. E. (1986). *Career development: A life-span developmental approach*. Hillsdale, NJ: Lawrence Erlbaum.

Vondracek, F. W., & Schulenberg, J. E. (1986). Career development in adolescence: Some conceptual and intervention issues. *Vocational Guidance Quarterly, 34,* 247–254.

Wakabayashi, M., & Graen, G. B. (1984). The Japanese career progress study: A seven-year follow-up. *Journal of Applied Psychology, 69,* 603–614.

Walsh, W. B. (1973). *Theories of person-environment interaction: Implications for the college student*. Iowa City: American College Testing Program.

Walsh, W. B. (1979). Vocational behavior and career development, 1978: A review. *Journal of Vocational Behavior, 15,* 119–154.

Walsh, W. B., & Betz, N. E. (1985). *Tests and assessment*. Englewood Cliffs, NJ: Prentice-Hall.

Walsh, W. B., Osipow, S. H., & Leonard, R. (1973). Self-esteem, self-consistency, and second vocational choice. *Journal of Counseling Psychology, 20,* 91–93.

Walter, V. (1985). *Sixteen PF Personal Career Development Profile*. Champaign, IL: Institute for Personality and Ability Testing.

Walz, G. R., & Bleuer, J. C. (Eds.). (1989). *Counseling software guide*. Alexandria, VA: American Association for Counseling and Development.

Wanous, J. P. (1973). Effects of a realistic job preview on job acceptance, job attitudes, and job survival. *Journal of Applied Psychology, 58,* 327–332.

Ward, L. G., Friedlander, M. L., Schoen, L. G., & Klein, L. G. (1985). Strategic self-presentation in supervision. *Journal of Counseling Psychology, 32,* 111–118.

Waterman, R. H., Jr. (1987). *The renewal factor: How to get and keep the competitive edge*. New York: Bantam Books.

Watkins, C. E., Jr. (1984). The individual psychology of Alfred Adler: Toward an Adlerian vocational theory. *Journal of Vocational Behavior, 28,* 28–47.

Watts, A. G., & Kidd, J. M. (1978). Evaluating the effectiveness of careers guidance: A review of the British research. *Journal of Occupational Psychology, 51,* 235–248.

Webb, E. J., Campbell, D. J., Schwartz, R. D., Sechrest, L., & Grove, J. B. (1981). *Nonreactive measures in the social sciences* (2nd ed.), Boston: Houghton-Mifflin.

Weiner, M. F. (1982). *Therapeutic impasse: Diagnosis, management, resolution.* New York: The Free Press.

Westbrook, B. W. (1983). Career maturity: The concept, the instrument, and the research. In W. B. Walsh & S. H. Osipow (Eds.), *Handbook of vocational psychology* (Vol. 1, pp. 263–303). Hillsdale, NJ: Lawrence Erlbaum.

Westbrook, B. W., & Parry-Hill, J. W., Jr. (1973). The measurement of Cognitive Vocational Maturity. *Journal of Vocational Behavior, 3,* 239–252.

Wholeben, B. E. (1988). Sixteen PF Personal Career Development Profile. In J. T. Kapes & M. M. Mastie (Eds.), *A counselor's guide to career assessment instruments* (2nd ed., pp. 238–242). Alexandria, VA: National Career Development Association.

Wiggins, J. D. (1987). Effective career exploration programs revisited. *Career Development Quarterly, 35,* 297–303.

Williamson, E. G., & Bordin, E. S. (1941). The evaluation of educational and vocational counseling: A critique of methodology of experiments. *Educational and Psychological Measurement, 1,* 5–25.

Winer, J. L., Cesari, J., Haase, R. F., & Bodden, J. L. (1979). Cognitive complexity and career maturity among college students. *Journal of Vocational Behavior, 15,* 186–192.

Wise, R. I. (1982). Opportunities for funding research on education and career development. In J. D. Krumboltz & D. A. Hamel (Eds.), *Assessing career development* (pp. 227–237). Palo Alto, CA: Mayfield.

Wolman, B. B. (1973). Concerning psychology and the philosophy of science. In B. B. Wolman (Ed.), *Handbook of General Psychology* (pp. 22–48). Englewood Cliffs, NJ: Prentice-Hall.

Worthington, E. L., Jr. (1984). Empirical investigation of supervision of counselors as they gain experience. *Journal of Counseling Psychology, 31,* 63–75.

Yalom, I. D. (1985). *The theory and practice of group counseling.* (3rd ed.). New York: Basic Books.

Yates, C., Johnson, N., & Johnson, J. (1979). Effects of the use of the vocational exploration group on career maturity. *Journal of Counseling Psychology, 26,* 368–370.

Yost, E. B., & Corbishley, M. A. (1987). *Career counseling: A psychological approach.* San Francisco: Jossey Bass.

Young, R. A. (1983). Career development of adolescents. *Journal of Youth and adolescence, 12,* 401–417.

Young, R. A., Friesen, J. D., & Pearson, H. M. (1988). Activities and interpersonal relations as dimensions of parental behavior in the career development of adolescents. *Youth and Society, 20,* 29–45.

Zager, J. J. (1982). *Self-esteem enhancement as an intervention for career indecision.* Unpublished doctoral dissertation, University of Maryland, College Park.

Zakay, D., & Barak, A. (1984). Meaning and career decision making. *Journal of Vocational Behavior, 24,* 1–14.

Zunker, V. G. (1986). *Career counseling: Applied concepts of life planning* (3rd ed.) Monterey, CA: Brooks/Cole.

Zytowski, D. G. (1976). Predictive validity of the Kuder Occupational Interest Survey: A twelve–nineteen–year follow-up. *Journal of Counseling Psychology, 23,* 221–233.

Zytowski, D. G. (1977). The effects of being interest-inventoried. *Journal of Vocational Behavior, 11,* 153–157.

Zytowski, D. G. (1978). Vocational behavior and career development, 1977: A review. *Journal of Vocational Behavior, 13,* 141–162.

Zytowski, D. G. (1985). *Kuder DD Occupational Interest Survey: Manual supplement.* Chicago: Science Research Associates.

Zytowski, D. G. (1988). Salience Inventory. In J. T. Kapes & M. M. Mastie (Eds.), *A counselor's guide to career assessment instruments* (2nd ed., pp. 151–154). Alexandria, VA: National Career Development Association.

Zytowski, D. G., & Borgen, F. H. (1983). Assessment. In W. B. Walsh & S. H. Osipow (Eds.), *Handbook of vocational psychology* (Vol. 2, pp. 5–40). Hillsdale, NJ: Lawrence Erlbaum.

Zytowski, D. G., & Laing, J. (1978). Validity of other-gender-normed scales on the Kuder Occupational Interest Survey. *Journal of Counseling Psychology, 25,* 205–209.

APPENDIX A

Vocational History Questionnaire

PURPOSE OF THE QUESTIONNAIRE

Providing a complete vocational history can accomplish two important objectives: (1) it can help you summarize your background and experience; and (2) it can provide valuable information to you and your counselor that will assist you in making a satisfactory career decision. The information that you give in this history is considered confidential.

Name _____   Date _____

Address _____   Date of birth _____

_____   Height _____

Telephone (home) _____   Weight _____

(office) _____   Age _____

Marital status (check one or more)

_____ Single   _____ Divorced

_____ Married   _____ Considering a divorce

_____ Engaged   _____ In a strong, supportive relationship

_____ Remarried   _____ Alone and depressed about it

_____ Separated   _____ Alone but okay about it

_____ Widowed

Father's current occupation _____

Brief history of father's career _____

_____

_____

_____

_____

_____

Mother's current occupation _____

Brief history of mother's career _____

_____

_____

_____

_____

_____

Briefly describe your parents' feelings about their careers.

Mother _____

_____

_____

Father _____

_____

_____

Describe your home life as a child and your relationship to each of your

parents _____

_____

_____

_____

_____

_____

	Maternal	*Paternal*
Grandfathers' occupations	_____	_____
Grandmothers' occupations	_____	_____

Your present job title	Year begun	Salary
_____	_____	_____

How did you obtain your job? _____

_____

_____

List several positive (+) and negative (−) aspects of your job:

(+) _____

(−) _____

Outline your advancement history _____

_____

_____

_____

Describe your feelings about your immediate supervisor _____

_____

_____

_____

Describe your goals for this job _____

_____

_____

_____

List the people who have had the most influence on your career development:

(1) _____	(6) _____
(2) _____	(7) _____
(3) _____	(8) _____
(4) _____	(9) _____
(5) _____	(10) _____

Which of the following persons are currently providing effective social support during your career decision process? (check as many as apply)

_____ Mother _____ Husband _____ Church member

_____ Father _____ Wife _____ Co-worker

_____ Grandmother(s) _____ Stepsibling _____ Foreman

_____ Grandfather(s) _____ Aunt(s) _____ Work supervisor

_____ Sister(s) _____ Uncle(s) _____ Colleague

_____ Brother(s) _____ Friend(s) _____ Mentor

_____ Girlfriend _____ Stepparent _____ Teacher, instructor or professor

_____ Boyfriend _____ Children _____ Academic adviser

_____ Fiancé _____ Minister _____ Counselor

_____ Ex-wife _____ Priest _____ Psychologist

_____ Ex-husband _____ Rabbi _____ Social worker-Psychiatrist

_____ Athletic coach _____ Neighbor _____ Career counselor

_____ Structured support group _____ Family doctor _____ Placement counselor

Which of the following have you done during the last month? (check as many as apply)

_____ Talked to friend about my career

_____ Read a book on careers

_____ Visited a new job site

_____ Read the want ads

_____ Took a test

_____ Talked to a recruiter

_____ Sent out my resumé

_____ Went to an employment agency

_____ Thought about my career

_____ Talked to a career counselor

_____ Read information about careers

_____ Talked to a person working in a job that interests me

Which of the following apply to you? (check as many as apply)

_____ Underestimate my ability

_____ Overestimate my ability

_____ Realistic about my ability

_____ Anxious about career decisions

_____ Unable to get going

_____ Lack information about jobs

_____ Make career plans

_____ Seek advice from others

_____ Need more information about jobs

_____ Don't know my interests

_____ Don't know my ability

_____ Confident of my ability to make a career choice

_____ Concerned that I will be unable to execute a career choice.

_____ Consider all sides of choice

_____ Open to new information

_____ Open to negative information

_____ In control of my career

_____ Blocked in my career

_____ Delayed or off schedule in my career

_____ Have few skills

_____ Have many skills

_____ Father dislikes my career choice

_____ Mother dislikes my career choice

_____ Using few of my skills

_____ Confident of my ability to implement a career choice

List your five main fears about work or a career:

(1) _____

(2) _____

(3) _____

(4) _____

(5) _____

What are your three main goals for career counseling?

(1) _____

_____

_____

(2) _____

_____

_____

(3) _____

_____

_____

What are the three best career decisions you have made?

(1) _____

_____

(2) _____

_____

(3) _____

_____

What are the three worst career decisions you have made?

(1) _____

_____

(2) _____

_____

(3) _____

_____

Describe your early career ambitions _____

_____

_____

_____

_____

_____

_____

Describe any career failures you have experienced ＿＿＿＿＿＿＿＿＿

＿＿＿＿＿＿＿＿＿＿＿＿＿＿＿＿＿＿＿＿＿＿＿＿＿＿＿

＿＿＿＿＿＿＿＿＿＿＿＿＿＿＿＿＿＿＿＿＿＿＿＿＿＿＿

＿＿＿＿＿＿＿＿＿＿＿＿＿＿＿＿＿＿＿＿＿＿＿＿＿＿＿

＿＿＿＿＿＿＿＿＿＿＿＿＿＿＿＿＿＿＿＿＿＿＿＿＿＿＿

Describe any career successes you have experienced ＿＿＿＿＿＿＿＿

＿＿＿＿＿＿＿＿＿＿＿＿＿＿＿＿＿＿＿＿＿＿＿＿＿＿＿

＿＿＿＿＿＿＿＿＿＿＿＿＿＿＿＿＿＿＿＿＿＿＿＿＿＿＿

＿＿＿＿＿＿＿＿＿＿＿＿＿＿＿＿＿＿＿＿＿＿＿＿＿＿＿

＿＿＿＿＿＿＿＿＿＿＿＿＿＿＿＿＿＿＿＿＿＿＿＿＿＿＿

Respond to the following statements:

(1) When I think about my present job, I feel ＿＿＿＿＿＿＿＿＿＿

＿＿＿＿＿＿＿＿＿＿＿＿＿＿＿＿＿＿＿＿＿＿＿＿＿＿＿

＿＿＿＿＿＿＿＿＿＿＿＿＿＿＿＿＿＿＿＿＿＿＿＿＿＿＿

(2) When I think about jobs I might have in the future, I feel ＿＿＿＿

＿＿＿＿＿＿＿＿＿＿＿＿＿＿＿＿＿＿＿＿＿＿＿＿＿＿＿

＿＿＿＿＿＿＿＿＿＿＿＿＿＿＿＿＿＿＿＿＿＿＿＿＿＿＿

(3) Making a career decision is ＿＿＿＿＿＿＿＿＿＿＿＿＿＿＿＿＿

＿＿＿＿＿＿＿＿＿＿＿＿＿＿＿＿＿＿＿＿＿＿＿＿＿＿＿

＿＿＿＿＿＿＿＿＿＿＿＿＿＿＿＿＿＿＿＿＿＿＿＿＿＿＿

(4) The important people around me think I should ＿＿＿＿＿＿＿＿

＿＿＿＿＿＿＿＿＿＿＿＿＿＿＿＿＿＿＿＿＿＿＿＿＿＿＿

＿＿＿＿＿＿＿＿＿＿＿＿＿＿＿＿＿＿＿＿＿＿＿＿＿＿＿

(5) What I really want from a job is _____

_____

_____

_____

_____

(6) I wish that I _____

_____

_____

_____

_____

Check highest level of education you have completed:

_____	1st grade	_____	Technical or junior college (1 year or less)
_____	2nd grade	_____	Technical or junior college (2 years)
_____	3rd grade	_____	Technical or junior college (graduate)
_____	4th grade	_____	Four-year college (1 year)
_____	5th grade	_____	Four-year college (2 years)
_____	6th grade	_____	Four-year college (3 years)
_____	7th grade	_____	Four-year college (graduate)
_____	8th grade	_____	Graduate school (1 year)
_____	9th grade	_____	Master's degree
_____	10th grade	_____	Master's degree + 30
_____	11th grade	_____	Doctorate
_____	12th grade	_____	Other _____

List all degrees, certificates, licenses, and advanced training you have received.

Degree/certificate	*Year*
_____	_____
_____	_____
_____	_____

List all of the jobs (both part- and full-time, paid and nonpaid) that you have held during each of the following periods of your life. Be specific.

Adolescence (ages 8–15)

Job title _____   Years _____

How obtained _____

Positive and negative aspects _____

_____

Job title _____   Years _____

How obtained _____

Positive and negative aspects _____

_____

Young adult (ages 16–21)

Job title _____   Years _____

How obtained _____

Positive and negative aspects _____

_____

Job title _____   Years _____

How obtained _____

Positive and negative aspects _____

_____

Job title _____   Years _____

How obtained _____

Positive and negative aspects _____

_____

Adult (ages 22–65)

Job title _____   Years _____

How obtained _____

Positive and negative aspects _____

_____

Job title _____   Years _____

How obtained _____

Positive and negative aspects _____

_____

Job title _____   Years _____

How obtained _____

Positive and negative aspects_____

_____

Job title _____   Years _____

How obtained _____

Positive and negative aspects _____

_____

Retirement (after age 65)

Job title _____   Years _____

How obtained _____

Positive and negative aspects _____

_____

Job title _____   Years _____

How obtained _____

Positive and negative aspects _____

_____

Describe any work situations that make you uncomfortable or anxious

_____

_____

_____

_____

_____

_____

Add any other information that would assist your career counselor in understanding your situation _____

_____

_____

_____

_____

APPENDIX B

Diagnostic Taxonomy of Adult Career Problems

The following presentation of the taxonomy begins with an outline of the four problem categories and the subcategories contained within each category. Following the outline a detailed description of problem categories, subcategories, and causal factors is presented.

DIAGNOSTIC TAXONOMY OUTLINE

Problem Categories and Subcategories

1.0 Problems in Career Decision Making
    1.1 Problems in Career Decision Making: Getting Started
    1.2 Problems in Career Decision Making: Information Gathering
    1.3 Problems in Career Decision Making: Generating, Evaluating, and Selecting Alternatives
    1.4 Problems in Career Decision Making: Formulating Plans for Implementing Decisions
2.0 Problems in Implementing Career Plans
    2.1 Problems in Implementing Career Plans: Characteristics of the Individual
    2.2 Problems in Implementing Career Plans: Characteristics External to the Individual
3.0 Problems in Organizational/Institutional Performance
    3.1 Problems in Performance: Deficiencies in Skills, Abilities, and Knowledge

3.2 Problems in Performance: Personal Factors

3.3 Problems in Performance: Conditions of the Organizational/Institutional Environment

4.0 Problems in Organizational/Institutional Adaptation

4.1 Problems in Organizational/Institutional Adaptation: Initial Entry

4.2 Problems in Organizational/Institutional Adaptation: Changes Over Time

4.3 Problems in Organizational/Institutional Adaptation: Interpersonal Relationships

DIAGNOSTIC TAXONOMY

1.0 Problems in Career Decision Making

This category includes problems which interfere with or retard satisfactory initiation and completion of the career decision-making process. For purposes of this taxonomy, the decision-making process is viewed as consisting of the following four phases:

1. Getting started, i.e., awareness of the need for a decision and the willingness to expend the time and effort necessary to know and complete the process
2. Information gathering
3. Generating, evaluating, and selecting alternatives
4. Formulating plans for implementing decisions

The process may be viewed as completed when a satisfactory decision and plans to implement that decision have been made. Problems with implementing plans (decisions) are not part of this category and are classified elsewhere.

Problems may be evident in any one or more of these phases. Career decision-making problems can occur at all stages of career development and are not confined to initial entry into the labor force. Hence, problems might be associated with labor force reentry, mid-life career change, and retirement.

The following subcategories 1.1 through 1.4 describe problems corresponding to the four phases of the decision-making process.

1.1 Problems in Career Decision Making: Getting Started

This subcategory includes problems which arise due to an individual's general orientation toward the decision-making process. This orientation determines whether the steps in decision making are undertaken as well as the quality of the steps that are taken. Problems usually involve some degree of avoidance or lack of awareness and/or knowledge of the decision-making process.

More specifically, this subcategory could include the following types of problems:

1. Lack of awareness of the need for a decision

   Example: The high school senior who feels life will continue as it is and he/she can just move along with the crowd

   Example: The employee whose company is reorganizing and does not recognize that he/she will have to make a position-change decision

2. Lack of knowledge of the decision-making process

   Example: The person who would like to make a career change, but does not know how to get started

   Example: The person who is confused as to the best sequence of steps to make a decision

3. Awareness of the need to make a decision, but avoidance of assuming personal responsibility for decision making

   Example: The student who keeps postponing appointments with the guidance counselor

   Example: The person who asks someone else to make the decision

1.2 Problems in Career Decision Making: Information Gathering

This subcategory includes problems in which the information essential to career decision making is lacking or interfering with the completion of the decision-making process. Career decision-making information encompasses information about the person (e.g., abilities, interests, and values) as well as the world of work (e.g., training programs, job opportunities, organizational settings, and retirement programs). This subcategory could include the following types of problems:

1. Inadequate, contradictory, and/or insufficient information

   Example: The preretiree who cannot obtain accurate information about retirement housing

   Example: The job candidate who has received conflicting reports about the stability of the organization under consideration

   Example: The rural youth who has limited access to career information

2. Information overload, i.e., excessive information which confuses the decision maker

   Example: The career explorer who has received an overabundance of career materials and is having difficulty determining the personal relevance of each

Example: The person who feels a compulsive need to collect more information than is necessary

3. Lack of knowledge as to how to gather information, i.e., where to obtain information, how to organize and to evaluate it

   Example: Persons who are unaware of existing sources and procedures for obtaining information

4. Unwillingness to accept the validity of the information because it does not agree with the person's self-concept

   Example: The rejected pre-med student who denies the validity of the medical school admission's tests

   Example: The aspiring truck driver who feels he/she is in better health than indicated by the qualifying physical examination

1.3 Problems in Career Decision Making: Generating, Evaluating, and Selecting Alternatives

This subcategory includes problems in which the process of generating, evaluating, and selecting career alternatives is impeded and/or results in unsatisfactory or inappropriate decisions. Problems are classified here when an individual has recognized the need to decide and has collected information but is stymied in the process of deciding among alternatives. Problems in this subcategory could include the following:

1. Difficulty deciding due to multiple career options, i.e., too many equally attractive career choices

   Example: The multipotential person who would probably do well in any number of careers

2. Failure to generate sufficient career options due to personal limitations such as health, resources, ability, and education

   Example: The unskilled, unemployed fifty-five-year-old with a sixth-grade education

   Example: The mentally retarded youth

3. The inability to decide due to the thwarting effects of anxiety such as fear of failure in attempting to fulfill the choice, fear of social disapproval, and/or fear of commitment to a course of action

   Example: The employee who procrastinates accepting a supervisory position for fear of peer disapproval

   Example: The student who purposively prolongs his/her education to avoid public commitment to an occupation

4. Unrealistic choice, i.e., aspiring either too low or too high, based upon criteria such as aptitudes, interests, values, resources, and personal circumstances

Example: The person who is determined to become a plumber despite low aptitude test scores required for this occupation

Example: The person who underestimates his/her capabilities and accepts a menial job

5. Interfering personal constraints which impede a choice such as interpersonal influences and conflicts, situational circumstances, resources, and health

   Example: The mid-life career changer who needs to reconstruct family circumstances before considering a career decision

   Example: The preretiree who has to delay making a retirement decision pending the improved health status of a dependent

6. The inability to evaluate alternatives due to lack of knowledge of the evaluation criteria—the criteria could include values, interests, aptitudes, skills, resources, health, age, and personal circumstances. The person knows the general process of career decision making, has collected appropriate information, generated alternatives, but is now having difficulty formulating and applying criteria for assessing alternatives

   Example: The person who is having difficulty prioritizing work values, e.g., security vs. autonomy

   Example: The person who is having difficulty assessing the implications of geographic relocation related to a job change

1.4 Problems in Career Decision Making: Formulating Plans for Implementing Decisions

This subcategory includes problems relating to formulating plans for implementing a career decision after a decision has been made. This subcategory does not include problems associated with the actual implementation of a decision, which are classified elsewhere. The formulation of plans consists primarily of cognitive activities that assist the person in thinking through how a decision will be implemented. In some instances, a person will have overlooked a key factor in a decision which surfaces during formulating plans, e.g., the increased cost of housing in another city, which might necessitate reevaluating the decision to relocate.

Problems in formulating plans typically emanate from the following sources:

1. Lack of knowledge of the necessary steps to formulate a plan

   Example: The person who wants to become a barber, but does not know the procedures for obtaining training

   Example: The person who would like to work as a grocery clerk, but does not know how to apply

2. Inability to utilize a future time perspective in planning

   Example: The breadwinner who is unable to foresee changing family responsibilities as they might interact with a career decision

   Example: The aspiring executive who is having difficulty projecting how long he/she should stay in the present job before attempting a move

3. Unwillingness and/or inability to acquire the necessary information to formulate a plan

   Example: The student who does not want to exert the effort to acquire housing information

   Example: The mechanic who wants to establish his/her own shop but delays exploring loan information

2.0 Problems in Implementing Career Plans

This category includes problems encountered in the process of implementing one's career plans. Individuals in this category are assumed to have made a satisfactory career decision and to have outlined a plan designed to implement that decision. Thus, the next critical step in their career development involves the successful implementation of the decision and the attainment of the desired career objectives.

Problems in implementation are in evidence when the individual's goals are being thwarted and/or when he/she cannot or does not orchestrate planning elements. Problems of this type typically occur due to two subcategories of factors: (1) characteristics of the individual, e.g., lack of motivation to complete the necessary steps in implementation, and (2) characteristics external to the individual, e.g., lack of available positions in the individual's chosen career field. The following subcategories 2.1 and 2.2 describe these two types of problems of implementation.

2.1 Problems in Implementing Career Plans: Characteristics of the Individual

This subcategory includes problems in implementation due to characteristics of the individual. These problems may arise from the following:

1. Failure of the individual to undertake the steps necessary to implement his/her plan

   Example: The individual who postpones beginning a job search through lack of motivation or fear of rejection

   Example: The individual who fails to implement plans for retirement because he or she wishes to deny its necessity

Example: The student who fails to apply for loan assistance to continue his/her education

2. Failure or inability to successfully complete the steps necessary for goal attainment

   Example: The individual who is unable to complete necessary educational or training programs

   Example: The individual whose lack of persistence, thoroughness, or realism in a job search results in failure to find a job

3. Adverse changes in the individual's physical or emotional condition

   Example: The young athlete whose plans are disrupted by a physical disability

2.2 Problems in Implementing Career Plans: Characteristics External to the Individual

A second major subcategory of problems in implementation describes external factors or circumstances which interfere with the individual's progress in implementing his or her career plans. Problems may arise due to the following:

1. Unfavorable economic, social, and cultural conditions

   Example: The individual whose attempts to find a job are complicated by an economic recession

   Example: The preretiree who finds that inflation has prevented his or her accumulation of sufficient financial resources upon which to retire

   Example: The prospective elementary school teacher who realizes that the decreasing birth rate has reduced the demand for persons in that profession

2. Unfavorable conditions in the organization or institution central to the implementation of one's plans

   Example: The individual who is discriminated against in hiring and/or promotion

   Example: The individual who loses his or her job when the employing organization goes out of business

3. Adverse conditions of or changes in the individual's family situation

   Example: The individual whose career plans are disrupted by the death or serious illness of a family member or significant other

   Example: The individual who must, perhaps unexpectedly, expend time and money to care for a child

Example: The partners in a dual-career relationship who must compromise their mobility if they are to stay together

3.0 Problems in Organizational/Institutional Performance

This category includes problems in which the individual is having difficulty achieving or maintaining an acceptable level of performance based upon either personal and/or organizational/institutional standards within an educational or work setting. The person could be satisfying work standards for the organization/institution, but falling short of his/her personal standards, or the reverse, e.g., the student who is getting passing grades, but aspires for much higher grades, or the mechanic who feels he/she is doing good work, but is not satisfying the boss. Performance problems can be manifested in a variety of ways such as poor quality or quantity of work output, absenteeism, interpersonal conflicts, sloppy work habits, tension, dishonesty, and accidents. Performance problems can be classified under three subcategories: (1) deficits in skills, abilities, and/or knowledge; (2) personal factors, e.g., poor emotional or physical health; and (3) conditions of the organizational/institutional environment, e.g., inadequate support facilities, supplies, and/or resources. The following subcategories 3.1 through 3.3 provide further elaboration of performance problems.

3.1 Problems in Performance: Deficiencies in Skills, Abilities, and Knowledge

This subcategory includes problems arising from deficits in the skills, abilities, and/or knowledge essential for satisfactory performance. The deficiency may exist due to the following:

1. Insufficient skills, abilities, and/or knowledge upon position entry, i.e., underqualified to perform satisfactorily
   Example: The person who was hired as a bank teller, through personal contacts, but lacks the mathematical proficiency to perform satisfactorily
   Example: The trainee who was given conditional admission status to a training program pending remedial correction of admission requirements such as reading or math
2. The deterioration of skills, abilities, and/or knowledge over time while in the position due to temporary assignment to another position, leave, and/or lack of continual practice of the skill
   Example: The construction worker who was assigned to the front office for an extended period of time and returns to his/her former assignment

Example: The welder who returns from a lengthy leave and has difficulty reestablishing his/her work rate quota

Example: The stenographer who loses his/her shorthand skills due to insufficient opportunities to take dictation

3. The failure to modify or update skills, abilities, and/or knowledge to stay abreast of job changes, i.e., job obsolescence due to new technology, tools, and knowledge

   Example: The accountant who has not learned computer technology

   Example: The nurse who has not kept pace with pharmaceutical changes

3.2 Problems in Performance: Personal Factors

This subcategory includes performance problems resulting from individual characteristics other than skills, abilities, and knowledge. Personal factors pertain primarily to the individual's values, attitudes, motivation, personality, health, and personal circumstances as they relate to satisfactory performance. The individual may possess the skills, abilities, and knowledge to perform satisfactorily but is not doing so due to interfering personal factors. Problems may arise due to the following:

1. Personality characteristics discrepant with the job, e.g., values, interests, and work habits

   Example: The overeducated, underemployed typist who prefers a more challenging position

   Example: The assembly line worker who needs a job, but hates the work and would rather be in an outdoor occupation

2. Debilitating physical and/or emotional disorders

   Example: The dock worker who is suffering from a bad back

   Example: The ambulatory psychotic who has trouble concentrating on the work

3. Adverse off-the-job personal circumstances and/or stressors, e.g., family pressures, financial problems, and personal conflicts

   Example: The employee whose father is being treated for a terminal illness

   Example: The employee who has overextended his/her financial obligations

4. The occurrence of interpersonal conflicts on the job which are specific to performance requirements, e.g., getting along with the boss, coworkers, customers, and clients

   Example: The crew chief who unduly harrasses his/her subordinates

   Example: The salesperson who is abrasive to customers

3.3 Problems in Performance: Conditions of the Organizational/Institutional Environment

This subcategory includes problems arising from conditions within the organizational/institutional environment which interfere with or inhibit the achievement of satisfactory performance. Interfering conditions typically stem from at least four aspects of the environment:

1. Ambiguous or inappropriate job requirements, e.g., lack of clarity of assignments, work overload, and conflicting assignments

   Example: The employee who has been given contradictory instructions from different supervisors

2. Deficiencies in the operational structure of the organization/institution

   Example: Employees who are unable to achieve their production quotas due to inefficient management coordination among work units

   Example: Employees whose morale is low due to frequent conflicts among top management

3. Inadequate support facilities, supplies, and resources, e.g., insufficient lighting, ventilation, tools, support personnel, and materials

   Example: The television cameraman who is unable to provide a quality picture due to inferior equipment

   Example: The appliance repairperson who is frequently behind schedule due to delays in obtaining parts

4. Insufficient reward system, e.g., compensation, fringe benefits, status, recognition, and opportunities for advancement

   Example: Employees who are rarely given credit for extra effort

   Example: Employees who perceive no opportunities for advancement

4.0 Problems in Organizational/Institutional Adaptation

This category includes problems in which the individual is having difficulties adjusting to and fitting into the organizational/institutional environment. Problems classified within this category involve difficulties in adjusting to organizational policies, regulations, rules, decorum, administrative structure, and to other members of the organization. The category excludes problems in performance and, rather, emphasizes the degree of adaptation of the individual to the total organizational environment. Problems in this category can be classified using three subcategories, i.e., (1) initial entry, (2) changes over time, and (3) interpersonal relationships. The following subcategories

4.1 to 4.3 describe these three types of problems in organizational/institutional adaptation.

4.1 Problems in Organizational/Institutional Adaptation: Initial Entry

This subcategory includes adjustment problems occurring during the period following initial entry to an institutional/organizational environment. These problems include the following:

1. Lack of knowledge of organizational rules and procedures
   Example: The individual who dresses inappropriately due to lack of knowledge of norms regarding acceptable attire
2. Failure to accept or adhere to organizational rules and procedures
   Example: The individual who fails to observe norms regarding interactions with subordinates
   Example: The individual who refuses to follow the directions of superiors
3. Inability to assimilate large quantities of new information, i.e., information overload
   Example: The individual who is overwhelmed by the amount he or she must learn quickly and, thus, becomes anxious and less effective
4. Discomfort in a new geographic location
   Example: The individual whose lack of familiarity with and comfort in a new city hinders his or her job satisfaction
5. Discrepancies between the individual's expectations and the realities of the institutional/organizational environment
   Example: The college student who anticipated a busy social life but has found that other students are more interested in studying at night
   Example: The person who finds that his or her job duties are different from what he/she had expected

4.2 Problems in Organizational/Institutional Adaptation: Changes Over Time

This subcategory includes problems in adjustment which occur after the individual has been with the organization long enough to have achieved an initial adjustment to the institution/organization. Adjustment problems in later stages of the individual's tenure with the institution/organization may be viewed as disruptions in the state of individual-environment congruence or balance that had been previously achieved. Such disruptions may occur for the following reasons:

1. Changes over the life span in one's attitudes, values, life style, career plans, or commitment to the organization which lead to incongruence between the individual and the environment

Example: The individual whose changing value system is no longer compatible with the values of the organization

Example: The individual for whom the stresses of life in a large city or of striving to reach the top of an organization are no longer tolerable

Example: The individual who, over time, has become bored with tasks and responsibilities which once provided personal satisfaction

2. Changes in the organizational/institutional environment which lead to incongruence between the individual and the environment, e.g., physical and administrative structure, policies, and procedures

    Example: The individual who finds that working conditions under new company management are intolerable

    Example: The individual who is dissatisfied with changes in promotional policies

    Example: The junior chemist who feels professionally isolated when his/her mentor is transferred to another division

4.3 Problems in Organizational/Institutional Adaptation: Interpersonal Relationships

This subcategory includes problems related to the individual's attempts to develop and maintain satisfactory relationships with persons sharing the same organizational/institutional environment. Relationships creating problems can be either with people to whom the individual must relate on a formal basis, e.g., supervisors and supervisees, or those with whom informal relationships are formed, e.g., others working in the same office and students in the same dormitory. Problems in interpersonal relationships may be due to the following:

1. Interpersonal conflicts arising from differences of opinion, style, values, mannerisms, etc.

    Example: The individual who is irritated by a coworker who whistles or talks to himself/herself

    Example: The individual who is continually arguing with a coworker who has differing political views

2. The occurrence of verbal or physical abuse or sexual harassment

    Example: The secretary who is continually bothered with sexual innuendos and advances from his/her boss

    Example: The meek employee who is always a victim of the company bully

Source: R.E. Campbell, J.V. Cellini, P.E. Shaltry, A.E. Long, and D. Pinkos, *A Diagnostic Taxonomy of Adult Career Problems* (Columbus, OH: The National Center for Research in Vocational Education, 1973), 56–66. Reprinted with permission.

APPENDIX C

National Career Development Association Ethical Standards

These Ethical Standards were developed by the National Board for Certified Counselors (NBCC), an independent, voluntary, not-for-profit organization incorporated in 1982. Titled "Code of Ethics" by NBCC and last amended in February 1987, the Ethical Standards were adopted by the National Career Development Association (NCDA) Board of Directions at its April 1987 meeting in New Orleans, LA. Only minor changes in wording (e.g., the addition of specific references to NCDA members) were made.

PREAMBLE. NCDA is an educational, scientific, and professional organization dedicated to the enhancement of the worth, dignity, potential, and uniqueness of each individual and, thus, to the service of society. This code of ethics enables the NCDA to clarify the nature of ethical responsibilities for present and future professional career counselors.

SECTION A: GENERAL

1. NCDA members influence the development of the profession by continuous efforts to improve professional practices, services, and research. Professional growth is continuous through the career counselor's career and is exemplified by the development of a philosophy that explains why and how a career counselor functions in the helping relationship. Career counselors must gather data on their effectiveness and be guided by their findings.

2. NCDA members have a responsibility to the clients they are serving and to the institutions within which the services are being performed. Career counselors also strive to assist the respective agency, organization, or institution in providing the highest caliber of professional services. The accept-

ance of employment in an institution implies that the career counselor is in agreement with the general polices and principles of the institution. Therefore, the professional activities of the career counselor are in accord with the objective of the institution. If, despite concerted efforts, the career counselor cannot reach agreement with the employer as to acceptable standards of conduct that allow for changes in institutional policy that are conducive to the positive growth and development of clients, then terminating the affiliation should be seriously considered.

3. Ethical behavior among professional associates (e.g., career counselors) must be expected at all times. When accessible information raises doubt as to the ethical behavior of professional colleagues, the NCDA member must take action to attempt to rectify this condition. Such action uses the respective institution's channels first and then uses procedures established by the American Association for Counseling and Development, of which NCDA is a division.

4. NCDA members neither claim nor imply professional qualifications which exceed those possessed, and are responsible for correcting any misrepresentations of these qualifications by others.

5. NCDA members must refuse a private fee or other remuneration for consultation or counseling with persons who are entitled to their services through the career counselor's employing institution or agency. The policies of some agencies may make explicit provisions for staff members to engage in private practice with agency clients. However, should agency clients desire private counseling or consulting services, they must be apprised of other options available to them. Career counselors must not divert to their private practices, legitimate clients in their primary agencies or of the institutions with which they are affiliated.

6. In establishing fees for professional counseling services, NCDA members must consider the financial status of clients and the respective locality. In the event that the established fee status is inappropriate for a client, assistance must be provided in finding comparable services of acceptable cost.

7. NCDA members seek only those positions in the delivery of professional services for which they are professional qualified.

8. NCDA members recognize their limitations and provide services or only use techniques for which they are qualified by training and/or experience. Career counselors recognize the need, and seek continuing education, to assure competent services.

9. NCDA members are aware of the intimacy in the counseling relationship, maintain respect for the client, and avoid engaging in activities that seek to meet their personal needs at the expense of the client.

10. NCDA members do not condone or engage in sexual harassment which is defined as deliberate or repeated comments, gestures, or physical contacts of a sexual nature.

11. NCDA members avoid bringing their personal or professional issues into the counseling relationship. Through an awareness of the impact of stereotyping and discrimination (i.e., biases based on age, disability, ethnicity, gender, race, religion, or sexual preference), career counselors guard the individual rights and personal dignity of the client in the counseling relationship.

12. NCDA members are accountable at all times for their behavior. They must be aware that all actions and behaviors of a counselor reflect on professional integrity and, when inappropriate, can damage the public trust in the counseling profession. To protect public confidence in the counseling profession, career counselors avoid public behavior that is clearly in violation of accepted moral and legal standards.

13. NCDA members have a social responsibility because their recommendations and professional actions may alter the lives of others. Career counselors remain fully cognizant of their impact and are alert to personal, social, organizational, financial, or political situations or pressures which might lead to misuse of their influence.

14. Products or services provided by NCDA members by means of classroom instruction, public lectures, demonstrations, written articles, radio or television programs, or other types of media must meet the criteria cited in Sections A through F of these Ethical Standards.

SECTION B: COUNSELING RELATIONSHIP

1. The primary obligation of NCDA members is to respect the integrity and promote the welfare of the client, regardless of whether the client is assisted individually or in a group relationship. In a group setting, the career counselor is also responsible for taking reasonable precautions to protect individuals from physical and/or psychological trauma resulting from interaction within the group.

2. The counseling relationship and information resulting from it remains confidential, consistent with the legal obligations of the NCDA member. In a group counseling setting, the career counselor sets a norm of confidentiality regarding all group participants' disclosures.

3. NCDA members know and take into account the traditions and practices of other professional groups with whom they work, and they cooperate fully with such groups. If a person is receiving similar services from another professional, career counselors do not offer their own services directly to such a person. If a career counselor is contacted by a person who is already receiving similar services from another professional, the career counselor carefully considers that professional relationship and proceeds with caution and sensitivity to the therapeutic issues as well as the client's welfare. Career

counselors discuss these issues with clients so as to minimize the risk of confusion and conflict.

4. When a client's condition indicates that there is a clear and imminent danger to the client or others, the NCDA member must take reasonable personal action or inform responsible authorities. Consultation with other professionals must be used where possible. The assumption of responsibility for the client's behavior must be taken only after careful deliberation, and the client must be involved in the resumption of responsibility as quickly as possible.

5. Records of the counseling relationship, including interview notes, test data, correspondence, audio or visual tape recordings, electronic data storage, and other documents are to be considered professional information for use in counseling. They should not be considered a part of the records of the institution or agency in which the NCDA member is employed unless specified by state statute or regulation. Revelation to others of counseling material must occur only upon the expressed consent of the client; career counselors must make provisions for maintaining confidentiality in the storage and disposal of records. Career counselors providing information to the public or to subordinates, peers, or supervisors have a responsibility to ensure that the content is general; unidentified client information should be accurate and unbiased, and should consist of objective, factual data.

6. NCDA members must ensure that data maintained in electronic storage are secure. The data must be limited to information that is appropriate and necessary for the services being provided and accessible only to appropriate staff members involved in the provision of services by using the best computer security methods available. Career counselors must also ensure that electronically stored data are destroyed when the information is no longer of value in providing services.

7. Data derived from a counseling relationship for use in counselor training or research shall be confined to content that can be disguised to ensure full protection of the identify of the subject/client and shall be obtained with informed consent.

8. NCDA members must inform clients before or at the time the counseling relationship commences, of the purposes, goals, techniques, rules and procedures, and limitations that may affect the relationship.

9. All methods of treatment by NCDA members must be clearly indicated to prospective recipients and safety precautions must be taken in their use.

10. NCDA members who have an administrative, supervisory and/or evaluative relationship with individuals seeking counseling services must not serve as the counselor and should refer the individuals to other professionals. Exceptions are made only in instances where an individual's situation warrants counseling intervention and another alternative is unavailable. Dual relationship with clients that might impair the career counselor's objectivi-

ty and professional judgment must be avoided and/or the counseling relationship terminated through referral to another competent professional.

11. When NCDA members determine an inability to be of professional assistance to a potential or existing client, they must, respectively, not initiate the counseling relationship or immediately terminate the relationship. In either event, the career counselor must suggest appropriate alternatives. Career counselors must be knowledgeable about referral resources so that a satisfactory referral can be initiated. In the event that the client declines a suggested referral, the career counselor is not obligated to continue the relationship.

12. NCDA members may choose to consult with any other professionally competent person about a client and must notify clients of this right. Career counselors must avoid placing a consultant in a conflict-of-interest situation that would preclude the consultant's being a proper party to the career counselor's efforts to help the client.

13. NCDA members who counsel clients from cultures different from their own must gain knowledge, personal awareness, and sensitivity pertinent to the client populations served and must incorporate culturally relevant techniques into their practice.

14. When NCDA members are engaged in intensive, short-term therapy, they must ensure that professional counseling assistance is available to the client(s) during and following the counseling.

15. NCDA members must screen prospective group counseling participants, especially when the emphasis is on self-understanding and growth through self-disclosure. Career counselors must maintain an awareness of each group participant's welfare throughout the group process.

16. When electronic data and systems are used as a component of counseling services, NCDA members must ensure that the computer application, and any information it contains, is appropriate for the respective needs of clients and is nondiscriminatory. Career counselors must ensure that they themselves have acquired a facilitation level of knowledge with any system they use including hands-on application, search experience, and understanding of the uses of all aspects of the computer-based system. In selecting and/or maintaining computer-based systems that contain career information, career counselors must ensure that the systems provide current, accurate, and locally relevant information. Career counselors must also ensure that clients are intellectually, emotionally, and physically compatible to using the computer application and understand its purpose and operation. Client use of a computer application must be evaluated to correct possible problems and assess subsequent needs.

17. NCDA members who develop self-help, stand-alone computer software for use by the general public must first ensure that it is initially designed to function in a stand-alone manner, as opposed to modifying software that was originally designed to require support from a counselor. Secondly, the

software must include program statements that provide the user with intended outcomes, suggestions for using the software, descriptions of inappropriately used applications, and descriptions of when and how counseling services might be beneficial. Finally the manual must include the qualifications of the developer, the development process, validation data, and operating procedures.

SECTION C: MEASUREMENT AND EVALUATION

1. NCDA members must provide specific orientation or information to an examinee prior to and following the administration of assessment instruments or techniques so that the results may be placed in proper perspective with other relevant factors. The purpose of testing and the explicit use of the results must be made known to an examinee prior to testing.

2. In selecting assessment instruments or techniques for use in a given situation or with a particular client, NCDA members must evaluate carefully the instrument's specific theoretical bases and characteristics, validity, reliability, and appropriateness. Career counselors are professionally responsible for using unvalidated information with special care.

3. When making statements to the public about assessment instruments or techniques, NCDA members must provide accurate information and avoid false claims or misconceptions concerning the meaning of psychometric terms. Special efforts are often required to avoid unwarranted connotations of terms such as IQ and grade-equivalent scores.

4. Because many types of assessment techniques exist, NCDA members must recognize the limits of their competence and perform only those functions for which they have received appropriate training.

5. NCDA members must note when tests are not administered under standard conditions or when unusual behavior or irregularities occur during a testing session and the results must be designated as invalid or of questionable validity. Unsupervised or inadequately supervised assessments, such as mail-in tests, are considered unethical. However, the use of standardized instruments that are designed to be self-administered and self-scored, such as interest inventories, is appropriate.

6. Because prior coaching or dissemination of test materials can invalidate test results, NCDA members are professionally obligated to maintain test security. In addition, conditions that produce most favorable test results must be made known to an examinee (e.g., penalty for guessing).

7. NCDA members must consider psychometric limitations when selecting and using an instrument, and must be cognizant of the limitations when interpreting the results. When tests are used to classify clients, career counselors must ensure that periodic review and/or re-testing are conducted to prevent client stereotyping.

8. An examinee's welfare, explicit prior understanding, and agreement are the factors used when determining who receives the test results. NCDA members must see that appropriate interpretation accompanies any release of individual or group test data (e.g., limitations of instrument and norms).

9. NCDA members must ensure that computer-generated test administration and scoring programs function properly thereby providing clients with accurate test results.

10. NCDA members who are responsible for making decisions based on assessment results, must have appropriate training and skills in educational and psychological measurement—including validation criteria, test research, and guidelines for test development and use.

11. NCDA members must be cautious when interpreting the results of instruments that possess insufficient technical data, and must explicitly state to examinees the specific purposes for the use of such instruments.

12. NCDA members must proceed with caution when attempting to evaluate and interpret performances of minority group members or other persons who are not represented in the norm group on which the instrument was standardized.

13. NCDA members who develop computer-based test interpretations to support the assessment process must ensure that the validity of the interpretations is established prior to the commercial distribution of the computer application.

14. NCDA members recognize that test results may become obsolete, and avoid the misuse of obsolete data.

15. NCDA members must avoid the appropriation, reproduction, or modification for published tests or parts thereof without acknowledgment and permission from the publisher.

SECTION D: RESEARCH AND PUBLICATION

1. NCDA members will adhere to relevant guidelines on research with human subjects. These include:

a. *Code of Federal Regulations,* Title 45, Subtitle A, Part 46, as currently issued.
b. American Psychological Association. (1982). *Ethical principles in the conduct of research with human participants.* Washington, DC: Author.
c. American Psychological Association. (1981). Research with human participants. *American Psychologist, 36,* 633–638.
d. Family Educational Rights and Privacy Act. (Buckley Amendment to P. L. 93-380 of the Laws of 1974).
e. Current federal regulations and various state privacy acts.

2. In planning research activities involving human subjects, NCDA members must be aware of and responsive to all pertinent ethical principles and ensure that the research problem, design, and execution are in full compliance with the principles.

3. The ultimate responsibility for ethical research lies with the principal researcher, though others involved in the research activities are ethically obligated and responsible for their own actions.

4. NCDA members who conduct research with human subjects are responsible for the subjects' welfare throughout the experiment and must take all reasonable precautions to avoid causing injurious psychological, physical, or social effects on their subjects.

5. NCDA members who conduct research must abide by the following basic elements of informed consent:

   a. a fair explanation of the procedures to be followed, including an identification or those which are experimental
   b. a description of the attendant discomforts and risks
   c. a description of the benefits to be expected
   d. a disclosure of appropriate alternative procedures that would be advantageous for subjects
   e. an offer to answer any inquiries concerning the procedures
   f. an instruction that subjects are free to withdraw their consent and to discontinue participation in the project or activity at any time

6. When reporting research results, explicit mention must be made of all the variables and conditions known to the NCDA member that may have affected the outcome of the study or the interpretation of the data.

7. NCDA members who conduct and report research investigations must do so in a manner that minimizes the possibility that the results will be misleading.

8. NCDA members are obligated to make available sufficient original research data to qualified others who may wish to replicate the study.

9. NCDA members who supply data, aid in the research of another person, report research results, or make original data available, must take due care to disguise the identity of respective subjects in the absence of specific authorization from the subject to do otherwise.

10.   When conducting and reporting research, NCDA members must be familiar with, and give recognition to, previous work on the topic, must observe all copyright laws, and must follow the principles of giving full credit to those to whom credit is due.

11. NCDA members must give due credit through joint authorship, acknowledgment, footnote statements, or other appropriate means to those

who have contributed significantly to the research and/or publication, in accordance with such contributions.

12. NCDA members should communicate to others the results of any research judged to be of professional value. Results that reflect unfavorably on institutions, programs, services, or vested interests must not be withheld.

13. NCDA members who agree to cooperate with another individual in research and/or publication must incur an obligation to cooperate as promised in terms of punctuality of performance and with full regard to the completeness and accuracy of the information required.

14. NCDA members must not submit the same manuscript, or one essentially similar in content, for simultaneous publication consideration by two or more journals. In addition, manuscripts that are published in whole or substantial part in another journal or published work should not be submitted for publication without acknowledgment and permission from the previous publication.

SECTION E: CONSULTING

Consultation refers to a voluntary relationship between a professional helper and help-needing individual, group, or social unit in which the consultant is providing help to the client(s) in defining and solving a work-related problem or potential work-related problem with a client or client system.

1. NCDA members, acting as consultants, must have a high degree of self-awareness of their own values, knowledge, skills, limitations, and needs in entering a helping relationship that involves human and/or organizational change. The focus of the consulting relationship must be on the issues to be resolved and not on the person(s) presenting the problem.

2. In the consulting relationship, the NCDA member and client must understand and agree upon the problem definition, subsequent goals, and predicted consequences of interventions selected.

3. NCDA members must be reasonably certain that they, or the organization represented, have the necessary competencies and resources for giving the kind of help that is needed or that may develop later, and that appropriate referral resources are available to the consultant.

4. NCDA members in a consulting relationship must encourage and cultivate client adaptability and growth toward self-direction. NCDA members must maintain this role consistently and not become a decision maker for clients or create a future dependency on the consultant.

5. NCDA members conscientiously adhere to the NCDA Ethical Standards when announcing consultant availability for services.

SECTION F: PRIVATE PRACTICE

1. NCDA members should assist the profession by facilitating the availability of counseling services in private as well as public settings.

2. In advertising services as private practitioners, NCDA members must advertise in a manner that accurately informs the public of the professional services, expertise, and counseling techniques available.

3. NCDA members who assume an executive leadership role in a private practice organization do not permit their names to be used in professional notices during periods of time when they are not actively engaged in the private practice of counseling.

4. NCDA members may list their highest relevant degree, type, and level of certification and/or license, address, telephone number, office hours, type and/or description of services, and other relevant information. Listed information must not contain false, inaccurate, misleading, partial, out-of-context, or otherwise deceptive material or statements.

5. NCDA members who are involved in a partnership or corporation with other professionals must, in compliance with the regulations of the locality, clearly specify the separate specialties of each member of the partnership or corporation.

6. NCDA members have an obligation to withdraw from a private-practice counseling relationship if it violates the NCDA Ethical Standards, if the mental or physical condition of the NCDA member renders it difficult to carry out an effective professional relationship, or if the counseling relationship is no longer productive for the client.

PROCEDURES FOR PROCESSING ETHICAL COMPLAINTS

As a division of the American Association for Counseling and Development (AACD), the National Career Development Association (NCDA) adheres to the guidelines and procedures for processing ethical complaints and the disciplinary sanctions adopted by AACD. A complaint against an NCDA member may be filed by any individual or group of individuals ("complainant"), whether or not the complainant is a member of NCDA. (Action will not be taken on anonymous complaints.) For specifics on how to file ethical complaints and a description of the guidelines and procedures for processing complaints, contact:

AACD Ethics Committee
c/o Executive Director
American Association for Counseling and Development
5999 Stevenson Avenue
Alexandria, VA 22304

APPENDIX D

Vocational Inventories for Use in Career Counseling and Research

CLASS 1: CRITERION-BASED INTEREST INVENTORIES: COLLEGE BOUND

Inventory	*Publisher*
Kuder Occupational Interest Survey (KOIS) Kuder & Diamond, 1979	CTB McGraw Hill 2500 Garden Road Monterey, CA 93940 408–649–8400
Jackson Vocational Interest Survey (JVIS) Jackson, 1977	Sigma Assessment Systems P.O. Box 610984 Port Huron, MI 48061–0984 800–265–1285
Strong Vocational Interest Blank (SVIB-SCII) Hansen & Campbell, 1985	Consulting Psychologists Press 577 College Avenue Palo Alto, CA 94306 415–857–1444

CLASS 2: CRITERION-BASED INTEREST INVENTORIES: NON-COLLEGE BOUND

Career Directions Inventory (CDI) Jackson, 1986	Research Psychologists Press P.O. Box 984 Port Huron, MI 800–265–1285

Exploring Career Options (ECO)
Andberg & Johansson, 1987

National Computer Systems
4401 West 76th Street
Minneapolis, MN 55435
612–829–3000

Career Assessment Inventory (CAI)
Johansson, 1982

National Computer Systems
4401 West 76th Street
Minneapolis, MN 55435
612–829–3000

CLASS 3: HOMOGENEOUS SELF-GUIDING INTEREST INVENTORIES

Interest Determination, Exploration,
and Assessment System (IDEAS)
Johansson, 1980

National Computer Systems
4401 West 76th Street
Minneapolis, MN 55435
612–829–3000

Self-Directed Search (SDS)
Holland, 1985b

Psychological Assessment
Resource (PAR)
P.O. Box 98
Odessa, FL 33556
800–331-TEST

CLASS 4: HOMOGENEOUS HAND OR MACHINE SCORED INTEREST INVENTORIES

California Occupational
Preference System (COPS)
Knapp & Knapp, 1984

Educational and Industrial
Testing Service (EDITS)
P.O. Box 7234
San Diego, CA 92107
619–222–1666

Unisex Edition of the ACT
Interest Inventory (UNIACT)
American College Testing Program

ACT Career Planning Program
P.O. Box 168
Iowa City, IA 52240
319–337–1000

Vocational Interest Inventory (VII)
Lunneborg, 1981

Western Psychological Services
12035 Wilshire Boulevard
Los Angeles, CA 90025
213–478–2061

Vocational Preference Inventory
(VPI)
Holland, 1985c

Psychological Assessment
Resources (PAR)
P.O. Box 98
Odessa, FL 33556
800–331–TEST

CLASS 5: CAREER MATURITY INVENTORIES

Adult Career Concerns Inventory (ACCI) Super, Thompson, & Lindeman, 1988	Consulting Psychologists Press 577 College Avenue Palo Alto, CA 94306 415–857–1444
Career Adjustment and Development Crites, 1982	Crites Career Center 1942 Broadway Boulder, CO 80302 303–938–6899
Career Development Inventory (CDI) (ACCI) Super, Thompson, & Lindeman, Jordaan, & Myers, 1984	Consulting Psychologists Press 577 College Avenue Palo Alto, CA 94306 415–857–1444
Career Maturity Inventory (CMI) Crites, 1978	CTB McGraw Hill 2500 Garden Road Monterey, CA 93940 408–649–8400
Cognitive Vocational Maturity Inventory (CVMT) Westbrook & Parry-Hill, 1973	Center for Occupational Education North Carolina State University Raleigh, NC 27607

CLASS 6: DECISIONAL STATUS INVENTORIES

Assessment of Career Decision Making (ACDM) Buck & Daniels, 1985	Western Psychological Services 12035 Wilshire Boulevard Los Angeles, CA 90025 213–478–2061
Career Decision Scale (CDS) Holland, 1985b	Psychological Assessment Resources (PAR) P.O. Box 98 Odessa, FL 33556 800–331–TEST
Career Exploration Inventory (CEI) Stumpf et al., 1983	Management Simulations Group New York University Tisch Hall 40 West 4th Street New York, NY 10012 212–998–4118
My Vocational Situation (MVS) Holland, Daiger, & Power, 1980	Consulting Psychologists Press 577 College Avenue Palo Alto, CA 94306 415–857–1444

CLASS 7: MEASURES OF PERSONAL AGENCY

Activities Survey
Osipow & Rooney, in press

Marathon Consulting and Press
330 Eastmoor Boulevard
Columbus, Ohio 43209-0189
614–292–1748

Career Beliefs Inventory (CBI)
Krumboltz, 1988

Consulting Psychologists Press
577 College Avenue
Palo Alto, CA 94306
415–857–1444

Career Self-Efficacy Scale
Betz & Hackett, 1981

Department of Psychology
Ohio State University
Columbus, Ohio 43210

Campbell Work Orientations
   Inventory
Campbell, 1986

Center for Creative Leadership
5000 Laurinda Drive
Greensboro, NC 27402-1660
919–288–7210

CLASS 8: VOCATIONAL CARD SORTS

Occusort
Jones, 1978

CTB McGraw Hill
2500 Garden Road
Monterey, CA 93940
408–649–8400

Vocational Exploration and
   Insight Kit (VEIK)
Holland and associates, 1977

Consulting Psychologists Press
577 College Ave.
Palo Alto, CA 94306
415–857–1444

CLASS 9: MEASURES OF PERSONAL STYLE, VALUES
AND NEEDS

Hall Occupational Orientation
   (HOOI)
Hall & Tarrier, 1976

Scholastic Testing Service
480 Meyer Road
Bensenville, IL 60106
312–766–7150

Level 1 Lifestyles Inventory
Human Synergistics, 1989

Human Synergistics
39819 Plymouth Road
Plymouth, MI 48170
313–459–1030

Management Skills Profile (MSP) Personnel Decisions Inc, 1989	Personnel Decisions, Inc Suite 2300 Foshay Tower 821 Marquette Avenue Minneapolis, MN 55402 612-339-0927
Managerial Style Questionnaire (MSQ) McBer & Co., 1981	McBer & Co. 137 Newbury Street Boston, MA 02116 617-437-7080
Minnesota Importance Questionnaire (MIQ) Rounds, Henly, Dawis, Lofquist, & Weiss, 1981	Vocational Psychology Research Work Adjustment Project Department of Psychology University of Minnesota Minneapolis, MN 55400 612-624-9646
Salience Inventory Nevill & Super, 1989	Consulting Psychologists Press 577 College Avenue Palo Alto, CA 94306 415-857-1444
Values Scale Super & Nevill, 1986	Consulting Psychologists Press 577 College Avenue Palo Alto, CA 94306 415-857-1444
Work Values Inventory (WVI) Super, 1970	Houghton Mifflin Inc. 1 Beacon Street Boston, MA 02107 617-725-5000

CLASS 10: WORK SAMPLE BATTERIES

McCaron-Dial Systems	McCarron-Dial Systems Dallas, TX 214-247-5945
Tower System ICD, 1977	ICD Rehabilitation and Research Center 340 East 24th Street New York, NY 10010 212-679-0100
VALPAR Component Work Samples VALPAR International Corporation, 1974	VALPAR International P.O. Box 5767 Tuscon, AZ 85703 602-293-1510

CLASS 11: ABILITY MEASURES

Armed Services Vocational
  Aptitude Battery (ASVAB)
U. S. Department of Defense, 1989

U. S. Military Processing
2500 Greenbay Road
North Chicago, IL 60064
800–323–0513

General Aptitude Test Battery
  (GATB)
U. S. Department of Labor, 1979

Division of Testing
U. S. Employment and Training
  Administration
U. S. Department of Labor
Washington, DC 20402
202–523–6666

Differential Apptitude Tests
  (DAT)
Bennett, Seashore, & Wesman,
  1982; 1984

Psychological Corporation
757 3rd Avenue
New York, NY 10017
512–299–1061

CLASS 12: MEASURES OF PERSONALITY

California Personality Inventory
  (CPI)
Gough, 1975

Consulting Psychologists Press
577 College Avenue
Palo Alto, CA 94306
415–857–1444

FIRO Awareness Scales
Shutz, 1978

Consulting Psychologists Press
577 College Avenue
Palo Alto, CA 94306
415–857–1444

Myers-Briggs Type Indicator
  (MBTI)
I. B. Briggs & McCaulley, 1985

Consulting Psychologists Press
577 College Avenue
Palo Alto, CA 94306
415–857–1444

Sixteen PF Personal Career Profile
Walter, 1975

Institute for Personality and
  Ability Testing (IPA)
P.O. Box 188
Champaign, IL 61820-0188
800–225–4728

CLASS 13: MEASURES OF WORK ENVIRONMENT

Maslach Burnout Inventory (MBI)
Maslach & Jackson, 1981

Consulting Psychologists Press
577 College Avenue
Palo Alto, CA 94306
415–857–1444

Occupational Stress Inventory
(OSI)
Osipow & Spokane, 1987

Psychological Assessment
Resources (PAR)
P.O. Box 98
Odessa, FL 33556
800–331–TEST

Work Environment Scale (WES)
Moos, 1986

Consulting Psychologists Press
577 College Avenue
Palo Alto, CA 94306
415–857–1444

APPENDIX E

Testing Competencies for Career Counselors

BASIC CONCEPTS

Concepts important to the informed *use* of tests are listed below. Persons with final responsibility for *evaluating* and *selecting* tests will require knowledge beyond these basic concepts.

Use the following key in responding to the statements:
  3 = I am able to apply the concept and explain it to others.
  2 = I have some knowledge but little experience in applying the concept.
  1 = I have little or no knowledge of this concept.
Enter the appropriate number in the blank at the left of each statement.

1. STATISTICS USED IN TESTING AND TEST MANUALS

_____ a. Mean, median, mode

_____ b. Standard deviation

_____ c. Frequency distribution

_____ d. Normal distribution

_____ e. Correlation coefficient

2. TYPES OF INSTRUMENTS

_____ a. Measures of maximum performance

_____ b. Measures of typical performance

_____ c. Similarities and differences among self-reports, self-ratings, inventories, and tests

_____ d. Similarities and differences among measures of intelligence, aptitude, ability, and achievement

3. SCORE REPORTING PROCEDURES

_____ a. Percentile ranks

_____ b. Standard scores (including stanines)

_____ c. Grade placement (equivalent) scores

_____ d. Score profiles and profile analysis

_____ e. Group similarity indices ("Your scores are similar to people who . . . ")

_____ f. Expectancy (experience) tables

_____ g. Estimates of probability of success and/or level of success; standard error of estimate

4. STANDARDIZATION AND NORMS

_____ a. Standardized administration and scoring

_____ b. Limitations of raw scores

_____ c. Types of norms (e.g., local, national, gender, grade); their applications and limitations

_____ d. Norm-based vs. criterion-referenced interpretation

5. RELIABILITY

_____ a. Meaning of test reliability

_____ b. Sources of measurement error

_____ c. Types of test reliability (test-retest; parallel forms; internal consistency, including split-half)

_____ d. Standard error of measurement and error bands

6. VALIDITY

_____ a. Meaning of test validity

_____ b. Implications of test use for validation procedures

_____ c. Types of test validity (content, criterion-related, construct)

_____ d. Factors affecting test validity (e.g., the "criterion problem")

_____ e. Differential validity of test batteries for diverse criteria

_____ f. Potential sources of bias affecting validity

RESPONSIBILITIES/COMPETENCIES

Test user responsibilities and concomitant competencies are listed in the next three sections.

Use the following key in responding to the statements:
3 = I do this routinely—as a regular practice.
2 = I have done this on occasion.
1 = I do not do this—but should give it consideration.
NA = Not applicable to the tests I am using.
Enter the appropriate number in the blank at the left of each statement.

PREPARING FOR TEST USE

_____ 1. Avoid unnecessary testing by determining whether existing information can meet the needs of your counselees and institution.

_____ 2. Consider advertisements for tests, promotional brochures, catalog descriptions, etc., in the same manner as advertisements for any commercial product in a competitive marketplace.

_____ 3. Obtain and review up-to-date copies of the administration, interpretation, and technical manuals for any test you are seriously considering. If not qualified to evaluate the test, obtain help from a qualified supervisor or consultant.

_____ 4. Read professional reviews of the test—e.g., in the *Journal of Counseling and Development,* the Buros series of *Mental Measurements Yearbooks, Test Critiques....*

_____ 5. Determine whether the test's reading level is appropriate to your counselees.

_____ 6. Verify that the test items, norms, and score reporting procedures minimize bias due to gender, cultural background, disability, or age.

_____ 7. Know whether you possess the qualifications (e.g., specific training and/or experience) required for use of a given test. Apply the same criteria to anyone with delegated responsibility for test use.

_____ 8. Determine whether research shows that the test measures what you want it to measure; evaluate the basis for any cut-off scores or decision rules advocated for score interpretation.

_____ 9. Avoid a test that requires the comparison of a counselee's raw scores unless research shows that equal raw scores for each of the test's scales (e.g., interest types) indicate equal amounts of the characteristic being measured.

_____ 10. Determine that computer-administered tests meet the same standards as traditional paper-and-pencil tests. For ability tests and other timed measures, determine that norms are appropriate to computerized administration.

_____ 11. Examine the basis for occupational attribute descriptions (e.g., relevant abilities, work activities) used to link counselee characteristics (e.g., abilities, interests) to occupations. Determine whether the descriptions and links are justified.

_____ 12. Before final adoption of a test, evaluate usability by administering and interpreting it to a small number of counselees. (See subsequent checklist items.) If possible, arrange to take the test yourself.

ADMINISTRATION AND SCORING

_____ 1. Acquire the training necessary to administer the test. Study the directions for administration and know whether additional materials (e.g., timer, scratch paper) are needed.

_____ 2. Provide a training session for test administrators and proctors.

_____ 3. Ensure that reasons for testing are understood and accepted by counselees—why the test is being given; what the test can and cannot do; who will receive the test results; how they will be used.

_____ 4. Maintain the security of test materials before, during, and after administration.

_____ 5. Provide a testing room and psychological climate that allow each counselee to achieve optimal performance.

_____ 6. Plan for special circumstances affecting the administration of the test (e.g., late arrivals, disabled persons, left handers).

_____ 7. Ensure that test administration directions are followed explicitly and completely.

_____ 8. Determine appropriate answers to questions about guessing, skipping questions, and using time efficiently.

_____ 9. Note unusual behavior by any person(s) being tested. If the test results are not invalidated, consider whether a report of the unusual behavior should accompany the scores.

_____ 10. Periodically rescore (perhaps with clerical help) a sample of machine-scored answer sheets to verify scoring accuracy.

_____ 11. Periodically rescore a sample of "self-scored tests" to verify scoring accuracy. Routinely check the scores of counselees who, in your judgment, may have difficulty with self-scoring.

_____ 12. Develop a system for dating, recording, maintaining the confidentiality of, and storing test results.

INTERPRETATION

_____ 1. Provide test interpretations based on documented bridges between scores and their real-world implications. That is, be sure your test interpretations, including those provided on the score report and/or a computer terminal, are warranted by research conducted on the test.

_____ 2. Initially, and periodically thereafter, discuss your test interpretations with a qualified colleague.

_____ 3. Review, with the counselee, the purpose and nature of the test— why the test was given (e.g., its relevance to counselee goals); what the test can and cannot do; who will receive the test results.

_____ 4. Obtain the consent of the counselee before using test results for purposes other than those described prior to testing.

_____ 5. Consider whether a counselee's reading level, gender, cultural background, disability, or age may have influenced the test results. Take such information into account in any reports of results.

_____ 6. Encourage counselees to discuss how they felt about the testing experience in general (e.g., did they see potential personal benefit?); their performance in particular; and any problems encountered (e.g., nervousness, fatigue, distractions).

_____ 7. Provide a simple explanation of measurement error and its implications, especially for score differences on profiles.

_____ 8. Help the counselee to think of test interpretations as hypotheses to be checked against past experience, compared with other information, tested via mutually planned activities, and periodically reviewed and modified.

_____ 9. Apply good counseling techniques to test interpretation by—attending to the counselee first and test results second (e.g., by listening attentively and encouraging feedback); allowing sufficient time for the counselee to assimilate information and ask questions; checking the counselee's understanding from time to time and correcting any misconceptions.

_____ 10. Help the counselee begin (or continue) the career planning process by cooperatively identifying career options, steps for exploring the options, and criteria for evaluating the options.

_____ 11. Monitor and encourage career planning activities through informal contacts, scheduled progress reports, or follow-through counseling sessions.

_____ 12. In general, observe the Golden Rule of Testing: "Administer and interpret unto others as you would have them do unto you."

Source: D.J. Prediger and N.J. Garfield, "Testing competencies and responsibilities: A checklist for counselors." In J.T. Hapes and M.M. Mastie (Eds.), *A Counselor's Guide to Career Assessment Instruments,* 2nd ed. (Alexandria, VA: National Career Development Association, 1988), 45–54. Copyright © 1988 by the American Association for Counseling and Development. Reproduced by permission.

APPENDIX F

Case Conference Outline

I. Identifying Data
   A. Age, sex, race, educational level, appearance, marital status, children
   B. Current occupation and length of time in occupation
   C. Referral source

II. Presenting Concern
   A. What does the client believe is their central concern

III. Observations from Interviewer
   A. General demeanor
   B. Personality style and dynamics
   C. History from form
   D. Family/support systems
   E. Tape transcriptions

IV. Course of Treatment
   A. Number of sessions
   B. Synopsis of sessions
   C. Treatment goals and plan
   D. Options considered
   E. Manner of facilitating gain
   F. Follow through

V. Tests and Assessment Data
   A. Interest Inventories (SDS, SCII, Kuder DD)
   B. Card Sort if any/constructs
   C. Decisional status/maturity
   D. Ability

VI. Outcomes
  A. Job status
  B. Feelings about situation
  C. Future plans
VII. Questions Considerations and Impediments
  A. Relationship to postulates as illustration
  B. Impeding mental health issues
  C. Key incidents facilitating movement

Author Index

Subject Index